Relentless Pursuit

Relentless Pursuit

A YEAR IN THE TRENCHES WITH

TEACH FOR AMERICA

Donna Foote

Alfred A. Knopf

New York   2008

THIS IS A BORZOI BOOK
PUBLISHED BY ALFRED A. KNOPF

www.aaknopf.com

Knopf, Borzoi Books, and the colophon are registered
trademarks of Random House, Inc.

Portions of this work originally appeared in *U.S. News & World Report*.

Library of Congress Cataloging-in-Publication Data
Foote, Donna, [date]
Relentless pursuit: a year in the trenches with Teach for America / Donna Foote—
1st ed.
p. cm.
ISBN 978-0-307-26571-5
1. Education, Urban—California—Los Angeles—Case Studies. 2. Urban high
schools—California—Los Angeles—Case studies. 3. High school teachers—
California—Los Angeles—Case studies. 4. First school teachers—California—Los
Angeles—Case studies. 5. Teach for America (Project) I. Title.
LC5133.L67F66 2008
371.1009794'94—dc22   2007034179

Manufactured in the United States of America
Published April 17, 2008
Reprinted Two Times
Fourth Printing, September 2008

To the loves in my life:

Jim, my rock
James, my light
Dad, my hero
And my mother, whom I miss every day

Contents

Relentless Pursuit

Lockdown

When the lights went off in room 241 during her fourth-period special ed biology class, Rachelle didn't think anything of it. The bells seemed to ring constantly at Locke High School. Why should she expect the lights to work?

This Monday was the first day of the first full week of the first year of the first job of her professional life. Never mind that she had had only five weeks of training. Over the summer, Rachelle Snyder, psychology major and former captain of the University of Pennsylvania soccer team, had become Miss Snyder—or sometimes just Miss—special education teacher at Locke High School in Watts. The transition had been surprisingly easy to make. Except for the fifteen pounds she gained, Teach For America's "institute," aka boot camp, didn't bother her. It was like soccer training: she woke up early, worked hard, got the job done. She was exhausted—they all were. But during breaks, when other teachers-in-training were having panic attacks, Rachelle would catnap on the concrete benches that line the walkway along Locke's inner quad, her long blond hair bunched up beneath her head like a pillow, trousers rolled up, her pale skin bathed in the harsh white light of the L.A. sun.

The day had started well. She'd gotten to school early, reviewed her lesson plan, and made sure that the desks were still arranged in clusters of four, exactly the way she'd left them on Friday. The morning had flown by. The kids in the early periods were attentive, eager to please. She particularly liked her girl-heavy third period. Three fourteen-year-olds had children of their own at home, and a fourth was pregnant. She found that out after she had the kids make peanut butter and jelly sandwiches as a way to introduce the idea of steps and procedures in science. "You think I don't know how to make peanut butter sandwiches?" asked one girl. "I got a baby at home and he always be screamin' for them."

Maybe it was Rachelle's blond hair and light blue eyes—the girls seemed drawn to her. Some even brought their friends to the classroom to get a look. "See!" they squealed. "She looks just like a Barbie doll!" Rachelle couldn't access their computerized Individualized Education Programs (IEPs), the government-mandated plans of instruction and services specially tailored to meet the specific needs of each student with a diagnosed learning disability. So she had no way of knowing how these smart, streetwise girls had come to be sitting there, hanging on her every word.

She had a pretty good idea how the twenty boys in her fourth-period class got there. They were in special ed because their behavior interfered with their ability to learn. It was certainly interfering with her ability to teach. These boys were rude, crude, and disrespectful. She didn't think it had anything to do with her gender, her race, or her youth. She was reasonably certain that they behaved badly with every authority figure.

It was only five days into the school year, and she felt she was already losing control of period four. She had been wrestling with how to handle all her special ed kids, but these boys were especially troubling. Her instinct was to try to win them over with kindness. They'd probably had enough tough single women in their lives. She wanted to show them something else. *Do I continue to be nice? If I do, will they break me?* As the boys straggled in, shorts hanging low on their hips, T-shirts on inside out, some with do-rags hugging their heads, she felt tense.

She worried about two of her African American students—cousins Martel and Deangelo—who'd almost gotten jumped on their way to school the Friday before. The boys had come into class that day subdued, scared to leave the building unless she walked them out. *What will they be like today?*

Then there was Raúl. Last week she'd handed out a survey asking generic questions about the kids' goals and attitudes toward school. Raúl's response stopped her cold. He said he hated teachers and liked to "kill." He drew a picture of a building with a boy on top firing a rifle. The bubble said "Die Fucker." There were stick figures on the ground running away from the words "Kill, Kill, Kill." Rachelle grabbed the seating chart and was surprised to find that the artist was a quiet little Latino kid, one of the few boys in class who didn't cause trouble. He kept his head down and his eyes averted. She didn't think he was looking for attention with his threatening handiwork; she thought he was an emotionally disturbed boy who needed help. She alerted the principal, Dr. Frank Wells, immediately. He seemed on top of things, but Raúl was one of some 3,100 kids in his charge. *Will Raúl be in class today? Will he have killing on his mind?*

Five, ten minutes had passed before everyone was seated. The day's lesson was about the scientific method. The kids were going to test the manufacturer's claim that the fertilizer Miracle-Gro was guaranteed to produce especially hardy plants. Each group of four was given seeds, a pot of soil, and a bucket of water. Only half the class had shown up, but Rachelle was actually relieved. The fewer there were, the more easily she could maintain control. After explaining the project, she'd moved from group to group—praising those busy at work, gently scolding those who were fooling around. The room hummed with the sound of the kids' voices as they prepared their pots. Rachelle began to relax.

Then the lights went off. At first it didn't seem like cause for alarm, but within minutes Rachelle could hear the sound of kids running up and down the stairwell and along the hallway outside her room. Her students heard the commotion, too. Suddenly, the vibe in the classroom changed. The kids were uneasy, distracted. The air felt charged, the room dangerous.

Rachelle peeked out the door. Students were literally running wild, shouting and jumping one another in the darkness. Graffiti artists had whipped out their markers and were signing the walls with gleeful abandon. The security guard who usually sat within ten feet of Rachelle's room was missing. She slammed the door shut.

"You are not leaving," she said to her students, her voice rising in fear. "Sit down. Let's get back to work."

But the kids were unsettled. Some were at the door, clamoring to get out. Others circled the desks, itching for trouble. When told to sit, they refused. When ordered to continue working, they said the experiment sucked. Rachelle tried to keep teaching. As she bent over to inspect one kid's pot, her T-shirt inched up her back, revealing a patch of bare white flesh above her hip-huggers. Dante, a tall, skinny black boy, made a farting noise. The classroom erupted in laughter. Encouraged, he announced in a high-pitched voice that he had to pee. Rachelle told him he was forbidden to leave the classroom.

Dante insisted that if he was not allowed to leave, he would pee in the classroom. As he began to lower his pants, the kids taunted him: "It's so small! Your dick is so small!" They dared him to make good on his threat. "She wants you! She wants to see you! Do it, do it! You want to do it!" they chanted.

He did it. Dante urinated in a water bucket right in the middle of Miss Snyder's class. Rachelle ordered the entire class out of the room: "You guys need to leave. NOW! Dante, you need to stay."

"I want to transfer out of this class," said one boy as he left the room. "It sucks."

"What about me?" pleaded Dante. "Can I get out of here?"

Things were different on the third floor. In room 301 there were only ten minutes left of Phillip Gedeon's geometry lesson when the screen for the LCD projector went blank. The classroom lights were already off; the new teacher assumed he had blown a fuse by running his personal Apple laptop and the school projector simultaneously. He wrapped up his lesson and gave his students their homework. As the kids prepared to leave, the sound of their chatter rose to a low rumble. Phillip stood stock-still, a finger raised to his lips.

"There is NO TALKING in this class," he said. "There needs to be silence. You need to be quiet. I'll wait." A stopwatch hung on a red cord around his neck. His new white shirt was still crisp, and the crease in his black trousers would have passed military muster. The noise stopped as abruptly as it had begun.

After less than a week on the job, Phillip was earning a reputation as one of the best of Locke's Teach For America recruits. During institute, TFA's summer training session, observers had streamed into Gedeon's summer school classroom. "Impressive," "very strong," and even "revolutionary" were the words used in his assessments. He had graduated weeks before from Connecticut College with a dual degree in mathematics and race relations. He had also taken education courses and ended his senior year by student teaching, so he was ahead of the pack when he entered Teach For America.

He had been nervous about starting his teaching career at Locke, but his nervousness came from concerns about working conditions at the troubled high school—not from doubts about his ability as a teacher. He wondered about the history of violence there, about the issue of crowding, about the teachers, about edgy race relations between the black and Latino students. But every time those thoughts seemed to take over, he reminded himself of the larger truth. *I have these kids for 170 days. There's a lot to accomplish. This is make-or-break time.*

From the beginning, his priority had been to establish order; once he had absolute authority over his students, he would teach. So he had spent much of the first few days of the school year laying out his expectations for student behavior and academic achievement. He was very direct. He listed his "nonnegotiables." Students could not speak without raising their hands. Students could not leave their seats without permission. Pencils were to be sharpened before class began. His rules were effective immediately. On the second day of school, students who came late to class were disciplined. Those slow to comply with Phillip's directions were told to leave the room. It was working. Just five days into the school year, Phillip seemed to have total control over the forty teenagers crammed into room 301.

Growing up in Springfield, Massachusetts, as the only child of a single black mother, Phillip had dreamed of being a teacher. Long before he had ever heard of Teach For America, he knew that education was the only way out for his people. The approach Teach For America promulgated was the same one that had worked for him as a child of the underclass; teachers had to set the bar high and then invest students with the tools and mind-set to reach it. TFA had been labeled messianic by some: recruits worked long hours, were expected to lead disciplined lives governed by a set of values that included humility and respect, and believed passionately in their mission. Phillip was a true disciple. He considered it a privilege to be a member.

Only days into his life's work, Phillip felt almost giddy. Things were going well. There was no place he would rather be than at Locke High School. His fears about racial tensions on campus had so far not been realized. And though he had been warned that Locke students could present discipline problems—especially in a school so steeped in the macho culture of the gangs—he hadn't encountered anything he couldn't handle.

Phillip concluded the fourth-period class in his usual way. The bell hadn't rung, but he took no notice. He didn't run his classroom on the bell system. He kept his students until the lesson was finished and all was quiet. If kids were late for their next class, it was no concern of his. Satisfied that everything was in order, he announced: "Class is dismissed. Have a nice day."

With that, Phillip swung open the door. All was quiet. Except for the eerie glow cast by emergency lights, the hallway was pitch-black. The kids hesitated. Phillip did not. He told them to proceed to their next class. The children ventured out into the darkness.

It didn't take long for the hallway calm to morph into chaos. Down at the other end of the third-floor corridor, Hrag Hamalian watched as he waited for his fifth-period biology class to arrive. He didn't like what he was seeing. Kids were careening down the windowless hall, screaming and yelling as they collided with one another. Fights were erupting, and there were no adults in sight. He didn't know what to do. *Am I in charge of policing the hallways? Or should I just deal with my own students?*

They kept him busy enough. Fifth period was his nightmare class. When he left school the Friday before, just four days into a two-year commitment with Teach For America, he'd been on the verge of tears. A fight had erupted in his fifth-period class that day, and he had completely mishandled it. It was probably his fault in the first place for not being sensitive to race issues. He wasn't thinking when he seated Cale, a tall, skinny black kid, with three Latino boys. Cale resisted the move, and before Hrag could intervene, he was taking swings at José, a compact Latino kid with a swagger. Hrag held José back and ordered Cale to stop. Then he lost it. He screamed at them both, and as his voice rose he could feel his body heat rising, too, inching up his neck and turning his face bright red. Hrag directed José back to his seat, but Cale was still throwing punches. The boys' anger was infectious; Hrag could feel the adrenaline coursing through his own body. He knew he had to get them out of the room before the other kids got into the action. The class watched in fascination as the two boys tumbled into the hallway. Hrag was physically fit—he had been a wrestler in high school—but he couldn't separate them. Finally, Hrag called security. When the fifty-year-old female guard arrived, his heart sank. He couldn't handle even one of these kids—how was she supposed to manage two? It came as no surprise when Cale squirmed out of her hold and bolted away.

In the end, Cale ended up in the dean's office, where he was suspended. José resumed his seat in class. Order in room 308 was restored, but Hrag was rattled. Later he learned that he had botched the whole episode. The rules at Locke were clear—even if they had never been communicated to him. First, the teacher never leaves the classroom unattended. Second, if a fight erupts, both kids go to the office and both are suspended. Third, teachers don't touch kids, not even with a finger. Hrag had allowed José to return to his seat because José had stopped when Hrag asked him to. But the way he handled his first crisis in the classroom had sent all the wrong messages. Hrag feared that it looked bad to the administration that he had felt compelled to send a kid to the dean's office so early in the school year. Worse, it signaled to his students that he was vulnerable. Hrag knew that if he didn't get a grip, if he didn't earn their respect quickly, this misstep would follow him through the entire year.

And so he had worried all weekend. He'd barely slept, and when he did finally nod off, he'd awakened with a knot in his stomach. He kept thinking about school, about the upcoming week, about the kid he had punished and the kid he had not. All the veteran teachers had warned him not to take things in the classroom personally. Well, for him that was impossible. He took things *very* personally.

What's happening to me? This is a complete mind blow!

Three months before, he'd been a party-loving senior at Boston College with a double major and great grades. Now he felt so . . . sad. Overnight he had gone from being a twenty-one-year-old kid with no responsibilities to a man who woke up before sunrise. The old fun-loving Hrag was gone. In his place was an overworked, stressed-out, lonely guy winging it as a teacher in a dysfunctional inner-city school thousands of miles from his home in New Jersey. More than one person had stopped to ask him what was wrong. He looked terrible. His hair was always a mess, his tie awry, his eyes heavy with fatigue behind his thick glasses. It wasn't just the hard work and the long hours that bothered him—or the fact that he had no girlfriend at a time when he needed one most. It was the idea that if he failed, it wasn't just him. His kids failed, too. *I feel like someone has his foot on my head and I'm underwater, and just when I think I have enough air, my head goes under again. Nothing is constant. There is nothing to rely on.*

Hrag hadn't expected to feel like this. Many of the TFA recruits had had a difficult time over the summer. Not him. For Hrag, the training had been a breeze. He had seen people break down in tears, and he had heard about corps members throwing up because they were so stressed out. He was shocked when his friend and roommate quit the program because he found it too intense. Hrag left the institute on a high. He felt more confident than ever.

Now here he was, standing in the doorway of his own classroom, dreading period five. As the kids streamed in, Hrag noticed a security guard walking his way with Cale in tow.

Oh no. He's back.

Before Hrag had a chance to work out how he would handle the irascible teenager, the boy slipped the guard's hold and disappeared into the crowd.

Another guard approached Hrag and instructed him to keep both his doors open so that the light coming from his windows would help illuminate the hallways. Hrag agreed. Then, as soon as the guard was gone, he shut both doors. There was no way he could allow his kids to witness the craziness outside and expect them to do any work.

"Yo!" Hrag boomed as he paced in front of the room. "We have work to do today. Sit down. Let's go."

The kids settled down. They were used to a darkened room; Hrag had been turning the lights off during this period anyway to cool them down after PE and lunch. Twice, administration officials walked into the classroom to tell Hrag to hold the kids in his room for the rest of the day, but not to let the class know. Of course, the kids were aware that there had been a blackout. They figured Locke hadn't paid the electric bill.

Taylor Rifkin and some of the other ninth-grade teachers were in the staff lunchroom finishing up a planning session for the first freshman social when the lights went out. Taylor was pleased that the veterans had invited her to join them. She hadn't expected them to be so welcoming to a new TFA teacher. The power failure barely registered with her. There had been plenty of little technical glitches these first few days of school; she figured this was just another one. Her fifth-period class was due to start in minutes, so she finished the fried chicken from the fast-food place up the street, clipped up her long brown hair, and made her way back to room A22, one of the makeshift bungalow classrooms on the outer reaches of the campus built years before to relieve overcrowding. Outside, the sunshine was blinding.

Her ninth-grade English students entered the bungalow joking that since there was no power, there would be no lesson that day. Taylor's green eyes flashed. "Class, I do not care whether we have power or not," she announced, carefully enunciating every word. "I am not prepared to let this class slip further behind my other classes because of a technical difficulty. We will continue our lesson as scheduled. Please open your books to page fifty-eight."

The students quieted down. Taylor knew they would. She had spent the previous week on rules and procedures. She was tough, no doubt about it. She didn't mind if the kids considered her a bitch. She wasn't the buddy-buddy type anyway. She was a realist. She had *x* number of ninth-graders—figure twenty in a class, five classes—one hundred or so. She wasn't going to be the teacher driving them home at night and baking them cookies. She was going to be the teacher who taught them English and actually gave them the strategies they needed to graduate. She didn't care if they loved English, and she didn't care if they hated her. What she cared about was helping them make it through the state standardized tests. That was her big goal. Forget the TFA do-gooder crap.

Still, even she was surprised by her tough-love shtick. *I didn't know I had this in me. Where did this voice come from? And the false enthusiasm? What an act! Whatever. It's working.*

It didn't come out of nowhere. As a communications major at the University of Southern California (USC), Taylor had gotten used to addressing large audiences. The toughness, she knew, was in her DNA. Though her parents were now neighbors of Oprah Winfrey's in Montecito, California, they had worked hard and long for that address. Her father started out as a teacher. The Rifkins made their fortune when they bought some of the first California Weight Watchers franchises and later sold them.

When Taylor was in the eighth grade, she became anorexic and lost forty pounds. Her parents pulled her out of school and had her admitted to the eating disorders program at UCLA Hospital. Taylor spent five weeks in treatment. When she was released, she returned to the alternative school in which she had been enrolled. The school administration asked her to address the student body and speak frankly about her ordeal. Taylor was ashamed and embarrassed, but she did it. After that, she was more cautious about revealing too much of herself to anyone. And she was careful not to try too hard to be perfect.

That wasn't easy. Particularly when she was surrounded by the type A high achievers in Teach For America. Taylor had a difficult time at the summer institute and was so put off by the experience that she didn't bother to attend the closing ceremonies. Her family had reservations, too. They didn't think she could handle the pressure.

But Taylor left TFA's summer school confident that she had mastered the key to being a successful teacher: classroom management. She learned that lesson the hard way. It still upset her to think about that day in mid-July. It was a Wednesday, her third day of teaching. She began by allowing the kids one minute to "get the talking out of them." She knew immediately that it was a big mistake. When she called the class to order, the chatter continued, and she tried to speak above them.

"I would like you to write a paragraph about your favorite childhood memory," she said, her voice raised. Another mistake.

"I don't have one," shouted one student.

"I wasn't born," quipped another.

"It was the day my dad beat me up," said the kid in the corner.

Taylor changed tack. "If you can't remember a childhood memory, then tell me what you did yesterday," she said.

"Nothin' " was the first response.

"Took naps" was the second.

It didn't get any better. Taylor decided to illustrate the elements of a good paragraph by using a handout with a line drawing of a stoplight. But the kids argued over which color went where. She herself became confused. When she suggested that yellow meant "slow down," they corrected her: "Not in L.A.!" Soon all the kids were talking out of turn. One kid started whistling; others took up the refrain.

She was paralyzed. *What do I do?* Finally, the faculty advisor observing in the back of the room had to step in to restore order. She kept the students after class and gave them a stern lecture. Then she gave Taylor one, too.

It stuck. The next day Taylor went in with guns blazing. She walked up and down the room and addressed the class: "You will NEVER disrespect me again," she barked. Then she proceeded to lay down the laws of her classroom. The kids were spellbound. Taylor never had a problem with discipline again. At the end of summer school, students came up to her and thanked her for maintaining control and allowing them to learn. They told her they wished she had been even stricter.

Now, in the darkened classroom, she began the lesson she had meticulously planned the night before on exploring narration and point of view in the short story. "Open your books," she repeated. "Check this out."

She stopped. Someone was talking.

"When I'm talking, you're not; when you're talking, I'm not," she said, repeating her pet phrase for what seemed like the hundredth time that day. "I'll wait till it's quiet." She stood staring at Billy, a Latino boy in the front row who'd been talking. "I'll wait . . . Raised hand, please. Thank you, Billy. Question?"

Taylor was halfway through the lesson when there was a knock on the door. She knew something was wrong as soon as she saw Mr. Wooden, one of the ninth-grade deans. He turned his face away from the students and spoke in a clipped whisper. The school was on lockdown. Under no circumstances was she to allow any student to leave the classroom. Taylor nodded knowingly. Meanwhile, her heart was racing. *What will I tell the kids when they ask why the dean came? What happened? Are we all in danger?*

She tried to pull herself together and continue the lesson. But it wasn't easy. As she taught, the internal monologue kept running through her head. *Taylor, keep calm, damn it! You are in control of this classroom. Don't let them know anything is wrong. Just keep teaching. Wait a second. Lockdown! We are all going to die! A terrorist is running in the hallways of the main building and is headed out here to the bungalows to kill us next!* All she could see were images of Columbine.

Now a kid was raising his hand—as required—and asking to go to the bathroom.

"No," she said. "You can't."

"Why not?" the student asked.

"Look," she said. "You can't go to the bathroom because nobody is leaving right now."

Twenty pairs of eyes were trained on her. Then Irvin, one of her smartest students, called out: "It's because we're on lockdown, isn't it?"

She could hear the fear in his voice for sure, but there was something else there, too, something knowing, almost cynical. Irvin had been down this road before.

"Yes, we are on lockdown," she conceded, as if this were as routine as lunch period. "There is nothing to worry about. But we will not be leaving this classroom until we are instructed to do so."

Taylor continued the lesson. By the end of the period, the lights were back on. There had been no foul play. Locke—and some two million other customers—had lost electricity when a utility worker at a distribution plant accidentally cut a power cable.

CHAPTER TWO

The School and the Movement

Although education has long been considered a cornerstone of American democracy, there was an achievement gap in this country long before Teach For America started sending graduates like Phillip, Taylor, Hrag, and Rachelle into schools like Locke. The shocking disparity in academic achievement between students in low-income areas (predominantly children of color) and their higher-income counterparts (usually white) reaches back to the earliest days of our nation's history and remains today—seemingly immutable. The potential consequences of this great divide are dire: to paraphrase Thomas Jefferson, no enduring nation can be both ignorant and free.

Until Teach For America decided that higher education's best and brightest would raise up K–12's lowest and poorest, the job of closing the gap was left to an educational system only marginally responsive to efforts at reform. But a swing in the civic sensibilities of America's young elite in the 1990s coincided with a federally backed move toward outcome-based instruction, and TFA—slowly at first, but then faster and faster—became a force for change. Not only did TFA fill spots in schools like Locke, which saw the teacher corps as a risk-free option, preferable to hiring longtime subs and district castaways; it also began to build a farm team of education reformers who held out hope for a more just and lasting change—a change that would close the gap once and for all. It was a change that seemed all but certain to occur when Locke was built.

Locke High School arose out of the ashes of the infamous Watts riots, a six-day spasm of racial violence in August 1965 that stunned the nation. The immediate cause of one of the bloodiest episodes of civil unrest in America's history was a routine traffic stop that turned ugly. It was an unbearably hot summer night. The police officer was white; the two brothers he pulled over on suspicion of drunken driving were black. Locals, driven out of their homes by the heat, gathered at the scene as twenty-one-year-old Marquette Frye took and failed a sobriety test, and then proceeded, along with his brother and mother, to resist arrest. Police reinforcements arrived, and so did more spectators. Within minutes, the size of the crowd swelled from twenty-five to one thousand; the mood morphed from curious to furious. Eventually, a half dozen or so people were arrested after tussling with police. As the last squad car left the scene, a bottle hit the rear fender of the black-and-white and shattered.

The riot had begun. When it finally ended nearly a week later, the siege covered an area twice the size of the island of Manhattan. A heavy toll had been exacted on the mostly black community of South Central Los Angeles: thirty-four people were dead, one thousand were injured, and more than six hundred buildings were damaged or destroyed. Some four thousand of the estimated ten thousand rioters who ravaged the city were hauled away in handcuffs. The financial losses were put at $40 million; the psychic cost was incalculable. When the rage was spent and an exhausted calm finally descended, the community looked like a charred battlefield.

The Watts riots occurred a little more than a year after the passage of the Civil Rights Act of 1964. The landmark federal legislation was aimed specifically at addressing and eliminating racial inequality; in fact, it protected the civil rights of all by banning discrimination based on race, color, religion, sex, or national origin. Though the law promised to usher in a new era in race relations, riots broke out in a number of cities within weeks of its passage. In the meantime, a number of states maneuvered to eviscerate some of the legislation's key reforms.

California was one such state. In a move to circumvent the fair-housing components of both the federal legislation and California's own Rumford Fair Housing Act of 1963, Proposition 14 was put on the 1964 ballot. Under the terms of the proposition, a new amendment would be added to the California Constitution that would give owners the right to decline to sell, lease, or rent property to anyone they chose, essentially legalizing race-based housing discrimination. The proposition passed by a whopping two-thirds majority, setting the stage, many believe, for the following summer's holocaust.

The city was still smoldering when California governor Pat Brown appointed ex-CIA chief John McCone to head a commission to investigate the causes of the civil unrest. In a report entitled "Violence in the City: An End or a Beginning?" the McCone Commission set out a detailed chronology of events, probed the riots' immediate and underlying causes, and suggested prescriptive actions to prevent a recurrence.

The violence caught the city by surprise. Just a year earlier, when other American cities had erupted in race riots, Los Angeles had remained quiet. Indeed, in 1964 the National Urban League named Los Angeles the best city in the country for "Negroes" to live in—and so it seemed. The McCone Commission noted that the opportunity to succeed in L.A. was "probably unequaled in any other major American city." It described the "Negro districts" of Los Angeles as "neither slums nor urban gems"; most housing units located there were single-family structures on well-maintained streets. Compared with conditions in most other large cities, the lot of blacks in Los Angeles was declared "superior."

But the report also conceded that the city should have seen "trouble gathering under the surface calm." A wave of black immigrants from the South had resulted in an explosion of the African American population of Los Angeles—from 75,000 in 1940 to 650,000 in 1965. The realities of life in southern California often collided with the newcomers' dreams. Los Angeles may have offered better living conditions than other, grittier cities, but it was far from color-blind.

It took the commission one hundred days to issue its report. Its conclusion: the area that gave rise to the violence was home to bad schools, chronically high unemployment rates, and "resentment, even hatred of police." Though some black leaders complained that the riots had been studied through the distorted lens of the ruling white middle class, the commission's analysis of the underpinnings of the riots was generally accepted.

The commission recommended urgent action to reverse a spiral of failure. The affected areas were in desperate need of jobs, better community policing, and improved schools. Failure to address the inequities, it warned, would be a costly mistake, a mere "curtain-raiser for what could blow up one day in the future."

The city's principal responses: the Los Angeles Human Relations Commission was established to liaise between the city and the community; the number of minorities on the police force was upped; the Martin Luther King/Drew Medical Center was opened, giving some 1.5 million people living in a ninety-four-square-mile radius easier access to a hospital; and the L.A. Watts Summer Games were established to engage disaffected black youth. The games, modeled after the Olympics, were first held in 1968 at the newly opened Locke High School.

But McCone's dark warning proved prophetic.

Twenty-seven years after the fatal Watts riots, Los Angeles erupted again. The spark that ignited six days of rioting in April 1992 was the aquittal of four white cops charged in the videotaped beating of black motorist Rodney King. But, as in the case of the Watts riots, underlying tensions in Los Angeles's black communities had been building for years. A deep economic recession exacerbated the situation. The verdict, which appeared to blacks to legitimize what seemed to be an open-and-shut case of police brutality, was the tipping point.

By the time the fires were extinguished, the soot had settled, and the acrid smell of incineration had finally wafted away, the Rodney King riots had made history as the costliest civil disturbance in American history. The toll—in lives and capital—dwarfed that of the Watts riots. Fifty-five people were dead, more than two thousand injured, and ten thousand arrested. Damages totaled one billion dollars.

The rioters this time were not only African American; Hispanics participated in almost equal numbers. For blacks, the riots were initially a reaction to perceived police brutality; for Hispanics it was seen as a giant giveaway. "People who never had, found an opportunity to have, and they took it," explains Zeus Cubias, chairman of the Locke math department in 2005, who was a senior at Locke at the time of the riots. The majority of Hispanics had no truck with Rodney King's plight—or that of his people. They believed King was wrong to resist arrest.

Though the epicenter of the manmade quake was north and west of the area surrounding Locke, all of South Los Angeles was shaken. Schools were shuttered, allowing students of enterprise to join in the mayhem. Those who didn't actively go out and loot happily participated in the "Great Riot Sale" later. Eighteen-year-old Cubias, looking ahead to college in the fall, managed to buy a new TV, a stereo system, and a mini refrigerator for fifty bucks.

The area around Locke High School was mostly residential (few commercial businesses had set up shop in the wake of the Watts riots), so property damage was not as extensive as it might have been. But those who did do business in the area either armed themselves to protect their property or lost their shops to looting. On Imperial Highway, the main east-west artery near Locke, snipers stood atop store rooftops with rifles trained on would-be trespassers. Most unguarded businesses were damaged and never reopened. Liquor stores were a notable exception. They were up and running within days.

When Locke High School opened its doors in 1967, it was a welcome addition to a blighted neighborhood. In the wake of the Watts riots, the city had promised change, and Locke was a symbol of hope, visible proof that the city meant business. The new school was named after Alain Leroy Locke, a Harvard man who became the first African American Rhodes Scholar. The name alone spoke volumes.

Early graduates of Locke enjoyed the glory days. At the time, the school was considered a state-of-the-art facility. The staff was hand-picked, and Locke was awash in money. Baseball Hall of Famers Eddie Murray and Ozzie Smith were proud graduates. So were songwriter Patrice Rushen and smooth-jazz artist Gerald Albright. The school's music program became renowned—the Locke Saints Marching Band played at NBA parties, opened for pop star Michael Jackson at the Forum, was featured in videos, and was hired out for parties. "When I came here to Locke High School, I thought I was a movie star because I made the band," recalls Corwin Twine, a 1984 graduate who returned to Locke as a world history teacher in 2001.

But violence remained a hallmark of the community. Within weeks of its opening, police were called to the campus to contain a "rock and bottle throwing" mêleé that erupted after dismissal. Locke made national headlines in January 1973 when a sixteen-year-old girl was killed in a drive-by shooting on her way home from school. That spring, two more Locke students were shot and wounded. The following year, Robert Briscoe, an eighteen-year-old student, was hit in the chest by a stray bullet while jogging on the school track. He died several hours later. As the violence ticked upward, the spurt of antipoverty programs initiated in the wake of the Watts riots faltered.

A seismic demographic shift was under way in inner-city Los Angeles. By 1980, the white population had largely fled, and the Hispanic population was beginning its meteoric rise. The number of African Americans, which until then had been the largest minority group in Los Angeles County, peaked at 926,000, representing 12 percent of the population. Then began its inexorable decline.

"The plague hit," explains Otis Yette, an assistant principal at Locke in 2005. "Crack cocaine descended upon us. Little gangs took over the neighborhoods. Murder was rampant. So the good people moved out. And the black working-class families disappeared." The black folk left behind, says Yette, were those with the fewest options open to them. Spanish-speaking immigrants—some legal, many not—began to move into the areas vacated by working- and middle-class blacks.

Zeus Cubias was one of the newly arrived in 1982, the oldest of three kids born to a homemaker and an upholsterer from El Salvador. The Cubias family settled into an apartment at Imperial and Main—just blocks from Locke—because it was the only affordable housing they could find. Within five months, little Alex, as he liked to be called, was speaking English. By the time he got to Locke High School in 1988, he was just another "knucklehead"—a kid who believed that if he attended school three days straight, he was entitled to take the rest of the week off. He spent more time on the handball courts than he did in the classrooms.

By then, the school had lost its luster. Over time, Locke's initially high test scores and graduation rates sank. The dropout rate rose. The school's legendary music program declined. When Locke got noticed at all, it was not for music; it was for murder and mayhem. In 1987, Manuel Diaz, a sixteen-year-old tenth-grader, was shot while running from a cop. In 1988, a sixteen-year-old ninth-grader named George Hernandez was hit by a gangbanger's bullet. Seventeen-year-old Walter Stewart died in a gang shooting the year after that.

The violence hit home for Zeus when his cousin Spanky, a member of Los Hang Out Boys (LHOB) gang, was killed. Spanky had dropped out of school and was working at his father's body shop just a few streets away from campus. One day a guy pulled up to the shop on a bicycle and said: "Hey, you Spanky?" Then he point-blank shot him dead. The shooter was a gangster, too. Word was out that Spanky had killed a rival homey days before. Spanky's death was payback.

After the shooting, Zeus wanted out. Out of South Los Angeles and far away from the forces that had taken Spanky's life. By then he had met the person who would change his life—an uncredentialied teacher of tenth-grade English at Locke. After Zeus wrote a paper on the movie *Batman,* which had been shown in class, the teacher pulled the wiry young Latino aside and gave him a graphic novel to read. Zeus devoured it, and before long he was reading William Faulkner short stories and taking AP classes. Cubias graduated from Locke in 1992 and started at the University of California at Santa Barbara that fall. He majored in math and decided to become a teacher. Once he was credentialed, he returned to the hood and got a job at his alma mater.

When Cubias started at Locke—just twenty-one years after it opened—the student body was 78 percent black and 20 percent Hispanic. Four years after he graduated, the ratio was fifty-fifty. During the 2005–2006 school year, Hispanics at Locke outnumbered blacks two to one.

Even as their numbers dwindled, blacks still enjoyed positions of power in the community. The local papers were black-owned; the administrative positions at Locke tended to be filled by African Americans. (For a few months during the 2005–2006 school year, there were two Spanish-speaking assistant principals on staff. By year's end, one was gone and the other had announced she was leaving.) When visiting artists came to Locke to entertain at lunch, they tended to be black rappers. The homecoming festivities were largely a black affair. Murals on the outer walls of the handball courts, which were used exclusively by Latinos, honored black leaders such as Dr. Martin Luther King Jr. Locke, like all schools in the district, celebrated African American History Month each February.

But the way of life in the neighborhood was Latino. Taco stands outnumbered soul-food takeouts. Billboards were written in Spanish. The majority of home buyers were Hispanic. Posters celebrating Latino history and culture started appearing in Locke's hallways. The king and queen of the 2006 prom—along with every other member of the court— were Hispanic. (The principal personally intervened in the voting and announced a "tie" for one spot in the court so that at least one black face would appear in the commemorative photo.)

The transition from black majority to Hispanic majority had not been a smooth one. Maribel Gonzalez, valedictorian of the Locke class of 1998, who went on to UCLA and joined Teach For America when she graduated, remembers that race riots occurred all four years of her time at Locke. After a while, she became inured to most of the racial jousting. But it was hard to forget the riot of 1997. Maribel was a junior. Fighting broke out between blacks and Latinos at lunch, and LAPD swat teams were called in. When order was restored and kids returned to class, a lockdown was declared. Cops surrounded the school, patrolled the nearby streets, and manned the traffic stops. When the bell rang at three o'clock, kids were released class by class. By the time Maribel left Locke that day, it was five-thirty. The incident that sparked the fracas? Two black students had inadvertently bumped into a Latino student, knocking a can of soda from his hands.

When former student Corwin Twine returned to Locke as a teacher in 2001, he was shocked. "I couldn't believe it," he recalls. "Kids were shooting dice, having sex, doing drugs—it was like a freaking war zone. And there were certain people working here who were scared. You could tell by the way they talked to the kids." Twine reassured one frightened white teacher: "Dude, they won't mess with you. They kill a white guy, you know how many cans and rocks they gonna turn over here?"

In 2005, the two cultures coexisted, uneasily. Most teachers made an effort to "integrate" the races in their classrooms. But outside, on the quad and the scruffy playing fields, the cultural turf was clearly demarcated. The handball courts belonged to the Latinos. The football field and basketball courts were all-black terrain. On the quad, Latinos would "kick" along the south boundary. Directly opposite, facing them, were the African American students. The cafeteria divided pretty much the same way: as you entered, it was blacks in the left-hand corner, Spanish speakers in the first few benches, special ed students tucked away in the right-hand corner. The area just outside the cafeteria—the eastern edge of the quad—was a kind of demilitarized zone bounded by two trees. The African American football players sat under one. Under the other was a group of Latinos, some of them athletes, too. The understanding was that between the trees there would always be peace. The treaty has yet to be broken.

Even in 1967, when Locke was a spanking new $5.4 million school built on 25½ acres in the middle of a moldered community, closing the achievement gap for all the at-risk students it enrolled was going to be an uphill battle. The 1965 McCone Commission had found that the achievement test scores for students in the city's disadvantaged neighborhoods, like Locke's, were "shockingly lower" than the citywide averages—in all subjects and at all grade levels.

But few could have imagined that forty years on so little would have changed. In the 2005–2006 school year, by virtually any and every measure—whether by state, federal, or private-research yardsticks—Locke was one of the lowest-performing schools in all of the Los Angeles Unified School District (LAUSD), if not in the state.

California has a grab bag of indexes used to calculate academic performance; they are as confusing as their acronyms. The state metric is the Academic Performance Index (API), a scale ranging from 200 to 1,000 that reflects a school's performance based on the results of statewide testing. Schools that fail to reach California's API performance target of 800 must hit specific annual growth objectives until they do. Failure to meet the growth goals results in penalties, which can include school reorganization or even a state takeover. In 2005, Locke's API was 488, the second lowest—by a hair—in LAUSD.

The feds' system of accountability for schools receiving antipoverty funds is called Adequate Yearly Progress (AYP) and is based on a set of requirements, including API growth. Schools that lag in their AYP for two consecutive years go to a Program Improvement (PI) plan in which the severity of the penalties increases over time, although the government doesn't spell out consequences past year five. Locke has been in PI since the 1997–1998 school year. The school met its API growth target in 2005–2006, and it graduated 332 students—the largest number in recent memory. But it still fell far short of reaching federal proficiency rates.

Research carried out by UCLA's Graduate School of Education and Information Studies in 2006 only underscored Locke's last-place status. UCLA found that Locke's "College Opportunity Ratio" was rock bottom in a study of nineteen of the city's lowest-performing high schools: for every 100 of the 979 ninth-graders who entered Locke in 2001, 24 graduated in 2005, and 3 completed the course requirements for admission to a California State University (CSU) or a University of California (UC) campus. Locke's ratio on another key UCLA indicator, the "Cumulative Promotion Index"—which calculates the probability that a student entering ninth grade will complete high school on time with a regular diploma—was the lowest of the low, at 15 percent.

Over the years, beleaguered Locke High School became the poster child for needed school reform in Los Angeles, a photo op for politicians and celebrities alike. Vice President George Bush visited Locke in 1988, and President Bill Clinton stopped by on a "poverty" tour in 1999. Tipper Gore, John McCain, and Maria Shriver all made house calls. The rapper Ice Cube appeared in 1993, and Muhammad Ali was there in 1996. Edward James Olmos, star of the movie *Stand and Deliver,* basketball legend Kareem Abdul-Jabbar, and jazz great Herbie Hancock have paid their respects as well.

The school district tried numerous interventions and reforms to turn things around. Administrators were hired and fired, the school was reorganized into small learning communities, after-school and Saturday classes were offered to beef up instruction, and gang-prevention measures were put in place. Lots of money was allocated; much of it was misspent.

Inevitably, the initiatives had as much staying power as did the staff forced to implement them; each year, up to fifty teachers dropped out of Locke. When Dr. Frank Wells took over as principal in 2004, he was the third person to hold the title in almost as many years. Things had gotten so bad that in 2001 local superintendent Sylvia Rousseau moved her district office to Locke and briefly ran the school herself. But since the arrival of Wells, the vibe on campus had changed. Locke was a safer school. Everyone said so—even the rotten, bottom-of-the-barrel teachers, the ones Wells referred to as "the residue," the ones who "grieved" him to the union every chance they got. Locke had fewer drug busts and fights, and the school district police had the numbers to prove it: the school had gone from first in the number of campus crime reports in LAUSD to thirteenth. Wells recited that factoid every chance he got.

Wells brought a lot to the table. He was an African American male with a commanding presence. As the only son of a single mother, he could relate to all the kids at Locke whose fathers were MIA. And he knew what it was like to grow up living week-to-week on government assistance. Most important, he had a reputation for raising test scores. As principal of a low-performing elementary school in northern California a few years before, he had made news with "soaring" scores under his leadership. His framed press clippings were hanging on the wood-paneled walls of the principal's conference room.

Wells made his mark at Locke immediately: trouble started on the second day of school. It was during lunch, and he was on the quad, the large grassy interior courtyard where kids naturally gathered during breaks. As the new principal stood there surveying the student body, two groups of rival gangbangers squared off in a furious scrum in the middle of the quad. It didn't last long. Campus security moved in, and the ringleaders were nabbed. When Wells asked for a list of the other kids involved—and anybody else known to associate with them—security presented him with some eighty names. Satisfied that he had identified the few kids responsible for the most trouble on campus, Wells kicked them out of Locke. Most, he suspected, would end up back in juvenile hall; some would be offered "opportunity transfers" to other schools. He called Superintendent Rousseau to let her know what he had done.

"I need to know if you will support me on this or if I should pack my bag," he said.

Rousseau told him to clean the school up; the district didn't need any more bad publicity coming out of Locke. Few on campus complained about what seemed to be a lack of due process for the alleged perpetrators; most were happy with Wells's housecleaning. But not everyone. Some higher-ups in the district questioned the legality of the expulsions. And the ejected students had their own way of registering their dissatisfaction. They carved a big C on the hood of the beautiful black Cadillac truck parked in the spot marked "Principal." The C, of course, stood for the Crips, the predominant gang at Locke.

Frank Wells was no stranger to violence. Like many of his childhood friends from the projects in Hunters Point, outside San Francisco, he had flirted with gang life. But he was lucky. Though he was a special ed student who didn't learn to read until he was thirteen, he graduated from high school, joined the army, and went on to college. Many of his friends were not as fortunate. Some ended up in jail. Two were shot dead.

Wells fell in love with Locke at first sight. He saw the barred windows, and he stood before the sliding steel gates while beefy Themus, the sad-eyed security guard, opened the iron door just wide enough for him to enter. He strode down the cement breezeway that separates the instructional wings from the strip of administrative offices where Superintendent Rousseau had set up camp. And he saw the corner principal's office with its revolving door. He climbed the stairs and noticed kids roaming the halls when they should have been in classrooms. And he noted the graffiti, the ragtag fields, the littered campus, and the cement walkways polka-dotted with blackened chewing gum. Across the street from the back of the bungalows was the run-down housing on Avalon Boulevard, rumored to be a Crips hideout. He certainly saw the on-site police station, the full-time parole officer's desk, the derelict student garden, and the child-care center for student mothers. The "tardy room," a holding pen for kids caught in the daily floor-by-floor truancy sweeps, was in plain sight—it took up a corner of the open-air cafeteria.

The test scores and school stats, of course, were another matter. Locke's 2004 API was 450—the lowest result in all of LAUSD. That gave Locke a statewide rank of 1 out of a possible 10—even among schools with similar demographic profiles. Results on the CAT/6, the norm-referenced tests that compare California students to their peers nationwide, were equally dismal. Only 11 percent of Locke's ninth-graders scored at the 50 percent level (the national average) on reading and math. Thirty-one percent of the freshman class was expected to graduate—a number just slightly lower than their parents' own graduation rates.

Wells submitted his application, and in the time it took him to drive home, the district was on the phone trying to set up an interview. Other candidates may have seen in Locke hopeless dysfunction. Frank Wells saw opportunity.

When Wells was named principal, Teach For America had already been a presence at Locke for a decade. But the number of recruits in any given year had never exceeded five, and in all, fewer than two dozen TFA alums had taught at Locke. That began to change when Dr. Rousseau signed a contract with TFA allowing recruits to train at Locke's summer school. At first Rousseau, now a professor of education at USC, was dubious. She was a product and proponent of teacher-ed programs. But the district was desperate for math and science teachers, and Rousseau reckoned a TFA recruit had to be better than a sub or what she called a "dying-on-the-vine" teacher. It worked out. TFA sent Locke quality teachers, and the dynamic at the school began to change. "TFA was a real asset for us," she recalls.

Under Wells, Locke became a TFA factory, home to the largest cluster of corps members in the Los Angeles region. In 2004, his first year, TFA sent nine corps members to Locke. The next year, when Phillip, Rachelle, Hrag, and Taylor joined the staff, they were among thirteen new Locke TFAers, bringing the total of first- or second-year recruits teaching at Locke to nearly two dozen. Five more staffers, including the new assistant principal Chad Soleo and the brilliant physics teacher Josh Hartford, who headed the School of Social Empowerment, one of six small learning communities at Locke, were star TFA alums.

"The TFA teachers come here with a missionary zeal," said Wells, explaining why he hired so many. "It must be a requirement of the program."

Good grades and a history of achievement were, too. The program was highly competitive. A record seventeen thousand people applied for two thousand spots in the 2005 corps. Among them were 12 percent of the senior class at Yale, 11 percent of the graduating classes of Dartmouth and Amherst College, and 8 percent from Princeton and Harvard. Founder Wendy Kopp once said that she wanted Teach For America to have the same cachet as a Rhodes Scholarship. In 2005 it did: Teach For America was *the* postgraduate program of choice for the elite of America's top universities.

Ultimately, only 12 percent of all applicants gained admission to TFA in 2005; two thirds of the Ivy Leaguers who applied didn't make the cut. The average GPA of those who did was 3.5, SAT scores averaged 1310, and 95 percent held leadership positions on their campuses or in their communities. Getting accepted at Teach For America was a big deal.

The selection process had actually changed little since 1990, when Wendy Kopp and her start-up team accepted 500 of the 2,500 college seniors who applied to join Teach For America's inaugural class. The first applicants submitted an essay application, underwent a tough personal interview, and had to present a five-minute lesson plan. In the interview, selectors probed for proof of the candidate's persistence, commitment, and intellectual heft. Kopp recalls in her book *One Day, All Children* that one of the questions posed to applicants was "(1) What is wind? Don't describe it, just tell me what it is. (2) Phenomenologists draw an analogy between religion and the wind, claiming that one can't see religion, only the manifestations of it—like synagogues, churches, and mosques. Similarly, one can't see the wind, only manifestations of it—waves in a wheat field, moving branches. What's another analogy you can draw to the wind?"

From the very beginning, Kopp believed that in order to make teaching attractive to her peers, tagged then as the "Me Generation," or even the "Mean Generation," there had to be an "aura of status and selectivity" around Teach For America. High-achieving college students like Kopp viewed teaching as a downwardly mobile career. Those who didn't go directly to graduate school after graduation tended to head for investment banks or marketing firms. To most, becoming a schoolteacher was unthinkable.

Kopp was going to change all that. The 1989 graduate of the Woodrow Wilson School of Public and International Affairs at Princeton University wrote her senior thesis on the idea of starting a "Teacher Corps" not unlike the Peace Corps. The mission would be to take on what she considered to be the number one civil rights issue of her generation: the educational achievement gap between the rich and the poor in America.

Nothing in Kopp's past, to that point, had suggested that education would become her issue or social justice her passion. Raised in University Park, an affluent, lily-white enclave of Dallas so insulated from urban realities that it was known as "the Bubble," Kopp didn't know exactly what she wanted to be when she grew up. She told her local newspaper, *The Dallas Morning News,* in 1985: "I would love a career that combines speaking and writing skills with economics and politics." She never seriously considered becoming a teacher.

Kopp was part of a generation of "extraordinarily bright, morally earnest, and incredibly industrious" students the author David Brooks wrote about in a much-noticed 2001 *Atlantic Monthly* article called "The Organization Kid." The cohort were rule-following team players who were not trying to buck the system but climb it, observed Brooks. Like others among Princeton's young meritocratic elite that Brooks deftly profiled, Kopp was goal-oriented—a straight-A student who was valedictorian at Highland Park High School, a perennial on the Best High Schools in America list. Kopp's credentials—even by today's overheated standards—were impressive. She was editor of the school newspaper two years running, president of the debate team, a member of the National Forensic League, the lead in the school play (Hannah in Neil Simon's *California Suite*), and a member of the National Honor Society. Kopp did community service through an organization called Right Turns, which counseled younger children about drug prevention. She also sat at the school's Round Table, a current-events discussion group. In the summers Kopp worked for her parents, Jay and Mary Pat, who published guide-books for conventioneers in Dallas and Houston. She loved to play tennis and was an avid jogger. Oh, and she also sewed her own dresses and skirts.

At Princeton she kept up the pace. Outside of the lecture hall, much of her energy went into the Foundation for Student Communication, a student-run organization that held three yearly conferences and pub-lished its own undergrad magazine called *Business Today,* the largest student-run magazine in the country. Within months of joining, Kopp was an associate editor writing about student entrepreneurs for the magazine. But *Business Today* was financially shaky, and soon enough Kopp was working the ad side as well. During an interview with a top executive for a story she was writing, Kopp mentioned the magazine's financial woes and suggested he might like to buy an ad. She made the sale then and there. More important, she learned an invaluable fund-raising lesson that would serve her well in the early days of Teach For America. Instead of hitting up lower-level executives for ads, she realized it was more efficient—and effective—to go right to the top. After that, ad revenues ceased to be a problem. By her senior year, Kopp was president of the foundation and editor and publisher of the magazine. Foundation revenues had jumped fivefold, from $300,000 to $1.4 million.

The idea for Teach For America was born at one of the foundation's conferences in November 1988. Kopp had handpicked a group of top executives and leading students to meet in San Francisco that year to dis-cuss the problems facing public school education. Among the many issues on the agenda was a session about teacher quality. Nearly all of the student participants claimed that they would be willing to teach in public schools if it were possible to do so without having degrees in educa-tion. Suddenly, Kopp had an idea. As she wrote in her 2001 book: "Why didn't this country have a national teaching corps of recent college grad-uates who would commit two years to teach in urban and rural schools?"

The rest of the tale is now part of TFA lore. Kopp was the very last person in the Woodrow Wilson School to declare a thesis topic that year; she couldn't find an advisor. So she went to the sociology department chair, Marvin Bressler, who promised to take her on if she agreed to propose mandatory national service as her thesis. Kopp ignored Bressler's suggestion. She had a better idea: she would write about creating a national teaching corps. When she made her case to Bressler, he quipped: "You are quite evidently deranged."

He was joking. Bressler was very impressed with Kopp; he just thought she suffered from excessive ambition. What she proposed seemed to him undoable. But, as Bressler recalls, Kopp was possessed of a kind of "innocent arrogance," which made it clear that she believed she had already thought of ways to overcome all the obstacles to her plans, and Bressler evidently had not. She was right, says Bressler with a chuckle. "She had this combination of midwestern idealism and a very good practical mind on how to do things, that made her dreams less extravagant," he remembers. "It was a kind of American conviction that if you have a good idea, it can be put into practice."

In April 1989, when she turned in a very detailed proposal for a national teaching corps that she calculated would take $2.5 million to get off the ground, Bressler dismissed it as "a glorified advertising campaign." Kopp defended her idea, Bressler came around, and the thesis earned an A.

Kopp recalls that her senior year was difficult. "I was in a funk," she confides seventeen years later from her small, simple office adorned only with a few photographs, among them one of her wedding to Richard Barth and another of her three small children on the beach. "I was tortured. I could not figure out what I wanted to spend my life doing." Kopp knew she wanted to make a difference in the world. But she was at a loss as to how to do that. So she reckoned she'd start with a corporate training program—"maybe do brand management, or investment banking, or management consulting." But her heart wasn't in it, and she kept searching for more meaningful work. She wrote to policy makers seeking internships, and she even fleetingly entertained the notion of teaching. When she discovered that she was too late for a spot in Princeton's small teaching program, she researched the maze of teacher certification requirements and talked with a recruiter for the New York City public school system. She gave up when she was told that New York didn't hire uncredentialed teachers until days before the school year began. But the experience made her wonder: *Why aren't we being recruited as aggressively to teach as we are being recruited to work on Wall Street?*

In the end, she applied to Morgan Stanley, McKinsey & Company,

Bain & Company, Procter & Gamble, and a commercial real estate venture. Kopp, impressive résumé aside, was turned down by every one of them. When she sent her idea for a teaching corps to the White House for consideration, her proposal was mistaken for a job application and she was rejected there as well.

So she decided to turn her thesis into reality. Though Bressler scoffed at the notion that Kopp could actually raise the $2.5 million needed to start a national teaching corps, he thought enough of the project to put her in touch with Princeton's director of development. The day after she turned in "A Plan and Argument for the Creation of a National Teacher Corps," Kopp whittled her thesis down to a thirty-page proposal and headed over to the college library for a listing of the country's top CEOs. Within a week, some thirty proposals went out across corporate America, each topped with an eye-catching red cover and a letter requesting a meeting. By the time Kopp graduated from Princeton, she had secured a $26,000 seed grant from Mobil and donated office space in Manhattan from Union Carbide.

With three trash bags of clothes and a sleeping bag, Kopp moved into a New York apartment with two other girls. She spent the summer crisscrossing the country in search of funders and wise counsel—with mixed results. It was hard to argue with her stated goal of closing the achievement gap. But was sending the teachers with the least amount of experience into the classrooms with the greatest need the right solution? Was it even fair? Skeptics argued that the way to close the achievement gap was to reform teacher education, not to undermine it by sending teachers into needy classrooms with a meager few weeks of training. What's more, they charged, TFA's limited two-year commitment would only add to the problem of teacher retention in underserved communities. TFA could actually turn out to be an enabler of dysfunctional school systems. Would providing underperforming school districts with ready-made teachers for the hardest-to-fill spots allow them to put off true reform?

Kopp had an answer for every concern. Her plan to close the achievement gap was based on a two-pronged theory of change. In the short term, she believed, the most talented graduates in the country would almost certainly be successful in the classroom if they worked relentlessly and were committed to the mission. In the longer term, she was convinced, the TFA experience would be so profound that it would inform whatever its members decided to do afterward. Inevitably, she reckoned,

TFA alums—the doctors, lawyers, journalists, academics, policy makers, and, yes, the schoolteachers and administrators who got hooked and never left—would eventually force and lead the systemic change necessary to level the educational playing field.

Professors in the schools of education may have complained about the possible negative consequences of hiring TFAers, but at least some superintendents in the trenches indicated they would jump at the chance to hire young college graduates from premier universities for their toughest slots. The alternative, they knew, was to contract with permanent subs—many with no training at all, some without even a college degree. In the face of a national teacher shortage, taking a chance on a TFA recruit was a no-brainer.

So Kopp forged ahead. That fall she assembled a skeleton crew to help realize her vision. Sustained by cold pizza over a seemingly endless string of all-nighters, the group of five moved into larger quarters (this time donated by Morgan Stanley) and began to work out how to recruit, select, train, and place a prospective five hundred new teachers.

In one respect, the selection process was easy. Kopp and her band were looking for people just like themselves—hard-driving, high-achieving twenty-somethings who, when contemplating their futures, were filled with a mix of idealism and indecision, in equal measure. "I think it's very hard for college seniors to think about their futures," Kopp explains. "At that age, you think the next two years are the rest of your life. It was certainly true for me. I assumed, honestly, I really believed all the momentum [for this movement] would exist after two years. I fully thought it would happen. I had no long-term plans for the future. None."

After researching selection models and consulting with successful principals, the start-up crew hammered out a rigorous admissions process. Long and heated debates resulted in a list of twelve character traits thought necessary to succeed in the classroom: persistence, commitment, integrity, flexibility, oral communication skills, enthusiasm, sensitivity, independence and assertiveness, ability to work within an organization, possession of self-evaluative skills, ability to operate without student approval, and conceptual ability/intellect. Candidates applying to Teach America—as it was tentatively called—would be judged on each trait based on a sliding six-point scale. (It turned out that Teach America was a name already taken by a medical company. Kopp tossed around a number of other names, like Teach U.S. or U.S. Teach. The idea of inserting the word "For" and making the name Teach For America came to her during a late-night ride on D.C.'s Metro. "Even better," she wrote in her book, "in that it was a call to action and communicated a sense of service.")

The first Teach For America Institute was held in June 1990 at the University of Southern California. Dr. Marvin Bressler was the keynote speaker. His advice to the five hundred graduates who came from one hundred colleges was fittingly self-effacing: "Whatever you do as teachers, never discourage your students."

The institute started on a high note, and then things went rapidly downhill. The eight weeks of training were disastrous, recalls Kopp. Corps members sparred with one another, the training was inadequate, the housing spartan; on top of all that, recruits were ineligble for the loan forgiveness from the federal government that TFA had promised them. People skills were not Kopp's strong suit; she holed herself up in a suite of dorm rooms to avoid all the conflict. Teach For America barely survived its first summer institute. There would be many more challenges during the so-called dark years of the early and mid-nineties, when the organization's very existence was at stake.

Linda Darling-Hammond, a highly regarded professor at Columbia University's Teachers College, almost sank the flagship in 1994 when she published a scathing critique of Teach For America in the September issue of the *Phi Delta Kappan,* the premier academic journal of the education community. Noting the unequal status of TFA recruits and their charges, Darling-Hammond alleged that the "frankly missionary program" was a quick fix that was harmful to students most in need of qualified teachers. For recruits, TFA's true beneficiaries, it was a handy "pit stop" on the road to their "real" jobs in law, medicine, or business. The "slapdash" teacher-training program devalued teaching as a profession, she continued. And the "revolving-door trip into and out of teaching" only exacerbated the critical problem of teacher retention in the ghetto. The assault hurt Kopp personally and Teach For America publicly. Funding, always an issue, became even more precarious. Some supporters got the jitters. Internecine fighting broke out among staff. Kopp wrote in her memoir that the organization at that point reminded her of *Lord of the Flies.*

The financial turnaround began in 1996; structural and programmatic improvements followed. By the time Teach For America was ten years old, fifteen hundred corps members were teaching in fifteen different placement sites. Over the decade, more than thirty thousand applicants had competed for five thousand teaching jobs in low-income communities across the country. On firmer footing, the ten-million-dollar organization began an ambitious five-year plan to grow in size and impact. Money flowed in as corporations and foundations lined up behind Gap founders Doris and Donald Fisher to underwrite TFA's expansion. What had started out as a small grassroots movement was poised to become one of the most successful—and sophisticated—nonprofits in the country.

But did it work? And how could you tell? In the beginning, there was no measurable way to assess success in the classroom. You just knew it when you saw it. But sometimes appearances did not match reality. Sometimes the teachers who seemed most successful—those who had the greatest rapport with students—were not the ones raising kids' test scores. Kopp knew that equal resources did not correspond to equal opportunity. In order to close the achievement gap, low-income kids needed to *achieve* at the same academic level as their more privileged peers. So TFA decided that student outcomes should be the barometer of a teacher's success.

"[Kopp] shifted the conversation from input to output, from what credentials people have to what results they get with their kids," observes TFA alum Dave Levin, cofounder of the successful KIPP schools, a chain of fifty-seven charter schools serving more than fourteen thousand students nationwide. "And that is a fundamental shift in the way education is viewed."

Such an approach flouted educational convention. To some, the idea of evaluating a teacher based on student test scores seemed to ignore the myriad factors that militate against academic success for children in disadvantaged communities. Teachers couldn't and shouldn't be held accountable for the broken homes, the poverty, and the violence that circumscribed student achievement in underserved schools. Education wasn't about numbers and metrics; it involved many intangibles, making it much more complicated than a simple teacher-student binary. For lack of a better measure, districts and unions tied teacher salaries to years of service and academic degrees.

TFA and some in the education establishment had been at odds since Kopp first wrote her thesis. Over the years, the issue of how to improve teacher quality has been the subject of exhaustive debate. While some, like Linda Darling-Hammond, have argued that the answer lies in improving the quality of teacher training, Kopp believes the answer is to be found in improving the quality of the teacher.

To some, the presumption that smart kids with five weeks of training could do the job smacked of hubris. "You probably wouldn't want to be injected by someone from an organization called Nurse For America," says UCLA's director of Urban Schooling Jeannie Oakes. "But we tend not to balk at someone inexperienced and untrained being put in some of the most challenging classroom situations in the U.S. TFA is at its root a stopgap measure."

"I guess we're asking two different questions," explains Kopp. "Some people out there believe that what we are doing is flying in the face of traditional notions about what needs to be done to improve education. For them, the starting question is how do we strengthen the profession of teaching; recruiting people to a short-term commitment seems like not the way to go.

"The question we're asking is: How as a society are we going to finally step back and make real progress to address the disparities in the educational opportunities [between the rich and poor]? We think the magnitude of the problem justifies out-of-the box solutions. We need to channel the energy of our most talented people in that direction."

Even as her organization has challenged the status quo in education, Kopp has tried to avoid direct confrontation with the powers that be. Politically nimble, TFA has not directly criticized school districts or the powerful unions that often control them. "TFA doesn't want to piss off the districts—the employers of their teachers," notes former Los Angeles mayor Richard Riordan, who was California's secretary of education from 2003 to 2005. "And it doesn't want to get into fights with the unions, which represent a mediocre bunch of people in a system with little or no accountability. TFA just wants to teach kids. So it's not solving the whole problem. It's going to take a revolution to do that, because under union control, there is no accountability, you can't fire teachers or principals—you can't even flunk students."

Though Kopp rejects the notion that the only path to the classroom is through campus-based teacher education programs and notes that many successful private schools employ noncertified teachers, TFA has formed strategic alliances with university credentialing and graduate programs—

like Loyola Marymount University in Los Angeles and University of Pennsylvania in Philadelphia—so that recruits satisfy state and federal teaching requirements. At the same time, she joins a growing number of like-minded education reformers, and the federal government, in openly encouraging the growth of alternative credentialing programs as a way of attracting more top-flight talent into the profession. A 2006 report from The Education Schools Project found that the vast majority of the country's university-level schools of education don't have the capacity to produce excellent teachers, and more than half of the teachers are educated in programs with the lowest admission standards—some of which accept 100 percent of applicants. Indeed, the National Council on Teacher Quality in 2004 reported that teaching attracts a "disproportionately high number of candidates from the lower end of the distribution of academic ability." That year, the average combined SAT score for college-bound seniors was 1026; the average of those intending to major in education was 965. (Future elementary school teachers tended to come from the bottom of the class; aspiring secondary school teachers were on a par with their peers.)

The 2006 report from The Education Schools Project found wide variations in curricula and approaches, amounting to a training universe that author Arthur Levine, former president of Columbia's Teachers College, likened to "Dodge City." The obvious conclusion: nobody knows what it takes to make a good teacher.

But Kopp believes the essence of good teaching *is* knowable. It isn't magic. After nearly a decade of sending thousands of teachers into scores of districts, she developed a theory about why certain teachers produced better student results than other equally committed teachers. She came to believe that good teaching was, in essence, the exercise of good leadership. Her theory was dubbed "Teaching as Leadership," or TAL. The idea was that excellent teachers—just like great leaders—set big goals, invest students in attaining the goals, work relentlessly to meet the goals, constantly assess progress, and improve over time.

By the new millennium, TFA had distilled the twelve original selection traits down to seven "competencies" that it believed were key to effective classroom leadership: achievement, perseverance, critical thinking, organizational ability, influencing/motivating skills, respect for others, and fit with TFA.

This time around, there was no guesswork involved. The organization spent countless hours identifying its most effective teachers, observing them at work, and breaking down their performances into discrete capabilities. TFA set student achievement goals and began using those benchmarks to develop a system by which to measure corps member effectiveness. In 2003, it rolled out IMPS—Information Management and Processing System—a database that allowed TFA to track corps member data across the program continuum.

It got a little help from its friends. As a pro bono project, top consulting firm McKinsey helped TFA redesign its recruiting and selection process. And when McKinsey partner Matt Kramer eventually joined the TFA staff, he pioneered a predictive selection model that could identify which candidates would make the best teachers. The model linked student achievement outcome results to individual corps members' incoming scores on the seven application competencies. As the data became more and more robust, TFA was able to identify a certain combination of teacher traits that were predictive of success in the classroom. Real people still presided over the interview process, but computers were increasingly relied upon to inform their decisions. By the time Hrag, Rachelle, Phillip, and Taylor applied, TFA had developed six distinct profiles of winning traits in successful teachers.

Teach For America's mission from the start had been to *recruit* and *train* the best and brightest to teach in America's lowest-performing schools. The organization never promised to figure out a way to *retain* them. In fact, it fully expected the majority of its corps members to leave the classroom after their two-year stint. TFA took the long view, guessing that TFA alums would assume positions of power in public life and ultimately figure out the retention piece as part of the larger solution to the achievement gap.

By 2005, the theory was bearing fruit. "I think most people deeply engaged in ed reform believe and know that TFA is producing an unprecedented and deep pipeline of people moving the ball forward on education reform," says Kopp. "I think we are going to see a dramatic growth in impact as our alums get older." Education reformers agree. "We think of TFA as a farm system for leaders," says Kevin Hall, a former TFA staffer who is chief operating officer of The Broad Education Foundation, one of the leading philanthropies funding school transformation. Jim Shelton, education program director for the mighty Gates Foundation, concurs. Noting that TFA has successfully seeded the educational-reform landscape with high-caliber human capital and talent that is "really, really smart and very, very good," he describes it as "one of the most important nonprofit organizations serving public education in America."

But the immediate and pressing problem of the recruitment and retention of quality teachers has yet to be solved. Nationwide, an estimated 14 percent of teachers leave the classroom in the first year, nearly half by the fifth. High attrition rates are especially pronounced in low-performing schools. In California's high-poverty schools, 10 percent of teachers transfer away each year. The result: in 2005, children in the state's lowest-performing schools were five times more likely to face a string of unprepared teachers than were kids in the highest-performing schools.

At Locke, the numbers were worse. In the 2005–2006 school year, approximately one third of the faculty was new and three fourths had been there fewer than five years. Thirty percent lacked a full credential. Three of the six assistant principals were in their first year as Locke administrators, and not a single one had been at the school longer than five years.

Locke students suffered the consequences. In the 2005–2006 school year, 32 percent of the classes in core academic courses were taught by teachers not qualified under federal law. And 302 classes were characterized as "teacher misassignments," meaning that teachers assigned to the class lacked a legally recognized certificate or credential for the course. Three teacher positions went unfilled—a marked improvement over the fourteen full-time teacher vacancies the year before.

There are excellent, experienced teachers at Locke. There just aren't enough of them, and there never have been. Seasoned teachers in general have always tended to gravitate to advantaged areas where working conditions are more favorable. And lousy teachers, not wanted at high-performing schools but protected by tenure, have too often ended up at low-income schools. School districts have been complicit. Unwilling or unable to expend the considerable time and resources required to fire a tenured teacher protected by a powerful union, they have allowed subpar teachers to shuffle from post to post in a practice known within LAUSD as the "dance of the lemons." Union laws have bound principals to accept any tenured transfer seeking an open position, regardless of past performance. The result: low-income schools became repositories for bad teachers. (In 2006, California governor Arnold Schwarzenegger pushed through a law that permits principals to reject transfers of underperforming teachers.)

Even without the new law, poor-performing schools have little control over the quality of the staff, because beggars can't be choosers. Without a large pool of applicants seeking tough inner-city posts, principals have had no choice but to take less experienced—and often less effective—teachers.

Ironically, TFA represents both the problem and the solution to one of the thorniest issues facing Locke. On the one hand, in 2005 TFA had become the school's primary hiring source, supplying nearly 20 percent of the teachers on staff. On the other hand, by the end of that year, nearly a dozen TFAers at Locke had resigned. Two never completed the first year of teaching; eight others left after fulfilling their two-year commitments. In one fell swoop, some of the school's most capable educators were gone. TFA fans and foes alike acknowledged the loss.

Dr. Wells felt betrayed. "TFA teachers are leaving in large numbers," he said bitterly. "The other teachers are always telling me to forget TFA; they are not committed to the community. I used to brush it aside as jealousy. But you invest in them, get them to a level of skill, and then they leave. I have to look for stability at the school. Last year I hired all TFAers for my vacancies. This year, I'm going to be looking for a significant number of non-TFA teachers."

Things didn't work out that way. Wells ended up gobbling up as many TFA teachers as he could at the Teach For America hiring fairs over the spring and summer. Reason trumped anger. He found the quality of the thirteen new TFA candidates he hired to teach in 2006 much higher than that of those from other, more traditional credentialing programs, and he thought the passion they displayed for the mission could not be faked.

Wells began to rethink his take on TFA. He started to see it as the educational equivalent of the U.S. Army. Enlistment in the military was for a finite period, he reasoned, but that didn't mean the country's highly trained volunteer army wasn't successful in battle. Quite the contrary. The United States boasted the finest fighting force in the world. TFAers were like soldiers: carefully selected volunteers who were well trained and, for the most part, highly effective—often more effective than the lifers. Wells decided he could live with the fact that he got them for only two years, as long as he knew there would be another crop of highly skilled, bushy-tailed recruits to replace them.

"Teach For America has literally saved this school," he said, acknowledging that recruits were among Locke's best teachers. "If it were not for TFA, Locke would be a school the state would refuse to take over, and be nationally recognized as the epitome of why public education doesn't work. TFA teachers fill the holes and offer kids the kind of rigor that allows the students to grow academically. If you took all the TFA teachers out of Locke, we would have forty percent roving subs and mass chaos. We would not be able to survive."

CHAPTER THREE

You're in the Army Now

In 1990, the New Teacher Center at the University of California, Santa Cruz, published an article that Teach For America still refers to today. Entitled "Phases of First-Year Teaching," it describes the stages new teachers move through during their first year. *Anticipation,* the short period that usually begins during training, comes first. The beginning teacher looks forward to the new career with a mix of excitement and anxiety. *Survival* follows close on its heels, soon after school starts. The overwhelmed teacher struggles to stay afloat. This period normally lasts six to eight weeks but can go on indefinitely. Then there is *Disillusionment,* a phase of profound disenchantment when new teachers question both their commitment and their competence. *Rejuvenation* eventually follows. For the lucky ones, it begins after winter break and continues well into spring. For the not-so-lucky, it can take weeks, if not months, to kick in. Finally, as the school year winds down, there is *Reflection,* the final phase of the cycle, in which the teacher begins to envision what the second year in the classroom will look like.

Some new teachers find it hard to imagine finishing the first year. Teaching in a low-income school right out of college is a shock to the system—like getting really old really quickly, if you ask some TFA recruits. You shed your old skin, the one you were so comfortable in. A new skin develops and a new person emerges, one who is completely different from the old person. When you're twenty-two, that takes some adjusting.

The article is illustrated with a graph. The line charting the five-stage cycle starts high, dips very low very fast, and then slowly, slowly rises—unevenly. There's nothing balanced or tidy about the drawing, and that's probably apt. The first year of teaching is messy, misshapen, lopsided. And that's if you've been in a traditional university-based credentialing program complete with student teaching and peer mentoring. Teach For America corps members become teachers of record after five weeks of training.

For most of the 2005 recruits, the anticipation phase was just a blur marked by hard work, long hours, and little sleep. It started almost as soon as the candidates accepted the TFA offer—when the institute six-course curriculum (called the six-pack), plus the independent classroom-observation assignment, arrived in the mail. The package of pastel-colored, spiral-bound texts covered everything from diversity and classroom management to literacy, learning theory, and TFA's central thesis, Teaching as Leadership (TAL). Before arriving, recruits were expected to read the texts and complete nine written exercises based on observations of experienced teachers at work. Many corps members (CMs) dispensed with the prep work; they arrived for their summer training cold.

Institute began on a sunny Sunday in early July, when some six hundred Teach For America recruits streamed onto the campus of California State University, Long Beach. They were dressed in tank tops and jeans, board shorts and T-shirts—some emblazoned with the TFA logo and the words CORPS 05. Gucci and Burberry bags could be spotted here and there, but most inductees toted suitcases or hauled huge backpacks. The famous blue pyramid, a campus landmark, towered in the near distance. It all felt very much like the first day of college as CMs found their dorm rooms and the shortest route to the cafeteria.

But any illusions corps members had about the rigor of the training to come were dispelled when they were given a thick three-ring binder with a letter of introduction and the institute calendar. A quick perusal of both made clear that institute would bear a much greater resemblance to boot camp than to a college orientation program. Gone was the most basic of university freedoms—the right to manage time. In its place was a carefully choreographed sixteen-hour day—every minute of which would be accounted for. There would be no more waking at nine or ten and pulling on a T-shirt and jeans for a midmorning class. Under the TFA regime, the working day began at dawn and went pretty much until midnight. There was a grown-up dress code, too. For men, that meant a button-down shirt, tie, and slacks. For women, it was a skirt or dress of "reasonable length," or slacks with a blouse.

Breakfast was served each morning beginning at 5:45. Big yellow buses packed with bleary-eyed CMs clutching red lunch totes left the Long Beach campus about an hour later, headed for school sites. On-campus training lasted the length of the school day—from 8 a.m. until 4:05, when the buses ferried exhausted CMs back to the dorms for a break and dinner before the evening sessions began at 6:30. The day didn't end three hours later when the nighttime workshops were wrapping up. After that, CMs were expected to prepare a lesson plan for the following day. Few got to bed before midnight, many not at all.

Locke was the school assignment site for 139 TFA recruits. The Locke cohort was divided by teaching subjects into nine groups of fourteen to sixteen CMs, each headed by a corps member advisor (CMA). Each CMA group was further divided into four-person teaching teams. The recruits bonded quickly. TFA encouraged this with various ice-breaking exercises, but it would have happened anyway. There was an up-against-the-wall mentality to the Locke institute—and a gallows sense of humor.

The first week was devoted entirely to curriculum course work. By the second week, recruits were working in classrooms with summer-school students. The TFA teacher-prep program stood the traditional student-teaching model on its head. Instead of having a student teacher shadowing a veteran educator at work, the TFA rookies took turns teaching while a paid faculty advisor (FA) from Locke's staff observed from the back of the room. In the mornings, team members taught summer school; in the afternoons they received feedback and sat in on specific curriculum tutorials, like "The Five-Step Lesson Plan" and "Building a Culture of Achievement." During week four, each recruit got to teach an entire day solo. By the end of the five-week crash course, student teaching was over. Each CM had spent the equivalent of about three full school days teaching. The next time they stood in front of a classroom of students, they would be the teachers of record.

Hrag Hamalian, toting his lone suitcase, arrived at Teach For America's summer institute dressed in a wife-beater T-shirt and shorts and thought: *Wahoo! It's L.A.!* Days later, he was sitting in slacks and a dress shirt at the welcoming ceremony, astonished at the turn his life had taken. Hrag, along with the other corps members assigned to do their teacher training at Locke High School, had rehearsed a cheer for the evening. It was like a rap: *Stop. Locke. Time to teach, Open up shop.* He was surprised—and not a little embarrassed—to be rapping during institute, but that hardly prepared him for the spectacle that was unfolding in the auditorium of Wilson High School in Long Beach. The gathering of all 639 trainees felt like a football rally, or even a religious revival—not a meeting of smart and serious college graduates and soon-to-be professional teachers.

For the welcoming ceremony, the L.A. institute corps was organized into groups, each representing a different training campus or permament-placement site. In they marched, bands of cheering coeds, each lot shouting louder than the last, until the noise was literally deafening. Standing in front, watching it all, stood Teach For America founder Wendy Kopp. Fifteen years before, she had presided at the first TFA institute just miles away. Corps members were clapping and chanting "TFA! . . . TFA! . . . TFA!" then, too. She had found the spontaneous enthusiasm disconcerting in 1990; the eardrum-piercing cheers and the near hysteria of 2005 were no less unsettling. She knew there was a fine line between exuberance and disillusionment. If she were a new CM, she mused, she would have been turned off. She wondered if others here felt the same way.

She might as well have been reading Hrag's mind. He didn't feel plugged in to the crazy energy that emanated from the hall. He did absolutely believe in the central TFA dogma—that all children deserve an opportunity to attain an excellent education—and he was impressed with Wendy Kopp's welcoming speech. When she stepped up to the podium, dressed in her customary well-tailored pantsuit, her long, light brown hair parted down the middle like a schoolgirl's, the hall was dead quiet.

Kopp's remarks could have been mistaken for those of a commanding officer sending troops off to battle. She started by saluting the corps members for choosing to dedicate the next two years of their lives to teaching in underserved schools. "This has to be the road less traveled," she said. "There had to be other options for you that were supported by family and friends." Kopp went on to recite the dreary statistics underscoring the achievement gap between the richest and poorest students in the nation all along the education continuum. Among children in low-performing American schools, she said:

- Fourth-graders read at a first-grade level.
- Once they reach high school, there is only a 50 percent chance that they will graduate.
- If they do graduate, they will leave school with the same skills as an eighth-grader.

"Education is the key to having choices, well-paying jobs, and participating in a democracy," Kopp said to a sea of upturned faces. "Our success depends on your remembering our fundamental purpose: to eliminate educational inequity. Your success depends on retaining a sense of *outrage* over those inequities. When you encounter your biggest challenges, remember the high stakes for your students. Remain centered on the fundamental purpose of Teach For America. Retaining a sense of purpose, outrage, and urgency is the foundation of creating a successful classroom."

Kopp reminded the recruits that the organization talks about teaching as leadership; that successful teachers possess the same skills and attributes as any effective leader. Then she suggested three things to help CMs center themselves in the coming months: "Really get to know your kids. Remind yourself constantly of the stakes. And take care of yourself."

Kopp's address was the final speech of the evening. Earlier, Jason Kamras, a 1996 TFA alum who had just been named National Teacher of the Year, spoke of his transformative experience as a corps member. Next up was a patented TFA production in which five institute staff members stood in a row across a darkened stage, heads bowed. Suddenly, a single speaker stepped forward into a spotlight, head now raised, and began to read from a diary chronicling the personal travails and triumphs of a TFA recruit. The short but moving presentation, called a "spark" in TFA-speak, concluded with the refrain "Why I Teach For America." When finished, the speaker faded back into the darkness and the light was trained on the next teacher, whose equally stirring testimonial also ended with the words "Why I Teach For America." On it went until each bowed and darkened head had been illuminated, and each person had shared a personal epiphany that underscored the need and urgency of the battle—not to mention the quiet satisfaction attained from joining it.

Hrag had found Wendy Kopp convincing. But the stage show was a bit too scripted, the canned "Why I Teach For America" mantra cheesy. He wasn't the rah-rah type, and he thought the notion that as individuals they could revamp a broken education system was skewed. He surveyed the scene with growing dismay. *What is going on? What am I doing here?*

Across the country in River Vale, New Jersey, Manuel Hamalian didn't have to attend the welcoming ceremony to understand what his son, Hrag, was doing there. Manuel was the one who had opened the TFA acceptance envelope that Hrag received that spring. He had carefully read the contents and called his son to tell him the news that he was in. Hrag didn't know if he would accept the offer, but he felt honored that it had been extended.

"They recruit on merit," Hrag had told his father. What he was really saying was: *I am one of the elite.*

"That's not it," his father had countered, speaking as always in his native Armenian tongue. Manuel had emigrated from the Middle East nineteen years earlier, bringing with him his wife, Baizar, his aging parents, and his two small children, Gareen and Hrag. Manuel held a degree in public health from the American University of Beirut, but in United States he commuted four hours each day to his job as a manager of a freight forwarding company. Baizar, who went by the American name Claire, was a nurse; she worked the night shift at a local hospital. Together they literally labored around the clock. The kids were never denied. They had everything they needed, even the things the family couldn't necessarily afford. Manuel's parents, both refugees from the Armenian genocide of 1915, stayed at home and babysat.

The Hamalians had high expectations for their children. They wanted them to find careers that would give them stability and security— and enable them to enjoy the pleasures of life that they themselves had often had to forgo. So far, the kids had not disappointed. Hrag was graduating from Boston College with a 3.56 GPA. Gareen had graduated from Columbia University and was attending Tufts School of Medicine.

Gareen was well on her way. Hrag was not. Not yet, anyway. The

Hamalians were mildly concerned. Manuel and Claire feared that a two-year stint with Teach For America could sidetrack their only son.

So Manuel had not shared Hrag's enthusiasm about the TFA acceptance letter. He was cautious, and he wanted his son to be, too. "They are really judging you on your character," Manuel had told Hrag over the phone. "They're looking for your type of person—someone who will make a commitment and not leave it."

Hrag had felt his anger rising. His parents had always been sparing in their praise. He had just won a spot in one of the most prestigious post-grad programs in the country. Only a few of the eleven who interviewed with him had been offered a position. *Everyone else knows Teach For America looks for the highest-achieving graduates. Why can't you see that?*

Manuel had kept on repeating: "They judge you by your character. I went through [the acceptance packet]. Nothing shows me you got accepted for achievement. You got accepted because you're not gonna leave."

Hrag first heard about the organization in high school when a TFA alum addressed his class. It sounded cool. He didn't really think about it again until his senior year at BC, when he had to decide what to do after graduation. TFA had sent him a personalized e-mail listing his accomplishments and inviting him to apply. At first it creeped him out—the idea that someone he didn't know knew him. But he was flattered, too—and curious. So he agreed to meet for coffee, and afterward the e-mails kept coming. There was no obvious career path ahead for Hrag, no law school, med school, or MBA program in his immediate future. He just knew he wanted to do something that he would enjoy. And if he was going to have to work hard all day, he wanted to have something to show for it when he came home at night. Gareen offered to arrange a meeting for Hrag with her friend Seth, who had just completed his TFA commitment. Seth had only positive things to say about the experience, though he did admit that during his first year he sometimes came home crying. Hrag was unfazed. *Well, that's not me. My first year will be hard; my second will be better. All in all it'll be such a great experience.*

Hrag applied and was invited to interview. The daylong process was scheduled for April 1—April Fools' Day. He knew it would be intense. Applicants were required to prepare and deliver a five-minute lesson plan. They had been sent reading material on educational issues in preparation for a group discussion and a one-on-one interview. Role-playing and problem-solving exercises were also on the agenda.

TFA made no secret of the seven attributes it was seeking in prospective corps members. Everything was posted on its increasingly sophisticated website and included in the mailings. But Hrag and the others had no way of knowing which combination of traits unlocked the door.

Hrag didn't spend much time worrying about it. He had been on several other interviews already, and he actually enjoyed the process. He was nimble, good on his feet; he liked showing folks what he could do. So he went in with a game plan designed to give TFA what it was looking for. He carefully prepared his mini-lesson. Hrag asked one of his favorite professors, Dr. Krauss, for help in adapting one of his particularly memorable lectures on evolution into a five-minute presentation. The night before his interview, Hrag staged a dry run of the suitably dumbed-down lesson using members of BC's Armenian Club as guinea pigs.

Hrag arrived at Boston's Prudential Center in a suit and tie. TFA selectors watched as each applicant delivered a lesson to the entire group. Hrag came armed for his with fifty colored plastic dinosaurs and a raft of photocopied handouts. The dinosaurs went flying when he simulated the crash of a meteor by pounding his fist on a desk. The dramatics effectively illustrated his point: in the event of a natural disaster, the animals with the broadest niche were most likely to survive. As he stuffed the toys back into a brown paper bag, he reckoned he had nailed the teaching exercise. Everyone else in the room appeared to think so, too.

As part of the initial application, candidates had been asked to write an essay describing a time when they were faced with a serious obstacle. Hrag had written about the summer he spent in Datev, a "Third World village tucked away in a forgotten corner of Armenia." Hrag and Gareen had traveled there on a service project sponsored by their local Armenian club. Though their parents weren't born in Armenia—Manuel was born in Syria, Claire in Lebanon—both were Armenian patriots. In America, the Hamalians had clung to the cultural roots of a country they themselves had never seen. Their social life revolved around the Armenian community in the greater New York area and their extended families that had settled there. Hrag and Gareen had grown up on their paternal grandfather's tales of the old country he had been forced to flee. The children were proud to be Armenian and thrilled to be able to visit their country to help rebuild a school there.

"Armenia was my homeland," Hrag wrote, "and no matter how far I was distanced from it as a result of the Diaspora of my people, I was determined to reconcile myself with it." He went on to tell the story of how he won over hostile Armenian villagers who seemed to resent the noblesse oblige of the visiting Armenian Americans. The breakthrough came when Hrag sent a stray soccer ball soaring over the heads of the young kids playing near the construction site. The children mobbed him for his amazing feat; before long, their parents were inviting him to dinner.

The TFA selector reading the essay drew brackets around the paragraphs outlining Hrag's success at winning over the villagers. Next to the brackets was the notation "I/M," TFA shorthand for "influencing and motivating others," one of the key competencies TFA had identified with the help of McKinsey consultants.

At one point in the seven-hour process, the candidates were split into two groups for a discussion based on readings the applicants had been sent. Hrag hadn't studied the articles; he scanned them even as he led the discussion. He didn't really know what he was talking about. What he did know was that TFA interviewers were watching the group to see who would step up and lead the conversation.

During the one-on-one interview, Hrag emphasized his leadership qualities. He spoke about the growth and success of the Armenian Club at Boston College under his stewardship. When he had first arrived at BC, the club was just about moribund. Because the club had only four members, getting himself elected president was easy. The hard part was finding a way to revive the organization. Hrag decided to scan the names of all the students on campus and e-mail the ones with names ending in "ian." The plan worked. Enrollment jumped to fifteen. With the club showing signs of life, Hrag started holding events on topics he thought would be of interest to Armenian Americans. He then convinced professors to give extra credit to anyone who showed up. The night before Hrag's interview, seventy people attended the club meeting and lecture, a number unheard of before his tenure.

Hrag had also gleaned that the organization put a premium on persistence. TFA called it relentless pursuit. It was the first of the organization's five core values. After all, TFA owed its existence to the fact that Kopp had persisted against all manner of seemingly insurmountable odds, especially in the first five years.

Hrag knew all about persistence. At Boston College, he had taken his GPA from a 3.18 as a freshman to a 3.78 as a junior. Before that, his career as a high school wrestler at Pascack Valley High School in Hillsdale, New Jersey, was an ode to persistence. The tale said as much about his father as it did about Hrag.

Hrag made it onto the varsity wrestling team as a sophomore, but he never won a single match that year. His father didn't care. He made it a point to attend every match. And through every one of them, Manuel silently endured the reproaches of another dad seated nearby—a father whose son actually won some matches. "Yank the kid," the guy would say. "It's embarrassing—to the boy as well as the team. You're hurting your own kid. Stop. It's painful to watch."

Manuel never responded.

Then, in what seemed nothing short of a miracle, Hrag took on the school's rival in his junior year—and won! And kept winning. In his senior year, he was ranked second in the league.

Hrag's first victory came in the only match of his wrestling career that Manuel wasn't able to make. It didn't matter. That night, when he arrived home and heard the news, Manuel heaved his teenaged son atop his shoulders and paraded him around the house like a Greek god. Hrag savored that moment as much as the victory.

The TFA staffers handling the interview process that day kept a score sheet for each applicant. Candidates were rated on the seven competencies along a sliding scale of 1 to 3, with 1 signifying an unacceptably low score, 2 indicating a solid performance, and 3 representing exemplary, the highest possible rating. Each score on each trait for each candidate was carefully entered, first on the work sheet, later into TFA's burgeoning computerized data bank.

At the end of the day, Hrag was tagged a "Best Bet," a candidate who had not met one of the six computer profiles that were predictive of success but who had shown great potential. On Hrag's documents, an obviously frustrated selector had asked that his application be reviewed, noting, "I feel like the rubric is not allowing me to select someone who I think might make a great corps member." After a "selection check" by headquarters, TFA "decided to admit on a BB b/c of strong PR spike."

Translation: Hrag was accepted to the corps as a "Best Bet" because of his strong score on perseverance.

Even after he was accepted by TFA, Hrag continued to go on other interviews. But as the school year came to a close, he realized that all the other positions seemed like glorified sales jobs. TFA was different. It offered Hrag an opportunity to do something good, to be in a position of power, and to feel proud about what he was doing. He signed up and asked to be sent to the West Coast. He was assigned to Los Angeles, close to Huntington Beach, the first place the Hamalians had lived after immigrating to the United States nearly two decades before. It all seemed to click. He bought a plane ticket, packed a bag, and flew west.

Hrag never saw the paperwork, but by early fall he begrudgingly acknowledged what Manuel Hamalian, in his fatherly wisdom, had known all along. Hrag had certainly shown leadership abilities, but it was his relentless pursuit of his goals—academic, athletic, and Armenian—that had tipped the scales in his favor. When Teach For America extended an offer to Hrag, they knew he was a keeper. He would never quit.

Hrag turned his anger on himself. Why hadn't he seen all this back then, in the beginning, before he had made a two-year commitment? He hated the fact that TFA—and his dad—knew right from the start what he had only recently come to understand. Though the thought of leaving had been on his mind since the very first day of school, quitting wasn't an option for a person like Hrag. If he left, he knew he would feel like a failure for the rest of his life. Besides, in the Hamalian family, there was no failing—not like that, anyway.

Hrag felt like he had been sucker punched. Sure, TFA had said it would be hard. But no one had explained that it would be *this* difficult. Nobody had warned him that the job would take over his life and rob him of his youth. *What about the others? Why were they drawn to this Mission Impossible?* Two thousand had signed up with Hrag, and nearly nine times as many had applied. He knew why *he* could never quit. Why were the others still hanging in there?

He couldn't put his finger on it, but there was something about the people in TFA that set them apart. At first he thought it must be a religious thing. There seemed to be a lot of Mormons and Christians in the program. His roommate at institute had been a missionary. Dave Buehrle, a TFA English teacher assigned to Locke, was an unabashed

Christian who had attended Calvin, a midwestern Christian college, and had stayed on a Christian missionary base while on a two-month internship in Hong Kong. Elissa Salas, a new special ed TFAer, had actually lived in a convent while doing social justice work in Washington, D.C., the previous summer.

And there was Phillip Gedeon, the new TFA geometry phenom. Hrag didn't know Phillip well, though they worked in the same wing on the third floor. Phillip, too, was a Christian. He believed it was his life's work to teach—that God had ordained it. That certainty was one of the arguments Phillip presented to his single mother when he informed her that he was moving across the country to teach in Los Angeles. She didn't like the idea of losing her only child, but it was hard to argue with God's wishes. Back east, Phillip belonged to the Evangelical Covenant Church. In the early months at Locke, he sometimes traveled with other TFA Christians to area churches. He kept God out of the classroom, but he enjoyed those Sunday-morning journeys in search of a religious home.

Hrag didn't know it, but TFA alum Chad Soleo, the "dean" of the Teach For America teachers at Locke, was also a Christian, though increasingly less faithful and more angry with the God who presided over Watts. Soleo had been baptized a Catholic and attended Catholic schools, but had never practiced after grade school. He was "born again" when he moved to California and became reacquainted with his extended family there. They were Evangelical Christians, and they took him in as one of their own. Though it meant a long commute to Locke, Chad decided to live with them in an Orange County suburb. During the summer between his first and second years at Teach For America, Chad traveled with his California family to China as a missionary. Officially, they were all there to teach English, but the deal was that they were free to speak about their faith to anyone over the age of eighteen. Chad's work during that crucial summer break had a profound effect on his decision to remain in education and to assume a leadership position at Locke. Because he was the only teacher among the small group of fellow Christians giving English-language instruction that summer, the others naturally deferred to him. He liked mentoring them. And they seemed happy to follow him.

Hrag himself was a sub-deacon—a *tbir*—in the Christian Orthodox Church. He was ordained during his sophomore year in high school.

Though he had not yet joined an Armenian church in Los Angeles, he and his family were active congregants at the weekly two-and-a-half-hour services at home. He wasn't fanatical about his faith—in fact, he considered himself more spiritual than religious. But a cross hung from the windshield of his red Ford Focus. He was a believer.

Of course, not everyone at TFA was. Some had no real ties to organized religion at all. Taylor Rifkin described herself as Jewish "light," though she was actually raised without any religion. Her mother was Episcopalian and her father was Jewish. Her baby boomer parents had attended a Unitarian church for a while, but Taylor found Sunday school hokey.

Rachelle Snyder belonged to no organized religion, unless being the youngest member of Greenpeace counted. Her parents, both lawyers, were attached to social justice causes, not churches. But they, too, had searched for a religious identity for their two kids. Rachelle's mother, Lynne Lasry, came from a family of Sephardic Jews, and her father, Allen, was raised Protestant but no longer practiced. They tried bringing their kids to a Unitarian church, but Allen couldn't suspend his disbelief. Now, as a young adult, Rachelle thought of herself as a spiritual person. She subscribed to what she believed was the message of all religions: to be honest, sincere, good, and just.

No, Hrag decided. There was something else going on with these TFAers. It wasn't necessarily an abiding belief in God. Maybe what drove them was an overwhelming sense of duty. A sense of passion. Or perhaps it was hubris—the unwavering conviction that no problem was insurmountable, that anything was possible. Hrag found himself studying his colleagues for clues. *What is it about these people?*

To be sure, there was a kind of postcollege Skull and Bones club feel to the organization. The idea that this was an exclusive society, a many-are-called-few-are-chosen-type deal, accounted for some of the attraction. The summer institute only added to the mystique. Everyone referred to it as boot camp. And TFA did little to discourage the notion. The long hours, the hard work, the sleep deprivation, the code of conduct, the constant critical feedback—it all fed into an almost cultlike feel. TFA even had its own acronym-laden language. Corps members were CMs. "Teaching as Leadership" was TAL. Corps member advisors were CMAs. Locke staffers hired to mentor corps members were FAs, faculty advisors. Student Achievement Plans were SAPs. TFA staffers assigned to monitor CMs during the school year were PDs—program directors.

There were even more acronyms at headquarters. EDs were executive directors of specific TFA regions. RDs were recruitment directors. RAs were recruitment associates. SAT stood for the fund-raising program Sponsor a Teacher. AKC stood for "awareness, knowledge, consideration"— TFA marketing terms for the levels of TFA infiltration on college campuses. POCs were "people of color," CSOPs were "career-specific one-pagers"—campus flyers. DLs were "deadlines"; POPs were "pockets of potential"; PDBs were "performance dashboards"; SPS meant "structured problem solving." The organization itself was TFA—Teach For America. CMs joked that TFA reminded them of two books: *1984* and *Brave New World.* Not everyone was kidding.

The question of who these fellow TFAers were and what exactly made them tick consumed Hrag. Whenever he went for a drink with the TFA teachers, the conversation revolved around work—the mission, the kids, the gap. Most times Hrag remained silent, hoping that the conversation would turn to something like college football or the war in Iraq— anything to escape being sucked into the TFA vortex. But it rarely did. So as the others nattered on, Hrag found himself thinking: *Do they really mean it? Do they really believe that the achievement gap is closable and that they will be the ones to close it?*

He was always shocked by his own conclusion: *Yes, they do. They really do believe.*

Teaching had always been in the back of Taylor's mind. It was kind of the family business. Her mother, Andrea, had a thriving career as an independent guidance counselor for high-paying, college-bound high school students. Her father, Fred Rifkin, had earned a lifetime teaching credential years before.

Taylor was in her teens when her dad was elected president of the Santa Barbara School Board. In 1998, he made the national news with the district's decision to scrap bilingual education. The public debates that preceded the vote were ugly. Opponents accused board members of racism, declaring the decision tantamount to ethnic cleansing. On the night of the historic vote, school board members were provided police protection. But the board stood fast. They had crunched the numbers.

The Latino kids in Santa Barbara couldn't pass proficiency tests in English or Spanish. Bilingual education wasn't working. It had to go.

Taylor was fully engaged in the debate. She tutored Latino kids after school and found that they never wanted to speak to her in Spanish. They begged her to use English. So she knew her father was right. But she attended Santa Barbara High School, where the cultural and socioeconomic divide between white and brown students was huge. The debate over bilingual education only widened the gulf.

Life at home was stressful. Fred Rifkin was suddenly a media star—it seemed his face was on TV every night and in the papers every morning. He received a death threat. And Taylor became anorexic. The thing she remembers most clearly from that time is sitting alone one night with her father as he cried and cried.

Education may have been in her blood, but during her senior year at USC, fear of the future was on her mind. She couldn't sleep. She was terrified that she would end up at a desk somewhere, bored silly. She dreaded graduation. What would she do with her life? She had already had a taste of Hollywood as a college intern at E! Entertainment TV. She knew then that writing press releases for the next J.Lo was not going to do it for her.

When she heard a presentation at USC by a TFA corps member, she was totally sold. It wasn't so much the inequity issue that resonated with Taylor. For her, it was the idea that she had something to share. And because her family was well-off, she could afford to be a low-paid humanitarian. So she figured she would join TFA for two years, with luck do some good, and worry about what to do with the rest of her life later.

She made TFA's first cut—the written application. But by then she had decided she didn't want the job. Her aunt told her she'd be miserable. Her brother Ryan warned her she wouldn't stand a chance of surviving in an inner-city school. Taylor had visions of working in dungeon-like conditions with staplers flying at her head. Because she was fairly susceptible to other people's opinions, she talked herself out of caring whether or not she got accepted. But as the date for the interview approached and she began to read over the materials, she remembered the reason she had applied in the first place. She believed in the mission; she felt moved to action.

Of course, she was terrified on the day of her interview. She knew

TFA was very competitive. There were fourteen other applicants with her at USC that day, all vying for a spot. She automatically assumed there was no way she would get in. What she didn't take into account was the fact that she had been on TFA's radar ever since she had attended the USC recruitment event. She was one of about twenty campus coeds who had been invited to a special TFA lunch that year, long before she had even decided to apply.

Taylor sized up the competition and began to gauge her chances. The mini-lessons were telling. Some people completely bombed—one girl taught for two minutes about how to write the letter *M*. Some had no stage presence. But others were clearly talented and put together really impressive lessons. Taylor adapted hers, on the U.S. Census, from a website; she put the finishing touches on her presentation at 3 a.m.—after partying in Hollywood. Still, she was comfortable in front of large audiences. The lesson went well.

She was chary of the next exercise—the group discussion. She knew she had to demonstrate presence without appearing to be a bully, and that would require a careful balancing act. The chat was about overcoming the achievement gap. One candidate insisted that parental involvement and after-school activities were key to raising student achievement. Taylor countered that parental involvement was problematic and that instruction had to take place within school hours, while students were a captive audience. She argued for double blocks of math and English and suggested cutting out electives until students were up to par on the basics. When the group broke for lunch at the end of the discussion, Taylor had decided she *really* wanted to teach for America. She was going to kick ass in the private interview.

She did. In fact, she had been impressing the selectors all day long. She ended up receiving 3s on all but two of the competencies. Her overall score gave her the highest rank possible, and an automatic green light for admission. She had no idea that she had scored so high, but she did know before she left that day that she would be offered a spot. When the interviewer invited questions at the conclusion of the one-on-one, Taylor didn't hesitate to use her favorite job-interview tactic.

"What kind of a candidate do you think I am for this job?" she asked, figuring the evaluator would be caught off guard and would have to answer truthfully.

"You are remarkable," came the response. "We rarely come across people like you."

After those words of high praise, summer institute should have been easy for Taylor. It wasn't. She felt totally unqualified. And she found that the competition to get into TFA didn't end with admission. All the new recruits were overachievers. They were all perfectionists. The five-week training blitz turned into a 24/7 academic decathlon.

It didn't help that every week each CM was given the equivalent of a report card. By then, Kopp's leadership principles had been codified into the TAL rubric: teachers had to establish ambitious goals, invest students to attain them, work relentlessly, and constantly improve. Those four objectives were further broken down into twenty individual skills deemed necessary for mastery. So, for example, to show mastery of TAL objective number one, establishing ambitious goals, a teacher would have to be proficient at two skills: setting a big goal that was measurable, and exhibiting high expectations for student achievement. Each week recruits were expected to master an increasingly larger basket of skills.

Like every part of the organization, the institute had its own big goal and objective ways of measuring mastery—for the individual CMs, the CMA groups, and the region as a whole. The institute goal was that every CM would rate either proficient or exemplary in 80 percent of the TAL skills. At the end of every week, CMs were assessed on each skill and given a grade ranging from 1, for "beginning proficiency," to 4, for "exemplary." The grades were fed into a computer, which then spit out an analysis. CMs who failed to make adequate progress were put on an individualized Corps Member Improvement Plan (CMIP) and monitored closely.

The CM's ranking and percentile vis-à-vis other CMs in the same CMA group were also calculated and stored. The data collected and analyzed each week was posted on the organization's internal dashboard so that comparisons on progress could be made region to region, training site to training site, corps member advisory group to corps member advisory group. As the results came back at the end of each week, the institute staff looked for trends and fine-tuned upcoming instruction to specifically address problem areas.

The CMs were all looking for good grades. Several of them went into bitch mode to get them. During one session with a particularly pedantic curriculum specialist, the CMs almost mutinied. The prof squelched the rebellion. She sternly admonished them for "crossing a line" and launched into a "teacher knows best" lecture. She urged them to look for the value, the application, in the instruction she was offering. The CMs pushed back. They insisted that they were being asked to do too much in too little time, or, conversely, that they were being forced to spend too much time on exercises of too little value. They were tired and frustrated from working ridiculously long hours on precious little sleep. They had been selected for their leadership qualities and yet were being asked to be passive participants in their training. They were being treated like sheep, not shepherds.

Taylor's was one of the lone discordant voices. She argued that it was unrealistic to assume that TFA would change the schedule or the courses. "I feel it, too," she said to a hot, stuffy classroom filled with irritable CMs. "Sometimes you think, 'Oh, this is tough.' It's like getting a shot. Just do it. Air the complaints and then let's rock and roll. We've got to do it. Let's just suck it up!"

The discussion went on for a few minutes more, during which the instructor assured them that "this dark time" would soon pass. But Taylor's against-the-current comments had broken the tide of dissent. Things continued to be tough at institute, but for the most part complaints were made in private.

By the time institute concluded, Taylor had had enough. After a great start, her Locke faculty advisor was now blowing hot and cold on her. Things weren't going that well with her CMA, either—they had sparred several times over the weeks. At one point, her CMA objected to the tone of Taylor's voice in the classroom. Taylor didn't defend herself; instead, she thanked the CMA for her advice. But she didn't buy it: *They're fourteen-year-old kids. When they're adults, I'll talk to them like adults.* Toward the end, it seemed like all-out war with her CMA and the members of her teaching team. Taylor got into a disagreement with one of her co-teachers and, unbeknownst to her, a meeting was called to hash things out. Taylor felt like she'd been ambushed; the CMA justified the group therapy session by reminding Taylor that teaching can be emotional at times. Taylor thought it was supposed to be professional.

She went AWOL. She left the meeting in tears, and instead of returning to the TFA dorms in Long Beach that night, she drove to her grandmother's house. She needed to calm down and get some sleep. Taylor didn't want to be on anybody else's roller coaster; her own ride was rocky enough. But the conflict didn't end there. The CMA took the problem further up the chain of command. The institute director ended up taking Taylor aside and asking if he could do anything to help. She was embarrassed. And angry. The incident had been blown out of proportion. *Why am I getting into trouble over this?*

The whole thing turned her off. She wasn't about to quit Teach For America, but she sure would have liked to leave its summer camp. She skipped the closing ceremonies, opting for a nap instead. She told herself she wasn't the typical TFA type anyway. The confrontation made her wonder: *What did I get myself into?*

It was a question she would ask herself again and again over the course of the year. But as September crept closer, the thought rarely left her mind. She was nightmare scared. Again, she couldn't sleep. *I'll quit. I won't make it. I'll die here at Locke High School. I know I will fail.* Her thoughts were terrifying. What made things worse was that she fully expected them to be realized; she expected to fail.

The night before the first day of school, she went to a barbecue at her brother's beach house. Evan had done well in the tech boom. He seemed to have it all going on—the wife, the dog, and a big bunch of friends all making big bunches of money. Her brother Ryan was there, and he tried to talk her out of going through with TFA, arguing that she couldn't handle the stress. She was the youngest of four; the whole family saw her as the immature baby sister.

But she was not backing out. Before she went to bed that night, she checked her stuff three times. She had already been to Kinko's, where she'd made hundreds of copies of handouts. When she arrived at Locke at 6 a.m. after a sleepless night, it was still dark. She stopped at the main office and discovered a few other insomniacs roaming the halls, then made the long walk back to the bungalows and her own classroom. When she got to A22, she concentrated on breathing. *In and out, in and out.* She put her desk where she wanted it and waited.

Though Taylor was expecting to teach ninth-grade English to the kids who streamed though the door, she spent that first period helping students with their schedules. All the ninth-graders with last names beginning with "Ro" through "Ru" had been sent to her room. They came in, sat down, and were stone-cold silent. They just sat there and stared. They looked as scared as she was.

. . .

Teach For America began basically as a garage start-up; as it grew and matured, it took on many of the characteristics of a successful, results-driven corporation. As TFA rounded the corner into financial and programmatic health in 2000, it embarked on an ambitious growth plan. In order to support the expansion, TFA reorganized its management structure. The vice presidents of the various arms of the organization—from program to development—reported to a new chief operating officer, Jerry Hauser, a 1990 alum who returned to TFA after Yale Law School and a stint at McKinsey. Hauser took over daily operations from Kopp. TFA set organizational goals, tracked progress, and continuously analyzed virtually every aspect of the enterprise in order to reach those goals.

Today, data analysis drives the organization's relentless pursuit of results. Meticulous records of all facets of the program and organization are stored and analyzed. The data collection begins in the recruiting process, when all campus interactions—e-mails, coffees, info sessions, canvassing—are fed into a sales-force software called Sales Logix. The collection runs through selection, training, and on-the-job performance. With a new emphasis on maintaining and enriching alumni records and relations, it basically never ends.

The analysis of the data it collects helps TFA track its own performance, make predictions during the selection process, and increase teacher effectiveness. It also allows TFA to identify good candidates for other jobs within the organization once CMs have completed their time in the classroom. Though in recent years TFA has increasingly gone outside the organization to fill positions in its top team (only 35 percent of its senior operating team are alums), 60 percent of its eight-hundred-member staff come from its own rank and file. TFA is so good at spotting talent that hot companies like Google and JPMorgan have chosen not to compete with it for new hires; in 2006 they both inked recruitment partnership deals with the organization. So, when looking to hire staffers to support the mission, TFA looks first to its own.

That's how Samir Bolar came to be one of six TFA program directors assigned to the Los Angeles region in 2005. The role of PD was to be part mentor, part nanny, part boss to the corps member—the human face of the TFA juggernaut. PDs were expected to ensure that CMs got the job done—that they set high student goals that resulted in significant student achievement. Each PD was assigned to monitor up to fifty CMs through four rounds of classroom observations and subsequent follow-up meetings over the course of the school year. Among Samir's charges were the twenty-two Teach For America CMs working at Locke High School in 2005.

Samir was a star TFA alum from the 2002 corps. He had joined TFA fresh out of the University of Texas at Austin with a double major in chemical engineering and English (he picked chemical engineering because it was the most challenging major he could find). At the end of his two years at Willowbrook Middle School in Compton, an incorporated inner-city community in South Los Angeles, his students earned the highest scores for eighth-grade algebra in the district. What's more, on the strength of their performance, the school's overall growth target actually quadrupled. Though TFA had set goals for significant gains, it had no systematic means of measurement in place during the 2002–2003 school year. But Samir did. He created a student tracking system on an Excel spreadsheet, adopted the TFA goal of 80 percent mastery for his kids, and charted their progress from day one. By any measure, Samir Bolar met the bar for excellence in teaching.

Willowbrook begged him to stay on, but, like many in TFA, he had bigger plans. At first he wanted to be a school principal, but a summer internship at the educational arm of the L.A.-based Broad Foundation opened his eyes to the breadth and depth of the growing educational reform movement. By summer's end, his new ambition was to open a series of technology-based charter schools. In order to do so, he thought he needed more critical-thinking and problem-solving skills. So he took a job in the private sector, working with Fortune 500 companies on IT issues.

His stint on the outside was short and unfulfilling. When TFA approached him about becoming a PD in mid-2005, he felt honored. It had never occurred to him that he might be PD material—he wasn't even sure how great a teacher he was, compared with other CMs. That kind of information was never shared; TFA considered humility to be one of its core values. It was leery of creating a superstar system.

Samir calculated that becoming a PD would be an ideal opportunity to hone the skills he would need to lead a cluster of schools. Not only would he learn the inner workings of a big school district like LAUSD, he would gain experience as a manager as he helped select and then support fifty new TFA teachers. He would get to see what good—and bad—

teaching looked like; what made a school function; what contributed to a school's failure. He accepted Teach For America's job offer and rejoined the fold in July 2005.

Samir was sent to Houston for one week of training. There he learned how to score teachers on the newly codified TAL rubric and was introduced to Co-Investigation, a new teacher-development program that was a direct result of TFA's push to improve teacher effectiveness. A reflective problem-solving approach, Co-Investigation was the result of an exhaustive eighteen-month internal study that drew from the work of various adult-learning theorists, including David Kolb and Robert Kegan. TFA introduced the self-help model because it knew that PD intervention alone would not suffice to move CMs through the continuous cycle of learning and improvement necessary to make significant gains in the classroom. The teachers had to learn how to help themselves. Though the idea of reflective practitioner work was not foreign to the world of teacher education, TFA's model was outcome-based, and heavily reliant on the use of data to assess progress.

Co-Investigation represented a paradigm shift in TFA's care and support of its teachers. Until then, when PDs met with TFA recruits, it had been an anecdotally driven discussion: the PD asked how things were going, the CM reported on areas of struggle, and the PD came up with a grab bag of tips and resources. The PD inevitably brought something valuable to the table, but it wasn't always the most purposeful in terms of the ultimate objective.

Under the Co-Investigation model, freewheeling PD-CM chats gave way to highly structured and tightly focused meetings centered on reaching the goal of significant student gains. Before each meeting, the CM was required to submit student assessment scores and to fill out a reflective guide gauging how well the CM was addressing the four TAL habits of an excellent teacher. After a classroom observation, the PD and CM met to identify the "key" teacher problem that was inhibiting student achievement. Then, together, they looked for potential causes, possible solutions, and future measures of success.

Like every other program on the TFA continuum, Co-Investigation was a work-in-progress. Throughout the 2005–2006 school year, the organization continued to refine and flesh out the new support model. In February 2006, it called all the PDs together once again and introduced Co-Investigation 2.0, a more nuanced version of the original. The second iteration probed more deeply into the cause of the key problem, determining whether it was due to knowledge, resources, or mind-set.

Applying the Co-Investigation model would be no easy task. Samir was responsible for supporting fifty corps members who were teaching every one of the secondary core subjects—across six school sites. During the waning days of the summer, he pored over curricula and state standards, trying to bone up in the subjects he was least familiar with. He studied the Teach For America summer institute curriculum, too, combing it for teaching strategies on everything from literacy to lesson planning. Among his flock were a gaggle of special ed teachers, many of them clustered at Locke. TFA had provided him with no particular insight into problems specific to special ed teachers. He didn't have a clue how best to support them.

As he headed to Locke for his first school visits, he was nervous. His experience as a teacher was limited to two years in a very small middle school. Locke was the biggest and the baddest of the schools he was assigned to; the idea of dealing with almost two dozen teachers there was overwhelming. Samir knew he looked young. He *was* young. Every time he arrived at a school and asked for a teacher's room assignment, he would be mistaken for a wet-behind-the-ears sub—not a professional TFA manager. It didn't get any better once he found the right classroom. At Locke, every classroom was locked from the inside. *Should I knock? Or should I wait until the end of the period? I don't want to intrude. How should I handle this?* Inevitably, Samir would knock. But rarely did he feel welcome as he flipped open his laptop and began to tap out a minute-by-minute account of a new TFA teacher at work.

He didn't feel very competent in Co-Investigation—in fact, he didn't even think it was the right way to support struggling new teachers. He knew from his own experience; after only a few weeks or even months in the classroom, a new teacher had neither the time nor the inclination to navel gaze about "key" problems. A new teacher didn't need a so-called thought partner. A new teacher needed a Mr. Fix-it.

His first few visits to Locke didn't exactly allay his concerns. Many of the second-year TFAers were openly hostile. Some of the first-years were, too. They felt like lab rats. They resented the intrusions, particularly in the beginning, when they were at their weakest as teachers. Samir's first meeting with Hrag was particularly uncomfortable. Hrag came right out with his qualms.

"So what is this relationship all about?" he demanded. "Are you here to tell me what I'm doing wrong?" Hrag's low-key, straightforward tone of voice intimidated Samir. He doubted very much if Hrag was disposed to take his advice.

Phillip didn't appear to need it. He was impressing just about everyone who walked into his classroom—and he had plenty of visitors, starting with the principal himself. Kids were in their seats, participating, even turning in homework. Unlike most of the corps members, Phillip had already assessed his kids by his first formal meeting with Samir. When asked what he would like Samir to look for, Phillip responded: "I feel like people look at my management and not necessarily at my teaching. I want you to tell me what you see." What could Samir say? He saw a very thorough, by-the-book teacher whose high expectations were having an unexpected effect on the kids. They appeared to be actively engaged in learning geometry.

Phillip was the exception. All the other CMs Samir visited were struggling. And it seemed that whenever he gave a suggestion, they rejected it as untenable—based on the expected reactions of their worst students. Samir urged them not to fall into that trap. "Don't model your class after your worst student," he argued. "Think of the middle-of-the-road student you could motivate. Sure, you will have some students who say FU—but that doesn't mean there are no rules. Maybe that student won't react the way we want, but let's talk about everyone else."

The new Co-Investigation model was intended to examine one key problem. Samir was seeing a multitude of key problems, ranging from bad classroom management to lousy lesson plans. He couldn't help himself: he wanted to help solve them all. So instead of zeroing in on one area of concern as he had been trained, he ended up addressing three or four issues at a time. By the end of an observation, his notes would be covered with critical comments. Samir was thrilled to be of so much help. But most CMs didn't share his enthusiasm. They resented it.

Samir was too swamped to bother reviewing the application files before his CM meetings. But he did look at all the information input from institute. Most times, when he saw a questionable review, it had to do with race. TFA always held a series of discussions centered on diversity over the course of institute. The idea was to get the issue of race out on the table and have people talk and think about it in ways they had not before. For many recruits, it was a scary discussion, and inevitably some made questionable statements. The idea that they might be perceived in certain ways based on the color of their skin was unnerving; the notion that race could have an adverse impact on teacher effectiveness seemed ridiculous. The discussions were often heated, the language aggressive. Some CMs of color suggested that white teachers were not equipped to teach minority students. Bullshit, came the angry response.

Taylor's file threw up a red flag. Sure enough, diversity had been an issue for her during institute. When another recruit questioned the motives of the white CMs for joining TFA, she bristled. *Yes, everyone knows that TFA can burnish a résumé, but that's not why whites are signing up in record numbers. Why can't people be taken at face value?* Samir knew something about that question himself. After the 9/11 terrorist attacks, he had been singled out for a particularly disturbing brand of bias. His family had immigrated to the United States from India when he was a child. Assuming he was a Muslim, his students called him Mr. Osama.

It was the note about Taylor's run-in with her CMA at institute that gave Samir pause. There had obviously been a lot of friction. In the file, the CMA suggested that Taylor had acted unprofessionally. Taylor, she alleged, had verbally attacked her. Samir steeled himself for their meeting. In his head he was expecting a lot of resistance. *Oh, I'm gonna have to watch out. She's going to challenge everything I say.*

For Taylor, the reality of day-to-day life in the classroom was actually much more bearable than the anticipation had been. Teaching felt natural to her. She wasn't faking it. She actually believed that she was providing her ninth-graders with a good education.

She had been careful from the very first day of school to create a safe environment for learning in her classroom. Over the summer she recoiled when she heard kids taunting one another: "Fuck you, you're stupid," or "Shut up, you dumb-ass nigga." She knew that kind of classroom culture made kids not want to come to school. If she was going to get them *out* of Locke, she first had to make sure they were *in* Locke. *I can't have an environment where kids are allowed to be mean to each other, or I'm screwed.* So when Taylor heard one kid tell another to shut up, she corrected her and asked the girl to rephrase what she had said. "May you stop talking so much, please," came the do-over in a heavy Spanish accent. That was better; in Taylor's classroom, at least, kids were going to feel free to express themselves, safe to make mistakes.

But a white, middle-class college graduate's idea of "safe" didn't necessarily correspond to a Locke ninth-grader's understanding of the word. Over the summer, when a fellow corps member gave her students the safe classroom speech, the kids laughed. "Look behind you, Miss," commanded one student. "How can you say this is a safe place?" The teacher turned around. There was a bullet hole in the window.

Later in the summer, CMs learned—only after the threat had passed—how potentially dangerous teaching at Locke could be. One morning, a student had come to school with a sawed-off shotgun hidden in a guitar case. Another student informed the front office, and a mad scramble was on to locate the gunman (gunchild?) before he could do any damage. When security found him, he was sitting quietly in class with the instrument case by his side.

Taylor had realized early on that at Locke anything could happen. Clearly, the only thing she would have any control over would be her own classroom. She worked hard to establish her authority—setting rules and getting to know her students. Her first test had come on the first day of summer school, during institute, when a cell phone rang in the middle of class. "There are no cell phones allowed in class," she said to the owner. "I need to take your phone." The student was big, much bigger than Taylor, and he was wearing a house arrest ankle bracelet. "No," he replied. Taylor stood there with her hand out, waiting. And hoping. Finally, the boy gave up the phone. And Taylor thought, *Maybe I have a chance of not dying here . . .*

Days into the school year, she had her kids fill out a survey about their goals. Almost everyone listed college. But there was a disconnect. Too many said "Nothing" when asked what they loved about English, and "Everything" when asked what they hated about it. Most couldn't name a favorite book. *How are these kids going to get to college if they don't read? It's one thing to have a dream; they need a plan to realize it.*

She waited until the end of the first week to introduce an ice-breaking activity she had picked up at institute. She asked the kids to list four things about themselves, one of which was untrue. Then the class had to guess which item was fiction. When things got a little noisy, Taylor simply said, "Excuse me," and there was absolute silence.

"Why are we doing this?" she asked. Hands shot up.

Then: "We're functioning as a what in here?"

"A team!" came the response.

"Are we competing against one another?" she demanded.

"No!" came the answer.

So the tone was set. Kids had goals, they knew and respected the rules, and they were bonding as a class. Taylor filled out the required TFA form with her self-reflections on how well she was incorporating the TAL habits into her teaching practice and submitted it. She was ready for Samir's visit.

At least she thought she was. When Samir came the following week and sat in the back of the room and watched, she couldn't tell what he was thinking. He was totally inscrutable. Afterward, when they talked, she got the message loud and clear. Samir told her that she had not yet set the big goal of 80 percent mastery with her students, and that was something she needed to do right away. She also needed to give her kids diagnostic tests ASAP so that she could begin to track their progress toward the big goal. Samir talked to her about student investment, too. He told Taylor she had to make the kids invested in coming to school. Something had to be special about Miss Rifkin's ninth-grade English class.

"Let them know you," he counseled. "Let your personality shine through."

Samir saw lots of positive things happening in room A22, but Taylor didn't focus on that part of the discussion. She heard only what she had failed to do. And at first she was defensive, particularly about the big goal stuff. *The big goal is all the kids are gonna get 80 percent or better? What the hell is that? It's not gonna happen. I want them to make it through the competency tests. That's my big goal. TFA says you have to rally around this big goal. But I know I wouldn't have gone for it in high school. Are they kidding me?*

She didn't like Samir's advice about letting the kids get to know her, either. She wasn't comfortable putting herself out there for them. She purposely held back. She wore the same black trousers and black ballerina shoes to school every day. And she never wore jewelry. The kids probably thought she was flat broke, without so much as a closet; little did they know she was living in a spacious apartment in posh Marina del Rey. No, they knew nothing about her, and she wanted to keep it that way. Teaching wasn't about her, it was about them. She didn't need to be their friend. She needed to be their teacher.

Taylor had always been a straight-A student. She graduated from high school with a 4.6, thanks to advanced classes, and had a 3.85 GPA when she applied to TFA. After Samir's visit, she felt like she had just gotten a B. That didn't sit well with her. But she knew she would have to follow up on Samir's suggestions, because if she didn't, she'd feel even worse. Besides, she needed TFA off her back. She barely had time to manage graduate school, lesson planning, and a long-distance romance. She didn't need to be thinking about big goals and relentless pursuits. So she went out and paid twenty-five dollars for a brightly colored cardboard racetrack, dutifully tacked it up on the bulletin board, and began to record the progress of each of her classroom "teams." She gave all her kids the Gates-MacGinitie diagnostic reading test (their reading levels ranged from third to tenth grade), and she had them write essays about their big goals. After she scored the diagnostics and read the essays, she gave them the official big goals talk.

A few weeks later, she gave it to them again. She had just gotten the results of the first school-mandated assessment, and saw that only 52 percent of her second-period class got 80 percent or higher.

"Raise your hand if your future goal is to go to college," she said. "Raise your hand if your goal is to be a professional." When all hands were raised, she said: "Well, it starts here. To be doing well in this class means getting eighty percent or above on all the tests and quizzes. Think to yourself, 'Am I one of the people getting eighty percent or higher?' "

Her words came in a steady stream. She paused only to toss out admonitions: "Take out your gum! . . . Excuse me! . . . No talking!" She pointed to a chart that she had made comparing period two's 52 percent with period three's 75 percent. She told the kids she knew they could do better. She talked about what it would take to reach the goal.

"What about studying?" asked Taylor. "Reading? What about attendance? Is it important?"

"Yes!" they shouted.

"Raise your hands, please," she scolded. "Why is it important to be in this class every day? Because we cover new material every day! You've got to be here! Okay. Our first big goal is eighty percent of students will show eighty percent mastery of the material. So, what are you waiting for? If you are not doing well in my class right now, why not? You've been here four weeks. The point is, what happens at Locke High School? Do you all make it? No! Only three hundred of you are going to graduate! Do I want all the people in this class to graduate? I DO!"

Taylor then asked them to write out their future goals once again, so that she could pin them on the back wall, the newly named Goal Wall. As they worked, she played some music: "You Can Get It If You Really Want" and the reggae song "Three Little Birds." Soon the Goal Wall was covered with teenaged dreams. Janine wanted to be a mortician, Vishon wanted to be a football player, and Guillermo wanted to win a scholarship so that he could get an MBA.

They all wanted to go to college. She ran the numbers for them—another TFA tactic. High school graduates made $280,000 more over a lifetime than school dropouts, she reported. College graduates made even more—$1 million more—than high school graduates. So, if the class goal and the personal goal weren't enough to motivate them to do well in school, Taylor asked them to consider the bottom line. A college education would show them the money.

By then she had run through all her prepared arguments for working hard in her class. What she really wanted to say to those who claimed they wanted a college education was: *Why do you come in here and screw around if this is what you really want?*

It broke her heart to think about it.

CHAPTER FOUR

The Men of Locke

The assembly—the first of the year—was by invitation only. The kids were told that TV court judge Joe Brown had requested a meeting with the "Men of Locke." Many of the kids had never heard of the good judge. But this offer was hard to refuse. After all, it was a free hall pass good for missing at least one period of school. So, on this sunny September morning, the Locke men poured out of their classrooms, walked across Saint Street, the internal campus road, and into the gym. They yanked up their drooping shorts and bounded up the bleachers. By the time Principal Frank Wells introduced Judge Joe Brown to his audience, it was standing room only. Most of the faces were black; some were Hispanic. The only females in the cavernous hall were school staff.

If the kids thought they were going to get the boilerplate "dare to dream" speech they had heard so many times before from the well-intentioned guest speakers occasionally bused in to motivate them, they were mistaken. The man with the mike had an entirely different message. And he delivered it in the cadence of a preacher from the Deep South, his voice rising and dipping, thundering one minute, cooing the next. In a mocking singsong he said: "I don't say: 'Now, boys and girls, you can be whatever you want to be.' " Switching to his hanging-judge voice, he exclaimed, "NO! Quit thinking you can be what you WANT to be. My message is: you can be what you NEED to be. What you NEED to be is about the business of being men."

Judge Brown explained, this time in the patient, avuncular tone of a community elder, that in the wake of the social and political upheaval of the sixties, the African American male had been abandoned and feminized. The primal betrayal had come at the hands of generations of young, feckless mothers who had themselves been abandoned, first by their own teenaged fathers, later by the boys for whom they unthinkingly opened their legs. The radical feminists had told the girls that they didn't need men at home, that they could do better on their own. The message stuck. The result, intoned Brown in full crescendo: "Sixty-eight percent of live births [among blacks] are born illegitimate. Most young brothers are being raised in households established by women. Now we got six, seven, eight, nine generations who don't know what a man is. If you got sons at home and you don't know what a man is good for, how the hell do you know how to raise one?"

Now he was pacing back and forth in the front of the gym beneath the basketball hoop, furiously spitting out words. "What the hell you puttin' on jewelry for? Look at yourself! You got a do-rag on your head like a damn Aunt Jemima. And the way you dress! Your pants are hangin' off your butts. What that means is you're doin' time. You're in the penitentiary and you've been spoken for. Someone is hittin' you up on a regular basis. You got 'em so low down so that when nobody's lookin' you're ready to bend down and give it up. And your big long T-shirt looks like a dress. You invitin' it! Where did that come from? That foolishness is because you don't know how to be men."

Brown reserved the most contempt for their single mothers. In high-pitched Ebonics he pantomimed the young ghetto mamas squealing on the phone to their men after their welfare checks from the first and the fifteenth arrived—and afterward in their bedrooms, satisfying their appetites as their children listened to the couplings through paper-thin walls. He dismissed the visiting men with their jewelry and nice cars as mere "houseboys—tricked out, turned out" in some grotesque gender reversal where the women produced the checks and the men primped and preened for the booty. "It used to be you worked hard to get what you wanted instead of living off a woman, but that's not true for a segment of black men."

In fact, too many black men lack ambition—or the means to succeed, said Brown. "You have no skills or occupation," he scolded. "And even if you wanted a job, the employer is callin' 911 because you look like you're about to hold the place up!"

Part preacher, part performer, Brown held the audience in his sway for nearly an hour, the kids seemingly mesmerized by the man if not the message. He acknowledged all the black superheroes that once sat in classrooms at schools like Locke. And he reminded his audience that the best and brightest of the stars—like Magic Johnson and Kareem Abdul-Jabbar—used their sports as a means to an end. Like Brown himself, they had recognized the value of an education. He ended the assembly with an appeal to all the boys at Locke—black and brown—to join forces and become the men they were supposed to be.

The kids clapped on cue, hitched up their sagging shorts as they clambered down from the hard wooden benches, and streamed out of the gym. The bright sun made the diamond studs in their ears and the burnished dog tags around their necks sparkle. The inside-out T-shirts reached their knees; some of the shorts nearly touched their ankles. Once the last kid entered the dark, cement-floored breezeway leading to the classrooms beyond, the sliding steel gates clanged shut and the click of the padlock secured the building. As the man-boys made their way back to class, it was hard to see what effect—if any—Joe Brown's tough talking had had on them.

But the judge was right when he said that the African American male is an endangered species. A 2005 report by the Los Angeles Urban League and the United Way of Greater Los Angeles entitled "The State of Black Los Angeles" found that blacks in general were twice as likely as other groups to be victims of violent crimes. They had had the overall highest death rate, the highest premature death rate, and the highest teen mortality rate in the city. Black males, in large part, accounted for the unacceptably high numbers. The most striking statistic was the homicide rate: black males were being killed at a rate four times higher than that of Hispanics, and twelve times higher than that of whites. The incarceration of black men aged eighteen to forty was 13 percent, and the probability that a black male born in 2001 would go to prison during his lifetime was 32 percent. According to an analysis of the 2000 census data by Steven Raphael of the University of California, Berkeley, among black school dropouts in their late twenties, on any given day, more were in prison—34 percent—than at work.

Locke principal Frank Wells knows something about young black males raised without fathers. He never knew his. It wasn't until Wells was established with a good job and a young stable family of his own that he decided to try to find his dad. He didn't want him to get the idea that he was looking for a father figure—or some money. His mother had told him a little bit about his dad, and Wells did some research on his own. Wells wanted to have a conversation with his father, to learn what could possibly cause a man to abandon his own child.

He found him living right there in the San Francisco area. While Wells had struggled all those years just to get by as his mother made beds and waited tables, his father had been driving a bus not very far away. When Frank Wells finally met his dad, he was struck by the resemblance between them. Wells introduced himself, though he didn't need to. His father had known his whereabouts all along. "I know who you are," he said. "You're my son." He seemed like a nice guy. Wells's dad explained why he had walked away. Back then, he didn't know nothin' about daddyhood, he said. He was a teenager, just like Wells's mother was, when she had him at seventeen. He went into the military and got on with his life. His boy was out of sight, out of mind.

Wells doesn't stay in touch much with his father, who went on to have several more families after his only son was born and recently retired after thirty-three years of bus driving. Though he has introduced his three kids to their grandfather, Wells doesn't feel comfortable calling him Dad. "I didn't have a dad, and I'm not looking for a dad," he says. "I met him to know who he is. I think that's just what happened in the projects. It was babies having babies that they weren't willing to take care of. I'm kind of numb about it. I'm not angry or upset. But I make a real effort to balance my life with my children and work."

Wells appreciated Judge Joe Brown's appearance at Locke. To the uninitiated, it may have seemed like a misogynist rant, but in Frank Wells's opinion, it was just what the Men of Locke needed to hear. "We don't grow up with a father, we don't have a male role model other than the local drug dealer and pimp, and so we have a misguided sense of what being a man is all about," he explains. "For them to hear from someone who looks like them, and who they can relate to, helps."

As principal of an increasingly Hispanic school where one third of the student body are classified as English-language learners, Wells was being forced to look more closely at the academic hurdles facing students whose first language is Spanish. But he believed it was the young African American males at Locke who needed the most attention.

After all, the kids at Locke with limited English proficiency (LEP) performed better on standardized tests than did African American students. And what that told Wells was that teachers were less tolerant of Locke's black kids. There was a reverse bias. He thought it must be a cultural thing. Hispanic students by and large were quiet, easier to manage. African American kids, he knew, were much more vocal, more apt to challenge authority. If they found a weakness, they were more likely to humiliate the teacher and take over the class. And that meant they got referred to the dean's office for discipline issues at much higher rates than the Hispanic kids did. The result: the black students received less instructional time and consequently scored lower than their Hispanic peers. Frank Wells believed that it was the African American students, especially the males, who were getting left behind.

"It is very complicated and complex and yet, at the same time, very simple," explains Wells. "Our African American boys are dealing with a multiplicity of issues that no other race has to face on a daily basis. They are dealing with the issue of retaining their manhood and surviving at the same time—in the absence of parents. They are targets if they are not in a gang. And if they are in a gang, they are either a victim or a victimizer. The foundation or the organization that has the leverage to interrupt the course of destruction is education. Other institutions have done a piss-poor job—resulting in high incarceration rates, high death rates, and other things destructive to that particular population."

Phillip Gedeon managed to avoid the path of self-destruction taken by so many other young black men. He owed his good fortune to his mother, Eunice Cole. Eunice was born in rural South Carolina and worked the cotton fields as a child. There were eight children in her family. When her older brother left home for Massachusetts, she followed him. It was there that she met the man who would become Phillip's father; he had come to the States from Saint Lucia, where he had played professional soccer. He was married when they met, though he had been separated from his wife for quite some time. The relationship with Eunice was intense—and short. Things were pretty much over by the time she gave birth. Eunice named the baby Phillip and gave him the middle name James, after her father, who died before he could see his new grandson. She called her first and only child PJ, short for Phillip James.

The life she built for PJ was as sheltered as any single working mother could provide. Until he was twelve, Eunice worked the second shift at the Smith & Wesson gun factory. She would drop PJ off at school, get things done around the house, then leave at two in the afternoon for the three-to-midnight shift. Eunice wanted it that way. She wanted to be home in the morning to get PJ off to school, and she wanted to be available for school conferences and activities during the day. After school, Phillip stayed with his aunt and two boy cousins who lived nearby. His aunt fed him dinner; if she wasn't free, Phillip ate with his landlord. He was not allowed to play outside. Eunice was afraid that she might lose him to the streets.

Phillip didn't have friends, and looking back, he realized he didn't have much of a childhood, either. He spent his days indoors—with his mother or another adult—where he created his own little world peopled with stuffed animals sitting at imaginary desks in a make-believe schoolhouse. He did the work of each of his "students," hung the results on the living room walls, and filled out their report cards. His mother bought him a chalkboard, and his approving teachers gave him old textbooks.

The first playdate of his life didn't occur until he was in middle school; his mother dropped him off at a skating rink and then picked him up at the precise time the playdate was over. Though Phillip got his driver's license, the keys to the car did not come along with it. He had to wait. When he was finally given the car, he used it only to go to work—he had no friends he wanted to hang out with. By the time he was actually able to form real friendships, he wasn't sure he wanted them. *They weigh me down. I don't have time for this.*

He learned early on that his father was not someone he could rely upon. His father wasn't a real presence in his life, but Phillip felt lucky to know him. Most of the other kids at school didn't have dads at all.

When Phillip started playing soccer as a boy, his mother, who loved the game, mentioned that his father had played professionally. His father ended up giving Phillip the occasional pointer. But the son wasn't the aggressive soccer player his father had been. In fact, that's what Phillip liked about the game: soccer was more about strategy and teamwork than male aggression.

When he did see his father, Phillip recognized much of himself in him. It wasn't just that they shared first and last names; they had the same complexion, the same hair, and, in some sense, the same personality. His father was so blunt that he often offended people. Over the years, more than one person had told Phillip that he was a bit harsh in his dealings with people. Phillip didn't see it that way. When asked his opinion, he gave it. Sometimes the truth hurt.

Though Phillip's father was a truck driver, his financial support was as inconsistent as his parenting. So Eunice worked full-time to make sure she and her son had food on the table and enough money to meet their needs. When she got laid off from Smith & Wesson, she went to school to learn computing skills and took temporary jobs. She eventually landed a permanent job on the seven-to-seven shift making envelopes in a factory. Her schedule was three days on and two days off. She was still working there when Phillip left for Los Angeles to Teach For America.

Phillip's mother raised him with morals. And he knew he would disappoint her if he strayed from them. He didn't feel the need to experiment with drugs or alcohol, and he had never dated. But he did feel driven to succeed at school. That came from his teachers, who seemed to take a special interest in his education. Neither of his parents had attended college.

The mentoring started in second grade with Miss Alice Ross. In middle school, he had his first African American math teacher, Miss Johnson. Phillip was not strong at math, but Miss Johnson told him he could be the best in the class. "I expect it from you—nothing less," she said. It was powerful. Other good teachers followed. When he got a D on his first essay assignment, his teacher worked with him every day after school; she was appalled at his writing but impressed by his determination. During his high school summers, Phillip attended a private boarding school, Northfield Mount Hermon, as part of an eight-week Upward Bound program for underserved kids. In eleventh grade he joined the school's

Teachers for Tomorrow club. He graduated from Springfield's High School of Science and Technology with a 3.9 GPA.

Phillip came to believe that a lot of his teachers saw him as their child. After his acceptance at Connecticut College, it was his guidance counselor who personally intervened and got the financial aid office to pay 95 percent of the costs—the tuition alone was more than his mother made in a year. Another fan, his high school computer teacher, Denise Cardona, actually threw a party for his college graduation four years later. She went all out, and more than a hundred guests celebrated Phillip's achievement.

It was at the graduation ceremony that Phillip's parents finally realized what his teachers had recognized early on: he was a passionate, hardworking young man with great promise. Phillip had struggled to get through college. He was a terrible test taker, and a B student. He found college to be a truly elitist society, particularly at a predominantly white, wealthy institution like Connecticut. The work seemed so hard and so abstract that Phillip sometimes wondered, *What is all this for?*

But he persevered. And he became a campus activist. Teach For America recognized his prominence on campus and tapped him to be a campus campaign manager. He worked hard for TFA and managed to get more undergrads to TFA's campus information sessions than ever before. While attending a weekend training retreat, he was moved to tears by what TFA's largely white, middle-class, top college grads were doing to close the achievement gap. He decided that he wanted to join the move-ment when he graduated. *If they are so successful, think what I, a single African American male, could do in the inner city!*

By then he had built up an impressive résumé. He was a math mentor through the college's office of community volunteers, and he was the chair of Intercultural Pride (I-Pride), an organization founded to encour-age an appreciation of multiculturalism and multiracialism. The summer before his senior year, he interned at the Connecticut Department of Edu-cation, where he designed the Connecticut Mastery Test Handbook. At his graduation, all his efforts were rewarded. The dean of the college named Phillip the winner of the Anna Lord Strauss Medal, an annual commendation given to the graduating senior who had done "outstand-ing work in public or community service." A copy of his bio—which listed his accomplishments and noted his "keen intellect," "perseverance," and effectiveness as a "visionary educator"—was included in the graduation program. When his name was announced, the crowd erupted into cheers. Eunice Cole was hugely proud. It was one of the most thrilling moments of Phillip's life.

That night when they got home, Phillip packed his bags—eight of them in all. He stripped his room bare and stored the rest of his belongings in boxes to be shipped out west once he was settled. When Phillip first told Eunice that he'd been offered a spot by Teach For America in Los Angeles, she was devastated. Then she went into denial. They would talk, she would ask if he had accepted, and he would tell her he had. The next time the subject came up, it would go the same way. Phillip would say he was going, and his mother would pretend he wasn't. Not until she saw his bags packed on graduation night did Eunice really understand that Phillip was actually leaving home for good.

As part of the TFA selection process on interview day, Phillip and the other applicants had to indicate which subjects and grade levels they wanted to teach, and what region they would like to be assigned to. As he was filling out the form, it struck Phillip that this was a life-changing moment. He was choosing his destiny. He made a pact with himself then and there. If he was accepted, he would not chicken out; he would join the movement. He was a spiritual person. He viewed Teach For America as another calling—like college.

San Francisco was his first choice. When the TFA packet came in the mail over the winter break, it was fat. Phillip knew he had made it. He thought: *San Francisco, here I come!* But he waited a few days before he opened the envelope, afraid. He reminded himself that wherever he had been placed was where God meant him to be; he would go where he was needed. Steeling himself, he opened the envelope. His eyes went immediately to the second line of the letter, where the words "Los Angeles" were printed in black ink. *Crap! L.A.! Racial tensions, gang violence, bad school system. That's not for me. Holy crap!* He mulled over how to tell his mother, then resigned himself to his fate. He knew that wherever he was sent, he would be helping students like himself, students whose life circumstances were associated with low academic performance—students of color, of low socioeconomic status, students who were only sons of single moms and absent fathers. So he reframed the story: *L.A. Land of the Stars. Sure. Why not?*

With the Watts and Rodney King riots, Los Angeles had earned a reputation for racial tensions. On the East Coast, the racism was more insidious. And constant. He was reminded of it every time he went into a store and was approached by an anxious clerk asking if he needed help. Or when he was told the waiting time for a table at a good restaurant was half an hour even though the place was empty. What was particularly galling to Phillip was, the bigots didn't want you to know they were being racist, so they would smile outwardly, while shooting you with daggers on the inside.

At Connecticut College there was no attempt to mask the racism. Two of his white roommates were openly contemptuous of minorities—though they never confronted Phillip face-to-face. A spate of hate crimes, directed at anyone who wasn't white, wealthy, Anglo-Saxon, and heterosexual, plagued the school. As chair of I-Pride in his sophomore year, Phillip helped organize a hate crimes symposium at which top state officials spoke. The ugly e-mails and crank calls that I-Pride received didn't seem to be targeted at him personally. But still, they stung.

Would it be more of the same in Los Angeles? What about Locke? Mindful that racial tensions could be a problem, Phillip purposely arranged his classroom desks in rows and drew up a chart with assigned seating. He decided that there would be no group work until he was sure he had his students under control. The strategy seemed to work. He didn't have the racial conflict in his classroom that other teachers complained of—maybe because the kids knew that he wouldn't stand for it.

Still, he noticed that kids—both blacks and Latinos—almost instinctively played the race card when challenged by a person in authority. During the fourth week of school, Phillip went head to head with a Mexican boy called Rafael who was constantly late for class. That day, Rafael walked in and slipped into the wrong seat. Phillip asked him to move to his assigned seat. The kid balked, but Phillip had already laid down the law. His students would do as he asked. Rafael refused. "What kind of a fucking class is this?" Rafael complained.

He kept it up. Phillip ignored him. Rafael raised his hand. Phillip continued the lesson. Then Rafael held up a sign that read: "Please help me, I have a question." Finally he charged: "You don't like me cuz I'm Mexican."

Phillip ordered him out of the room. Out in the hallway, the battle of wills continued until Rafael threatened to vomit and went to the nurse's office. Later, another teacher told Phillip Rafael's story. It turned out that Rafael's parents were in and out of his life, so he had been living with his sister and her boyfriend, a big-time gangbanger with clout. He had raped Rafael while his sister looked on—in silence. Just thinking about it made Phillip cry. Rafael's aggressiveness had nothing to do with the fact that Rafael was brown and Phillip was black.

The truth was, in Los Angeles Phillip didn't really think much about being black. He felt free of the racial baggage he'd carried around in the Northeast. The only time he was ever conscious of his color was when he was driving his silver Honda Accord and he happened to see a cop. He could almost read the officer's mind: *Here's a black man in a nice car with his windows down listening to loud music* . . . But so far, at least, Phillip had not been stopped. People were amazed. Even white TFAers had been pulled over when driving near Locke. For different reasons, of course.

"What are you doing in this area?" the officer would ask. And then: "I'll escort you out of here."

Phillip may not have felt particularly black; many of the white teachers didn't feel particularly white. During the first few days of summer school, Taylor had been acutely aware of her skin color. As the days and weeks went by, she rarely thought about it.

But the kids at Locke did think about race, and they were confounded by it. They grew up believing that the white man was the oppressor. Many of their teachers had reinforced the point, and their limited life experiences had confirmed it. In their neighborhoods, the only white person they ever saw was the occasional cop—and interactions with the police often ended unhappily. In their minds, to be white was to be powerful, usually wealthy, and undoubtedly racist.

So a white teacher—particularly a hardworking one who obviously enjoyed kids—was a conundrum. Oftentimes, the kids were in denial. They simply decided the teacher was not white.

When one of Taylor's kids complained that a black teacher had cursed at her, she mused: "The white people here, I don't know why white people want to be here." Then she stopped. "Are you white?"

Taylor responded with a question. "What do you think?"

The child was nonplussed. "I don't know."

Hrag's heritage was the source of heated debate among his students. More than once he had to break up an argument, only to discover that the kids were bickering over his identity.

"Hey, Mr. H," said one black girl in the middle of a lesson about stem cells. "What's your race?"

Hrag had been told Armenian gangs were active in Los Angeles. He knew Locke was a gang school. He didn't want to put himself in any unnecessary danger because of his ethnicity. So he punted. "What's my race?" he answered.

"You not white, right?" she said by way of explanation.

Someone argued that he was Hawaiian. *What about me is Hawaiian? . . . Aah. Hamalian sounds like Hawaiian.* Other kids guessed Irish or Norwegian. They couldn't figure him out.

"Do you live in Beverly Hills?" asked one kid.

"Do you drive a Ferrari?" asked another.

"No, I don't live in Beverly Hills and I don't drive a Ferrari. I drive a Ford Focus," he said to a chorus of derisive laughter.

So they figured he couldn't be white—he didn't act like a rich guy from Beverly Hills, and he didn't look like a surfer dude. But he wasn't Hispanic, even though he spoke fluent Spanish. So what was he?

At first, he couldn't understand why his kids were so obsessed with his race. Then it dawned on him. *They have no perception of what white is. On TV, all the white people drive nice cars. White for them is not a race. It's more like a bunch of people who have no idea—about who they are and how they live. They think I'm not white, because I'm here.*

Even Phillip found himself being confused for the Man. When he refused to let a black kid go to the bathroom once, the kid charged: "It's because I'm black. You're a racist!"

"I'm as black as you are!" countered Phillip, incredulous.

"No, you're not, your skin is white." Phillip just looked at the kid and burst out laughing.

Rachelle's pale complexion, light blue eyes, and long blond hair made it hard to mistake her for anything other than a stereotypical California girl. She found it was much harder for her kids to process her skin color than it was for her to process theirs. During TFA diversity seminars in the summer, recruits were urged to explore their own hidden biases and to begin "unpacking privilege," a reference to a 1988 essay entitled "White Privilege: Unpacking the Invisible Knapsack," in which the author, Peggy McIntosh, refuted the myth of American meritocracy and exposed the unearned benefits and privileges attached to being identified as "white." One of the texts for the summer institute curriculum had been devoted to the issue of diversity. In it, TFA urged its members to engage in the process of "knowing thyself"—of thinking critically about internalized and often unrealized biases, and to consider the ways in which identity-based status bestows unmerited advantages. A documentary film exploring racial biases called *The Color of Fear* was shown at a diversity session one night in Long Beach; recruits of color were resentful when many white CMs skipped the discussion afterward. For many recruits, the message telegraphed at institute was: whites were prejudiced—even if they didn't realize it—just by virtue of their whiteness.

But Rachelle didn't feel that way. When she walked into the classroom, she didn't think, *Oh, I'm teaching a black or a Latino kid.* No. In her classroom, she didn't see kids of color, she saw kids with problems—caused by the limitations imposed on them by their color and circumstances.

For her, race didn't mean a great deal. It never had. But she found herself stepping back and imagining how other people—other white people—might see her kids. She knew how sweet and bright the girls on the soccer team were. But how would people in Beverly Hills perceive them if they were walking down Rodeo Drive? Darling or dangerous? There was no doubt: they would be dismissed at a glance as poor kids from the ghetto. It was so frustrating, because Rachelle knew something the white folks on the West Side didn't know. She knew for sure that *her* kids could do whatever *their* kids could do—if only they had the same zip codes.

She thought about her own life of privilege. She had grown up in Mission Hills, the historical section of San Diego that overlooks the harbor. Her parents were both attorneys. Her father, Allen, taught law at the University of San Diego; Rachelle had often played there as a child. Her mother, Lynne, was a prominent San Diego litigator who had been nominated to the federal bench during the Clinton administration.

Rachelle attended La Jolla High School, and through middle school had been enrolled in the seminar program, the San Diego school district's academic track for students who tested into the gifted-and-talented program. Rachelle had hated high school. She wasn't interested in her classes and couldn't stand all the rules. By the time graduation rolled around, Rachelle couldn't wait to get out of high school and away from home.

Now she empathized with her students whose IEPs read "oppositional defiant disorder." She had suffered from the same thing. Only in San Diego, it was called teenaged brattiness.

As difficult as it had seemed at the time, Rachelle now appreciated how carefree her adolescence had actually been. She had never been afraid to walk home from school. Nor did she ever have to worry about how she dressed. When she thought about clothes, it was in the context of what the boys would think, not whether the colors she picked could get her killed. Though both of her parents worked, one of them was always home at night to help with homework.

Rachelle wrestled with the issue of white privilege and internalized bias. On the one hand, she respected the racial identities of her kids and the barriers and limitations they faced. On the other hand, she didn't care what anyone said: some of the behavior she saw in her classroom would be considered unacceptable in any culture.

The cursing was unbelievable, the use of the word "nigga" absolutely shocking. In fact, it might have been the most frequently used term in the Locke high schoolers' vocabulary. Even some of the staff used it. One young boy came to Rachelle and complained that another teacher had called him a dumb-ass nigga. When Rachelle asked a veteran of Locke if that could be true, he explained, "Yes, it's true. It's because she's black. Black people talk shit. All black people talk like that."

Hispanics did, too. Zeus Cubias remembers that it wasn't until he got to college that he realized he wasn't a nigga. "Nigga" was used by black and Latino alike—as a term both of endearment and of derision, depending on the tone of voice and the context. Rachelle didn't care how they used the word, or why. It had to go. She was sick of hearing it.

So she gave her nigga speech. It was at the end of the second week of school. She hadn't meant to talk about the cursing; she certainly hadn't prepared her remarks. It all just poured out of her. It started, as so many things did, with Kenyon, a really smart kid with a really bad attitude. He was one of seven children born to a single mother. Though some had different fathers, each child had a name that started with a *K*. Kenyon was a strikingly beautiful child with a dark, flawless complexion—and he was big trouble.

"Did you know Miss G's a racist?" he asked, referring to another white special ed TFA teacher named Jill Greitzer. "Well, she is. She's a racist, and you are, too."

"Really?" Rachelle said. At that point, Rachelle didn't know who Miss G was, though later in the school year they would become fast friends. She tried to get the class back on track, but Kenyon kept winding her up. Racial slurs were flying through the air. So, before she knew it, she had launched into a lecture about the *n* word. She assumed they couldn't possibly know the genesis of the word or they wouldn't be using it with such abandon. She explained that "nigga" was another way of saying "nigger," a word that was a pernicious racial slur.

"Think the word over," she told the boys. "Your people had to struggle. I think you can say the word to your friends. I don't think we should be oversensitive. But you should know what you're saying, and where the word comes from—because not everyone takes it the way in which you say it. So say whatever you want to your friends. But don't say that word in this classroom, and here's why: words can be hurtful. You don't pick a Mexican kid and call him a wetback." As she talked, she could sense this little life lesson wasn't going as she'd hoped. The kids didn't get it. And she felt out of it, too, as she rambled on and on. *I can't believe this is happening.*

"We call Jaime a wetback," said one of the other black students, referring to one of their Mexican classmates. "He don't care."

"Then show *me* some respect," she responded. "Those are my rules. You don't use that language in my class."

By this point, Rachelle was almost crying. The kids thought the whole thing was funny.

The following week, Kenyon struck again. He walked into class, as usual, in his long black sweatshirt. The hood was pulled up over his head, concealing a do-rag. Do-rags violated the dress code, a code that was rarely enforced, though Rachelle had no way of knowing that so early in the school year. Rachelle told Kenyon to remove the do-rag and pointed to his assigned seat. Kenyon ignored the order, insisting that he had not been assigned a seat.

"I'm not arguing with you," replied Rachelle. "This is your seat. Move your butt. And take the do-rag off."

As Kenyon started negotiations, Rachelle started writing a referral, the form needed to send a kid to the office.

"I'll take it off. Will you not send me to the office?" he pleaded.

"I'm not here to play games with you," Rachelle replied, her voice rising. "I'm not negotiating with little boys!"

"So why should I take it off?" shot back Kenyon. He started air punching her face.

"Kenyon, come here with me. This is unacceptable. I'm calling security!" she threatened. To the others she said: "Get the book out and turn to the page I told you."

Kenyon removed his do-rag and stood in the doorway. She turned her attention back to the rest of the class and asked if they had done their homework. Only one person had. Eduardo, a Latino gangbanger, pulled his out, crumpled it into a ball, and threw it into the wastebasket.

Now Rachelle introduced the day's lesson—about false advertising and the need to test products scientifically. By this time, Kenyon had slipped back into his seat.

"Do you guys remember what we talked about yesterday?" she asked.

Kenyon's hand shot up. She ignored him. "I remember, I remember!" he cried. "But no. She won't pick on a black boy. She's racist."

There was a knock on the door, and Kenyon stood up to answer it. When Rachelle saw that it was another one of the troublemakers coming to class ten minutes late, she refused to allow him in. "Go away, Jesse," she ordered. "Don't touch my door!"

"Why? What'd I do?" Jesse said. Now he and Kenyon started to mix it up in the hallway as the rest of the class watched.

Rachelle turned to the other nine kids in the class and said: "You should not have to suffer. This is not your fault."

And Kenyon said to the class, "You're racist, just like her." To Rachelle, he said, "You! You shut up!" Then he reentered the room and threatened to throw the file cabinet out the window.

Now Rachelle was really angry. "You are not allowed in my class now! Do not tell me to shut up! I am sick of this! Sick of this crap!" She took him into the hall. Usually, a security guard sat just feet from her door. Today the seat was empty. She needed help. She needed to get him out of the room and down to the dean's office. There was no one in sight.

Inside the classroom, two Latino boys were throwing gang signs. Others doodled. A few got up to stretch and began to roam around the room. By the time security arrived, the bell had rung. Class was over, and Rachelle had not taught more than a minute of biology.

"What we did today was a complete waste of time," she said as the students rose to leave. "I want you guys in my class. I don't want you not to succeed. But I can't even teach a class!"

Fourth period was the last class of her day. It usually left her exhausted, often angry.

I have to stay calm. I am so appalled. I've never seen people act this way. They are so rude. I don't care where they come from. You don't act that way! Why am I wasting my time? They don't even listen to me. They make me want to quit!

She didn't know how to teach them—or even what to teach them. Should she show them first how to conform—how to be white—so people wouldn't judge them and they could blend into society? Or should she accept the bad behavior as part of who they were?

She wanted to tell them what she really thought: *When you act like this, you are confirming all the stereotypes. When you use profanities or take something from my desk and say: "You don't know, Miss Synder, this is the hood, this is how things go down, you got to get what you got to get," I want to say: "Don't act that way, don't talk that way. You are really rude. You have bad social manners. You are really bad with eye contact." Maybe it's no big deal if you're talking to your friends, but if you ever want to leave here . . .*

Maybe I don't know how you grew up. But you don't know how I grew up, either. Maybe it is white privilege. And it's not fair, it's not right. But it is true. People will judge you. I'm not saying the white way of interacting is superior, I'm saying it's more professional. You get pigeonholed. And I want to shake you and say "Why don't you wow people? Why don't you show them who you are?"

When Chad Soleo thought about race, and the school, and the community, and the plight of the young black males of Locke, he sometimes caught himself slipping into places he never thought he would go. But there were some things that just didn't escape notice—like who the loudest, most obnoxious students running down the halls were. He didn't want to say it was the black kids, but he saw what he saw. And it was at moments like those that he would find himself thinking things he philosophically and politically didn't want to be thinking—and hoping there was another explanation. Some people would say those kids were crack babies. And they probably were.

Because there was no doubt in his mind that a family could be out of Watts within one generation. If a poor family came and the parents worked their butts off to make sure their kids had a roof over their heads and a place to do homework, if they emphasized school and the need to go to college, there was every reason to believe they could and would get there. The opportunity was there. There were scholarships, and grants, a lot of money. If the student qualified, it was there. It was Chad's hope that when those kids finished college, they would return to their communities as leaders; but it was his job to make sure that they didn't have to return, that they had other options, and that as a result their children would, too. Leaving Watts was not an impossible dream.

Chad wondered about the families who didn't leave, who never made it out, who had been there for generations. Some of them were admirable community leaders who chose to stay and whose kids were going to college, and making money, not living in the projects in absolute poverty. They owned property in Watts. But those who stayed, mired in poverty? The renters? You had to believe that they were not doing what it takes to get their families out. They were not emphasizing the importance of education; they were letting their kids run amok. They didn't have it easy, definitely not. But you had to ask: *Why aren't you valuing education? Why aren't you seeing it as a ticket out for your kids? Because it is, it is the ticket out.*

He was not naïve. He knew there were circumstances that kept people from getting opportunities. But they didn't always come to mind when dealing with a tough kid. Instead he found himself thinking: *Why are you talking to me this way? Why won't you listen?* Then he would call the parent and everything would become clear. *Ah. That's why. You say you went to Locke, too? Okay. Now I understand. This kid doesn't prioritize school because you don't—and apparently didn't.* And he wouldn't have wanted to go there, but there he was, and he couldn't help but wonder what the kid would be like with different parents.

For the most part, he thought it was healthy, these musings; mentally embarrassing but healthy. *If I don't question the perceptions, then how do I help create solutions? If I don't explore the reasons, how do I come up with interventions to reengage black boys?*

He also knew there was a point—one he hoped never to reach—

when a person could become too cynical. Chad was reminded of a conversation he had had with a teacher, a TFA alum, who was still working at Locke when he first arrived. She said, "I really do think we should build a wall around this community and let them shoot each other. And don't let anybody in, and don't let anybody out, and let the community take care of itself." Chad would not dignify the statement with a comment. But he thought: *I'm embarrassed to know you. You need to go.* He knew that she couldn't have started out that way because Teach For America doesn't appeal to people like that. She made the comment during her fourth year at Locke. She left after that.

Now he was in his fourth year at Locke, and he was a newly named assistant principal, in charge of the counseling office. Not only did he have to create a master schedule to accommodate some 3,100 students and 131 teachers, he also had to manage a dozen counseling office staffers. He was younger than just about every one of them. Some, if not all, resented his success, which even at Locke, where a second-year teacher could practically run a department, was meteoric.

Chad had come to Locke in the fall of 2001 as a Teach For America recruit. He thought of his two-year commitment then as a useful detour on the way to law school. Teach For America could get him to Los Angeles, delay graduate school long enough for him to afford the tuition, and really challenge him—which he liked. But more important, it would put something really valuable on his résumé. It would open doors.

The gibe that TFA really stood for Teach For Awhile wasn't that far off the mark. In fact, there was an unspoken expectation that after completing their commitment, most corps members would move on to something else. TFA actually encouraged it. As valuable as two years in the classroom was to the mission, Kopp knew it would never be enough to close the achievement gap. Teach For America had to groom an army of leaders to take the fight beyond the classroom and into the corridors of power. So it forged partnerships with top graduate schools and prestigious private-sector firms that agreed to grant two-year deferrals for corps members. And the opportunities provided post-classroom became a key component in the marketing of TFA. A two-year stint in the classroom would give recruits a chance to do something valuable, with immediate impact, right out of school. And far from derailing the ambitious, it would actually help set them up, paving the way for their future careers.

But by the end of his second year at Locke, Chad had forgotten about law school. He had become a teacher. He couldn't have been more surprised. Teaching wasn't a serious career move for a person with ambition. It didn't pay enough money, and it didn't command enough respect; Chad wanted both.

The thing was, Chad had taken to teaching right from the start. He had actually enjoyed Teach For America's intensive five-week training institute in Houston. A classic type A personality, Chad found himself up until 2 a.m. every night perfecting lesson plans. Others chafed under the workload. He thrived on it. He was psyched when he heard founder Wendy Kopp speak at the opening ceremony, and he was still psyched when he got a job at Locke. Chad realized that Locke was a low-performing school—those were TFA's only clients. But he didn't know it was arguably *the* lowest-performing high school in all of LAUSD. And if he had been told that Locke was a de facto gangland battleground, it hadn't sunk in.

Chad had arrived at a school in free-fall. Attendance was low, truancy high. His tenth-grade students lacked the most fundamental skills; a good percentage of them were reading at a third-grade level. Fights were an almost daily occurrence. Though he never felt personally threatened, he could feel the danger in the air. Everyone could. If you worked at Locke, you were always holding your breath, just waiting for the inevitable spark that would ignite a fire.

The siege mentality drew many of the younger teachers together. Chad found a lifelong friend in Josh Hartford, the only other first-year TFA recruit assigned to Locke that year. The two of them reached out to the five other TFAers then on staff, and to some others, such as Vanessa Morris, the young UCLA alum who had become a nationally board-certified teacher—a feat unparalleled at the school. The veteran teachers may have resented the tight clique of young turks, but no one disputed their dedication, teaching skills, enthusiasm, and love for their students.

Within two months of Chad's arrival at Locke, the principal who had hired him was gone. Shortly after school began in September, Locke was the site of what the media called a bloody "mêlée." Chad and Josh Hartford watched in amazement as LAPD officers descended upon the campus to restore order after black and brown students engaged in a particularly ferocious battle during lunch. Weeks later, the principal was transferred, and local superintendent Sylvia Rousseau moved in.

June 2003 marked the end of Chad's two-year TFA commitment. He had seen the achievement gap narrow in his English classes. He had experienced the thrill of taking on a reading intervention class and turning it into a book circle where the ten kids who actually showed up had advanced several grade levels by the semester's end. Chad was a gifted teacher who had moved his students—academically and personally—and he reveled in their success.

He also experienced failure—and a loss so profound that it threatened to plunge him into despair. The boy was a gangbanger, only fifteen years old. His name was Angel de Jesus Cervantes, and by October, when he was shot dead in an alley, he had started coming regularly to Chad's class. The day after his death, students came to Chad's room crying, wanting to know what had happened to Angel. Chad had no idea. He was having trouble wrapping his head around the fact that his fifteen-year-old student was really dead. So he went down to the counseling office and asked how to verify whether a student had actually been killed.

"Well, what do you want to see? The dead body?" came the reply from a usually empathetic counselor. *No, I want to know what it is I'm supposed to do with these students crying in the hallway!*

Chad took the kids to the library, where Angel's girlfriend fell to the floor in hysterics. Chad had never seen anything so emotionally god-awful in his life. And he couldn't think of a thing to say. In the end he mumbled something about how everything would be "all right."

But nothing about it was all right. Angel's was the first funeral Chad had ever attended. All Angel's homeys were there—dressed in Bloods' red, arms crossed, gang signs flashing. Chad was incensed. *This is all so wrong. He had started coming to my class. And now he's dead.*

The kids seemed to get over the slaying more easily than Chad did. He couldn't stop thinking about it. The school never made an announcement that Angel had been shot and killed. When another teacher heard of the death, his response shocked Chad: "Oh, he was a gangbanger any-way," he said, as if that made his murder okay. Though Chad had been in South Los Angeles long enough to have a sense of the community and the gang violence that pervaded it, he hadn't been prepared to feel the way he did when he watched that fifteen-year-old—a boy he had known and presumably touched—being put into the ground.

Angel was the first student of many that Chad would lose in the next four years. Most, not surprisingly, were victims of gang violence; Los Angeles is the uncontested gang capital of the world. A 2006 gang study commissioned by the city council estimated that some 720 gangs call Los Angeles home. Despite 23 antigang programs that cost $82 million a year, gang violence in the city overall rose 14 percent in 2006. The increase in South Los Angeles—home to Locke High School—was 25 percent.

Throughout the 2005–2006 school year, school police had a small eight-by-ten-inch map tacked to the wall of the campus police station. Its title: "Southeast Division Gang Map, Black, 2003." At first glance the map looked like a lightly colored jigsaw puzzle. Locke High School was just a three-eighths-inch square in the middle, toward the top of the page. Surrounding it was a patchwork of pastel-colored geometric shapes. But they were not jagged puzzle pieces; they represented square footage, carefully surveyed gang-owned turf. What was painfully obvious was that the tiny neutral patch, marked with a red flag, the symbol for a school, was hopelessly landlocked, hemmed in on every side by warring gangs.

Locke is a Crips school; the black gangs that surround it are all sets of that notorious Los Angeles street gang. Blue is the Crips' color; their rivals, the Bloods, wear red. Dick Fukuda, the dean of discipline at Locke, reckoned there were more than a dozen Crips gangs operating on campus and in the surrounding community in 2006. Unlike the Bloods, whose various splinter groups tend to get along, the Crips are often at war with one another. The most active gangs at Locke are the Back Street Crips, the Broadway Gangster Crips, the Front Street Crips, and the East Coast Crips. It's hard to say how many students are hard-core gangbangers; probably fewer than 500, maybe even fewer than 250. But there are plenty of wannabes, kids who tag along, dress the dress, talk the talk; and there are "associates," too, the gangbangers-in-training, doing a kind of fraternity rush before being courted in as full-fledged members. For some kids, membership in a gang is a given, a birthright. Siblings, parents, even grandparents have gang connections. It's a family affair.

Not surprisingly, gangs break down strictly along racial lines. The primary Hispanic gang that operates in South Los Angeles is called South Los—Spanglish for Los Del Sud, a gang that originated in Mexico. South Los is a deadly force in the community, but it is not as active on campus as it once was. The Latino action at Locke comes from the tagging crews, or the "cliques," loose groups of wannabes that "kick," or hang around, together. The cliques can be violent, but they tend not to deal in drugs.

The highly selective tagging crews are not usually violent, but their handiwork is considered a crime. The names of the crews change constantly; their modus operandi does not. A tagger needs only a marker, a moniker, and a paintable surface. Locke High School offers a broad and inviting canvas. Every bit of it—floors, walls, ceilings, desks, doors, the runner on the stairs, and the cement benches on the quad—is covered in graffiti. In an effort to deglamorize the artistic vandalism, Dr. Wells invited Locke taggers to display their signs on the outer walls of the school's handball courts during the 2005 school year. Soon, the hand-painted murals of Dr. Martin Luther King Jr. and other black leaders were obscured by wall-to-wall graffiti. The experiment was short-lived. There was no notable decrease in tagging elsewhere on campus, and the district ordered that the walls be cleaned up. During the 2005–2006 school year, Locke employed three men, full-time, five days a week, to handle graffiti outbreaks. It was a task for a sorcerer's apprentice. The more the graffiti was painted over, the more it popped up elsewhere. WET PAINT signs posted all over campus marked the spots.

Every student on campus has a working knowledge of gangs. It's a necessity. At Locke, many kids must pass through several gang enclaves to get to school. Knowing how to navigate the terrain can be a matter of life or death. That means students have to watch where they go, how they dress (red is out of the question), and what they say. Bulging backpacks are often filled with clothes—not books—so that students can change colors as they traverse enemy territory. Even so, Locke students get jumped frequently on the treacherous journey to and from school. Wary of the danger, some kids join a gang simply for protection. It's called getting "jumped" in. The kids who don't "bang" often spend their days behind closed doors, rarely venturing outside—much as Phillip Gedeon did during his childhood in Springfield, Massachusetts.

Few escape their urban childhoods unscathed. A 2006 report by

Marlene Wong, director of crisis counseling and intervention at LAUSD, revealed that between 85 and 91 percent of children in eighteen district schools had been touched by violence. Teenagers are wounded—and die—at shockingly high rates. Carla German, hired in 2005 to be Locke's first-ever psychiatric social worker, guessed that by the middle of the 2005–2006 school year, nearly a dozen Locke students—or Locke dropouts—had died violent deaths since the first day of school. She couldn't be sure of the exact numbers. That's because no one knows how many students enrolled at Locke actually attend—much less how many drop off the rolls due to transience or death. "Shootings are a common occurrence here," says German. "There are always kids dying, kids losing friends. The thing about kids in this community, they have such a tough skin, they normalize it all very quickly."

That's what happened in early December 2005, when seventeen-year-old Carmen Duncan was killed by her own sister in a fight over a photograph. While the two Locke students were getting ready for school, they argued, and the older sister took a pair of scissors and stabbed the younger one to death. Word spread quickly that day as kids arrived at school. But there was no announcement of the tragedy on the intercom, nor was there a school assembly for mourning or public discussion. Wells sent a memo to the staff advising that counselors were on hand to help grieving students. Few came.

The case of Deliesh Allen, who had been a Locke sophomore earlier that spring, was different. Her death, perhaps because it was so random, perhaps because it was a slow news day, rocked the school and the community. Press conferences were called and tougher antiviolence measures promised. Dr. Wells, just seven months into his new position, spoke at the funeral. The program from the service was sealed beneath the glass that topped his office desk.

It was 3 p.m. on Friday, Saint Patrick's Day 2005, and school was just letting out. Fifteen-year-old Deliesh was standing on the sidewalk fifty steps or so from the school's back gate, waiting for her aunt to pick her up. She chose the wrong spot. Directly across the street was an apartment believed to be a stronghold of the infamous Back Street Crips. Suddenly, gunshots rang out. The young girl collapsed, a single bullet lodged in her brain.

School police officer Harold Salazar was in his car patrolling the perimeter of the school at release time that day when he got a call from a campus aide. "I think we have shots fired and I believe somebody is down" came the message. Salazar called for LAPD backup and made a loop around the campus. Traffic was bad as he turned onto Avalon Boulevard, heading for the school's back entrance. Looking to the right, he saw a crowd. Everyone was staring at the ground. The aide was right. Somebody *was* down. It was the east side of the campus. Salazar figured it was the Back Street Crips. What he hadn't reckoned on was that the victim was a young African American female. When he leapt from the car and saw the teenager lying on the ground unconscious, barely breathing, he pulled up short. *A child. Crap.* He had seen shootings before. But never a schoolgirl, never one that he knew attended Locke. As he cleared the area and set up the crime scene, he couldn't help thinking about his own kids. *You send them to school and you think they're safe. And then they die.*

The local fire department was just two blocks away and arrived within a minute or so. Deliesh was rushed to the hospital, where she died after eight days on life support.

The hunt for her assailant began immediately. A cop at the crime scene heard someone say, "It was Snoopy." The officer called over to the Locke police station and asked if anyone knew a kid by that name. Snoopy was the moniker for a gangbanger named Dejuan Hines. An index card with all of Hines's information was crammed into the over-stuffed, well-thumbed file box kept at the campus police station. He was arrested later that night. "I actually got along with the guy; he was respectful," recalls Salazar. "He wasn't one of the real knuckleheads. I'd deal with this kid, two, three times a week. He was one of those guys, if you tell him something, he'd say all right, and call you sir. What I think happened was he was shooting at a passing car or something."

On March 8, 2006, a few weeks shy of the one-year anniversary of the Deliesh Allen shooting, Dejuan Hines was convicted of second-degree murder and attempted murder. He was sentenced to eighty-two years to life in prison. He was eighteen years old when he killed Deliesh. He was a high school dropout.

Deliesh's death only underscored what Chad already knew. It was after Angel's funeral that he understood that he wasn't going to be in and out of Locke in two years. He hadn't finished what he had come to do. He was a get-it-done-and-be-done-with-it type of guy. Too late, he realized that that was a terrible personality to have in a low-performing high school. Because you never felt like the job was done. You always felt like a failure. And because you couldn't stand that feeling, you ended up trying even harder, working even more. Chad knew why he was at Locke, and he knew that Angel's death was something he would have to remember if he was going to continue to be effective there. *Remember how you feel, remember the kids, remember Angel.*

He probably couldn't have left Locke even if he wanted to. It felt like home. He couldn't leave the kids, and he couldn't leave the band of teachers he had come to love. They were all young, mostly white, mainly single, many of them TFAers. They called one another by their last names, but they were closer than family. They worked together and drank beers together at Sharkeez, a dumpy surfer bar on the edge of Manhattan Beach. Some even lived together.

So, he re-upped. But more and more, the satisfaction he felt at his students' achievements was replaced by a nagging sense of frustration with school bureaucracy and the slow pace of change. In two and a half years of teaching he had already been through two principals; the third was waiting in the wings. Student attendance and test scores remained appallingly low, school crime unacceptably high. The school was too big, the district too political. Chad Soleo worked as hard as was humanly possible, but at Locke, nothing stuck. Not the teaching, not the teachers, not the administrators, not even the kids.

He began to think about expanding his reach. As a teacher he knew the problems; as an administrator maybe he could fix them. He visited successful charter schools, and he pored over the literature on education reform. At around that time, the school was ordered by the district to reorganize into small learning communities—a consequence of failing to make academic progress under No Child Left Behind. Dr. Rousseau addressed the Locke faculty. "Dream!" she said. "Think about what a good school should be." Staff proposals for six small academies were due in weeks. Chad drew up an outline for a plan and asked his friends and colleagues to help him flesh it out. In September, the School of Social Empowerment (SE) was up and running. The next year, recognizing Chad's success in leading his small school, Wells asked him if he had thought about becoming a school administrator. Chad had reservations about Wells. Safety and security had improved under his leadership, but he thought Wells lacked the kind of instructional vision required at a school like Locke. He put aside his misgivings, though. Wells was making him an offer he couldn't refuse.

"Yes," he replied. "I have thought about administration, and yes, I would like to join your staff."

CHAPTER FIVE

Locked In

It's like a prison. Even the teachers are locked in. No wonder the kids act this way. Phillip was in a bad mood as the police officer slid the gate open just wide enough for him to exit the football field, then promptly locked it shut again. He was sick of all the gates and the locks. What good did they do, anyway? Weapons still made their way onto campus, property still managed to go missing, kids still ditched classes. He was tired of being locked in, locked down, locked out.

He should have felt great. It was homecoming weekend, the sun was shining on this first Saturday in November, and the Locke Saints were winning the game against rival Fremont High. Behind him, the cheerleaders were chanting: LET'S GO, LOCKE SAINTS, LET'S GO! LET'S GO LOCKE SAINTS, LET'S GO! The stands weren't full, but the three hundred or so people who had paid the seven-dollar admission fee and submitted to a scan by a wand-waving cop were having fun. Whole families were there. Little girls waved pom-poms in time with the cheerleaders; blue and yellow balloons fastened to the fence bobbed in the breeze. Frank Wells, a former football player himself, stood on the sidelines, shoulder-to-shoulder with the players, his arms akimbo in his Locke bomber jacket. The fans were mostly African American. Sports at

Locke tended to divide strictly along racial lines. Blacks played football; Hispanics played soccer.

Because of security issues, it wasn't often that the blue-and-gold Saints team played at home. Homecoming was special. The daylong festivities began in the morning when the once famous Locke Saints Marching Band led the annual parade through the neighborhood and onto the campus. Kickoff was at 1 p.m. Then later, at seven, the homecoming dance would begin. Throughout the day, security was tight. Three uniformed school police officers manned the field's sliding entrance gate, unlocking and locking it after each arrival and departure.

Phillip was wearing jeans. More than a few heads turned in surprise at the sight of him out of professional attire, but he had already put in several hours of work in his third-floor classroom. He would probably log in several more before the dance that evening. He was exhausted. His allergies were acting up *(was it the L.A. air?)*, and he hadn't had time to sort out his medical benefits and get a prescription refilled since he'd moved to the city. It felt like all he did was work. The only time he was able to relax was when he returned to the apartment he shared with three women—all first-year TFAers like himself. Their place was in Baldwin Hills, a black middle-class neighborhood only a short drive from Locke. It wasn't until they moved in that they realized that thirteen years before, the neighborhood had been ravaged in the Rodney King riots. Now their apartment building was filled with professionals—many of them teachers in L.A. Unified. The four roommates took turns cooking; over nightly meals they shared their war stories. They got along perfectly. Phillip's only complaint was that on occasion someone forgot and put his coffee mug in the dishwasher.

He felt burned out. But he wasn't the only one. Just walking down the halls each day, he could see people dragging. It was only November, and already a lot of the teachers were saying this would be their last year at Locke. Not Phillip. He had a plan from which he would not deviate. He would stay at Locke for four years, and during that time he would get his master's in administration from Loyola Marymount University. He didn't want to be a principal, but it made sense to get certified for administration. From there he would most probably move to another school, where he would work while earning his doctorate. Finally, he would get a Ph.D. He knew that eventually he would leave the classroom, and just the thought of that day's arrival made him sad. He loved teaching. Still, working at Locke was so taxing. People said the atmosphere on campus had changed for the better since Wells took over. But judging by the chaos he saw all around him, school and district policies had not. *The system is failing, and it's making me fail.*

Classes were too big and the school too dysfunctional for one teacher to effect real change in student achievement. Ten-week grades were due, and Phillip still didn't know exactly how many students he had. In his seventh-period class, only half of the thirty-six students enrolled ever showed up. In his fourth-period class, there were forty-five names on his roster in a room that had only forty-one desks. Most of the time it wasn't a problem—there were always at least five students absent; some of them he had never even seen. But it was annoying. Each day, one particularly good-natured student would come in, sit at the front table, and wait to see which desk would be empty. Then, satisfied that the real owner was a no-show, the student would take a seat and get to work. Phillip could have requested more desks, but that would have sent the wrong message to the administration. That would be saying that he was okay with an oversized class, and he was not okay with that at all. The way to raise student achievement was to lower class size, not to pack the kids in like sardines and assume there'd always be enough room because attendance was so poor.

Other things bugged him, too. Like the fact that there was a deaf boy in Rachelle Snyder's class who had no aide to sign for him, and the fact that some kids assigned to honors English couldn't really read, and the fact that faculty meetings were like grade-school food fights, and the phones didn't work, and access to copy paper was based on politics—if you were one of the anointed, you got paper; if you were not, you had to beg, borrow, or steal. That's literally what he had had to do to get a computer for his classroom. He begged. The school didn't have enough working machines, so rather than wait or do without, Phillip logged on to www.donorschoose.org and published his sob story. The website was designed to match donors with needy causes in low-income school districts. Some rich philanthropist trolling the site saw Phillip's proposal and funded the purchase of a Sony VAIO laptop for him.

The heady days when he first arrived in Los Angeles seemed like a mirage. Teaching at a place like Locke was a grind, an uphill climb with no summit in sight. And the kids! They came to school with so much baggage, baggage that no first-year teacher could possibly help carry.

His most recent heartbreak was Darius. Darius had been absent from school for three or four weeks, and when he finally returned, Phillip asked him where he had been.

"You don't wanna know," Darius replied.

"Yes, I do," insisted Phillip. "Tell us the story."

"I was at home," he explained. "I got into this fight with this kid and he lost, so he came to my house several times with guns."

"What else?" prompted Phillip.

"He's been threatening to kill me and my family, so my mom wouldn't let me go out. We got a TRO [temporary restraining order]. Then she thought I should go back to school."

"How is this going to come to a closing, a resolution?" asked Phillip.

"One of us is gonna have to shoot the other," came his simple reply. "Whoever shoots first solves the problem."

Phillip was taken aback. "Is it worth it?"

Darius looked at him and said, "You got to do what you got to do."

Everyone else in the class just sat there. There was no outrage, no shock, no embarrassment. It was business as usual. Phillip didn't know what to do with what he had just learned. *Who do I go to? He already has a TRO. Do I send work home? Who would pick it up? What should I do?*

Phillip had much in common with his students; he, too, was raised in a low-income community by a single mother. But he had never lived in a neighborhood like this. He had never experienced the kind of pressure or fear that Darius knew. He could sympathize, he could imagine, but he could never feel what Darius was feeling. The only answer for Darius's situation, he decided, was to make the time that he had with him meaningful, to make the moments in Mr. Gedeon's class the best moments of Darius's day.

But that did not address the larger problem, and it certainly didn't allay his own fears about Darius's safety. Now, when Darius was not in class, Phillip couldn't help but wonder: *Is this the day? Is this the day I'm gonna get the notice he's either in jail or dead?*

One day, way back in September, a note was left on his desk that read: "Hey Mr. G. I Love the way you teach our first period. You help me a lot in class. I really appreciate you helping me. Guess who? Thanks 5:30 p.m." Phillip tacked the letter to the bulletin board next to his desk.

He kept it there to read on days like this, when everything seemed so futile.

The first inkling that teaching at Locke was going to be tougher than he thought came when Phillip got the results of the first benchmark assessments, monthly tests that Dr. Wells required teachers to give to track achievement. Ninety-five percent of his students had failed. At the math department meeting afterward, Phillip realized that the other teachers had equally disappointing results; the kids had all bombed.

When Phillip handed out the scores to his students, they were surprised. He had given them the grades they deserved; they were used to getting the grades they needed. *Am I being too hard? Are the questions too difficult?* No, he decided. The questions had come directly from the work he had been presenting in class. *Then why are my students failing?*

Phillip was not in the habit of blaming himself. He decided that the problem was homework. His kids didn't do it. That was going to change.

First he decided to cut the number of nightly homework problems from an overwhelming twenty to a more manageable handful. Then he decided that the kids themselves would correct the homework in class, instead of handing it in to him for marking. That way there would be immediate feedback—kids wouldn't have to wait weeks to get their work back, if Phillip even got around to grading it. They would see that there was a meaningful relationship between the nightly homework and the weekly test results. The pace of the class would change, too. The lessons would be slower, more deliberate. Finally, failure to do homework would have consequences: a dreaded Saturday-school detention.

Phillip came up with his plan after reading through the "free writes," essays critiquing his class that he had solicited from his students. He found out that his emphasis on homework was the exception at Locke, not the rule. Most teachers didn't give it, or if they did, they didn't really expect to get it back. So it was tough; he was making a big deal about something that nobody else cared about. Phillip believed that Locke needed a schoolwide policy on homework. Without it, kids could not succeed. Limited resources were not the problem at Locke. The problem was that there was no culture of achievement.

It wasn't the kids' fault; it was the responsibility of parents and teachers to instill good work habits in their children. Phillip tried to put himself in his students' shoes: *If I were a student and no one forced me to do homework and I had a teacher giving it to me, and not grading it, why would I do it? I would think: "I have homework and there's a lot of it, so why do it?" Especially if I were a student who had been passing all the time.*

Phillip got positive feedback at the school's open house in early October. Attendance schoolwide for the event was low. But a whopping twenty-two out of two hundred parents had dropped in on room 301. Phillip used the time to try to create some accountability from parents. The next day, he tried to do the same with his students. He spoke for five minutes and took no questions. The kids needed a reality check.

When he started to speak, the look on the faces before him was *I don't care.* But as he continued, he could see that his words were having an effect.

"Let's talk about reality," he barked. "What do people think about Locke High School? The reality is the people on the outside—the school board members, the politicians, and the government officials—make decisions every day that affect you. But they don't care about all your trials and tribulations and who you really are. What they care about is what you show them. All they see is the test scores, the grades, the attitude. They don't see what we as teachers see on a daily basis. Talking to your parents made me realize that teachers are not the only ones in this struggle. The parents support us and want you to succeed. But you have to realize what people from outside the community think of you. They don't spend money on this school on a daily basis because you tell them on a daily basis that you are not worth it. Why spend money when you don't do the work? Why buy computers when you don't perform even at a basic level?

"You have to understand that every action has one of two consequences: you can either support their beliefs that you are unworthy and that you don't care so why should they, or you can show them that they are wrong. How? You be the students they think you cannot be. Study. Do your homework. Come to class and do as well as you can. You need to make a choice. Every time you do something, think of the consequences. Are you supporting or disproving their theories about who you are?

"The cards are stacked against you. But that doesn't give you an excuse not to play the game. That should give you the excuse, the motivation, to work twice as hard."

There was silence. He had their absolute attention. Now the look on their faces said *You're right*.

Seeing that, he launched into a lesson about biconditional and conditional statements.

While Phillip worried that all his kids were failing, one of Hrag's biggest problems was that too many of his students were passing. He didn't know how to grade. There was no schoolwide policy, so he just did what almost everyone else in the biology department did. The bottom line was, if you came to Mr. H's class and did the lab work, you passed. Hrag gave out homework maybe once a week—any more often, he figured, and they wouldn't do it. The tests he gave counted for only 15 percent of the final grade, though the kids didn't know that. Surprisingly, the results on the first couple of quizzes were outstanding—the average was 80 percent and the tests were *real* biology! Since then, though, the scores had dipped into the 60s. He wasn't sure what to make of the drop. He worried that the kids weren't conceptualizing the material he was presenting. But he had so little time to think about what he was teaching and how he was doing that he was hard-pressed to make any adjustments.

His life had gone from carefree to crazed in a matter of months. During his senior year at BC, Hrag had been able to kick back some. After a Thursday night of partying, he'd wake up at 2 p.m. on Friday, go to his one scheduled class, and then rev up for the weekend's festivities. Now he was rising before dawn and working late into the night. He was getting five hours of sleep—if he slept at all. On top of that, for the first time in his life he had to cook and clean for himself. He felt like he was sixty years old. When he woke up in the morning and looked in the mirror, he thought, *I am my dad*.

In addition to teaching five periods of biology every day, he was attending night school from four to ten two evenings a week. All recruits had to be enrolled in a credentialing program as a term of their employment by LAUSD. It helped meet No Child Left Behind requirements, and it helped blunt charges that TFA teachers were ill prepared. But grad school was a joke, every TFAer agreed. Loyola Marymount University had designed a special curriculum for busy TFAers, which got them a credential and a master's in two years—for four thousand dollars! But TFAers went to class after a long day of work, and most zoned out instead of tuning in. While the professors lectured, they were on their laptops, multitasking. They'd be catching up on e-mail, entering grades, and preparing lessons—while keeping one ear half open in case something interesting was said. Most found that very little of what LMU offered was applicable to life in the classroom. So they saw grad school as just another drain on their time and energy, and put it at the bottom of their list of priorities. Hrag had heard that the feeling was mutual. A lot of professors at LMU refused to teach TFAers. They thought they were obnoxious.

What Hrag hadn't realized before he started was that teaching was not a regular job. It enveloped his whole life. It was the first thing he thought of when he woke up, and it was on his mind on the weekends when he walked down to the beach to try to relax. All he ever thought of was school. He wasn't just a teacher—he was a referee, a counselor, a doctor—eighty things bundled into one. And that made him even more nervous. He had this thing in his stomach, this growing tightness. He told himself it was just the stress of the first couple of months, but he wasn't so sure. He read somewhere that after cops, teachers drank the most alcohol. He believed it; the job could drive anyone to drink.

After two years at Locke, he thought, he was going to be scarred. He was scarred already. He knew he would never forget the drunks on street corners he saw at 6 a.m. on the way to work, or tough little José and troubled Cale. He would always remember the kid who sat there shivering and licking his lips throughout class—*is he on drugs or just hungry?* And the gangbangers and the kids who looked like they'd been beaten. And the boy he often drove home from school because he lived so far away. He felt, too, for the kids who came to class every day to "get their learning on" against all odds. Yes, Teach For America was life-changing. He might not end up being an educator—at this point there was NO WAY—but down the line, years from now, he knew he would care about the achievement gap when 95 percent of the world did not.

Hrag lived in the little surfer town of Hermosa Beach with another TFA recruit, Mackey Brown, a guy he had known at BC. Mackey was a super-organized, very disciplined, work-like-crazy math teacher. He *never* stopped. Sometimes Hrag would beg him to slow down and take a break. And Mackey would tell him that working *was* his break. Mackey tried to keep Hrag moving, too. After classes at LMU, Mackey would insist they go to the gym. At 10 p.m., Hrag was dead tired and Mackey was ready to lift weights.

They, like so many roommates, were the Odd Couple. Hrag was constantly complaining; Mackey was unfailingly chirpy. Mackey was orderly; Hrag was kind of spacy, forever losing things. They didn't eat together, and after a while they didn't talk much, either. Mackey loved to hash out the day; Hrag couldn't bear even thinking about it. By the time he got home at night, Hrag didn't know if he could make it through the next day, much less discuss the one he had just survived. Hrag hung out with TFA friends who taught at different schools; he saw enough of the Locke teachers at work. Mackey was always working; he hardly went out at all.

But they carpooled to Locke. The routine never varied. Mackey knocked on Hrag's bedroom door at 5:30 a.m. "Hrag, you need to get up," he'd say. In response to the silence, Mackey would keep it up, nagging him to get going. Hrag would lie in his bed and think: *Go ahead. Just go ahead. Knock on my door one more time, and I'll rip it off its hinges!* But really, he was grateful. There were mornings when Hrag would simply announce: "I'm not going!" But because Mackey was on the other side of the door waiting, he would eventually get up and get dressed and go to work.

Hrag's old college buddies noticed the changes in him. He set aside several hours every Saturday morning for e-mails and phone calls, desperately wanting to stay connected. They all took note of his newfound maturity—and the fact that he had stopped cracking all those corny jokes for which he was famous. They also said they respected what he was doing, and admired him. That felt good. The glory was there—at twenty-one, Hrag was a teacher in a position of power. By contrast, his friends' lives seemed mundane—they sat at desks, crunched numbers, drove home, watched TV, and went to sleep. Being a TFA teacher was by far the hardest thing he had ever done, but he'd pick this pressure-cooker life of his over anyone else's any day.

Hrag spoke to his parents every day. Their attitude toward TFA was changing. They were proud to have a son getting his master's while teaching full-time in an inner-city school, and at such a young age! They decided to visit him for his twenty-second birthday, on October 16. Hrag figured they came because he had been complaining so much—they must have thought he was on the verge of losing it.

When the Hamalians had first immigrated to the United States, they lived for a short time in Huntington Beach. Manuel worked repairing industrial parts through a mobile franchise company. Few men would take jobs in the inner-city neighborhoods; it was considered too dangerous. But Manuel took whatever business came his way. He ended up working in Watts nearly every day, and he made a lot of friends there. Now things had come full circle. His son's first real job in America was in Watts, too. Neither of them had known what he was in for.

The Hamalians arrived on Friday. That night they took Hrag out to dinner, then went to visit some of his mother's family. It was late when they arrived, but all the cousins had come home to meet the Hamalians. Hrag shook everyone's hand, sat down, and promptly passed out.

His parents came to school on Monday. Hrag wouldn't let them observe his fifth-period class because he was worried that the kids might act out—and he might, too. Hrag was perfectly fine with having his parents know he was having a hard time. But they had never seen him really lose it. And in fifth period he had been losing it—a lot. Just the week before he had slammed a meter stick so hard that he almost broke it. The kids loved it when they got to him. He'd see them snickering, and that would make him even angrier. It would take some kid saying "Mr. H, why are you taking your anger out on us?" to calm him down. Then he felt awful. But even Mackey reached the breaking point sometimes. Hrag was thrilled to hear that he had snapped a clipboard in three.

Manuel and Claire got to see Hrag at his best. His third-period kids were enthusiastic and totally engaged. His parents were impressed. His father, as always, made some very astute observations. Manuel had grown up in a similar community—when he and Claire were married in Beirut, snipers stood atop the church. Locke looked to him like a typical high school; the kids in Hrag's biology class behaved like typical ninth-graders.

"You think these kids are a special case," Manuel said. "But in ninth grade, I guarantee you that you listened to at most fifty percent of what your teachers said."

And it was true. Hrag couldn't remember half of what he supposedly learned in high school. Actually, it was worse than that. Hrag recalled that he had cruised through an entire year of ninth-grade science without listening to a single word the teacher said. When it came time for the final at the end of the year, he had freaked out and started crying.

"What's wrong with you?" Manuel had demanded.

"I don't know a thing," Hrag had confessed.

Manuel had patiently sat him down, opened the book, and helped Hrag learn what he had missed over the course of the year. Hrag ended up getting an A.

Sometimes Hrag assumed that because his kids had been cheated all their lives, they couldn't follow directions or weren't capable of grasping what he was trying to teach. After talking to his father, he changed his mind: *No. They are fourteen. They could give a crap.*

But there was a big difference. Most of these kids didn't have a Manuel or a Claire at home holding their feet to the fire, checking on homework, helping them study.

It was good to see his folks. So often in high school Hrag had resented the way his parents had tried to shelter him. He and his sister, Gareen, were kept close to home, close to their Armenian identity and roots. When they were little, there were plenty of cousins around, so it didn't really matter. But as Hrag got older and wanted to spread his wings, he chafed at the restraints Manuel and Claire imposed. Up until his junior year in high school, he was forbidden to go to parties—even the ones right across the street. His parents thought there would be drugs, sex, and alcohol—and, of course, they were right. Now Hrag was grateful for their vigilance and forgiving of their protective excesses. It was gratifying to hear them effuse over his performance in the classroom. Their affirmation made him think that maybe he wasn't such a bad teacher after all.

Hrag realized he had it a lot easier than most of the other TFAers. He, at least, had Vanessa Morris, head of the science department. Morris had taken Hrag and the other new biology teacher, Jinsue Choi, under her wing. Her style of teaching biology was inquiry-based. Because her students' literacy skills were so low, Morris rarely referred to the textbook; instead she used hands-on labs to lead her kids to discovery. She had been at Locke for five years and was part of Chad's extended circle of young activist teachers. Like them, she coaxed pretty darn good results from her students. Seeing her teach was like watching a master magician. She glided from task to task with ease, handling behavioral issues with equanimity and presenting new scientific concepts with childlike delight. The period sped by, and inevitably, by its conclusion, Morris had worked her magic—the kids had been tricked into learning.

She didn't have written-out lesson plans to give Hrag and Jinsue, but every Tuesday morning at seven o'clock she met with them for forty-five minutes to talk through her plans for the week and share the labs that would accompany her lessons. Hrag lapped it all up. At night, he and Jinsue would get on the phone and figure out how to adapt her outlines to their classrooms. Morris was incredibly generous; Hrag often spent his lunch periods in her room picking her brain. But he didn't feel right about always being on the receiving end, and he sensed that Morris didn't like the situation, either. Before long, Hrag and Jinsue, the two tech-savvy neophytes, were sharing their custom-made PowerPoints with their department chair. The collaboration felt good, and the kids seemed to be learning. Hrag's loyalty to Morris—and to Jinsue—was unshakable. Every time he contemplated quitting, he thought of how he would be letting Morris down, and leaving became unthinkable.

Hrag was one of the few TFA science teachers in the L.A. cohort to be supported by a school leader, and probably the only one able to incorporate an inquiry-based system with labs into instruction. Many of the other TFA teachers were at a complete loss. When they left institute in the summer, instead of lesson plans and mentoring, they were given a pat on the back and told: "Go!" Most taught out of the textbook, but the majority of their kids could not read at grade level, and behavior management became a huge problem. Seeing the others' struggles and mindful of how much help he was being given, Hrag saved every one of his lesson plans to pass on to next year's biology teachers. Some nights he even scribbled notes to himself about what had worked and what hadn't. He saw no reason why each new CM should have to reinvent the wheel.

Hrag bitched, but he was really enjoying the kids, and he sensed that the kids were enjoying him, too. He joked around a lot. It kept his students engaged—and kept him from dying of boredom. Every time he got strict and serious, he could tell the kids were tuning him out. Most periods—with the exception of the incorrigible fifth—took his angry outbursts to heart. When he raised his voice in disapproval, the rowdy kids would turn into docile children, frown, and put their heads down. "Let's start over," he'd suggest. "I got off on a bad note, and so did you." They would come around, but it would take a few minutes. They became upset, too, if he was absent. They worried that he was quitting, that he wouldn't come back.

They really *did* seem to be learning, probably more than he had in high school. Hrag had learned how to take notes in high school, and that no doubt prepared him for college. But he didn't end up knowing anything about biology, and he thought that his students did. So, on the rare occasion that he allowed himself to think about it, he decided that what he was doing was a good thing, that he was doing a good job, a job he could be proud of, and that it was something that he would look back on as a moment in his life in which he had shined. Then, quickly, he'd go back to worrying. *I feel like a commando. I go into the jungle, but the jungle keeps changing. I don't know who I'm fighting.*

Taylor knew exactly what Hrag meant. She woke each morning feeling like a warrior about to go into battle. But she also felt soldier-strong. So much of the job was about finding that toughness inside that you didn't know you had, that part of you strong enough to take a beating and get up and do it again. She felt so good about what she was doing that she would have taught at Locke High School without pay. *This is the biggest accomplishment I've ever had—maybe the biggest I ever will have.*

She was amazed at herself—and so was her family and everyone else who knew her. People had probably thought that because she came from money, she would never do something like teach. Now, when they found out that she was working in a classroom in Watts, they were blown away. "You do WHAT?" they would say. And from the way they said it she could tell they thought she was either crazy or a miracle worker. Taylor realized she could never have a normal conversation at a cocktail party again. At one boozy affair in Hollywood, a glassy-eyed aging boomer effused: "Wow! You're changing lives!" Then, without skipping a beat: "Do you know where the rest of the soda is?"

She felt that her own life was changing, in ways big and small. For one thing, she couldn't go shopping anymore. She used to be frivolous with her money, going out and buying things she didn't need. Now, when she went shopping for herself, it weighed on her conscience. Her parents helped pay the rent (they told her they would think of her stint with Teach For America as the equivalent of two years of graduate school and subsidize her accordingly), but Taylor put herself on a budget. When her father gave her fifty dollars in spending money, she used it to buy books for her kids.

I've grown up overnight. I was in college; now I'm in a classroom, learning by doing, and getting a master's degree. It's happened so fast. I want it to slow down.

Though Taylor had been a sorority girl at USC, she had never really felt comfortable in groups. But now she was in this gigantic fraternity called TFA, and it felt right. She had never before met people like these. They were all so smart, so hardworking and capable. She loved them.

Some of them were really fun, too. Like Dan Ehrenfeld. Dan also taught English at Locke, and he had been in her teaching collaborative during summer institute. Raised in San Diego and a graduate of Wesleyan University, he was cool and laid-back. He made Taylor think, and he always made her laugh. On Friday afternoons he'd come to Taylor's bungalow and listen to music while she swept the classroom floor. Some nights they would get together to plan lessons; most times they'd just hang out. Taylor was afraid to see Dan teach. She imagined that with his freewheeling style, the kids probably ran roughshod over him. But his laissez-faire approach was the perfect foil to Taylor's perfectionism. Whenever she got down on herself and remembered that she really didn't know what she was doing, she just called Dan. "Don't worry about it," he'd say. "You couldn't be worse than me. No one's worse than me."

TFA was all-consuming. Her boyfriend lived in another city, and the distance and the job began to take a toll on the relationship. She found herself relating more to her fellow teachers than to him. When she heard that Hrag Hamalian was about to get a new class of repeating biology students—halfway through the first semester—she brought him a donut to cheer him up. He looked like he was on the verge of hysterical laughter. She had heard from others that he went out every night. He was kind of cute.

One day Hrag called her about a project they were working on.

"You sound upset," he said.

"I am," she replied. "This job is overwhelming."

"Taylor, you're one of the strong ones," said Hrag. "You can't break. We'll all break. You have to hold it together. It's not a competition. Are you still here? Then you have to give yourself credit. We all do."

He calmed her down. *Nice guy,* she thought.

Her feelings about Samir were more complicated. She dreaded his visits to her classroom, but she needed him. "Rip me apart," she told him. "I want to get better." Samir was pleasantly surprised. Taylor, the CM he had worried most about meeting, had turned out to be the one most receptive to Co-Investigation. Every time he gave her a "delta"— TFA jargon for something she could improve upon—she got to work. By his next visit, the change would be made. When Samir wasn't available,

Taylor reached out to others, stealing ideas and strategies and adapting them to her classes. She became the darling of the literacy coaches from UCLA who helped the new English teachers at Locke. Mrs. Jauregui, the Locke assistant principal in charge of the ninth grade, took notice, too. She declared Taylor a "natural," a potential master teacher.

Taylor looked upon Chad, the former TFAer turned administrator, as a god. In the real world, his abilities would probably be taken for granted. In a place like Locke, where the sands were always shifting and the administration was long on promises and short on follow-through, Chad's straightforward approach earned him genius status. He ran the once-a-month TFA Saturday-morning professional development sessions for the Locke English teachers. At his meetings, Taylor actually learned stuff. At the larger faculty meetings, she usually pulled out her laptop and worked on lesson plans as speaker after speaker droned on.

But Taylor paid attention when Chad was in charge. He had been an ace English teacher, and he happily shared his best practices with the new recruits. He also took his job as administrator very seriously. Dr. Wells had decreed that each department give regular benchmark assessments to track student and teacher performance throughout the year. Chad thought Wells's idea was a good one, and he worked with the young English teachers to help them develop a common curriculum and rigorous assessments. To ensure buy-in, he paid them for their planning time.

Many teachers regarded the assessments as just another ill-considered drain on their time, especially since they were already required to give the district's own periodic assessments. So they ignored Wells's directive. Behind closed doors, they were free to teach whatever they wanted, and they also felt free to create their own assessments. If they didn't have time or the inclination to grade them all, they estimated the average scores and just submitted those. The benchmarks were a bust.

Still, Taylor took them seriously. She began to teach to the tests that she and a few other ninth-grade English teachers had coauthored with Chad's guidance. And her kids' scores started to climb. But instead of making her happy, the results worried her. *Are they really learning? Do they understand the concepts? Am I placing too much emphasis on test results and not enough on the fact that these kids can't read?*

She shifted gears. Instead of focusing so much on testing, she decided her priority would be reading. She wanted her students to be able to compete in society. That couldn't happen unless they could read. Somebody had remarked that the achievement gap was really a literacy gap. She agreed. She would see seniors struggling over words and think: *How did this happen?* If she could get her kids hooked on books, she would have done her job.

So she cast about for reading strategies. She got some help from Jessica Miller, a second-year TFA English teacher at Locke. Miller wasn't the warm-and-fuzzy type, but she had managed to get her kids' reading levels up by two years. Taylor picked her brain. Following Miller's lead, Taylor began to build structure into her classes. Now, she started each day with a grammar "warm-up," a simple ten-minute review of a single grammatical rule, like subject-verb agreement or the possessive case. The warm-up was a way to get kids settled in their seats and working on something as Taylor took care of administrative tasks like attendance. Twice a week, she gave students a twenty-minute block for silent sustained reading (SSR) and tips to aid comprehension. She distributed Post-its so that kids could flag important passages as they read. And she taught them to look for clues—like foreshadowing—in the narratives to enhance understanding.

In the beginning of the year, she often led "guided practice" in essay writing, standing at the whiteboard and modeling exactly what she wanted to see her students do. Samir urged her to let her kids do more of the work themselves. That was hard—she didn't want them to mess up—but she slowly, slowly began to let them discover for themselves what worked and what didn't. When they were learning to write persuasive essays, Taylor chose the newly announced NBA dress code as a topic. She made the kids pull information from texts like the NBA website and the *Los Angeles Times* sports pages to support their positions. Some fell on their faces, but many of them astonished her with the complexity of their thoughts and writing.

Taylor refused to wage the battle over homework. She thought that if she drove them hard in class, that was enough. It was unrealistic to expect these kids to go home, find a safe, quiet spot, do their homework, and get help from a responsible adult if they were stuck. Equally unrealistic was the expectation that she would grade one hundred papers a night! So she tried to cover everything in fifty-minute periods, and if her students weren't finished by the time the bell rang, she held them until they were. Without the homework issue, she got less resistance and more engagement in class.

Her teacher personality began to change as well. She put aside her uniform of black trousers and black shoes and began to wear different outfits. She was still plenty tough; she had no compunction about ejecting a student for the tiniest infraction. But she found herself letting her guard down sometimes, too. She got nicer, and the kids responded. Some did total turnarounds when she was supersweet. Soon they began to come to her classroom after school just to hang out. One day, Taylor confided that she had lost a friend to a drug overdose, precipitating a flood of empathy from students who had also lost loved ones. One of her more vexing students, Marisa, told Taylor that her father had killed her mother when she was just two years old. "I love you, Miss Rifkin," she said, hugging her like a child. Taylor hugged her back and thought: *I love you, too.*

Rachelle had a dream about the kids. She was in her classroom and a bad guy was trying to get in. She ran to the door to try to stop him. She was halfway there when she woke up.

The dream was strange, because in waking life, Rachelle never really felt unsafe at Locke—or in the neighborhood. She didn't think twice about leaving campus, crossing Avalon, and stopping at a bodega to buy spicy chips for the girls on the soccer team before practice. The bars on the cashier's booth didn't bother her; neither did the run-down storefront. She didn't know that the Crips headquarters was rumored to be just doors away; and if she had known it, that probably wouldn't have stopped her. There were intimations of danger all around her; she just chose to ignore them.

During the first week of school, Raúl had scared her with his drawing of a rooftop gunman. After Rachelle alerted the office, sessions were set up with the school's psychiatric social worker, and the family was summoned to school for a meeting. Raúl lived with his grandparents; he said his father was in the hospital because he drank too much. It was clear that there was some pathology in the home and Raúl was socially maladjusted—though his IEP, the instructional road map required by law for every student assigned to special ed, mentioned nothing about emotional issues. Raúl didn't participate in class and turned his head to avoid eye contact with Rachelle. When she gave the kids a test, his paper came back with an F scribbled at the top with the words "think I need a F because I very bad in class I don't went I'm going to be good any more I'm sorry. I will not get a good grade because I'm stupid. I don't know if I like this class any more."

As the weeks passed and Rachelle got to know her students better, she thought it unlikely that Raúl would ever live out his murderous fantasies. The little guy worked hard—probably harder than anyone else in the class. And Rachelle worked hard to draw him out. She offered to accompany him to his therapy sessions, and in her loud, chaotic classroom, where it would have been easy for him to get lost, she made a point of acknowledging his presence. Eventually, someone figured out that Raúl was enrolled in two biology classes, and he was transferred out of Rachelle's fourth period. But not before Rachelle was rewarded with a small victory. One day, Raúl raised his hand in class!

It took a few months before Rachelle could get a code from the special ed office to access her kids' IEPs. The documents were supposed to be based on an in-depth assessment of each kid's specific learning disability. Preparing a proper IEP was an involved process that could take weeks, requiring meetings with parents and input from general ed teachers. If done correctly, they were invaluable tools for a special ed teacher. Not the IEPs Rachelle was handed. Many were hopelessly out of date, and most were incomplete or had obviously been slapped together at the eleventh hour. Based on what she was learning in graduate school about disability law, most of Locke's IEPs were out of compliance. When she was finally able to access them, most read: "specific learning disability." *What the hell does "specific learning disability" mean?*

What it ended up meaning for Rachelle was that in her first year of teaching special ed, she didn't know much at all about any of her kids. She had no idea what was impeding their ability to achieve—and causing the out-of-control behavior she often witnessed. No doubt some of the kids were acting out simply because they were frustrated by their learning disabilities, but others seemed handicapped by severe emotional issues.

Many appeared to be meeting expectations; they were stuck in the special ed ghetto, which was a real stigma among an already marginalized student population. One day, midway through the first semester, one of Rachelle's hardest-working students came to see her at lunch. "Miss Snyder," she said, sobbing. "You didn't tell me this was special ed!"

Little wonder she was upset. It didn't take Rachelle long to realize that the special ed kids at Locke routinely got the shaft.

She tried to buck them up. "You guys are fine," she would say. "I'm not babysitting. Whoever told you that you have a problem hasn't met you in the context of your life. Do your work and get out of here!"

At one of the first science faculty meetings, Rachelle was stunned to discover that special ed students had not been allotted any lab equipment. No goggles, no beakers, nothing. Nor had they been assigned a proper biology lab. Room 241 was practically a closet; there was no space for sinks, or Bunsen burners, or a refrigerator, or the other features of a biology lab. The official justification for the small room was that special ed classes had fewer students, but still! *Couldn't the kids at least be supplied with goggles?* Rachelle made some inquiries and was told that in fifteen years no one had ever asked for lab supplies for special ed kids. So she decided to take matters into her own hands. She slipped into the supply room and "borrowed" a couple of microscopes so she could give the kids their first-ever lab. She was seething. *They think because these kids are special ed they can't do labs? Shouldn't they be exposed to the same curriculum as the other kids? Especially since half of these kids don't belong in special ed in the first place?*

Rachelle was convinced that many of her kids had been misassigned. She had heard that some parents insisted on having their children in special ed. If they were foster parents, they got more money for kids with disabilities. If the child had been in trouble with the law, the special ed designation could keep him out of jail, or at least buy some time. As far as she could tell, the department had become a dumping ground for all the kids no one knew what to do with. Most of them were just badly behaved and had been slotted into special ed to minimize the damage they could wreak in a regular classroom of forty-five kids.

But others had so much going on outside the classroom that it consumed them. Take Eduardo, a big, sullen Latino boy who so far had done zero work in her class. He was obviously bright. What was he doing in room 241?

One day at the end of September, Rachelle was teaching her fourth-period kids how to take notes in preparation for an upcoming exam. The notes were projected on the front board, and the kids were dutifully copying them. Eduardo, dressed in a long, inside-out black T-shirt, just sat there frowning, a faux diamond sparkling in his pierced ear. Then, in what was becoming his classroom MO, he crumpled his paper into a ball and drained it into the wastebasket. "I made it!" he proclaimed.

"Yeah, you made it," replied Rachelle. "But I'm not impressed. How are you going to do on the test?"

"I'll just flunk it," he said, drumming loudly on his desk.

"You need to at least be quiet," said Rachelle. "If you fail, you fail by yourself." Then she turned to the others. Eduardo stood to leave.

"No! Sit back down!" she ordered, as some of the others stood and the low classroom murmur rose a decibel. Now she tried a usually reliable bribe. "If you sit down, I'll play the radio." Eduardo remained standing and the talking continued.

"I'm not talking over you!" she warned—to no effect. Finally, defeated, she said in disgust, "Okay. Forget it."

Eduardo sat back down and she walked over to his desk to find out why he was refusing to work. He unloaded. He told her that three days before, on Monday, he had been jumped on the way to school by a bunch of Bloods because he was wearing a blue T-shirt. He was still upset by the incident—and obviously frustrated. He didn't give a fuck about his schoolwork, he said.

Rachelle listened, and when he stopped talking she said: "Do you feel safe now?"

Eduardo jumped up and began to pace like a caged animal. Then, at her urging, he took his seat again.

"I want you to graduate; I want you to leave Locke," she said, whispering so the others couldn't hear. "I don't want you to have to worry about what color you're wearing."

"I want to get out of the ghetto," he replied, his voice steady and serious.

"You *can* get out," she urged. "With an education. You are a smart boy. You can do this. But you have to get this work done to leave here." As she talked, Eduardo pointed his forefinger at another kid and flipped his thumb down, as if to shoot him. He didn't appear to be listening. Rachelle switched tack and started to joke: "What color is it okay to wear? Brown? Pink? Should we get you a pink shirt?"

He ignored her jests. "Why do I need to copy it?" he asked, referring to the notes on the board, his fingers urgently rapping on the desk.

"It's the way your brain processes information," she explained as his drumming became louder and more insistent. "Stop!" she finally said, her voice rising with impatience. "Please stop. I'm gonna go nuts, man. Just stop. Get it done. Do you want to go to the office?"

"No," he said.

"If you have to put your head on the desk, then just do it," she said. Now he was up again and headed toward the door. Rachelle stood at the threshold, her arms spread wide, blocking the exit.

"I'm leaving," said Eduardo.

"No," she replied. "Sit down. Stay for a minute." Eduardo began pacing again. In the meantime, she turned her attention to Dante, who was back after his two-week detention for urinating in her classroom. "We need to get you caught up, Dante," she said. "Is it nice to be back?"

"I don't know," he said as the bell rang. "I'm just kidding. It feels good. It feels good. Good-bye, Miss Snyder!"

"Thank you very much, sweetheart," she said, smiling at Dante's attempt to joke. As she was talking to Dante, Eduardo slipped away. It would be weeks before she saw him again.

TFA expected each teacher to set a big student achievement goal of 80 percent mastery of state standards. Rachelle decided the brass ring for her students would be a little different. She wanted 80 percent to get a C or higher, the minimum grade required for admission to a state university. The first test she gave showed her just how high that bar would be for many of them. A few of her students did well, like her all-girl class, which averaged 75 percent. They proved her point; they had no business being in special ed. But some of the others! She had had no idea that there were so many ways to misinterpret a question. Her fourth-period class of unruly boys made her heart sink. They got an average grade of 20 percent.

Rachelle decided that, given the range of her students' abilities, her grading policy would be based on attendance and work in class. The only way to fail Miss Snyder's biology class was going to be not to show up. Even so, some kids ended up flunking. It was sad, because there probably was a reason they were ditching her class; she probably wasn't engaging them. But when the time came to write out the F's, she didn't feel nearly as bad as she thought she would.

TFA had urged all the CMs to assess their kids as early as possible.

Rachelle tested her students for science content knowledge but soon realized that the problem in room 241 was actually a lack of basic reading and writing skills. When she gave them the San Diego Quick Assessment, she discovered that most of her kids were reading at a third-grade level. More than a few couldn't read at all. She could tell they were secretly embarrassed. They all wanted to do better; they all wanted to know how to read. So she decided she needed to do more literacy work with them. How could they use a textbook if they couldn't read?

But she was a biology teacher, not a literacy coach. That presented a dilemma. While it was no doubt good for her students to be able to conduct biology experiments, she knew that being literate would be of more benefit to them. *It's criminal to allow them to graduate from high school without being able to read! I want to teach them how to read, and push them into general ed. But I don't feel qualified. I need to be more active. I need to get qualified to teach them.*

Rachelle started searching on the Internet for material on literacy. The stuff was kind of childish, but if her kids couldn't do it, how would they ever make it in the world? She found a picture of a kitchen to be used as a prompt to write a sentence. But then she thought: *Do they even know the words for all the parts of a kitchen?*

Still, she pushed ahead. Everything she did in class had to do with literacy. At least once a week, she reviewed grammar and simple sentence structure. She even worked on spelling. They misspelled nearly every term she gave them; one kid even managed to misspell *DNA*! It wasn't exactly biology, but who knew? There were no consequences at Locke. She could be playing patty-cake in room 241 and no one would be the wiser.

CHAPTER SIX

Dropping Out

Chad was feeling worn out and ugly, but he had been teaching long enough to know that this was just about the time when every teacher was at a low point. It was late fall. The adrenaline surge from the opening days of school had petered out. Thanksgiving was approaching, but that break hardly counted; it only whetted the appetite. Christmas was a long way off. For some reason, Chad had fooled himself into thinking that things would be different in this new job, that as an administrator he would have more power, more control, that he'd be happier.

What he had was more responsibility, more headaches, more in-your-face evidence that a big, underperforming school in a big, underperforming district was a tough ship to turn around. He now found himself doing all the things he had bad-mouthed the previous year's administration for. Like all the other assistant principals, he was spending a disproportionate amount of his time just putting out fires, or, as Wells liked to say, responding to 911s. The yellow-jacketed security team couldn't handle all the safety issues at Locke. APs had to pitch in, too. Each administrator was assigned a specific area of the campus to monitor during lunch breaks, and in the event of a 415, the campus code for a fight, if they were within reach, they were expected to drop whatever they were doing and respond.

As a teacher, Chad had railed against the administration's failure to effectively address academic issues; as an administrator he now understood that safety had to be a priority. And he now found, oddly enough, that his presence alone could defuse a potentially explosive situation.

Wells's first order of business in 2004 had been to create a safe school environment, and that had actually worked to Chad's advantage as a small schools coordinator. While Wells was busy establishing his authority on campus that fall, Chad and his partners were basically given free rein over their small school, which they had named the School of Social Empowerment. SE was one of the six small schools carved out of Locke that year in compliance with a district directive to reorganize or face a possible state takeover.

A few teachers, like Chad and four or five other core SE founders, saw the mandate as an opportunity for real change; they worked all spring and summer on their plans. Most of the rest, more skeptical, didn't bother. Locke already had three or four so-called academies, founded on grants that had long ago run out. Many veterans saw the small learning communities as a new iteration of the old academies, yet another half-baked idea handed down from above. They had no appetite for spinning their wheels on a reform with no shelf life, so they chose a school or were assigned to one, and reported to work in September. SE teachers insisted that those students who wished to join their school be allowed to. The rest of the schools had no substantive plans and thus no demands, so kids were assigned by lottery.

The deconstruction of Locke into small learning communities was in line with a growing national movement, supported by the Gates Foundation and other school reformers, to replace the failing large high school exemplar with one in which instruction took place in smaller, more intimate "learning academies." The hope was that the small schools on the big campuses would foster a much-needed feeling of intimacy and investment, making both teachers and students more accountable for academic achievement.

Locke's reorganization was announced in the spring of 2004, and it came just in time for Chad. It was his third year of teaching, and he didn't think he could go on at Locke much longer. He had been reading everything he could about the small-schools movement, and over beers at

Sharkeez he and the other happy hour regulars would fantasize: *What would happen if we started our own small school?*

Earlier in the school year, he had even gone so far as to contact Steve Barr, the charismatic political activist who was putting LAUSD on notice by creating successful charter schools in Los Angeles's toughest neighborhoods. Barr, founder of Rock the Vote, was a firebrand from the sixties who had adopted education reform as his latest cause. His goal was not to found *x* number of charter schools in Los Angeles; he wanted nothing less than the overhaul of the entire L.A. Unified School District. He reckoned that if his Green Dot schools showed the way, the community would demand that LAUSD replicate their success by establishing similar small, autonomous schools staffed by skilled teachers and visionary principals.

Barr met with Chad and a group of like-minded Locke teachers. Could Barr help them set up a charter school at Locke? The idea was interesting, but Barr encouraged the Locke corps to teach at one of his Green Dot schools first. Nothing came of the talks. Barr wasn't ready to take on a big school like Locke. Chad and the others weren't ready to give up on it.

When Dr. Rousseau announced the plans for the school's reorganization, everything clicked. By signing up with Rousseau, Chad and the others could effect the change they longed for without having to abandon their kids at Locke. It was like a dream come true.

They began to hammer out a plan. They decided that more instructional time was needed if their kids were to succeed, so they added an extra period to the day. SE's seventh period would officially be called College Prep Seminar, though everyone referred to it as guidance. It would be modeled after the highly successful college-prep program for underachieving students called AVID. Later, once the school was established, SE took on the intractable issue of truancy. In its second year, Andy Osterhaus, a young, commanding chemistry teacher who had left his home in Washington State to teach in Los Angeles's mean streets, was made attendance czar. Mr. O got time out of the classroom to chase down ditchers. SE's attendance rates started to climb.

SE's emphasis on attendance, and the extra period of instruction, got results. Test scores rose. So, too, did resentment among many of the staff. SE was the "white" school (meaning there were no black teachers), and SE got special privileges: an attendance czar (a position no one else planned or asked for) and a separate schedule to accommodate a longer day (which no one else wanted).

But few disputed that the entire large school benefited from SE's success. It was contagious. For the first time in several years, Locke was able to test enough students to qualify for a state academic performance score (API) and a federal annual yearly progress score (AYP), the two complementary yet confusing yardsticks for achievement. The very fact that the school earned a score at all was considered a triumph. That the school showed improvement by meeting the target the government had set for growth that year was cause for celebration. Though Locke's API score was the second lowest in LAUSD at the end of the 2004–2005 school year, the entire faculty was buoyed by the upward trend.

Wells had set the stage for improvement by ejecting troublemakers and making security a priority. He basked in the accomplishment and was determined to repeat it. In 2005, his second year as principal and Chad's first as an administrator, Wells summoned the ninth-grade students to an assembly during the first full week of school. He and his posse of deans were going to head off misconduct at the pass by laying down the law right from the beginning.

Dr. Magee, the AP in charge of safety and security, started off the meeting in the open-air cafeteria. "Welcome! You all are the graduating class of what year?" he asked the ninth-graders seated on benches before him. There was no response.

"You don't know?" he chided. "Okay, it's '09. Say it at the same time. I need you to say: 'The class of 2009.' " The kids begrudgingly complied. "Now, look to the left and right of you. Statistics tell us that a lot of your counterparts are not going to be in the graduating class with you. It's always the way it happens. Now look to the left and right of you and say: 'I'll be graduating, and I hope you graduate, too.' " The kids mumbled the refrain.

Then he introduced the freshman class to Dr. Wells. Wells, dressed in a suit and tie with a stern demeanor to match, knew how to get the attention of a crowd of yappy fourteen-year-olds. Just as he finished saying "Good morning, class of 2009!" but before he could begin his talk, he made his move. "One thing I don't tolerate is talking," he barked. Then, turning to the security guards, he pointed out two girls who were chatting: "Send those two girls home," he ordered. As the girls were marched out, Wells addressed the remaining kids: "This is an assembly. If you don't listen and cooperate, you don't stay at school. We take conduct very seriously here."

Wells went through the litany of dos and don'ts—which turned out to be mostly don'ts. First came the dress code: "You can't wear hats here unless they say 'Locke High School.' Effective immediately, we take hats. You can't wear wave caps or do-rags. We take them and trash them. Any red, blue, purple, or white T-shirts? Today's the last day you can wear them. What do we do if you wear a white T-shirt? We send you home, period. We instituted this rule last year because of safety issues. It is not open for negotiation. Students are prohibited from wearing any gang attire. Period. And at Locke, we wear clothes properly—no showing the midriff, no overly revealing stuff, no pants drooping."

Next up were cell phones: kids could have them, but they'd better not be visible. If the phones were lost or stolen, it was not the school's problem.

Then the code of conduct: "We take fighting and violence very seriously," Wells announced. "There is an automatic five-day suspension, and we don't care who started it. In most cases you are hauled out of school. There is zero tolerance. If you are thinking about fighting, think again." He added that the school banned the use of profanities, expected students to adhere to instructions from staff, and required daily attendance.

"Defiance can get you suspended," he warned. "And if you are suspended, you can't come back till you meet with school police. If you are sick, you need to come back with your parent. When you miss a class, we call home. Cutting is prohibited. Any ninth-grade student ditching first lunch gets an immediate Saturday detention. And if you fail to attend that, you get a two-hundred-fifty-dollar fine. We are very serious. Detention is not very nice. It gets real ugly. But we don't want you to go down that road.

"Robbing and stealing, we don't do that. Those culprits go to the youth authority. I'm not gonna mention weapons, because any kid with a weapon is in Big-Time Trouble. Not only that, they automatically go to jail. We take that very seriously."

The last thing he mentioned was "teaching and learning." The school took them very seriously, too. Wells announced that there was a "Saturday academy" for students who could use extra help with their school-work, and he explained why: "We know if we don't help you in ninth grade, you struggle. And by tenth and eleventh, you drop out. We don't want that."

Wells left the issue of lockdown—which by pure happenstance was declared only hours later—to Dr. Magee, who explained that in most cases lockdown was declared when police were looking for a suspect in the area. For obvious reasons, during lockdown no one was allowed on or off campus, and students were restricted to their classrooms. It was not suprising, then, that some students freaked hours later when the school went dark. In one second-floor classroom that faced the street, kids figured there was an L.A. terrorist group on the loose just outside the window: "We gonna die!" they screamed when told that no one could leave the room.

After Magee came Mrs. Jauregui, who tried to explain a bell system that confused teachers and students alike. The school was on two sched-ules. Three of the small schools were on a seven-period day that ended at 3:15. The others, including the two ninth-grade academics, were on a six-period schedule, with dismissal at 2:55. Lunches were staggered to accommodate the two different timetables. The upshot: sometimes when the bells rang, it was hard to tell for whom they tolled.

Mrs. Jauregui had touched on one of the most divisive issues at Locke, though the kids had no way of knowing that. The schools that had insisted on the longer school day argued that the students needed the extra time to enhance academics. Opponents—and there were many—argued that the seventh period was an added burden to teachers, and that the academic benefits were unproven and hardly outweighed the mass confusion caused by the competing bell schedules. What's more, the longer day appeared to violate the union contract governing teacher work minutes.

The kids didn't care about the bells. The only questions they raised concerned the seemingly draconian T-shirt policy. Why couldn't they wear colored T-shirts? What about shirts with writing on them?

"We don't want anyone getting shot" was the explanation from one of the ninth-grade deans. "That's why we came out with the T-shirt rule. Don't get mad at us because you can't wear colors."

They didn't get mad. They simply ignored the dictums—just about every one of them. Kids wore whatever color T-shirts they wanted, with

the exception of the Bloods' red, of course. Many girls wore tight cloth-
ing and exposed their bellies; nearly all the boys dressed in regulation
gangsta wear—baggy pants, long T-shirts, do-rags, and plenty of bling.
Profanities and pejorative language were parts of everyday speech. Ditching was rampant. The school police kept a whole drawerful of confis-
cated weapons, real and pseudo. And, at least in the beginning of the
year, before students settled into the school routine, fights occurred virtually every day.

You could see it happening. One kid would grab his belt buckle and
give it a shake, and with that subtle gesture a fight would begin. Dismissal
was always a dicey time, and the two different bell schedules didn't help.
Every administrator was expected to be on supervision then. Dr. Wells
himself stood sentry on a street corner a block or so away from the
entrance to school as kids navigated the busy north-south traffic on San
Pedro. One day in early September, Chad watched as Latinos and blacks
squared off right in front of the entrance, just minutes after the dismissal
bell sounded.

His first big confrontation came a few weeks later. He was standing,
as he always did, in the area just outside the cafeteria, in the southeast
corner of the quad, close to where the Hispanic activists on campus
kicked, when a guy walked by with his girlfriend. Chad heard her say,
pointing to another student some yards away, "Isn't that the kid you're
looking for?" Chad decided to follow them. And sure enough, they
turned the corner, and the boy jumped a Latino kid. Chad was the only
supervisor in sight. Within seconds, he was in the middle of a nasty fist-
fight. He had found that generally, if he could duck in and push the kids
away from each other, they wouldn't hit him. Not this time. Chad ended
up on the ground, pinning one of the kids down while he held him in a
headlock. The school police came quickly; the brawl was probably over
within a minute. As the cops took the kids away, Chad got up and dusted
himself off. He was fine—until he realized that his keys to the school were
missing. The football players who had watched the fight said they saw
the keys tumble from his pocket in the scuffle. Someone had grabbed
them while Chad was down.

Chad offered a one-hundred-dollar reward for their return. There
were no takers. So the school had to be rekeyed—at a cost of nine thousand dollars. Until they were changed, all the school locks were jammed
with nails.

Being on the other side of the great divide between teachers and administrators was chastening for Chad. He used to think all administrators were stupid. How else to explain the problems at Locke? There were five or six well-paid people in the top administration positions, but the school was a mess. As head of the School of Social Empowerment, Chad sat in on a lot of supervisory meetings, and he was always shocked by some of the stuff the APs presented. *Are they blind, stupid? Can't they manage at all?* When he got the job, he knew he could be really effective. He thought: *Cool. I'm an intelligent person.* But as he sat in on the smaller meetings, with just the principal and his APs, Chad had an epiphany: *These are very intelligent men and women.* Mrs. Jauregui was in the doctorate program at USC. Dr. Wells had some valuable ideas and a good rapport with students. Another AP, whom Chad had regarded as the dumbest man on the planet, turned out to have some well-thought-out plans that unfortunately ended up being poorly executed. *No, the problem is time. There's not enough time to do everything the job requires.*

Chad was swamped. He had spent the summer designing the master schedule but had yet to be paid as an administrator because he had never found the time to turn in the paperwork. Most of September was consumed in fine-tuning the schedule, getting guidance counselors into their offices, and organizing a filing system. He wanted to make the counseling office functional, efficient, and dependable. He had countless meetings to attend, and as an administrator he had to get into classrooms to evaluate the teaching. And, of course, there were always the 911s. He would have liked to give the new Teach For America recruits more support, but he didn't have the time or the energy.

He had also made a lifestyle change when he became an AP. Until then he had shared an apartment with Martha Mata, a fellow teacher at Locke. With the new job, Chad decided to live on his own. He also felt less comfortable bellying up to the bar with Locke teachers at Friday-night happy hours. He was still close to his teacher friends, but the relationships had changed. There was a distance between them now, because there were many work-related issues Chad could no longer talk about. He knew the Social Empowerment teachers trusted him to look after their interests at inner-circle supervisory meetings, but sometimes the interests of SE diverged from the needs of the school at large. Chad found himself doing a delicate balancing act. It wasn't easy. He felt pulled in opposite directions.

And there was no safety net. Chad couldn't depend on Wells. In fact, he felt like Wells was constantly undermining him. Chad was in charge of the incredibly complicated schedule of students, teachers, and room assignments. But a disturbing pattern had been established. Chad would make a difficult scheduling decision and run it by Wells, who would approve it. Then the teacher adversely affected would receive the news, run to Wells for relief, and the order would be reversed. Chad couldn't believe it: *I look like a moron, he looks like a savior, and I'm back to square one!*

From Chad's vantage point, Wells was a man who just couldn't say no. Even to crummy teachers. One teacher, a poorly performing long-time sub, went to Wells insisting that the math prep assigned to her by Chad be taken off her schedule. Wells agreed and ordered Chad to make the change. When Chad dragged his feet, the teacher threatened to file a grievance because, she said, under No Child Left Behind, she wasn't qualified to teach math. Chad looked at her and laughed. He thought of a hundred things he could have said—in his opinion, she wasn't qualified to teach *anything*—but as a supervisor he had to watch his mouth. The way he saw it, if someone was unhappy—especially if that someone was a teacher who shouldn't be at the school anyway—then let her be unhappy and leave the school. But that wasn't Wells's way. Wells was a people pleaser.

Chad's relationship with Wells grew strained. He began to think of Wells as a spin doctor. He believed him—to a point. Things took a turn for the worse in early November when one of the local district directors stopped Chad on campus for a chat. He asked Chad if Wells had talked to him about his position. Wells had not.

"No?" asked the district official, seeming surprised. "Well, we're bringing in a candidate for your position, and we're pretty sure we're going to go with her. She'll be here next week, and I'd like you to take her around campus."

Chad was stunned. He knew when Wells offered him the job that it was technically an interim position. Although Chad had an administrator's credential, he didn't have the additional certification needed to head the counseling office. In practical terms, it didn't matter. Chad referred the counseling issues directly to the counselors and the psychiatric social worker. The other stuff—the master schedule, the teacher observations, the supervision of the counselors, and all the odds and ends that Wells threw his way—Chad could and did do. And he did them well. Now he was being replaced!

He couldn't believe it. *You're kidding me! Not only am I being replaced, but you expect me to train my replacement? And Wells hasn't even run this by me?*

But he simply said: "What are you going to have me do?"

The answer threw Chad for another loop. Locke was creating a new position that was supposed to ensure cultural literacy in all the English and English-language learners' classes. Like so many positions within LAUSD, the job description was vague. Chad wasn't even sure what cultural literacy was; he figured it had to do with making instruction meaningful to students who were learning English as a second language. That certainly was not Chad's area of expertise; he didn't even speak Spanish. But he said, "Thanks for the opportunity. I've learned a lot as head of counseling, and I'm sure I'll learn a lot in this new position." There must have been some hesitancy in his voice, because the district director responded, "I'm pretty convinced you could run a school better than so many others. You'll do fine." With that, he walked away.

Chad made a beeline for Wells's office, but he didn't get to see him. So he drove home, made three phone calls to try to line up a job, and then met a friend in Manhattan Beach. Over cocktails, he rehearsed what he would say to Wells.

He went in the next day still angry. "I shouldn't have had to hear this from someone else," he told Wells. Chad conceded that he did not have the extra certification, but he argued that in his vision of how the job should be done, it wasn't necessary. He went on to enumerate his duties and accomplishments, and concluded with three words: "You owe me."

"You're right," Chad recalls Wells saying. "But I didn't tell you because I have no intention of hiring her. You have my word: you are in this office. No one will replace you. When she comes on campus, I will be there and she will not be hired."

Wells said all the right things. And when Elena Enriquez-Salazar came on campus, Wells didn't hire her. The district did, over his objections. Two weeks later she was on staff. Chad was asked to draw up a list of her duties and was assured that he could keep whatever parts of the job he liked. A few days later, a county coordinator of the college-prep program AVID phoned and asked Chad if he'd be interested in a liaison position for the district's AVID programs the following September. She had heard through the grapevine that Chad had been screwed, and that he was pissed.

"Absolutely, put my name in," replied Chad. "I don't know what will occur between now and next week, let alone next September."

He certainly wasn't prepared for what happened next.

Chad knew that all the TFA first-years were struggling. The surprise would have been if they were *not* feeling overwhelmed by classroom challenges. But Chad also knew the tough kind of person TFA recruits. He was one of them! So, aside from a small beer party he had thrown for them before school began, and his input with the English department, Chad hadn't really kept up with the incoming TFA class of '05. He figured most were slogging through the tough survival and disillusionment phases *(Who wasn't? He certainly was as a new administrator),* but he counted on rejuvenation to come after the winter break. Chad knew Phillip Gedeon was doing relatively well because Wells had been singing his praises. Chad hadn't seen Taylor Rifkin teach, but Mrs. Jaurequi had, and loved her. He had heard nothing about Rachelle Snyder—maybe because there was no coordinator for special ed—but he assumed no news was good news on that front. No one had actually been into Hrag Hamalian's class to observe, but Hamalian had certainly made his presence known. Hrag had been bugging Chad to do something about his schedule, and Chad didn't appreciate his in-your-face-approach. Chad had recently reconstituted Hrag's second period to accommodate recent transfers from other schools. The newcomers kept on coming throughout the semester, making it impossible for Hrag to teach new material. Still, Hrag taught only one subject—biology—and he had a great mentor, Vanessa Morris. Chad thought the guy had it made, compared with some of the other new folks, like Dave Buehrle and Heather Fieldsteel.

Those two had four different classes to teach, referred to as "preps," each requiring its own preparation time. Chad felt bad about them. He knew he had given them a bear of a schedule. But they were among the best of the new TFAers at Locke, and they had been assigned to SE, the most functional of the small schools. He figured if anyone could handle the stress, they could. Still, Josh Hartford, who had taken over as the SE coordinator, was worried that their workloads were too heavy. Chad knew he was right, but what could he do? He had too many bigger issues to address. Chad assumed that if they were really in trouble, they would speak up.

Both Dave and Heather had been speaking up—to fellow TFA teachers. By homecoming weekend in early November, Dave had decided to bolt. Heather was two steps behind him.

It was a tough call, but Dave made it, and he wasn't backing down. His fiancée, Emily, had also applied to Teach For America but had been rejected. She still lived in the Midwest, and he missed her badly. With the workload he was shouldering, they barely had time to even chat on the phone.

Dave had been one of the most promising of all the recruits. When he applied, he had a 3.58 GPA in film and a minor in English from Calvin College. He was a resident assistant, a community volunteer, and owner of his own small business: Buehrle Lawn Care Service. He was also a devout Christian. He had spent a semester studying at Oak Hill Theological College, a conservative evangelical seminary in England, and during a film internship in Hong Kong had volunteered at a Christian missionary base. After his daylong interview with TFA, there was no doubt about his suitability. With a 3 in two key traits—IMP (influencing and motivating) and PR (perseverance), he fit one of the TFA profiles for automatic admission. The TFA selector wrote at the bottom of his competency-scoring sheet: "Wow! Strong PR and IMP—Dave should be, based on evidence today, a strong CM!" During institute, Dave did not disappoint. He ended his five weeks of training with the highest objective average score of any of the CMs assigned to Locke.

Dave was drawn to the mission. He believed in working for social justice, in taking a stand and making a difference. He wanted to close the achievement gap, to overcome prejudice and racism, and he couldn't picture himself as a nine-to-fiver. He loved the idea of doing something short-term, high-impact, and unique, and then seeing what would happen.

He seemed to be a natural. Although he was thin and pale, almost frail-looking, with blond hair and blue eyes, he could be bold in front of a classroom of teenagers. And he was creative. During his very first week of teaching at summer institute, he introduced the formula for writing a persuasive essay with a confidence and flair few other CMs yet possessed.

He started the lesson with the statement "I'm not gonna lie to you." The class sat up. He continued: "This will revolutionize your life." They sat up a little taller. "If you have a notebook, get it out. You're gonna want to write this down." Now he had their full attention. Every kid in the classroom flipped open a pad as Buehrle wrote the word "*oppositio*" on the board. "The principle behind *oppositio* is so crazy! If you're making an argument, you state the other side's position!" After explaining the rationale for the writing strategy, he continued: "You are now ready to learn the *knock out* sequence for writing a persuasive essay. If you know this, it will change your life!" Buehrle wrote down five steps, explaining and modeling each. In the coming weeks, he would bravely write and sing a rap song and invite the principal outside to the quad to see his kids perform.

He was no less energetic once the school year began. But he was not just teaching twelfth-grade English for SE—he also had drama, a math lab, and a guidance period. Some preps required more work than others. His math-tutor lab, for example, was a relatively easy prep because there was no lecture involved—it was a class designed for remedial work. But drama and twelfth-grade honors English required lots of work. The result: Buehrle never stopped; he was stressed beyond belief. He didn't feel human. And he had underestimated how much he would miss Emily.

In room 209, where Buehrle taught, a quote by Frederick Buechner, a Presbyterian minister and author, was posted on the wall: "Your calling is where your heart's deep gladness and the world's deep hunger meet." The words spoke to him. He didn't believe God expected him to be a slave to a job. He also felt bound to do something important, to make a difference. He knew that there was a point at which those two impulses met— and the person who found and recognized that juncture would end up living life the way it should be lived. Dave wanted to find that sweet spot.

Buehrle believed in the TFA mission. But he wasn't happy with the way TFA was forcing him to carry it out. Ever since he'd received his letter of acceptance, he had found the organization cold, distant, blind to corps members' humanity. TFA was too scientific, too data driven. Not that it shared all its data. When someone at institute had asked about the TFA dropout rate, the TFA bigwig got squirrely.

The mission came first. All the other things that make a life full— friends, health, sanity, happiness—didn't seem to matter. TFA set these high goals and made you strive relentlessly, then made you feel inferior when you didn't reach them. Samir always found things he said Dave could do better. And Dave thought: *It's not like I'm twiddling my thumbs, like I'm not working at it.*

The breaking point came during a phone conversation with Emily, when she said: "You don't laugh anymore, Dave. I can't make you laugh. You don't seem like yourself." And the truth was, he didn't feel like himself. He was an optimistic person with a joy and passion for life. But he could no longer see the beauty in things that used to make him happy. He got to thinking: *What if I don't do this—even for a year? What if I ended this sooner?*

He raised the question with Emily. They both agreed to pray on it. Soon afterward, he flew home to see her. Emily said he needed to make up his mind. He wrestled with a decision that he knew would affect him for the rest of his life. It wasn't in his personality to quit. If he hadn't been in the relationship with Emily, leaving wouldn't have even been a consideration. But he *was* in the relationship, and Emily was the woman he adored, and with whom he intended to spend the rest of his life. This relationship was more important than the job. He asked himself what made sense: What had he been called to do and led to by God, a God who had been faithful to him in every decision he had ever made before? Buehrle decided he would teach until Christmas and quit. At last he felt at peace.

TFA had been the most difficult thing he had ever done, and the decision to quit was the toughest he had ever made. He looked around at the TFA teachers at Locke—at Chad Soleo and Josh Hartford and others in SE—and knew they were doing amazing things. And he loved his kids. The students in his math lab had created a rap song based on Dave's classroom mantras. First they'd start tapping out a beat, then they started rhyming refrains like: "Please sign the tardy log . . . Stop! . . . I don't appreciate!" It made him laugh. And it didn't make leaving any easier. His relationship with TFA was more complicated. It was love-hate. That's why he decided to write out and hand in his resignation letter before he told Chad and TFA. He was not going to be talked out of quitting. The letter would help him stick to his guns.

He had confided in a few of his closest TFA friends almost as soon as he made his decision. The news took them by surprise, but no one blamed him. Most thought that in similar circumstances they would have done the same.

Heather Fieldsteel was sad to see Dave go, but her overriding emotion was jealousy. She, more than anyone else, could identify with him. She, too, had gotten a terrible workload: four preps. That was after she went to Wells and begged to have the fifth prep, a math lab, taken away. He agreed, but it hadn't helped much. She was still underwater, and the thought of quitting was tempting. But now that Dave was going, her options had narrowed. If she left, too, she'd be letting down so many people—not the least of whom were her kids. Dave's students were now going to be stuck with a permanent sub for the rest of the year. She couldn't do that to her kids. She didn't think she could live with the guilt.

When Buehrle approached Chad during the last week of November and asked for a meeting, Chad didn't think much about it. In fact, he was busy and tried to put Buehrle off. But Buehrle persisted, eventually following Chad to the parking lot, where he handed him a letter.

"Is this something we can have a quick conversation about?" Chad asked impatiently. He was rushing to an off-site meeting. Dave suggested Chad start by reading his letter. So Chad opened it right there, in the parking lot. The first word his eyes landed on was "resignation." *Oh shit!* He skipped the part about the reason, saw "December 16," and thought: *Terrible date.* Then he was flooded with regret. He hadn't adjusted Buehrle's schedule when he knew he was struggling. Whenever he saw Dave, he seemed to be in total control, and Chad had thought, *Well, we're overwhelming him, and he's doing okay.* Chad was determined to do something for Dave. He just hadn't gotten to it.

I read him wrong. I didn't see this coming. Damn it, we've lost Buehrle! How resolute is he? I'll do whatever we need to do to solve his issues.

It was a Wednesday and Chad would be off campus until Friday. He told Dave that he would accept the letter but would not act on it. He warned him that quitting was more complicated than he might think. Dave should consider talking to Loyola Marymount, where he was enrolled in the master's program, and Chad urged him to call Samir at TFA as soon as possible. While he was talking, his mind was racing. *Maybe TFA can convince him—or guilt-trip him—into staying, at least until the end of the semester. And when he hears he might owe LMU ten thousand dollars in tuition, he might change his mind.*

Dave must have called Samir right away, because that evening Chad got a phone call from Felicia Cuesta, TFA's managing director of program in Los Angeles. TFA hadn't seen it coming, either, she said. Clearly, the schedule was difficult, and Dave had mentioned that to Samir. But when Samir visited room 209, he had liked what he had seen.

In his resignation letter, Dave didn't dwell on his grueling schedule. He talked about how the stress of the job was preventing him from seeing the beauty in life and how difficult it was to maintain a relationship with his fiancée from three thousand miles away. No job was more important than that relationship.

Aha! So, it's the fiancée, thought Chad, which somehow made the news more bearable. He and Felicia worked out a strategy. The short-term goal was to get Buehrle to agree to stay past the Christmas break, at least through the end of January, when the first semester would end. The longer goal was to get him to finish the year—and then, they hoped, two. Chad would immediately relieve Buehrle of at least one of his preps, even if he had to take it over himself. If that worked, and he agreed to finish the semester, Felicia would dangle the possibility of a transfer to a location closer to home, so he could honor his two-year commitment. Chad and Buehrle met a few days later. Dave didn't bite. He was leaving Locke on December 16.

It wasn't Chad's place to talk about broken promises; he would leave that to the TFA folks. In truth, Chad felt partially responsible because he had saddled Buehrle with that ungodly schedule in the first place. But, on the other hand, he thought: *What the hell! You signed up. This is a real commitment and you should hang in there. You have a responsibility to your kids, if not to TFA.*

Samir Bolar knew full well that some CMs never made it out of the disillusionment phase. All fall he had been dealing with one recruit at another school who had e-mailed him: "I hate my job, I hate my job, I hate my job! Give me one good reason why I shouldn't quit!" Samir swung into action. He arranged to have her co-teach with a successful teacher at her school who had many of the same kids but achieved much different results. He also had the struggling teacher observe three other first-year teachers at another L.A. high school—three first-year teachers who were also stretched but who had managed to put a visible management system into place in their classrooms. It was touch-and-go with this CM, but Samir would do everything in his power to help turn things around for her—because the stakes were so high. The loss of a Teach For America recruit was devastating—to the students, to the teachers, to the credibility of the organization, and possibly even to the recruit, who would no doubt carry that burden of defeat for a lifetime. It didn't help the recruit's program director much, either.

When Samir got the phone call from Buehrle, he was in the middle of the first of two selection rounds for TFA. Every PD was required to participate in the crucial selection process; it was hard work, but Samir relished the idea of helping to choose some of the teachers he would be supporting the following year. Besides, as a PD, he had a special appreciation for the traits and competencies needed to survive and flourish as a Teach For America recruit. It was an interesting juxtaposition: to have Dave call and say "I'm leaving" at the same time that he was asking potential candidates the final question, "Are there any circumstances under which you would quit before finishing your two-year commitment?"

Dave had not been on Samir's watch list. Samir knew Dave had a fiancée, but it wasn't like he was closed off or a shut-in. Samir had seen him at the TFA events—the introduction picnic and the one-hundred day party at a club in Hollywood. He knew that he lived with a few other guys from TFA, and from what he could see, he was getting out and creating a life for himself beyond the classroom. When Samir and Dave met at the end of round one—the first of the four classroom observations—Dave had seemed happy.

Dave *did* have a lot of preps, and he seemed a bit overwhelmed with the long-term planning procedures. After round two, Samir wasn't sure Dave yet had the kids' full attention, and he didn't know if Dave even expected it. Sometimes Dave just taught right through all the chatter. But he was a very creative teacher, and Samir had no doubt that he would make significant gains. Dave had mentioned that he was overworked—but, Samir thought, so were they all! Still, he realized that this disaster might have been avoided if the problem had been addressed sooner. *I feel like we weren't looking out for his interests.*

What bothered Samir the most was that he didn't really have a chance to address the problem; Dave made his decision before saying a word to him—or to Chad. Samir's hunch was that Dave had been complaining to friends and family and had been urged by them to pack it in and go on home. *When did it happen—when he didn't believe we wanted the best for him?*

Samir asked to see him. They met at Starbucks, where Samir offered Dave everything he could to get him to stay—including a position in

Chicago by June. Dave insisted that he believed in the TFA mission. But he said he didn't feel fulfilled, and his relationship with his fiancée was falling apart. Samir countered that any meaningful job would be demanding and would take a toll on his personal life. The key to satisfaction is in finding the balance between the personal and professional. Maybe it wasn't teaching that was the problem; maybe it was Dave's inability to balance the job and his love life.

Samir appealed to Dave's sense of duty. "You feel committed to the movement," he argued. "You feel the injustices being suffered, and you understood when you signed up that there was a degree of sacrifice required."

The two sat for hours, and when Samir had nothing left to say, Dave announced: "Samir, I'm finished."

After Dave called, Samir had immediately pulled up his application and file. The essay he had submitted in response to the prompt: "Describe a time when you confronted a serious obstacle" was entitled "The Opposite of Loneliness Is Deep Fulfillment." In it Dave described his experience as an intern for a film company in Hong Kong, where despite a profound sense of loneliness, he had found real meaning. Samir thought it strange: Dave's circumstances at Locke were not that different from those he described in his essay. The persistence he had demonstrated in Hong Kong led TFA to believe he was an ideal candidate. What happened?

Samir wouldn't be the only TFAer combing through Buehrle's application. The national selection team would be on the job, too. They would take Buerhle's application—and all the data that had been collected on him to date—and add it to the information already compiled on other early leavers, looking for trends. They would also carefully review his file to see what clues should have red-flagged his lack of commitment. Though he cited the fiancée factor, other conditions may have come into play. They would search for answers in his history of involvement at college, and they would no doubt reexamine his essay. His TFA selector had given him a spike in perseverance. Now New York would look closely at its own methods. Perhaps selection had taken Buehrle too much at his word. How could TFA have read this better?

The regional team strategized, too. It was decided that all the PDs would initiate weekly e-mail check-ins with their CMs. Teachers deemed to be in danger of quitting would be targeted for extra attention. At the same time, the regional office would put out the word to any other wavering CMs that quitting was not an option. Each job had an impact on the mission as a whole. It was important that CMs didn't get the idea that TFA was something they could walk away from.

After reviewing Dave's file, Samir contacted his TFA roommates. He wanted their insights into why Dave was leaving, and how, or if, he might be persuaded to stay. He also wanted to gauge whether they were wobbly, too. After talking to them, Samir was confident that Dan Ehrenfeld, another English teacher at Locke, was solid. But he discovered that Dave's other roommate, Grant, was also thinking about leaving.

Samir felt terrible. TFA's national retention rate over two years was 88 percent. Los Angeles's was higher. There was a lot of pressure from headquarters to raise the national retention rate; there was a lot of pressure from downtown Los Angeles to maintain its impressive record. By mid-December, something like seven CMs from the L.A. region had quit. Dave was the second TFAer to leave Locke alone—earlier Allison Momot, another first-year English teacher, had resigned for medical reasons. Now people were warning him to watch out for Fieldsteel as well.

The rumor was that she might not return after the Christmas break. Samir had not explicitly asked her if she was thinking of leaving the corps, but he did ask her how she was doing, whether she was feeling supported, how he could help her. If he had learned anything from Dave's situation, it was how important constant communication was. He would never again assume that because he hadn't heard from a CM, everything was okay. With fifty CMs to feed and water, he had been too busy to do a weekly check-in. That was going to change. *How am I to know what's going on in their minds? I don't even know if they trust me to be somebody they can confide in.*

In his gut, he didn't think Fieldsteel would leave. She was so good, and he didn't think she'd be putting in the effort she was if she wasn't getting some satisfaction, some sense that she was having an impact. But, then again, he had never suspected Dave would bail. He had to be careful. With Buehrle and Momot gone, it was two down, and who knew how many more to go!

Neither Chad nor TFA could change Buehrle's mind. Buehrle told the SE folks he was packing it in, and the word spread like wildfire. Some of his students cried. When the other first-years heard, they were very supportive. Most of the other teachers at Locke were not as sanguine. They saw him as leaving his kids high and dry, and screwing his colleagues to boot. The anti-TFA lobby at Locke took Buehrle's desertion as further evidence of the dangers of hiring TFA teachers. *Typical. They come and they go. They are not committed to this community. They end up doing more harm than good.*

But nothing surprised Chad more than Dr. Wells's response, when Chad said, "I've got some bad news. I got the resignation of Buehrle effective December sixteenth."

Wells didn't skip a beat, recalls Chad. "That's an opportunity," said Wells. "Because I've observed Buehrle and he's pathetic. This is a chance to get someone else."

Chad was speechless. He was expecting an administrator-to-administrator conversation about how they had made mistakes in not supporting the kid. Not this! Because *(a) Buehrle is not pathetic, and (b) Where in the world does he think we can get someone good in there to take his place? We already have two permanent subs working in the English department!*

Then he wondered: *Could he have Buehrle mixed up with another teacher?*

CHAPTER SEVEN

What the Hell Am I Doing?

Taylor was one of the first in the corps to know that Dave Buehrle was planning his Great Escape. She and Dan, Dave's roommate, hung out together. The three of them had gone to dinner one night toward the end of October, and Dave had told them then that he was quitting. Taylor admired Dave. The administration loved him, and he was regarded as one of the better TFA recruits at Locke. He got there early and stayed late. He was still working flat out for Locke, even when he knew he was going to resign! Taylor thought his kids were lucky to have had him, if only for a semester. But boy, his leaving was going to cause a lot of trouble. No one would want to blame it on Chad Soleo, but you had to think that if Chad hadn't given the poor guy four preps, he might not be leaving, and his kids might not be looking at half a year with a long-term sub—or worse, one of the crummy tenured teachers Locke couldn't get rid of.

Taylor worried about how the news would be received. There was a real stigma attached to quitting. It wasn't so much about not having the right stuff, though there was some of that. No, it was more about the kids. They got to you. It was as if they were your own children, so leaving them became unimaginable. How do you quit when these kids are depending on you? When they worry when you're out a day, scared that you won't come back? Taylor could never do it. But she wasn't about to second-guess Dave.

Dave believed they were all chasing something they could never catch. TFA, he said, trumpeted the success of teachers making "significant gains," and because the CMs are all psycho, and because they have always been told they can do anything they set their minds to, they chase this impossible goal, running themselves ragged to change the world. *But on what distant planet?* The reality, he said, is you can't force kids to make significant gains. There are so many other factors involved, and what are significant gains, anyway? And what is supposed to happen to your own life while you're tilting at windmills? Are you just supposed to put it on hold? Dave and his fiancée couldn't do it; they were miserable. "The TFA lifestyle is not sustainable," he concluded.

He's right, Taylor thought, *the lifestyle isn't sustainable.* She felt good about what she was doing, but she was overwhelmed. With the expectations of Locke, TFA, LMU, and even the UCLA literacy coaches at school, there was no time in her day for a social life. Sometimes, she wished she worked just for LAUSD and not for TFA, because LAUSD didn't make so many demands on a teacher. It was hard to bad-mouth TFA when the organization had given her such a wonderful opportunity. But she'd never been worked so hard—or been so emotionally drained. Like all the other CMs, Taylor was used to being good at whatever she tried. Now she thought: *I suck. I am a first-year teacher who doesn't know how to teach. I don't know how to be good at this.*

Her meetings with Samir left her feeling lousy. Even so, she would take his notes and put them on the table in her bathroom as a reminder of the things she had to improve upon. Just looking at them made her feel bad. She figured she could work twenty-four hours a day and still not be good enough. TFA was like the parent you could never please. She knew she was falling into an anorexic mind-set. When she wasn't reminding herself to be careful, her mother was. "Taylor, you're not trying to be the best, are you?" she would fret.

One Wednesday in early November, Taylor thought for the first time: *You know, I don't want to be here.* A week later, she drove home in tears. Teaching was challenging enough; now she had to deal with racial and cultural tensions that had been building in her classroom since mid-October.

It all started the morning she found the words "brown pride" scribbled all over her classroom. The tagging enraged her. She felt violated, as if someone had broken into her home.

Gustavo, one of the few Latino kids on the football team, ratted the taggers out. It was two girls—one of whom, Lucia, was a favorite of Taylor's. The other was a tough gangbanger named Estrella. The pair ditched school for two days afterward. When they returned, Taylor was ready for them.

"As far as I'm concerned, you were tagging on my desks!" she charged, over their vehement denials. "You are a couple of liars. I *know* it was you. You are not touching my stuff! Get out! It's your choice. Go to the dean's office or Mr. Sampson's class next door."

When they returned with the one-hundred-word essay she required for admittance back into her class, Taylor handed them graffiti remover and ordered them to scrub the desks. She stood with one arm on the door. "If you have attitude, I don't need you here. Go. Transfer out!" They cleaned the desks and stayed. Not long after that, Estrella got beaten up in a fight and was out of school for a while with her injuries. When she came back, Taylor simply said, "I'm sorry about what happened. Let's get you caught up." They'd been friends since then.

But the tensions among her students continued. The day she finally broke down and cried, she'd had to mediate three separate incidents with clear racial and cultural overtones. It was a nightmare. The first occurred when a Latino kid who rarely showed up took the seat normally occupied by Mighty Mikel, a little black kid with a big personality and a propensity for anger. "Nigga, you get the fuck outta my fuckin' seat, motherfucker!" Mikel demanded. Taylor threw Mikel out of the room without even giving him a destination or an assignment. During the next period, an explosive fight erupted between a black girl, one of Taylor's best students, whom she had chosen to be a class tutor, and a Hispanic boy. This time, both were ejected from class. The third incident was the one that made her cry: a girl fight was planned for right after school in the alley of 109th Street. Taylor kept one of the putative street wrestlers, Breana, after school.

"I heard about the fight," Taylor told her. "I know where it is, and I called the cops. Your friends are big blabbermouths. You are fourteen years old! And you fight! You have to be crazy, Breana! I don't see a good future for you! What can I do to help you?" Taylor was in the girl's face, competing with the incessant knocking on the door and the school-yard chant beyond it: "Fight! Fight! Fight!" Breana promised to reform. The fight never went down. The cops followed the kids there and broke it up before it could begin.

These kids had so much anger. Their short fuses freaked Taylor out. Even the girls were explosive—even the ones you didn't think had it in them sometimes erupted. Through her tears, Taylor made some decisions. The next unit she taught would be about race. The other teachers were doing Hemingway and Anne Frank. Not Taylor. She needed to address the serious cultural issues in her classroom.

In her graduate class at LMU, one text theorized that the educational system in the United States was created for the white hegemonic culture and could not accommodate or appreciate the needs of the Hispanic student, who too often dropped out in frustration as a result. LMU—and TFA—were big into multicultural textbooks, and Taylor knew that all kids want to read things that remind them of themselves. She was afraid that her instruction until then had been too white. From now on, her classes were going to confront racial issues head-on.

Her epiphany coincided with a two-day break from the classroom. The first day would be spent in professional development with the other ninth-grade teachers. On the second day she was going on a TFA-sponsored "excellent school" visit to Marlborough, an exclusive all-girls campus in tony Hancock Park. The only thing Taylor knew about the school was what she had gleaned while in the hospital. She had the impression that Marlborough was a feeder school for the UCLA eating-disorder unit.

But now Marlborough was a revelation. Its halls were strewn with backpacks. The concept of leaving a bag in a hallway unattended was mind-boggling to Taylor. But that was just the beginning. The first classroom she visited had no desks. The girls were sitting on sofas arranged in a semicircle and discussing epic metaphors in The Odyssey. They didn't use a whiteboard, and wrote in their notebooks as they went. It was like a college class. The instruction was literature-based. Taylor watched in amazement as ninth-grade girls engaged in real discussion.

When she returned to Locke, the kids knew right away that something was up. They were uneasy. She told them that she had gone to visit another school. They immediately assumed she was looking to leave Locke. "You leaving school? You going? You like that school? Were the kids quiet there? Do you like them better?" The questions came so rapidly she couldn't answer them all.

"I'm not going anywhere," she said. In fact, she was just getting started. She was going to push her students to a higher level. The rest of the world might think they were dumb, but Taylor knew better. They were crazy smart.

She had taken away a lot from her day at Marlborough. For starters, she was going to rearrange the desks in her classroom so that the space was circular and more conducive to discussion. To enhance comprehension, she was going to introduce close readings, which would require that she stop and ask questions about the text as students read aloud. The questions would stimulate conversation and make the students think critically about what they were reading.

Taylor understood that much of what Marlborough was doing assumed prior knowledge and that classroom management was not an issue there. So she was not surprised when her first stab at a meaningful conversation with her Locke ninth-graders went sideways fast. There were some kids she just couldn't shut up, and there was nothing more disheartening than to have a kid raise his hand out of nowhere, only to get drowned out by someone else talking over him. But she could see right away that the kids were more engaged, and she knew the close readings would make them examine the text more critically. As far as classroom management went, she decided to take the advice of one of her LMU profs. She was going to treat them like adults in the hope that they would act like adults. No longer would she send kids to the dean's office, or even to another colleague's room to write an essay as punishment. Now, when a kid misbehaved, she would just say: "If you feel the need to step outside, go on out and come back when you feel better and are ready to learn."

For the first close read, Taylor picked *Always Running* by Luis Rodríguez, a book about a boy who emigrates from Mexico with his family and settles near Locke High School, where he joins a gang. Praised by TFAers and the mainstream press for its raw depiction of life among Los Angeles's gangs, the book was banned by some school districts, including LAUSD. But Taylor didn't know that. She assumed she couldn't find copies of the book in the school book room because it was so disorganized, so she photocopied each chapter as they went along.

She started the book with a class discussion guided by four statements about immigration. The first was: *Immigration is an easy, painless process.*

Challenging hands shot up.

Selena said, "I disagree. Some people cross over and die."

"I got papers," Alfredo volunteered.

"Why do you say that?" Taylor asked. "Do you think people will accuse you of being illegal if you don't agree that immigration is easy?"

"I do," he said.

"It's not that easy, because you could get shot," Ricardo opined. "They got rifles that go *pop pop*. You don't jump quickly, you dead."

When Taylor asked rhetorically if any of them knew someone who had immigrated to the United States, they all laughed.

The next statement: *Americans embrace and accept all who choose to immigrate to the U.S.*

"I don't agree," Mariana said. "That is not true."

"I disagree," Alfredo said. "Arnold Schwarzenegger—they were gonna give us a license but he decided no. He's an idiot, since he's an immigrant, too."

Xavier said Schwarzenegger was from England. Alejandro said no, he was from Japan. And then Ricardo asked Taylor if she embraced immigrants.

"Yes, my family came from Russia," she replied. "My family was Jewish. They came from nothing."

"Didn't they kill people? Did they get to meet Hitler?" they wanted to know.

Statement number three: *Growing up in Watts is difficult.*

"I agree," said Eleesha. "People dying young, getting killed."

"Ah, that happens everywhere," said Alejandro. "It happens here—not every day."

"What if you walked in Beverly Hills, would it be the same?" Taylor asked.

"The same thing could happen, but even worse," said Alfredo. "You have to go on the freeway."

Taylor taught *Always Running* until she got a visit from her administrator, Mrs. Jauregui, who reluctantly informed her that the book was not district-approved for ninth-graders. It was too racy. Though the kids were really into it, Taylor stopped teaching it as instructed. But she thought, *I can't believe I could get into trouble for teaching a great book while other teachers sleep at their desks.*

The Monday after the long Thanksgiving weekend was hard for Hrag. He had flown out of Los Angeles the Wednesday before, as soon as school was finished, excited to be going home for the first time since June. Thanksgiving had always been his favorite holiday; it was the *whatever* holiday. So relaxing, no pressure; all you had to do was eat deep-fried turkey with all the trimmings plus a side of lamb, Armenian-style, and pass out. Hrag had obliged. He felt like he was home from college. He parked himself in front of the TV. He had assumed that he'd hit the local bars every night, but when he got home he didn't want to go out. He just wanted to see his parents and sister. *And to stop thinking about teaching.* His family was dying to hear all about his experiences in the hood, but he refused to talk about it.

It felt so good to be home and to have his parents taking care of him. Learning to cook, clean, and shop for himself in Los Angeles had been a shock to his system—yet another thing that made him feel old. But he had quickly gotten into a routine. On Sundays, he went grocery shopping for the week. He bought chicken, tortillas, and the fixings for salad. Then he cooked up all the chicken and stored it in Tupperware. He was careful to keep his food separate from Mackey's. It was kind of weird. Hrag and Mackey never shared a meal. Although they had attended Boston College together, they hadn't come into Teach For America as close friends. Hrag had tremendous respect for Mackey, but theirs wasn't a I'll-cook-tonight-you-take-tomorrow type of relationship.

The only TFA Locke teacher Hrag really felt a connection with was Rachelle. They had a lot in common. They both taught biology, and they seemed to approach the job in the same way. Rachelle didn't appear to be working herself to death, even though, as a special ed teacher, she had her hands full. Like Hrag, she did her work, but she was realistic about the job.

He and Rachelle had been invited to attend a weekend science conference in Palm Springs. They got to know each other better on the hundred-mile drive, and when they arrived at the hotel where the conference was being held, they sunbathed by the pool before checking in. It was so liberating. Hrag could joke around with Rachelle. Everyone else at TFA was so wound up and so on top of things. Take Taylor Rifkin. She acted really laid-back, but at work she was fiercely engaged and efficient.

Hrag hadn't bonded with any of Locke's male TFAers. Though he and Phillip shared the same hallway, they rarely spoke. And Mackey and he were friends, but they were very different people. They had stopped carpooling to school fairly early on. They weren't on the same clock. Mackey liked to get to school early and didn't mind staying late—he was the kind of guy who went out of his way to stop and chat with other teachers. Hrag, on the other hand, didn't want to spend any more time than necessary at work. He was never late for school, but he wasn't exactly an early riser. He had difficulty making small talk, and when he was done working, he wanted to get the hell out of Locke.

The Monday after Thanksgiving, Hrag arrived at school uncharacteristically early, well before 7 a.m., so he could get to his room and prepare for the day. But after he parked, he couldn't get out of his car. That awful knot in his stomach was back. He was so nervous, he couldn't bring himself to open the car door, so he tilted back the driver's seat, closed his eyes, and just lay there, half asleep, half awake. When Mackey arrived twenty minutes later and saw Hrag stretched out behind the wheel, eyes closed, he panicked. Pounding on the car window he cried: *"What are you doing? What are you doing?"*

Hrag asked himself the same question again and again. Time and experience didn't make it easier to answer. It just kept rattling around in his head, growing louder and more insistent as the days passed.

The question was loudest during fifth period. He had had trouble keeping order in period five from day one, when Cale and José got into their fight. He had yet to get it right. He couldn't figure out how these kids thought. They had all kinds of issues. He discovered that one student who was driving him nuts couldn't understand a word of English and belonged in a bilingual class. Another girl had the same problem, but he couldn't get her switched out. He didn't know what to do; he didn't speak Spanish well enough to teach biology in that language. Hrag noticed that kids came into class cut up. One boy brought Hrag a book of his poetry and it was filled with blood. The poetry was pretty good; the blood was disgusting. And José had a huge scar on his cheek. Hrag couldn't bring himself to ask how it got there.

José was already in the juvenile court system, on probation; a school suspension would send him to jail. Hrag liked the kid. If they were the same age, he thought, they would probably be friends. But as a student, José was Hrag's worst nightmare. The kid couldn't sit still, and he was an instigator. On the days he came to class, he brought trouble with him. And Hrag's newly adopted classroom-management policy, in which he sent the errant student to a nearby classroom to write a one-page reflective essay, didn't work with José. Other kids hated writing; just the thought of it whipped them into shape. Not José. If Hrag sent him out and demanded three pages, José would dutifully come back with three pages. And the thing was, his work was thoughtful and surprisingly well written. A reader would think the kid was a choirboy. Far from it; José was a failing student who lived with his mom and had some kind of problem with male authority. Managing him was exhausting. Hrag toyed with the idea of switching him to Vanessa Morris's class, thinking that José might perform better for a female. But he was reluctant to let him go. He didn't want Morris to think he couldn't handle the kid.

But José was incorrigible. One Monday in mid-November, right before the parent-teacher conferences, Hrag walked into his room to find "FUCK YOU MR. H" scrawled across the board. The message was signed "SNAPS." At first, Hrag was unfazed. Yet another *whatever* moment at Locke. He got some alcohol and wiped it off—only to discover that Snaps had tagged the entire classroom. "Snaps" was scribbled on the walls, on Hrag's desk, on the door, on José's chair, and on the table where he sat.

It was José. Hrag *knew* it. But just to be sure, he started making casual inquiries. "Anyone know Snaps?" he asked the kids in another class.

"Why?"

"You guys tell me," responded Hrag. "Does the name start with a *J*?"

"No," came the answer, accompanied by a knowing smile.

When everyone had left the room, a girl who sat in the front row, a quiet girl who did her work, confided that she had seen Snaps. It was clear that she was referring to José.

Hrag confronted him. "I don't have proof," he conceded. "But kids talk, and I know you did it. I'm trying to help you, José. I don't appreciate an FU on the board."

"Yeah, man, you've been disrespected," allowed José. "But I didn't do it."

When Hrag called José's mother, she wanted to know if Hrag had proof that José was the tagger. Then she said she didn't know what to do with him and gave Hrag his father's number. Hrag told José that he had called home.

"Man, why do you care so much about me?" he asked. "No one else cares. You know I come [to class]. I wish you'd lay off my back. Stop caring."

José had caught him off guard. Hrag had already typed a letter to the dean detailing his offenses. Now he decided not to hand it in.

Unlike José, Cale was not an instigator. He was a reactor. There was something about the kid that scared Hrag, and fascinated him, too. Cale should have been failing biology. But he came to class fairly often, and when he wasn't there, he made a habit of coming in at lunch and making up the work he had missed. Like so many other kids at Locke, Cale had never been trained to sit and learn; he had been trained to get through the system. So he was getting a B.

He wasn't a bad kid—yet. But he seemed to have deep-rooted problems. Again, Hrag thought it was a male thing. The kid was looking for a father figure. As far as Hrag could tell, he lived with his aunt and his grandmother; he couldn't figure out if he had parents around or not. Every time he asked, the grandmother or aunt would mumble something about what a rough childhood the boy had had. Still, Cale was always fashionably dressed. And when he applied himself, he could do anything that was asked of him.

When Cale came in at lunch, Hrag would shoot the breeze with him, trying to build a rapport, trying to get him to understand how to behave in class. Like many of the other boys, Cale didn't know how to act around girls—he was always putting his hands on them and being surprised to find his touch unwelcome. One day when Cale came in during lunch, he asked for Hrag's phone number. Hrag told him he wouldn't give it to him until he had earned his trust. After Cale left, Hrag realized that the kid had stolen three different things from his desk, random things like a glue stick and big markers, but still, it was creepy. Later Hrag learned that the petty theft had occurred on the day Cale's father was getting out of jail.

Not long after that, Cale was suspended. He had gone into a new teacher's room holding a pair of scissors behind his back. The teacher was a big guy, but he was freaked out. He didn't know Cale, and Cale apparently didn't know him. The teacher pulled his desk in front of him to put some distance between himself and Cale, and then asked the kid to put the scissors down. Cale just grinned and ran away.

Of course, he was caught. He was another kid who had already had brushes with the law—exactly the kind of kid Wells was happy to show to the door. Knowing that Hrag had had trouble with Cale in the past, the dean asked him to prepare a list of Cale's infractions.

Cale was clearly living on borrowed time, but he still came in at lunch and tried, in his awkward way, to connect. "Have you been to Jamba Juice?" he would ask. "Wanna go with me?" And Hrag would say, "Yeah, behave for a week and we'll go to Jamba Juice." It seemed to be working. Cale started working on the class stem-cell project, and his behavior improved. Then, ten minutes into class one day, two African American girls warned Hrag that he had better shut Cale up. Hrag did not want to interrupt the lab; he asked them to ignore Cale. Seconds later, one of the girls shouted at Cale: "I'm gonna have my brother fucking kill you!" Then all hell broke loose. The girl bolted out of her seat, scream-ing. Hrag had no idea what Cale had said or done to provoke her. "I'll kick you out, Cale, and you can't afford to get kicked out!" he warned. But Cale was unreachable. When Hrag did send him out, Cale an-nounced that he *wanted* to go to the dean's office.

The dean called, Hrag told him what had occurred, and that was it. Cale was gone. It took multiple phone calls to his grandmother to find out what happened to him. Hrag figured he'd just been recycled—kicked out of Locke and given an "opportunity transfer" to another poorly per-forming school in the district. And he was right. Hrag felt terrible, like it was his fault.

Then there was the cutter. You didn't have to be a shrink to know that cutting was rampant among America's young. It was a form of release, a stress reliever. Hrag had a friend in college who did it. It relo-cated the pain. So it wasn't like he had never seen it before. It was just that he had never seen lacerations so deep and so disfiguring as the ones he noticed on the young girl in his second-period class one day. She was late (he didn't know it, but she spent first period every day across the street with her baby at the day-care center), and he yelled at her. Instead of giving him crap like most kids would, she just sat there and hung her head. That made Hrag feel rotten, so he kept going over to her, trying to make up. He sensed she had problems. She had a big scar on her face, and she was always saying outrageous things and putting on shows for attention. At one point, she claimed she could speak Japanese. Another time, she bragged that she was going to France. "Are you okay?" he asked again. She wouldn't answer.

Then he noticed her wrist. There were deep cuts, carved in a pattern, and they were starting to scab over.

He kept her after class. "You need to talk to someone," he said.

"Nothing's wrong," she said.

"Then what happened to you?" he demanded to know.

"It's a burn."

"I want you to talk to me," he pleaded. She left.

Later that day, she handed him a note with a phone number and a name on it. "It's my mom," she explained.

Hrag had graduate school that night, but in between classes he called the number. The person who answered the phone was a basketball coach from another school. She said that the young mother had been through serious trauma, but she refused to give any details. "I'm trying to get her help, and it would be great if you could help out, too," she said.

"I don't know what I can do to help," replied Hrag. "I'm a biology teacher." The next morning the phone rang at six o'clock. It was the coach. She and Hrag worked out a plan to get the girl counseling. But after that, she stopped coming to class. Hrag fretted over her safety—and the role he was so ill equipped to play.

Who am I kidding? I don't know what I'm doing. The fact that it's left to me to identify a girl who is on the verge of killing herself is ridiculous. You can fake the teaching, but when it comes to this stuff, you can't. How can it be that I'm the one diagnosing or even realizing that this girl is in trouble? I don't even know who her guidance counselor is. If something happens, I could be held liable. I don't know who to go to. And if I don't write it on my hand, I won't remember to even report it. It's crazy. Oh God, I hope she's okay.

It wasn't just the troubled kids who kept Hrag up at night. It was all the kids at this dysfunctional school who were consigned to live in this crappy neighborhood in this screwed-up school district. The parent-teacher conferences in mid-November had him questioning anew what the hell he was doing.

Only eight parents showed up. It was strange. Some kids were there all alone, and Hrag didn't want to ask why, knowing that a sizable percentage of the students at Locke lived in foster homes. Most of the parents who did show up had kids who were model citizens. But not all. One boy, a very social African American kid in fifth period who fancied himself a ladies' man, walked into room 308 with a big black man who introduced himself as Norman. The kid was having some academic issues, and Norman wanted to know why.

"He talks a lot in class," explained Hrag.

"SHUT HIM DOWN!" thundered Norman, pounding the desk for emphasis. When Hrag explained that the talking prevented him from doing all his work in class, Norman pounded the desk again and repeated: "SHUT HIM DOWN!"

Hrag steered the conversation toward the class stem-cell project that would culminate in a research paper and the fourth annual Locke High School stem-cell debate. It was important that the boy do well on the paper, Hrag counseled. Norman listened intently. His sister was a nurse. School was important. Norman turned to his young charge:

"Bio: PAID!" he declared, slamming the desk with his fist as if stamping a bill. "Math," he continued, with another pound of the desk. "PAID! Talking in class: McDONALD'S!"

Hrag struggled not to laugh. The stamp he used on the kids' papers just happened to say PAID.

Norman asked about attendance. Hrag went down his roll and reported that the kid had missed class two times. Norman's face clouded over in anger. Rechecking, Hrag realized he had confused him with another student.

"You're a lucky boy," said Norman, after Hrag corrected his mistake. "You were about to get cut!"

Whoa!

The exchange ended when Norman declared Hrag the best of all the teachers he had visited that night and urged him to call him anytime. But Norman got Hrag thinking: *What the hell am I doing? By teaching them some biology facts, are they really learning anything they will ever get* PAID *for? When they don't even know how to read?*

When Hrag graduated from high school, he might not have been able to give an exact definition of a DNA polymerase, but he could take a concept, analyze it, discuss it, and then write about it. At Locke, he was teaching his kids some facts about biology, so he probably was closing their *knowledge* gap. But the achievement gap? *When somebody doesn't know how to read, or is reading at a third-grade level, that's not a gap, that's a gigantic, stone-wall barrier.* Just thinking about it depressed him. Sometimes he wanted to throw the biology book out the window, close up shop, and show them how to write a sentence.

Sometimes Rachelle felt lost at Locke, and she had nowhere to go for help. She was not assigned to a small school, and she didn't feel like a full-fledged member of the biology department. The graduate school courses she was taking at California State University, Dominguez Hills, tended to be too theoretical, and Samir Bolar, though obviously intelligent and perfectly nice, had no experience in special ed. That left the special ed department, which was totally dysfunctional. There had been no coordinator during the first few months of the school year. When one was finally named, her focus was on completing IEPs, not showing Rachelle and the other four new TFA special ed teachers the ropes.

The other new TFAers assigned to special ed were called resource teachers, and their job was to give one-on-one assistance to students who had been mainstreamed into general ed classes. It was difficult; the resource position was new to Locke and the TFA teachers were making it up as they went along. But they bonded over the frustrations and the challenges. By midyear, they were a formidable fighting force at the school. They demanded a special room for their students and ruffled many feathers in the process. When the administration finally found them an old art room, they spent their weekends renovating and painting it. Rachelle liked them and admired their ferocious advocacy on behalf of their kids, but she wasn't part of their team. Among the other first-year TFA special ed teachers, she was pretty much a one-woman band.

So every night Rachelle went home to the apartment she shared with two other TFAers and spent at least an hour and a half puzzling over what to teach the next day. Even on the rare occasion when she felt like she had put together a good lesson plan, she arrived at school feeling apprehensive. As the morning progressed and period four loomed larger, the sense of foreboding grew and deepened. Things there had gone from bad to worse.

Some days—too many days—she just wanted to quit. She would be teaching, or trying to, and the whole time she would be thinking that she didn't want to be there: *Fine. Walk out. Go. It's okay.*

But she just couldn't do it. So she found herself living day to day, longing for the weekends and then finding them disappointing, too. She had met some nice people through TFA. Like Hrag. He made her laugh; he always looked miserable, too. But she thought some of the others were geeks. She had hated the cheerleading at the opening ceremony, and now she hated all the earnestness. Everyone was so uptight. With the TFA crowd, all you did was sit around and talk about students and how you were all going to close the achievement gap.

Things weren't much better outside the TFA circle. She didn't feel like she fit into the L.A. scene. When she went to a club in Hollywood with a few friends, they were turned away. She figured it was because they weren't emaciated enough and didn't look like supermodels. She had always had a boyfriend in high school—and one in college, too, until her junior year when she studied abroad in Italy. It would have been nice to have a boyfriend now. But she didn't know how to meet people as a teacher, and besides, she didn't have time for a relationship. She figured this was just going to be that kind of year—an all-work, no-play deal.

So she scheduled trips to break things up. In fact, she had missed a few days of school and was feeling guilty about it. She had taken time off for a trip to New York, and she had returned to Philadelphia for Penn's homecoming weekend. The surprising thing was, when it came time to go, she hadn't really wanted to leave the kids. Of course, she was dying to see her old friends. (She wore a fake engagement ring to Penn to see what kind of reaction she would get.) But once there, she missed her students.

It was weird. She had thought it would be easy to slip back into college life. After all, she had been gone only five months. But so much had changed in that time. She found it strange just to spend a whole weekend going out and hearing people speak proper English. She realized it must have sounded snobby, but it was true: hearing grammatically correct English was shocking. Sometimes even she didn't speak right. After having spent so much time in Watts, she often found herself mimicking the kids' speech patterns and reminding herself that "Do you feel me?" is not a standard way of saying "Do you understand?"

Everyone at Penn knew that she was in TFA. They all wanted to hear her war stories, but they really had no idea. None of them actually wanted to cross the boundary and see for themselves firsthand. It was just: *Tell us more! Tell us more stories about your ghetto kids.*

The reality was, she loved her ghetto kids, and she believed that what she was doing was valuable and cool. She didn't know how much they were learning, but she was definitely connecting—especially with her soccer girls. Originally, she had planned just to help out with the girls' JV team, but when she arrived for the first practice, she was introduced to the girls as a coach. She wasn't able to make all the practices or even the games because of graduate school, but when she was there, she worked the girls hard, and they responded.

She may have been their coach, but they called her *guerita*, Spanish for "pretty little white girl." They didn't seem to have any adults in their lives to talk to; they began to confide in Rachelle. The Latina soccer girls came from very traditional Catholic families. Many of them wouldn't even use tampons because of their religion, but they were very curious about sex. They wanted to know what a real relationship with a boy was like, what was normal, what was appropriate for a boy to say and do. Rachelle counseled them much as she herself had been counseled: "No means no," she would say. "For real. If you say no, there is no argument, no discussion." She knew that many of their mothers had been children themselves when they had their first babies, so somebody wasn't saying no.

There was an infant-care facility right across the street to care for the babies of Locke students. The teenaged mothers dropped their babies off before school and usually spent one period a day there learning parenting skills. At any given time, there were up to two dozen Locke babies enrolled in the day-care program. But the total number of young mothers at Locke was much higher, because many girls, especially the Latinas, preferred to leave their babies at home for their own mothers to watch.

Pregnancies often went unnoticed at Locke. Classes were large, and students didn't necessarily know who to go to for help. Guidance counselors had hundreds of kids to manage, and it wasn't up to individual teachers to advise pregnant students of their rights (if they even knew what those rights were). So, often, unless a teacher took a particular interest, a pregnant student did not come to the attention of the administration. That meant many girls were never aware that there were government programs to ensure that their education continued throughout pregnancy, delivery, and recovery. Many just ditched school for however long it took to have the baby and bounce back from childbirth. Others simply dropped out.

Rachelle didn't want the lives of these smart—and yet incredibly unsophisticated—girls to be short-circuited. Playing competitive sports was one healthy activity that might help keep them in school.

Rachelle had started playing when she was five, and she ran off the field the first time she scored a goal. She was a tomboy; she played on a boys' soccer team until seventh grade because the girls' teams were too girly. She played club soccer after that and eventually joined the Surf Soccer Club, one of the best teams in the country. The competition to make the squad was stiff. Rachelle was used to being the best, but she had had to work harder for Surf, and when she did make the team, she didn't get to play much. The coach was incredibly challenging. He didn't even bother to learn a player's name until she had proved herself worthy. You either quit in frustration or you dug in. There were girls on the team who broke. Rachelle dug in.

During one game, her coach pulled her out and said: "You're either stupid or bad." Rachelle thought: *Well, I know I'm not stupid, so I guess I must be bad.* There were many times when she didn't want to go to practice and a million times when she wanted to quit. But she stuck with it. On one trip to the East Coast, the coach played her for only two minutes and then pulled her, saying: "I can't trust you." It was so upsetting. She had trained so much and worked so hard. Later in the game, another player got hurt and the coach was forced to put Rachelle back in. It was during that trip that Penn recruited her.

After that, the coach started playing her more. By the time she played her last game before going to college, her team was competing in the nationals. They lost in the finals, but Rachelle ended up scoring the most goals of the tournament. The next year, the team won it all.

Soccer had been good to her. It helped her get into the University of Pennsylvania, and it was the thing that had kept her on the right track in high school, when it would have been easy to screw up. With soccer practice four or five times a week and travel on weekends, she didn't have time to get into trouble. Her dad traveled to every one of her games, and when she played for Penn, he bought a bunch of Southwest Airlines vouchers and flew to every one of those games, too. That was his way of showing that he cared—especially during those tough teenage years when Rachelle was so rebellious. Whenever her parents said turn left, Rachelle automatically turned right. She gave them a hard time. Everything back then was a big FU.

Now she realized how lucky she was to have had two loving, involved parents. Though both had busy careers, Rachelle and her brother were far from latchkey kids; their paternal grandparents picked them up from school each day. She had a great relationship with her parents now. They were very proud of her for joining Teach For America, and impressed with how she was handling the work and the responsibility. One of Rachelle's enduring childhood memories was of her mother working late at night, surrounded by legal briefs. When Rachelle drove home to San Diego for her father's birthday and spent much of her time planning lessons, her mother remarked at how similar Rachelle's prep work was to her own.

Ironically, Rachelle was experiencing as a teacher some of the issues her parents had faced. She was trying to build a relationship with the kids while commanding their respect. It was hard, especially as a female. She had to be careful. She was conscious of how she dressed. (Even so, some at Locke took issue with the holes in her jeans and the tank tops she occasionally wore on student-free days.) Once when she used the Spanish word *"ese,"* meaning homey or buddy, to address one of her favorite students, the kid frowned and corrected her. "It doesn't sound right, you saying 'ese,' " he said. And sometimes, when one of the boys would give her a hug, she would think, *Is this too close to the line?*

So far, at least, they had never challenged her sexually. In fact, the only snide comments or crass sexual innuendos she had heard came from her colleagues, not her charges. She easily fended off the occasional unwanted advance or inappropriate remark at Locke. She hadn't expected it to be an issue at Teach For America. But over the summer, when she effused over how cute one of her students was, a corps member trilled: *"How* cute, Rachelle?" There was no mistaking the insinuation. Rachelle was insulted.

Because TFAers were not much older than some of their students, physical contact was a tricky issue for all of them. On the last day of summer school during institute, one of Hrag's female students kissed him on the cheek. Without thinking, he kissed her back, and was horrified. *Oh my God! What just happened?*

Rachelle sometimes wished that she were a school counselor instead of a special ed teacher. She didn't feel comfortable in the role of enforcer. But she soon understood that moms had the power in most families, particularly the black households, so she didn't hesitate to take advantage of that with a phone call home. The boys begged her not to; they did not want to cross their mothers. But often it was the only thing that worked. So when Dante threw a nasty temper tantrum one day, Rachelle picked up the phone and called his mom. He was going crazy, screaming and throwing his backpack around. The security guard outside Rachelle's door had tried to help, but it somehow became a race thing: "Dante, I know she's white, and you don't trust her because of that, but you have to trust the people who have your best interests in mind," he said, trying to get Dante to respond to Rachelle. It was another jolting reminder to Rachelle of how many things at Locke got filtered through a colored lens—even issues that had nothing to do with race.

When Dante finally calmed down, Rachelle drove him home. At first his mother was apprehensive because she figured Dante had done something wrong. But Rachelle didn't talk about his bad behavior. She marveled at his little sister's perfect attendance certificate and gave Dante a special project to do at home. After that, Dante turned a corner. He still had anger-management issues; kids teased him because he talked funny, and he had trouble reading, which bothered him. But he wanted to please Miss Snyder, so his outbursts became much less frequent.

Rachelle broke through to Deangelo the same way. Deangelo was a sweet kid with a short fuse. He and his cousin Martel were inseparable. They made an impression on her the very first week of school when they were afraid to walk home because they had been threatened by a bunch of gangbangers. But they were tough to handle. Martel was especially difficult, and Deangelo fed off his negative energy. They fought like cubs at play, poking and taunting each other with expletives and racial slurs. Rachelle would be trying to teach, and the two of them would be going at it.

Deangelo: You ugly, nigga. You gay. You a faggot. You a slut.

Martel: Shut up, bitch. Fuck you.

Deangelo: Fat black jerk.

Martel: Fuck you, bitch. Don't get mad, get glad, motherfucker.

As tiresome as they were, Rachelle knew that Deangelo wanted to succeed. But he had a hard time remembering assignments. She decided to help by calling him at home to remind him of his homework. She ended up talking to his mother, who had just finished a course of radiation for cancer and was undergoing chemo. She had spent the day in bed and told Rachelle that she wasn't doing very well. When Rachelle responded with the obligatory "Let me know if there's anything I can do to help," Deangelo's mom jumped on the offer. She wanted fruit. Could Rachelle bring her some fruit? So Rachelle and Deangelo went grocery shopping. They drove to a nearby food warehouse and picked up pears, pineapples, bananas, and tortillas. When they delivered the food, Rachelle made Deangelo show her the science report he had completed in middle school. Her interest made a difference. Deangelo started really trying. He even urged Martel to stop the cussing and do some work.

In the days leading up to the December break, even the most difficult kids got into the Christmas spirit. One of the highlights of the last week was the guest appearance of Mr. H. Rachelle enjoyed Hrag. They'd been hanging out together ever since Palm Springs. Hrag had put her in charge of getting Mackey to relax. She would call him up periodically and tease, "Mackey, are you working?" It was great to have Hrag in her room teaching her fourth-period class. He presented a mini-lesson on the breakdown of proteins in the digestive system. There were only four kids there that day, but they were all on their best behavior, and when Hrag left, Rachelle thanked them.

"Oh, we weren't good, Miss Snyder, we just didn't want to embarrass ourselves!" explained Martel. Then, noting the Christmas present Hrag had left on Rachelle's desk, he added: "Is that another boyfriend?"

The next day, Rachelle gave the boys a little quiz and promised to double their scores as a Christmas gift. Then she handed out photocopies of an outline of a human body and asked the kids to label the parts. The boys talked and laughed as they worked. It always surprised Rachelle: they liked being busy; they loved filling out work sheets! When she asked if everyone in the room celebrated Christmas, Martel bristled: "What you think? We black. We sit home doin' nothin'?" But the moment of tension passed, and soon they were all clapping and singing—and even dancing—to the hit hip-hop single "Laffy Taffy" by D4L and "Yo Quiero Saber" by Ivy Queen, the reggaeton diva.

Rachelle had been counting the days until the Christmas break. Her plan had been to do absolutely nothing. Things didn't work out that way.

Locke was hopelessly out of compliance with its IEPs: unless they were completed by January 28, the school could face a possible takeover. So special ed teachers were asked to come in over the break to work on them. Rachelle had fifteen to complete. Not only did the IEPs require input from general ed teachers, but they couldn't be closed without a parent's signature. Though she had scheduled multiple meetings with parents and guardians, many had been no-shows. So, before heading down to San Diego for the Christmas holiday, she spent the first week of her break working on IEPs. When she wasn't filling out paperwork, she was knocking on doors in Watts making house calls.

Still, on the last day of school before the three-week vacation, she was almost giddy. The staff Christmas party was in Hobbs Hall that afternoon. Faculty meetings at Locke often erupted into shouting matches—who knew what would happen at a Christmas party? She had heard that Dave Buehrle was leaving, and it was a safe bet that most of the TFAers would be there to say good-bye.

As it turned out, she never made it to the Christmas party. A fifteen-year-old girl she had never met before came into her room and asked to borrow her phone. Her name was Sharita, and she lived in a foster home. Rachelle asked her what was up.

Sharita needed to find somewhere to go. For the past year she had been living with a single mother who had one biological daughter. Sharita had just found out that she was pregnant with her middle school boyfriend's baby, and when her foster mom heard the good news, she kicked her out of the house. Sharita could sleep on the porch if she wanted, but she was no longer welcome inside. So Sharita collected her things, stuffed them into two garbage bags, and came to school to try to find someone to take her in. She had some numbers of long-lost relatives, but either the numbers were wrong or the people answering the calls had no interest in being reacquainted with a pregnant fifteen-year-old with no resources.

Sharita had never gotten to touch or even see her own mother, a drug addict who died of an overdose when Sharita was ten. As far as she knew, her father lived in Palmdale, but she was not allowed to see him. For most of her young life, she had lived with an aunt who was a prostitute. By age ten, Sharita was working off the books at a liquor store to help buy food and diapers for the babies her aunt kept having. Sharita ran away after being raped repeatedly by an older cousin.

She was happy to be pregnant.

"But what are you going to do with a baby?" asked Rachelle.

"If I'm old enough to open my legs, I'm old enough to take responsibility for what I've done," reasoned Sharita.

Rachelle stood by as the child dialed number after number. She didn't know what to do. Eventually, she took her downstairs to see Carla German, Locke's psychiatric social worker. German tried to contact Sharita's social worker, but because of the Christmas holiday, the woman was on an extended three-to-four-hour lunch break and couldn't be reached.

Sharita begged Rachelle to take her home with her. She wanted Rachelle to adopt her. And Rachelle actually entertained the possibility. *I can adopt her. What the hell? No! I can't. I'm almost as irresponsible as she is.*

"You'll get eight hundred dollars a month," Sharita assured her. "I'll be really good, I promise!"

Rachelle knew she couldn't take the girl home with her, but she didn't know what else to do. She found Dr. Wells at the Christmas party and asked him to intervene. He told her to call school security, but they were gone. Finally, there was no other option; they called the police. Rachelle remained at school with Sharita until five-thirty. Carla German stayed until the cops came and took the girl away.

As Rachelle left, she pressed her phone number into the child's hand. She felt sure Sharita would call, but she never did. In fact, no one ever heard from Sharita again. The earth may just as well have opened up and swallowed her whole.

Rachelle drove home crying. When she told her father Sharita's saga, he reassured her. If she didn't cry over something like that, he said, she couldn't possibly have a soul.

In mathematics, there was clarity, a right answer and a wrong answer. Phillip had the quintessential math personality. English or history teachers might approach their disciplines with an "Okay, let's think this thing through." Phillip's style was "Let's call it what it is. Break this rule, there are consequences." Crying over a failing grade didn't work with him. Emotion simply didn't enter into the equation. "Sorry," he would say. "You missed the boat." People said he was hard on his kids.

And they were right. He didn't expect talking when he was talking, and when it happened, he got angry. Some things were just not subject to compromise.

One day he ordered a particularly vexing girl to Saturday school for her bad attitude. The child ran out of the room crying hysterically. She was on probation, and one more offense could send her to jail. "I hate this class!" she screamed. "He's so mean. I'm gonna go to jail because of him!" Phillip reckoned he should have felt bad for the girl. But he didn't. He didn't feel anything. He was simply doing what he had said he would do. He asked his colleagues how they would have handled the situation, and they all agreed that they would not have written the referral. Maybe not, but Phillip could see the effect that attitude had in their classrooms. In Phillip's classes, the kids watched one another's behavior and called out anyone who was not following classroom procedures.

Relatively speaking, he thought he had more of a standing with the kids than did most teachers. He could feel it when he walked down the hall that was the home to his small school, SE. He didn't know all the students at Locke, but they seemed to know him. One day he interrupted an argument between two girls by ordering the one he knew, Rakesha, to class. Her friend started mocking Phillip, repeating what he had said, exaggerating each word. Rakesha turned to her and snapped: "Cool it! That's Mr. Gedeon!"

Phillip believed that when you're strict about the small stuff, you eliminate a lot of the bigger problems. He tried to nip things in the bud. Tardiness, talking, cussing, not doing homework—all were tantamount to disrupting his class. In Phillip's book, even saying "Shut up" was prohibited; he lumped that expression in with all the other profanities that had made their way into the everyday speech pattern of the Locke student body.

He had not had a student directly disrespect him: no objects thrown, no "Mr. G, you are this," or "Mr. G, you are that." Kids had said stuff, but never to his face. Because if he did hear something, he would demand that the student look him in the eye and repeat it, and the kid would suddenly be at a loss for words. Once the moment passed, Phillip never pushed the point; he always moved on. He would just say: "This is the end of the discussion. There is no need to argue. If you want to discuss it, you can come back on your own time."

There had never been a fight in room 301 because Phillip had never let anything rise to that level. To be sure, he had had students walk out, but that didn't bother him. "Walk out," he'd say. "You're not offending me. I want you to walk out so I can write you up."

His kids knew the limits. And he felt that his students, particularly the black males, saw something in him. One day, at the end of the first semester, a black kid named Carnell said, in front of the whole class: "Mr. G, you are the best teacher I ever had." Phillip thought he was just playing around, but soon other kids jumped in and agreed. It was strange to hear kids saying that about a math teacher, since most hated the subject. Maybe it was because Phillip was a black male. Maybe they found in him a kindred spirit, or maybe they wanted to impress him.

He was not a demonstrative person. And he didn't date. Relationships take time, and he didn't have any to spare. If something came along, that would be one thing. But he certainly wasn't going to seek it out or put any effort into it. He did have a social life, though. TFA didn't have many official social events—a welcoming picnic and a one-hundred-day celebration—but he went to both. The L.A. region recruits often got together, and teachers at Locke partied, too. He enjoyed eating and drinking and swapping stories about school and college. Most nights he ate with his roommates, but he and Dan Ehrenfeld and Dave Buehrle tried to get together once a week for a meal, and he sometimes saw Taylor outside of school, too. He became great friends with a UCLA alum who taught math at Locke named Amber Hardy. They met once a week and watched *American Idol* together. And he and Heather Fieldsteel had a running competition to see who could visit the other more during their breaks. He enjoyed the collegiality at Locke, especially among the TFA folks. In fact, he didn't know how a teacher could make it at a place like Locke without the support of colleagues.

But the focus of his life remained his work and his students. He made no apologies for that. He considered all the other stuff—posting TFA mastery charts, submitting proof of lesson planning to the front office—unimportant. He wasn't going to run around decorating his classroom or writing down lesson plans when he needed to be grading. Fine him, fire him—they could do what they had to do. He would do what he had to do.

The fact was, there were plenty of rules at Locke; there just weren't any consequences. Phillip knew they weren't going to fire him. They weren't even going to write him up. Nobody got written up! Even TFA had no real power over him—or any of the other recruits. Corps members were paid by the districts that employed them, not by the organization that had recruited them. Phillip ignored all the time-wasting directives. If he appeared arrogant or insubordinate, so what? He didn't worry about what people thought of him.

What mattered was his teaching, and that spoke for itself. After a poor first showing, his students' scores on the monthly assessments were up. He was buoyed by the results. Some of his kids got B's for the first time in their lives. Homework had become a priority, Saturday school an empty threat. Phillip put kids' names on the board for Saturday school when they didn't do their homework, but they never had to go—they all made up the missing work.

He was blackmailing them, and it was working. They were beginning to see the connection between homework and achievement. When they corrected their homework together in class, Phillip insisted that they ask him questions. He wanted to get them talking about math, comfortable with asking questions. They were not only learning geometry, Phillip was teaching them language skills, conversational skills, and if-I-don't-know-the-answer-I-can-ask skills. The kids weren't even close to TFA goals of 80 percent mastery. Maybe 50 percent were making a B or better (and that's if you didn't count the ones who were chronic ditchers or had other big impediments to achievement). As far as Phillip was concerned, though, this turnaround was major.

Phillip had asked his mother to choose which holiday she wanted to share with him: Thanksgiving or Christmas. She chose Christmas. So for the Thanksgiving holiday, he got a cheap $220 JetBlue ticket and flew to New York to spend time with a teacher friend who worked for the Peace Games Program, a nonprofit organization that promotes tolerance and conflict resolution to schoolchildren. In New York, Phillip felt totally disconnected from his real life. He didn't have to worry about Locke or TFA. He walked the streets all day long, slept in late, saw Ground Zero, and did Times Square. He sat in on a class that his friend taught. One thing he didn't do was see his father. His father had left his wife and was living with his girlfriend in New York. He had a new life. Phillip refused to be a part of it.

As it turned out, Phillip didn't go home for Christmas after all. He hadn't really been looking forward to it in the first place. The Massachusetts winter was cold and dreary, and the snowstorms had already begun. His mother worried about his traveling in bad weather, and she didn't have any extra vacation time to spend with him anyway.

So Phillip stayed in Los Angeles. He slept in and went to bed late. He watched his favorite TV shows—*Forensic Files* and *The Golden Girls*. He spent time with Emily, another teacher friend, and together they planned lessons and went out for drinks and the occasional dinner.

But mostly he worked. Over the three-week hiatus, he managed to prepare the upcoming chapter and develop lesson plans and work sheets for the two remaining weeks of the first semester. In his spare time he was on the phone, consulting with other teachers about their math programs and best practices. And he spent a lot of time thinking—reflecting back on the first four months of his teaching career and looking ahead to all that he hoped to accomplish in the coming months. *What could make my students more successful?*

He decided to make some adjustments. Even before the break, he had approached Zeus Cubias, the math department chair, and his own small-school leader, Josh Hartford, about reteaching Geometry A to his failing students. It was an idea that had never been tried at Locke. In the past, students who failed the first semester of geometry (Geometry A) advanced to Geometry B the second semester and retook Geometry A in summer school. Phillip didn't think that made any sense. Though others in the department disagreed, he believed that Geometry A and B were linked, that one built on the other. He wanted his students to pass Geometry A before proceeding to Geometry B. He wanted his failing students back with him. He knew where they were academically, and he thought if he had them for one more semester, they would have a real chance to succeed.

The whole idea for repeating the class came from the notion that the students who were really being left behind were the smart ones, because he was constantly having to stop and slow down for the low achievers. His arguments won the day. Phillip began advising his failing students of their new option, and he forwarded their names to Chad's office for scheduling. For some kids, the idea of repeating the class was incentive enough to work harder.

Phillip had some other innovations in mind as well. He decided that he would start using his side whiteboard more effectively. Under the title "Coming Attractions" he was going to list the dates for activities, tests, and assignments that were coming up. He would also post the lesson plan for each day, and across the top of the board would be the California State Standards for Geometry, so the kids could see the connection between what they were learning in class and what was required of them by law.

Phillip was going to change his whole style of teaching as well. When school first began, his classroom was very structured—even the desks were in rows. Now, as the first semester was drawing to a close and his students knew his expectations, he wanted to move away from direct instruction to group investigations. He wanted his kids to do presentations, to work on projects, to not only pass his class, but to excel. He couldn't wait for the next semester to begin.

CHAPTER EIGHT

Disillusionment

Christmastime made Samir Bolar nervous. He knew that virtually all his CMs were still struggling, and he didn't like the idea of them being at home, back in familiar surroundings, with friends and family who might be reacting to their inevitable horror stories with concern instead of encouragement. This was a tricky time in their development as teachers, a time when they needed someone they trusted to tell them to hang in there. The last thing they needed to hear was "What the heck are you doing?" Samir had sent each of his fifty corps members a holiday e-mail. Over the break, he wanted desperately to call them, to check in, to make sure they were still on board. But he kept his distance.

It was hard. He knew that some first-year teachers never make it out of the disillusionment phase. Dave Buehrle was a case in point. Samir was still smarting over that train wreck. He had to be careful. Looking over his roster, he could see a few faint signs of smoke. There could be other derailments coming down the track.

He kept running Buehrle's resignation over in his head. Dan Ehrenfeld had told Samir that his roommate Dave was a very religious guy, someone who wanted to do ministry work. If that was true, Samir didn't see how he could have just left his kids. Jessica Miller, a second-year

TFAer who had taught many of Dave's kids the year before, complained bitterly to Samir. She had worked so hard with those students; the idea that they were likely to spend the rest of the school year with a permanent sub was just galling. Samir was really bothered by the thought, too. *If only Dave and his fiancée realized the impact on the students and the other teachers at Locke.*

Samir convinced himself that Dave had quit because of the "fiancée factor." But it was hard not to look at his own role in the disaster. That was, after all, the TFA way. At institute, trainees had been taught about the concept of internal versus external locus-of-control orientation, aspects of personality that TFA believed played a crucial role in teacher success. According to this theory of psychology, the person with an external locus of control believes that outside factors dictate behavior and events. An internal locus-of-control personality is certain that it is within each person's power to determine his own destiny.

TFA knew that the CMs with an external locus of control were apt to cite a host of outside circumstances that militated against student success as a way of absolving themselves of responsibility for results. By contrast, the most effective teachers had internal loci of control. They took full personal responsibility for student achievement, refusing to blame outside factors, such as truancy and lack of parental support, for underperformance.

The early reflective guides submitted by many of Samir's CMs tended to list attendance or school dysfunction as key teacher problems. It was a point of view that Samir struggled to wrest away from them. He urged them to look at the things they could have power over, the areas where they could effect change. That's what Dave should have been doing. It's what Samir was doing now: *What about me? What could I have done to prevent Dave from leaving?*

To be sure, Samir had been struggling with the Co-Investigation model that TFA had just developed. He didn't think it was particularly helpful, and he didn't feel he was especially good at it. The bottom line was: he really didn't know how to have a highly structured conversation and still reach out to CMs with useful suggestions. Samir had the best of intentions, but the copious notes he gave them after classroom observations were seen as more critical than constructive. Some CMs read his comments and wept.

Samir changed his approach. He knew that the new teachers were critical enough of themselves on a daily basis; it was hard for them to internalize criticism from someone else. So he stopped typing out a minute-by-minute replay of what he observed in the classroom. And he started each meeting by noting all the good things he saw going on. He cooled it on the negative comments, jotting down clarifying questions instead.

But it was tough to get corps members to buy in. Among the fifty CMs on his watch, Samir had a few who must have flown in under the radar; they were not giving it their all. And he had neither the pay factor to motivate them nor the fear factor to intimidate them. The district hired them and paid their starting salaries of $37,000. Only the district could fire them. The sole incentive Samir had to offer corps members was the satisfaction of helping kids.

For most, that was enough. They took the job seriously and worked tirelessly. If they weren't totally on board, it was because they had too many other pressing things to do. They considered TFA's post-institute demands a hassle. So their reflective guides ended up being anything but—some gave no thought to the questions or to their answers. Some didn't bother sending data in at all. Too many thought the whole notion of Co-Investigation was nonsense: *Why do we have to do this? Why does the root cause have to be our fault? Why is TFA blaming us?* Samir would explain that Co-Investigation was actually all about self-reflective problem solving. They needed a systematic way of finding the answers to their problems on their own. TFA believed Co-Investigation would help them do that. The CMs weren't going for it.

Hrag seemed almost hostile. When asked to send in his reflective guide, he would sometimes respond in curt single sentences. And in the beginning, he didn't get around to sending in student data, making a true Co-Investigation difficult. Samir could tell that Hrag didn't really trust him. Hrag obviously felt he had already been overevaluated during institute. The guy was worn out and frustrated and defensive. He didn't think his kids were learning, and he wasn't sure it was possible for him to teach them—given that half of them never showed up for class.

Phillip still gave off the vibe that he didn't need Samir's help. He would start off a meeting by saying, "I know people think such and such about me, but . . ." Then he would go on to justify his teaching style and methods. Samir spent most of the hour agreeing with him, but it was as if Phillip couldn't hear him. When Samir did bring up key problems, it was hard to get Phillip to acknowledge teacher causes. It was discouraging; Samir got the impression that Phillip didn't really care if Samir was there or not. That was tough to handle. If there was anyone Samir felt capable of helping, it was another math teacher.

Rachelle was a problem, too. She was having a tough time with classroom management, particularly during fourth period. The story about Dante peeing in her classroom during the lockdown in early September was now part of Locke lore. People felt sorry for Rachelle. *Rachelle* felt sorry for Rachelle—especially since when she returned to the classroom the next morning, no one had cleaned up the mess. Rachelle had to deal with the urine-filled bucket herself.

Samir's round-one visit to her classroom was a disaster. Instead of teaching biology, Rachelle had had her kids doing an acrostic puzzle. It was a Friday, a day when attendance was always low and attention spans especially short. Rachelle hadn't wanted to start a new chapter. So it was a filler day, a day without a real purpose. When Samir asked her what she was doing, Rachelle said "confidence building," and even as she was sputtering out the words, she felt totally lame. Samir sympathized with her plight. Several kids were primary school readers. The rest were not much farther ahead. The kids had biology textbooks, but they were stacked along the walls; no one could read them. Samir urged Rachelle not to lower her standards. She *had* to keep her activities content-related. She *had* to squeeze in some biology.

He had difficulty arranging subsequent meetings with her. She wasn't available at night, so their conversations were always held in her classroom after her last class. Things would inevitably come up—someone would call or poke a head in the door—and she would end up canceling or cutting their sessions short. And she never sent Samir her data. Without evidence of how her students were performing, their conversations were anecdotally driven. Samir fretted that their meetings were not as useful as they might have been, since they never got to plumb the core issues that were hobbling Rachelle as a teacher. When the hour was up, neither party felt particularly satisfied.

Taylor was different. Their meetings were amazing. She was always prepared, and she had the TFA core value of humility in spades. She dutifully sent in her data, and her reflective guides were thoughtful. She was eager to improve, welcomed his input, and, though she might initially resist a suggestion, inevitably embraced it. She was a self-starter, too.

When Samir wasn't around, she reached out to others for help. And though she was stoked about her successes, she was never satisfied with them. She was in relentless pursuit of the mission.

Still, the round-one meeting with her at the beginning of the year had been rocky. The very first thing Taylor said to Samir was "Tell me how to get better." But telling her how to get better wasn't what he had been instructed to do during his one-week training in Houston. He was supposed to be a "thought partner" to Taylor, to help her understand and find a solution to one key issue impeding student progress. It was hard for her—and for the others—to understand why he didn't just give her the concrete help she needed, why he wasn't just feeding her a few tricks of the trade.

Sometimes he didn't have any tricks to offer. After all, his experience as an educator was limited. He had been wildly successful as an eighth-grade math teacher, but he had taught for only two years, and it had been at a very small middle school. He had lots of ideas for his math CMs, but when he came across problems he himself had not encountered, he didn't know what to say. Because he felt especially insecure about helping out special ed or English teachers, he sometimes overcompensated by offering too many suggestions. When that happened, he got pushback from them for being too commanding, not collaborative enough. He felt like he just couldn't win.

It was stressful. Samir found himself endlessly replaying his Co-Investigation conversations in his head and wondering if he had said the right things. He was constantly asking the other five PDs in the L.A. office for their advice. And then, based on their input, he would pester the CMs with phone calls and e-mails telling them the things he should have said and didn't. He was already working lunatic hours, but the more anxious he became, the longer and harder he worked. He was doing three or four observations during the day, then three one-on-one meetings after school that lasted until seven or eight in the evening.

The organization was lean and nimble—or stretched too thin, depending on your view. Overseeing struggling CMs was not Samir's only responsibility. He was assigned to manage a lot of side projects—like setting up recruitment fairs, organizing social events for the L.A. corps, and arranging alumni meet-and-greets. In fact, Samir was actively involved in every aspect of the program right across the continuum: recruitment, selection, matriculation, school placement, support, and alumni affairs. That was cool; he got to fulfill the mission at every stage. But it meant late nights and long weekends. He was being paid $50,000 a year for seventy-hour workweeks. He was as overwhelmed as the recruits he supported.

Of course, he was being evaluated himself. Felicia Cuesta and another member of the L.A. staff sat in on some of his early one-hour Co-Investigation meetings. He would spend an inordinate amount of time reviewing his observation notes with the CM before launching into a detailed discussion of three or four problems that stood out. Then, with his bosses looking on, he and the CM would chart out causes and solutions for all the issues. It was way too much for one meeting—everything got muddled.

Cuesta asked him why he conducted his meetings that way; had he been trained wrong? Samir insisted the problem was the system: Co-Investigation wasn't a good model for supporting struggling CMs, especially CMs who were already resentful of the added burden TFA placed on them by requiring them to write reflective guides and collect student data. The novice teachers had too many other things to attend to. What they needed from their PD were practical solutions to pressing problems.

Samir was dispatched to observe several other PDs who were having more success with Co-Investigation. And he began to get it. Over the Christmas break and into the new semester, he did a fair amount of self-reflection. TFA had received the midterm surveys on corps member satisfaction. Cuesta presented Samir with the feedback from the fifty CMs under his management. He didn't exactly get rave reviews. In the open-ended comments, Rachelle said that she "didn't feel much interaction with TFA on a personal level." Hrag noted that "there is help . . . but thinly spread." Taylor said that the CMs "often do not feel emotionally supported by TFA." Phillip didn't offer any comments at all.

Samir was crushed. He took the comments as thinly veiled rebukes. He felt like a failure, and he didn't know what to do to turn things around. The year was halfway over, two of the four observation rounds were in the can, and his reviews were lukewarm at best. Some of the CMs he had spent the most time with marked "somewhat agree" when asked if the PD had been very helpful. Others, whom he had felt he might have been neglecting, gave him high marks. Samir felt superfluous.

And nervous. He knew that even though some CMs just dashed off responses with very little thought, the CM survey was one of the most scrutinized pieces of information within TFA. Recruit feedback often led to changes within the program itself—and promotions for the PDs deemed most effective. TFA put a high premium on CM satisfaction. An analysis of the significant gains data overlaid on the CM survey results indicated that the most satisfied corps members tended to be the ones making the most significant gains. By contrast, dissatisfied corps members actually posed a threat to the mission; they were unlikely to stay allied with the movement as alumni and, in fact, could hurt recruitment and development through negative word of mouth. So the results of the corps satisfaction survey were demoralizing for Samir. He may have been one of the organization's most effective teachers, but he was nowhere near one of its most effective PDs.

Instinctively, he began to think critically about what his niche was. Samir had the most CMs to attend to, but his were also the most clustered. At Locke alone, he managed twenty-two teachers. He realized that the teachers at Locke had many more resources available to them than most other CMs. The Locke crew had access to a specially hired new-teacher coach and attended compulsory professional development meetings with literacy coaches from UCLA. Plus, they had a lot of TFA alums still teaching at Locke—and they had one another. Samir's advice, then, was not always necessary. If CMs needed something, they could get it down the hall. Samir decided that he had to be more interactive with his Locke teachers. He needed to be more encouraging on the front end, to relate to them more and critique them less.

Samir was not alone in feeling demoralized. Typically, teachers begin to pull out of the disillusionment phase after Christmas. For many in the Locke contingent, that wasn't happening.

Taylor had spent much of her extended break "awfulizing."

It didn't really make sense, because she actually ended 2005 on a high. The vibe in her classroom was cool; the energy was good. The kids were really into her. Taylor found it strange. She wasn't that much older than her students—she almost wanted them to call her by her first name. The girls especially liked to hang out in her room, and she liked talking to them. They wanted to know all about her, and the world from which she came. They asked about her boyfriend and about college, and if she went to football games and parties. She told them all about the beer-keg stands at USC where students, suspended by their legs, drank beer upside down.

She wanted to be honest with them. She decided she would answer any question they asked. Except one. If they wanted to know about ditching, that was another story.

She was getting lots of positive feedback from the school. One assistant vice principal, Mr. Yette, had asked her to take over a twelfth-grade English class from a longtime tenured teacher. It was all hush-hush. He said that he wanted to make sure that all the seniors had portfolios and would graduate in June. Taylor took that as a compliment. The two UCLA literacy coaches also saw the promise in Taylor and took her under their wings. Chad Soleo was happy to hear all the good reports. One of his trusted colleagues literally gushed whenever she visited Taylor's bungalow. Taylor knew it was tough to keep new teachers, and she appreciated all the kudos, but even she thought it was all a little over-the-top: *I could tell them I'm gonna write "shit" and "fuck" all over the walls and they might say, "What a good idea!"*

Samir was the exception. He spooked her. When she saw him at the one-hundred-days celebration at the Hollywood nightclub in early fall, he had a drink in his hand and was talking and laughing. Not long after that, he came into her classroom, said two words, and left after forty-five minutes.

She was giving a grammar lesson the day Samir came in, and even as she was lecturing, she knew he'd be tripping out about it. The lecture was too long, and the lesson that followed wasn't thematically linked. She couldn't bring herself to read the e-mail he sent afterward. She knew it would get her down, and then she wouldn't want to meet him for the follow-up. Samir was pretty amazing. His notes were minute-by-minute, and he'd write things like "12:35, student's head on desk." It was scary and nerve-wracking whenever anyone came in to observe her. But when it was TFA, she felt like the weight of the world and all the poor children of America were resting on her performance. Again and again she thought: *TFA is the parent you cannot please. You can jump through hoops and still not get there and not know what to do to make them happy. What if my numbers don't go up? What if they go down?*

On the day before school let out for Christmas, Samir brought his supervisors into Taylor's room to observe *him*. He had called at twelve-thirty that day to warn her—and to ask Taylor to e-mail her data and fill him in on what she wanted to talk about. When they showed up at three-thirty, she was listening to Prince at full volume and the room was abuzz with kids coming in and out. Samir walked in looking like the consummate professional and proceeded to do a great job. He was so smart and so articulate! He was able to pinpoint things Taylor hadn't even thought of, and he gave her very concrete, very specific things to do. She was so grateful for his help. She talked him up to his bosses. He was an amazingly talented guy. He was growing on her.

That night she was scheduled to meet the man who had "adopted" her through Teach For America's Sponsor a Teacher program. Sponsor a Teacher is one of TFA's major fund-raising efforts directed at individuals and small companies, and it accounted for 16 percent of the organization's funding base in 2006. SAT, as it is called, requires a donation of at least $5,000 to help defray the annual $12,500 cost of recruiting, selecting, training, and supporting a corps member. During summer institute, corps members had been asked if they were willing to be sponsored. Taylor signed right up. Based on a short spiel she wrote about herself, TFA had matched her with John Wong, a young guy who worked for the Capital Group, a giant investment management firm based in Los Angeles.

Taylor had looked forward to the meeting with Wong. It was being held at Loyola Marymount. Taylor knew exactly how it would go. Like everything else that TFA did, it would be professional—indeed, beyond professional. The affair would start on time and end when scheduled. There would be drinks, food tables, and the obligatory speakers. From there, it would be a sorority rush. Having been a Greek at USC, she had the rush down. She knew exactly what was required of her. It was a connection thing. She understood that the donor wanted to see her, in the same way that people who send money to some poor kid in Africa or Asia always want a photograph. And if they could converse with her, all the better. One of the L.A. coordinators had called and then e-mailed the major talking points to her. TFA wanted to keep everyone on message. The sponsor would want to hear all the good things his money was doing; the teachers should try to accentuate the positive.

When Taylor got the cue (a look from one of the coordinators), she turned it on. She told Wong all about her TFA experience at Locke, regaling him with classroom anecdotes and showing him pictures of her kids that she had taken with her cell phone. She told him the reason she had joined—that she had wanted to do something meaningful, something that would give her a lot of responsibility and make her proud. And she asked about his reasons for donating. She was touched by his humility. He confided that he wished he had done something similar, that he was in awe of what she was doing. Taylor was perfectly capable of faking her enthusiasm, but she didn't have to. She spoke from the heart. She was genuinely interested to meet someone who had given five thousand dollars—not because he needed a tax write-off, like so many people she knew in Santa Barbara, but because he had found a cause that he truly believed in. She invited her sponsor to come to Locke to see her teach and meet her kids, and she thanked him for his generosity.

Afterward she met Mackey, Hrag, and Rachelle at Sharkeez. She had recently been hanging out with Mackey some—they both worked in the bungalows on the edge of campus and shared a lot of the same students. And she had always liked Hrag, though she had heard he was a bit of a ladies' man. But it was the first time she had ever been out with Rachelle, and she really enjoyed getting to know her. Rachelle seemed to have it all in perspective. She worked hard, but she made it look easy. She wasn't obsessively driven like so many other TFA women Taylor knew. So it was fun. Taylor had given up drinking—she suffered from vertigo and alcohol made her feel sick—but the others had a few. Taylor thought that Mackey might have a little crush on Rachelle, but it didn't seem to be going anywhere. When Mackey said he wanted to leave, Hrag drove him back to the apartment they shared in Hermosa Beach, just down the road. Taylor went along for the ride, and Rachelle headed home. Taylor ended up spending the night on Hrag's couch. And her car, which was parked illegally, got towed.

But it didn't matter. It was the last day of school before break. She tied her mane of chestnut hair in a ponytail topped with a black headband, put on a festive red velvet jacket, and turned every one of her classes that day into a Christmas party. It was probably a no-no as far as TFA was concerned, but she decided not to teach. She wrote "MERRY CHRISTMAS" across the whiteboard, put on some music, and watched as her kids had dance-offs. She felt great. The karma in room A22 was good, and she was leaving the next morning for a family vacation in Mexico.

But over the break, the ebullience gave way to anxiety. She couldn't sleep at night. When she was able to rest, she woke up with her heart racing. She was thinking bad thoughts, generating awful, negative emotions.

A lot of it was eating-disorder stuff—wanting to be perfect and not being able to let go of that. She didn't want to have that negative thinking in her head. It was such a weight. But there it was: she was awfulizing.

Thinking back, she realized things had been tough for her since Halloween. She had been waking up at 4 a.m., unable to breathe and worried about what would happen when she got to school. She had weird dreams. One time she dreamed that they had bused a whole bunch of white kids into Locke; she was teaching white kids! In her real life, she couldn't imagine ever teaching white kids. How could she?

Her dad talked her down. He was the person she spoke to the most—about everything. Having been a teacher himself, he empathized with her situation and was a font of wisdom. He was the one who told her early on to draw a line between her professional and private lives. He told her not to bring work home—even if it meant staying at school until five or six to finish up. And when she was worried that she wasn't improving her kids' reading levels, he was the one who said, "Look for the smallest successes and hold on to them." So, during the break, when she was driving to see her boyfriend and awfulizing all the way, she turned to her father for help. Over the car phone, he reminded her that *she* was creating the anxiety, that *she* was generating the awful ideas. She could also generate positive ideas. "You need to find the positive and make that your reality," he advised. "Every day go in there and find something that makes it work for you."

Her best friend since first grade, Allisha, said just about the same thing. She suggested that Taylor start reciting daily affirmations. She needed to ask for peace and give her fears to a higher authority. She needed to "let go and let God." She recited the AA prayer, and suddenly it made sense: "God grant me the serenity to accept the things I cannot change, courage to change the things I can, and wisdom to know the difference." It was like an epiphany: *I should focus on what I can control and see where the chips fall, and I am going to be happy and not let it get to me.*

From then on, she did her affirmations every day. She would walk around her apartment saying out loud: "Today I choose to have peace in my life. I do not choose fear. My students need me. I'm happy." And by the time she got to school, she would be okay. She was more than okay: she was very happy. She loved the job. She was doing a good thing—not perfectly, but it was the right thing for her.

. . .

Phillip could have done with some of the same bucking up. He felt like he had PMS. He was depressed, and he found himself tearing up easily. It happened to him every two months or so. He would spiral down and feel awful for some days, then cycle back up and feel good for weeks on end, only to inevitably fall again into another short depression.

When he returned to school after the Christmas break, he thought he was well rested. But, in fact, he came back burned out. And the kids seemed rowdier than usual. Over the break, graffiti artists had been out in force. The entire façade of the school entrance had been tagged. Inside, Phillip caught kids gambling in the hallways. It probably had something to do with it being the end of the semester—the kids figured they didn't have much to lose. The bells were bonkers, too. For some periods they would ring three times; for others they didn't ring at all.

He had a lot to accomplish before the end of the semester. He had slowed down instruction to help with comprehension and retention, but that came at a cost. His classes were behind. Even so, he determined to push ahead with his plan to do more activities to promote hands-on learning. On the first Tuesday back, Phillip introduced a lesson on corresponding parts by giving each student a protractor, a work sheet, and a triangle. As the kids chattered, he warned them that there would be no more activities in the future if they couldn't come in, be silent, and follow directions.

"I want you to put your hands together," he said. "I didn't say put your lips together! When we're talking about corresponding parts we're talking about the relationship between two things—matching up. When you put your hands together, what's matching up? Corresponding fingers! Are all your fingers identical? Do they all match up the same size?"

The kids shouted: "No!"

Phillip corrected them. "Your hands should be the same size," he said. "So they are congruent. We are going to take this idea and relate it to shapes." He told them to start doing their work sheets. He wanted them to match triangles by finding corresponding angles and sides.

A few minutes later Dr. Wells came in and sat down in the back of the room next to Phillip's desk. He watched as Phillip modeled what he wanted the kids to do on the classroom's overhead projector. As they worked, Phillip moved to the whiteboard in the front of the classroom, where he began to review the problems. He finished up the lesson by reiterating the concept and reciting the principles that they had discovered by manipulating the protractors and triangles. Moments before the class ended, Dr. Wells left the room. On Phillip's desk was a yellow sheet of paper that was folded in two. Dr. Wells had written "Mr. Gedeon" on the outside; there was a smiley face below.

The entire time that Wells was in his classroom Phillip was thinking: *Why is he here? What is he doing? What is he writing down?* Phillip figured the principal had been in his room more than ten times since the year began, three to five times in the first week alone. He felt uncomfortable. And this third-period class was one of his wildest, not the class you necessarily wanted your boss to observe. It was the one period of the day when people would be perfectly justified in criticizing Phillip's classroom management. It was heavily African American male, and Phillip ran a slightly looser ship than usual. Though profane language was forbidden in room 301, there were a couple of black students who habitually swore in class. They would immediately self-correct with "My bad, my bad," and they never used the words maliciously. At first Phillip addressed the issue every time he heard a curse word. But after a while, he let it go. He saw the other side of the two offenders—he saw the sweetness in Andrew and the intelligence in Lemarr. If he couldn't get past the bad language, he realized he would miss so much in them—and they were capable of doing such great things!

Phillip didn't read the yellow note. He never read classroom observations right away. He preferred to wait until he had some distance and time to reflect on his own performance before reading someone else's take on it. Phillip was unhappy with the way the lesson had unfolded.

That afternoon he was about ten minutes late for the faculty meeting. He dreaded going to them. At best, they were boring, a waste of time. At worst, they degenerated into ugly shouting matches. Phillip would never forget the first faculty meeting of the year. When the union rep challenged Dr. Wells and became disruptive, he threw her out of Hobbs Hall. That set the tone for the year. So Phillip was in no hurry to get to the first meeting after Christmas break. When he slipped into his seat, Wells was talking about some teacher he had seen that day. He was reminding the staff to have the day's agenda posted on the board and objectives identified for all the students to see. Phillip always did that, so he tuned it all out. Later, when they broke into smaller department meetings, Wells came by, put his hand on Phillip's shoulder, and asked the group, "Have you seen Mr. Gedeon teach? You need to. He gives administrators like me hope. I saw a master teacher at work. I was utterly amazed." Then to Phillip he said: "Keep up the good work!"

When Dr. Wells left, the teasing began. It was embarrassing. Phillip felt awkward around Wells. The guy was always smiling at him. And Phillip didn't want to let him down. The next day, another teacher stopped him to tell him what Wells had said in the beginning of the faculty meeting, before Phillip arrived. Wells didn't name Phillip then, but it wasn't hard to figure out which math teacher he was talking about. Wells explained that he had intended to stay for a only a few minutes, before seeing the science class next door, but he became so engaged in the math lesson that he stayed. "He did not say that!" returned Phillip.

"I'm telling you, he did," the other teacher insisted. "He was speaking about you!"

At first he was blown away by the praise. Then it began to bother him. He knew that when one teacher gets singled out for praise, the others get resentful. It had happened to other teachers at Locke. When you have shown results, people don't like you—either because they can't do as well or because they can, and do, and are not similarly recognized. Phillip didn't need to be praised in front of a crowd. He already had a reputation for speaking his mind—and for not being a team player. It would have been much better if Wells had taken him aside and said those things privately.

But what really got to him that week was the realization that, at Locke, he really was considered one of the best teachers. That was crazy! *If I'm one of the best, what does that say about everyone else?* He knew his kids were learning and achieving. But he was a first-year teacher; he had so much more to learn. He was only doing what should be the norm for every teacher: setting high expectations, holding his kids accountable, and working his butt off. There was nothing amazing about it. It should have been standard operating procedure.

That was one of the problems. There were no standard operating procedures at Locke. There were no systems at all. The school wasn't set up for success.

Classes needed to be smaller and longer. Kids needed to be tracked. The students failing all their classes needed to be doing double of everything: English two times a day, math two times a day. If a kid couldn't write a history paper or read a textbook, why give him history? First teach him how to read. When he was up to level, then he could double up on science or history.

Someone had to stand up and say no to the status quo. The number of kids just falling through the cracks was breaking his heart. By the end of that first week back, Phillip was drained. He walked around his class-room in a daze. When he finally did get it together to go home, he had a bite to eat and went to bed. It was eight-thirty.

Why am I here? What can I do? How do I give both myself and my students hope?

Once she finished work on her IEPs, Rachelle did just what she promised herself she would do over the Christmas break: nothing. She relaxed, saw a few friends, chilled. But she found herself thinking about her kids. She wasn't stressing over how she was going to teach them mitosis. She was wondering what they were doing for Christmas, and worrying, too: *I hope they have family around. I hope they're happy.*

They were thinking about her, too, because a few of them phoned. One boy, Mario, a lovely Hispanic kid, called and said, "Hi, Miss." When Rachelle asked who was speaking, he insisted that she guess. Rachelle got it wrong; she thought it was a girl on the other end of the line. "Is everything okay?" she asked.

"I'm gonna ride my bike," he replied. "I just wanted to say hi."

It made her feel good. *That's what I've got going for me. I'm not good at special ed or teaching. In fact, I'm pretty bad. But I think most of them know I care.*

But she knew that wasn't enough. She had to make changes in her classroom. She had spent the first few months on the scientific method. She was bored with the material; she could only imagine how the kids felt. She was going to pick up the pace. At first she didn't know how much the kids could do, and she didn't want to stress them out. Now she knew they were perfectly capable of achieving. There was so much to learn in biology that was cool—Samir had made that point the last time he was in. He said that her kids were learning. And he had some sugges-tions that he thought could help them even more.

She was going to get better organized, too. She had recently connected with a second-year TFAer named Jill Greitzer, who taught special ed algebra to many of the same students Rachelle taught. Rachelle went to see Miss G teach and was really impressed with how she ran her classroom. She decided to adopt many of the techniques she saw.

Miss G was into setting small goals. She had a daily activity log in which students rated their performance in class. Then she compared their assessments with her own, added up the totals, and gave the kids daily grades. That way they could see what happened when they didn't come to school and what happened when they worked hard.

Rachelle was going to get stricter, too, even though it was against her nature. Like Miss G, she was going to have the kids sign contracts. And there would be new rules. She wasn't going to open the door to kids who were late for class. Under the new behavior plan, kids would be given classroom jobs; there would be rewards. Twenty tickets got you a lunch with Rachelle. The big prize was dinner. Other people coming into her room might think: *What the hell is going on here? It looks like a circus.* But she was going to hang on to the small gains and remember that these boys were just kids.

She vowed to work harder herself. Truth be told, she felt like she'd been slacking off.

She ditched her plan to teach literacy. She didn't know how to do it. And it didn't appear that anyone else did, either. Locke's UCLA literacy coach for science devoted two entire professional development days to "read-alouds," a strategy to aid comprehension. It was maddening. Rachelle got the concept immediately; she didn't need to waste two days reviewing it. Besides, her kids were not just "below level." She had kids who didn't even make phonemic connections, who didn't know the sounds certain letters made. She could spend three days just teaching the word "cat."

Her four-to-nine evening credentialing classes at Cal State, Dominguez Hills, twice a week weren't any more helpful. For the most part, they were a waste of time. She couldn't understand how anyone could major in education. It seemed that if she had really paid attention, she would have learned everything she needed to know at the five-week summer institute. In fact, even that could have been condensed!

What was particularly upsetting was that as useless as she thought the credentialing program was, she felt like she was falling behind. Her dad suggested that it was probably because she was exhausted. And that was true: she knew from experience that tired kids had trouble focusing. It was no different for adult students.

At one point, early on, it looked like she was going to get kicked out of the credentialing program over some bureacratic snafu. *Sweet! That frees up my nights!* But her mother put on her attorney's hat and informed her that without being in a credentialing program, she could get fired for teaching under false pretenses. State law required that every teacher of record be credentialed or working toward a credential. "You don't want to get fired, do you?" her mother asked.

"Yes, yes, I do want to get fired!" she replied. "I really do!"

She really didn't. She liked her job. And she loved the kids. She wanted to expand their horizons, to give them experiences beyond Watts. But even that proved difficult. She had signed up to take a handpicked group of students to see a play in Pasadena. It was disappointing. Only one kid showed up. And when she arranged through some friends with Hollywood connections to have Kenyon play basketball with Snoop Dogg, he was a no-show.

Then, one day, she got a call from someone she had met at the Palm Springs science conference that she and Hrag had attended a few months before. Rachelle had signed her name to every flyer she found at the conference—she was looking for freebies for her kids. One of the things she apparently signed up for was a field trip. When the phone rang, the voice on the other end wanted to know if Rachelle was serious about taking her kids to an outdoor learning camp. The shortest, cheapest program his company offered was a three-day academic camping trip to Catalina, the biggest of the Channel Islands, located just off the coast of southern California. The cost was $190 per child, and the instruction was pitched to a fifth-grade level. There was an opening at the end of May.

It sounded perfect. Most of her kids had never been on a boat—or even to the beach, though it was only a twenty-minute ride from school. Most had never been *anywhere* beyond Watts. Rachelle's mind began to race. *How cool would that be? But is it feasible? Is it even worth doing? Where will the money come from?*

She began to plan. Maybe she would get online and apply to donorschoose.org for a grant. Or maybe the school would pay. Or maybe not; there would almost certainly be liability issues. But Rachelle would argue that the kids who were allowed to go would be carefully chosen.

She was not going to take anyone who could potentially embarrass her or the school. She'd start the ball rolling and set good citizenship as one of the prerequisites for being included.

She knew she could take only a limited number of students. And as far as she was concerned, they were all going to be from the special ed department. No offense to Vanessa Morris, the science department chair, but her general ed kids were not welcome. The last science field trip had been to the aquarium in Long Beach. Hrag's kids had all gotten to go. Special ed kids had not. They were not on the radar at Locke. Rachelle's students were second-class citizens in a lot of other ways—they didn't need to be put down at school, too. So, no, this would be a special trip for special ed. She'd ask Jill Greitzer if she wanted to come along. Between the two of them, they would decide who'd be on the boat.

There was, of course, the little matter of running it by Dr. Wells. His first reaction was positive. He said the field trip would be a great use of Title I money, the federal funds granted to schools whose children live below the poverty line. Rachelle nearly jumped for joy. She intended to surprise the kids once all the details were worked out. But she couldn't help herself—she was so excited that she told them. They were going to Catalina!

CHAPTER NINE

The Corps

Every Tuesday at 9 a.m., like clockwork, Samir Bolar and the other Los Angeles program directors met in the conference room in TFA's Los Angeles regional headquarters downtown. The TFA offices were on the ninth floor of a twelve-story building. The first thing Samir saw when he stepped off the elevator and into the office was a banner printed with Teach For America's core values. The vision statement "One day, all children in this nation will have the opportunity to attain an excellent education" was written along the bottom.

The L.A. suite also posted the Teach For America Los Angeles time line, a snapshot of TFA's history there over the past fifteen years, and a not-too-subtle reminder to staff and visitors alike that Teach For America is an organization that keeps score.

Los Angeles was one of the six original charter sites in 1990, when TFA fielded its first class of five hundred corps members; it also hosted the first summer training institute, a tumultuous affair, as disorganized and chaotic as it was inspirational, according to founder Wendy Kopp. That inaugural year, close to 100 recruits were assigned to Los Angeles. Over the remaining years of the decade, the size of the L.A. corps waxed and waned with the organization's fortunes. In 2002, Los Angeles had

500 alumni. By 2005, when Hrag, Taylor, Phillip, and Rachelle entered the corps, TFA had more than doubled the incoming Los Angeles teachers to 223, making a total of 276 CMs teaching more than 22,000 students in 82 schools in the Los Angeles area. Most of the TFAers were employed by LAUSD. But in a district with more than 35,000 teachers, their numbers were tiny.

And the achievement gap in L.A.—and in virtually every other region in which TFA operated—persisted. "I think if you look at the overall statistics, you will not see a significant narrowing of the gap," conceded Kopp as the organization began its second five-year growth push. "That's one of the reasons we don't feel satisfied. That fuels our sense of urgency."

Los Angeles was exactly the kind of city TFA was built to serve. In few regions in the country was the gap more pernicious than in the City of Angels, home to the second-largest school district in the country. In the 2005 National Assessment of Educational Progress (NAEP), the kids in LAUSD's low-income areas were three grade levels behind their wealthier peers, and seven times less likely to graduate from college. The district's dropout rates were among the highest in the state, test scores among the lowest. Governor Arnold Schwarzenegger characterized the way LAUSD was run as "horrible." An independent audit of the troubled district in 2007 concurred; the 115-page report described a pervasive and shocking lack of accountability throughout the district on all levels.

But Los Angeles had deep pockets. Of the $2.6 million raised from funding sources in the Los Angeles region in 2005, 31 percent came from individual contributors to TFA's Sponsor a Teacher program. Perennials on Hollywood's A-list—Casey Wasserman, Jeffrey and Marilyn Katzenberg, Paul Newman, Jerry and Linda Bruckheimer, and Sherry Lansing—were among them.

Much had changed since Los Angeles had hosted the first four summer institutes. Wendy Kopp traveled to the West Coast often then, mining for gold. In those days, Teach For America's financial health was precarious; too often it lurched from paycheck to paycheck, forcing Kopp to spend much of her time raising money. She used the same tactics at TFA that she had employed at the struggling business magazine she headed as an undergrad at Princeton: she went right to the top. In her book, *One Day, All Children,* she recounts sneaking into one of Mike Milken's lectures at the UCLA business school. Afterward she introduced herself. Milken was pleased to meet her and offered to fly her back to the East Coast on his private jet the next day. They spent the three-and-a-half-hour transcontinental journey in earnest debate. Nearing touch-down, she asked the infamous financier and philanthropist for a million dollars. The money would make the difference between life and death for Teach For America, she told him. Milken seemed inclined to write the check but in the end didn't pony up. Others did—against all odds.

"She goes to where her fear is," explains Greg Good, an alum who was TFA's Los Angeles executive director in the mid-1990s. Good re-members traveling around L.A. in his Honda Accord hatchback hitting up the city's top guns for cash, his long dark hair flowing, a cigarette hanging out of his mouth, with Kopp, dressed in business attire, riding shotgun. By then the early seed money from the foundations had dried up. TFA was forced to turn to private funders, corporations, and the gov-ernment to survive. Kopp became a traveling saleswoman. She bunked in Good's Venice pad and arose each morning at five for her daily run. Then she spent the rest of the day and night shaking money out of trees. She excelled at it, but, as Good recalls, she wasn't necessarily comfortable with it. Inevitably, he says, just before walking into a high-level meeting, Kopp would turn to him and confide: "I am scared to death." And then she would walk through the door, deliver a compelling pitch, and, cool as a cucumber, conclude with "I'd love to see you come in at a million dol-lars." The first time she did it, Good nearly fell out of his chair. She was like a laser beam, plowing right through her fear, drawn to the challenge. She didn't always succeed, but she never let TFA fail.

It came perilously close. In 1994, Kopp recalls in her book, there was open rebellion at TFA's summer institute when she invited questions from the corps at a meeting midway through the training. Angry recruits stood on chairs, shouting out their complaints. Among the many: Kopp herself had never taught. Kopp suffered, observes Good, from the pedestal syn-drome. Because she was so engaged in the business of just keeping TFA alive, she wasn't present at every on-the-ground team meeting. The result was that she was seen by some as remote, removed from the trenches, a kind of figurehead—revered but not loved. Because her head was so far above the parapet, she made an easy target when the going got rough.

In the early days, it got rough a lot. Kopp maintained her cool throughout the institute ordeal, now remembered as "the night of a thousand suggestions," but there were more assaults ahead. It was just weeks later that Linda Darling-Hammond published her scorching analysis of TFA, "Who Will Speak for the Chidren? How TFA Hurts Urban Schools and Students," in *Phi Delta Kappan.*

"It is clear from the evidence," wrote Darling-Hammond, "that TFA is bad policy and bad education. It is bad for the recruits because they are ill-prepared. . . . It is bad for the schools in which they teach, because the recruits often create staffing disruptions and drains on school resources. . . . It is bad for the children because they are often poorly taught. . . . Finally, TFA is bad for teaching. By clinging to faulty assumptions about what teachers need to know and by producing so many teaching failures, it undermines the profession's efforts to raise standards and create accountability."

The blistering critique from such a big name in the field of education caused some of the organization's major supporters to balk and cast a pall over the efficacy of the mission that would last for years to come. When the fiscal year drew to a close at the end of September, TFA had a $1.2 million deficit.

It was make-or-break time. Kopp and her top money man, Richard Barth, who later became her husband, cut two million dollars from the budget, resulting in the termination of the sixty program directors. TEACH!, a TFA initiative set up to help school districts recruit and develop teaching talent, was shuttered. Another TFA start-up called the Learning Project, a summer school program headed by TFA's very first hire, Daniel Oscar, had already left the TFA stable to become an independent nonprofit. Having finished pruning, Kopp launched a three-year plan to transform TFA into a "stable, thriving institution."

The years of struggle had taken a toll on morale and tainted the mission's culture. Kopp moved to define the organization's core operating principles. Over time, the foundation of how TFA works was articulated in five core values: relentless pursuit of results; sense of possibility; disciplined thought; respect and humility; and integrity.

Kopp knew that in order to succeed, TFA needed better management—and it had to start at the top. She herself had to become a much more effective manager of a much improved product. But she was a young twenty-something who was learning on the job. And she didn't have the stereotypic personality of a dynamic leader. There was no flash, no flourish to Wendy Kopp. No memorable anecdotes, either—except those that underscored a clarity of focus and an unshakable confidence that caused her to work harder and longer than anyone else around her. Kopp, a runner of marathons, could go the distance. Oscar recalls one particularly exhausting night in the early days when everyone was crashing, and Kopp sent them all home at 1 a.m. to get some much needed rest. She stayed on, alone in an empty New York high-rise, endlessly making copies at the point when others on the team didn't have the strength to push the start button.

"She can't be described as charismatic," notes Dr. Bressler, her Princeton thesis advisor. "She's not eloquent, and she doesn't have the attributes associated with extraordinary leadership. What she does have is a kind of calm conviction that the thing is possible, and she conveys that. She's almost amused at a recitation of obstacles."

She was new to managing, but she embodied the key TFA operating principle of "constant learning." An autodidact on business management, she read voraciously and picked the brains of every smart person she encountered. Like the organization she led, she was obsessed with getting better. (Ironically, she consulted with Linda Darling-Hammond in the very beginning, when TFA was not much more than a senior thesis.) Nick Glover, a vice chairman for Whittle Communications, advised Kopp on how to structure the organization and management team in the very early nineties. By the end of the decade, TFA had developed formal working relationships with a number of consulting firms, including the Monitor Group, which assisted in the development of the 2005 and 2010 growth plans, and McKinsey & Company, which helped with selection and recruitment. Several of the outside consultants eventually took jobs with TFA—including Matt Kramer, from McKinsey, who was named president in 2007.

According to members of her top management team, Kopp was strongly influenced by the writing of Jim Collins, author of the bestselling books on business management *Built to Last* and *Good to Great.* In *Good to Great and the Social Sectors,* Collins describes a great organization as one that "delivers superior performance and makes a distinctive impact over a long time." He also notes the hallmarks of great leaders: they are ambitious for their institution—not themselves—and possess a paradoxical blend of personal humility and intense professional will. The goals TFA announced when launching the 2010 five-year plan read like Collins's definition of a great institution. As for his take on the distinguishing characteristics of great leaders, Kopp has them in spades say those close to her—and she looks for those qualities in the people she hires.

That doesn't mean she—or the organization she heads—is "nice" in the conventional sense of the word. " 'Nice' is not part of the self-concept," observes Matt Kramer. "Civility and humility are there, but that's not the same thing as nice. Nice is saying it matters more how people *feel* than how they *perform*, and whether they deliver results. Nice is: 'Here's what we're working on, we didn't get to where we're going, but that's okay.'

"That's not the way it is at TFA. At TFA, if something doesn't happen, it's terrible, we think about what we did wrong, and we really dive in and change things because we hate when we don't deliver results. And if somebody says, 'That hurts my feelings,' well, the thinking would be: *It's not about you, it's about delivering results. You don't let your personal emotions get in the way of results.* High-performing organizations are not *nice* places to work, but they are very *challenging* places to work, and because of that, they attract people who like challenges. The question is always: What's good the for kids?"

Richard Riordan, mayor of Los Angeles from 1993 to 2001 and California secretary for education under Arnold Schwarzenegger, was on the TFA advisory committee early on, and he agrees. He and Kopp were fellow Princeton alums; the idea for Teach For America struck him as perfect. Riordan compares Kopp to Mother Teresa, who—he is quick to point out—may have been one of the most giving persons on earth but not necessarily the nicest.

"Wendy wasn't some sweet bouncing young girl that God sent down from a star," he recalls. "She was a tough doer who really believed in what she was doing. To be a champion, sometimes you have to be pretty tough, and that describes Wendy."

According to Jerry Hauser, an alum who taught in Compton, California, in the inaugural corps and who returned to TFA in 1999, after law school and a stint at McKinsey, to preside over the first five-year growth plan, Kopp is a caring person who remembers birthdays and takes a real interest in others' lives. But that's not what sets her apart as a leader.

What makes her unique is her "relentless pursuit of results," he says. "She sets goals nobody thinks can ever happen, and she runs into obstacles, and she persists. The relentless pursuit of results, that's the phrase that best captures Wendy."

Hauser recalls a particularly tense board meeting at the end of the first year of the expansion plan that was "classic Wendy." It was the week after the 9/11 attacks, and things seemed pretty bleak. It didn't look like there was going to be a lot of funding money around; the stock market had tanked by 25 percent. The board appeared ready to rethink the expansion. Then Kopp spoke. She said if ever there was a time to keep growing and going, it was then. It was critical that TFA do it for the country. She argued that the original plan was sound; TFA should stick to it. Some members of the board were skeptical and warned that they would keep a close eye on progress; if they didn't like what they were seeing, they would ask TFA to change course. That never became an issue. The expansion unfolded pretty much as planned.

Kopp had called on that same steely determination when she tried to steady the TFA ship in the mid-nineties. After slashing the budget, TFA launched a three-year plan to broaden its funding base, deepen its management bench, and build its reputation. It also decided to get some more grown-ups involved in the mission by strengthening its national board and creating regional boards. Especially after the Linda Darling-Hammond crisis, Kopp realized a bunch of twenty-five-year-olds couldn't do the job entirely on their own—they needed friends in high places.

For a while, it looked as if Kopp's resolve to right her listing organization might have come too late. The federal government, which in 1994 had given TFA a $2 million grant as a member of the newly created network of community-service organizations called AmeriCorps, was not convinced of TFA's viability. In the spring of 1995, the Corporation for National and Community Service threatened to deny renewal of the AmeriCorps grant unless TFA cut another $1 million from its already skeletal budget and agreed to accept the government's $5,000 a year education awards for recruits. Kopp said yes, but even with the government's infusion of $2 million and pledges of another half million dollars, TFA still needed another $150,000 to survive.

It was the summer of 1995, and for the first time in the six years of TFA's existence, Wendy Kopp broke down in tears during the local directors meeting in Houston. "She cracked," recalls Good, who tends to speak in military metaphors when discussing TFA. "There had been a deluge of volleys—Linda Darling-Hammond, AmeriCorps, and the financial factors, with Wendy flying all over the place begging for money—and it all came to a head. Though she had an amazing capacity to not take things personally, and had withstood so many attacks through the years, I think she finally felt the weight of the personal attacks." Good remembers that Kopp was addressing the group when suddenly she just stopped talking. He had to pause for a second and think: *Is Wendy crying?* Then she walked out of the room. Good caught up with her.

"I will go to war for Teach For America," he said, surprising himself with the intensity of his own feelings of loyalty to Kopp and TFA. When Kopp returned to the meeting, she was still teary-eyed, and she apologized for that. Now, standing before them, the show of confidence was over. The personal bravura had disappeared. Kopp told the gathering of the financial crisis at hand. As Good recalls, she sent out a very powerful message through her tears. "She said we had to change. Period. Because if we didn't, we would not survive."

That was a turning point. By the end of the conference, Kopp had managed to scrape the money together. More important, she had rallied the troops. The so-called dark years were over. TFA had a big goal and a detailed plan for how to reach it. Kopp and her team took off on a relentless pursuit of results.

By the time TFA celebrated its tenth anniversary in 2000, the financial woes that had plagued the early years had been put to rest; the organization had been operating on a surplus for four successive years. Applications had more than doubled from the all-time low of fewer than 2,000 in 1996 to 4,100 in 2000. American VIPs such as Oprah Winfrey, Henry Kissinger, and football coach Mike Ditka—as well as CEOs from America's top corporations—had been lining up since 1997 to be guest teachers during the organization's annual "Teach For America Week." And Wendy Kopp, hailed by *Time* magazine in 1994 as one of the country's most promising young leaders, was given the unofficial Washington imprimatur when President Bill Clinton invited her, together with other young leaders, to the White House for dinner and discussion. That same year, she met with presidential candidate and Texas governor George W. Bush, who was a fan of TFA's work in his home state. After his election, Laura Bush named Teach For America one of the special causes she would publicly support as First Lady. In 2002, the president called Kopp one of America's "quiet heroes."

TFA entered the new century stronger and smarter. "We'd been pursuing plans to make sure that we would survive over the long haul," says Hauser. "And then in the spring of 2000, we thought: *Gosh, we've kind of done it! Our day-to-day existence is not in question.*" The immediate next thought was: *What's next?* The choice was do more of the same, or step it up to a higher level to make a bigger impact.

TFA wanted to ratchet it up. As it turns out, so did Don and Doris Fisher, founders of the Gap. The Fishers were supporters of KIPP, Knowledge Is Power Program, a chain of inner-city charter schools started by two former TFA teachers, Dave Levin and Mike Feinberg. The KIPP schools were staffed to a large extent by TFA alums. One way to grow the KIPP engine, reckoned the Fishers, would be to increase the pool of TFA teachers from which KIPP could recruit.

Kopp got a call from the manager of the Fisher family's Pisces Foundation one day in May 2000. The Fishers were interested in expanding Teach For America. Could Kopp meet them at their New York apartment? The meeting lasted an hour. The Fishers ended up giving TFA an $8.3 million grant over three years, which TFA matched on a one-to-one basis in four months. That cash infusion was to put Teach For America on a path of aggressive growth that would help it become one of the most highly touted social entrepreneurships of the new millennium.

TFA had always relied on the kindness of strangers—and of rich men. In 1990, it was Ross Perot's $500,000 challenge grant (TFA had to match it three-to-one) that funded the training and placement of the very first corps of five hundred. A decade later, the Fishers, with a grant of exponentially higher magnitude, allowed TFA to think big. In order to truly close the achievement gap, the organization knew it would have to greatly expand its impact. The only way to do that would be to grow in size.

Once again, TFA set goals. In five years, it wanted to double the number of corps members to four thousand. It would beef up training and support of its teachers to increase their effectiveness, and it would better cultivate alumni as agents of change. The idea was to get *more* corps members to move *more* students, to achieve *more* academic gains. At the same time, it needed *more* alumni in its leadership pipeline.

All the big rocks were already in place. TFA had a program that it believed worked, and it had a strong, distinct corps of results-driven high achievers. But it lacked the sophistication and maturity of a great business enterprise. It needed to broaden its financial base, build up its organizational capacity, and attract more managerial talent.

Every facet of the organization was to be affected by the decision to grow in size and impact: on the program continuum, TFA would enhance recruitment, selection, training and teacher development, alumni affairs, program design, and regional operations. Supporting the growth would be offices of marketing and communications, finance and operations, growth strategy and development, and human assets. Using frameworks and rubrics, it set goals, made action plans, got feedback, collected and analyzed data, and held itself accountable for the results. What emerged was a twenty-first-century hybrid—an organization with the soul of a nonprofit and the brains of a Fortune 500.

TFA had been underinvesting in recruitment—and missing a lot of potentially great candidates as a result. In order to meet its target of four thousand CMs teaching by 2005, it would have to significantly increase the number of applicants.

Until then, TFA's approach to recruiting had been fairly straightforward: it advertised, held information sessions, and then picked the best from whoever applied. But TFA was competing against sophisticated recruiters with big budgets, like Goldman Sachs and the other elite investment banks and consulting firms—and it had to fight against the negative image of teaching as a profession. With advice from McKinsey, and under the leadership of Elissa Clapp, a 1996 alum, TFA began to beef up its infrastructure to support a more vigorous recruitment effort. The country was divided into recruitment territories, the number of recruitment offices was doubled, and progress was tracked.

And a big new head-hunting strategy was crafted. Rather than waiting to see who would show up for its info sessions, TFA was going to aggressively seek out the people it wanted to apply. "Just casting a wide net would be leaving too much to chance," explains Clapp. "Given the scope and the extremely high selection bar, we had to go out and proactively find those individuals most likely to be accepted." Enlisting the help of professors, school administrators, recent alums, and campus activists to identify school leaders and high achievers, TFA then personally reached out to them, principally through e-mail, but later through personal meetings and phone calls. The targeted online communication appealed to tech-savvy coeds. Phillip Gedeon received repeated e-mails from TFA seeking to recruit him as a campus manager before curiosity finally got the best of him and he responded. TFA had Hrag Hamalian in its sights, too, identifying him early as a campus leader. Recruiters also marketed TFA through campus information sessions, job fairs, and strategically placed posters and flyers. But it put a lot of stock in one-on-one coffees and small dinners with potential candidates, many of whom had been preselected for special wooing.

TFA got to know its target audience better through market research conducted by the Monitor Group. The research revealed that ten years on, TFA was perceived as a grassrootsy, do-gooder organization. To meet its expansion goals, the organization needed to better articulate the power of the TFA experience and reposition itself as smart, serious, and purposeful—an important alternative to Goldman Sachs or grad school. Research also indicated that TFA was reaching only one type of altruists. There was another group of socially conscious people out there who were long-term changers, too, but who thought the way to remake the world was through law school or some other postgraduate study program. TFA believed it could tap into that cohort if it could demonstrate that teaching in a high-needs community could actually provide the kind of insight and perspective that would make them better agents of change. And, far from foreclosing on other career options down the road, the set of "enablers" that TFA had created—the grad school and corporate partnerships— could actually expand them. The argument was that a two-year stint with Teach For America was a win-win proposition: good for low-performing students, good for high-achieving recruits.

Melissa Golden became TFA's brand czar in 2001. She was one of the first non-alums to join TFA's top leadership team, and her input was key. Golden helped to reposition the brand by making sure that potential recruits and supporters understood that there were two parts to the TFA mission. In the short term, TFA teachers would make an immediate, catalytic impact in lower-income classrooms; longer term, they would join a burgeoning army of teacher leaders who, transformed by their teaching experience, would force systemic change to ensure educational equity, whether or not they stayed in the classroom beyond their two-year commitment.

Since the beginning, TFA had been on the defensive about the short-term nature of the teaching commitment, particularly when talking to school districts and funders. By emphasizing the longer-term goal of the mission, TFA was able to neutralize some of the well-founded concerns around the issue of teacher churning in underperforming schools. It was hard to argue with the idea that true educational reform would require people in leadership positions beyond the classroom. In identifying America's future leaders—in law, medicine, public policy, journalism, academia, business, politics, and education—and engaging them in this life-altering mission, TFA believed that it was setting the stage for the transformation of the American system of public education. Out of the TFA incubator would come the smart, driven leaders—across all professional disciplines—who would close the gap for good.

Once TFA had better articulated its theory of change, it moved quickly to bring uniformity to the look and feel of the brand. Until then, the regions had been left to their own devices to create recruiting materials. The result was that TFA was sending out mixed messages. Under Golden's policing, the marketing team developed general talking points to keep everyone within the organization on point. Recruiters and selectors were provided with scripts to use when interacting with potential candidates. TFA adopted a uniform color palette for internal and external use, and it centralized the creation of all its promotional material. It also built up its website, using it as a key recruitment tool for a generation that had grown up on the Internet. Like everything else about TFA, the site was a work-in-progress, constantly evolving to meet TFA's changing needs and growing sophistication.

Kopp believed that there had always been a social-service impulse among American youth—TFA just happened to tap into the urge to make an impact at a time when there were fewer avenues open to them. But ongoing market research—both internal and external—increasingly showed that there were important differences between the first generation of TFAers, Generation X, and the Millennials, or Generation Y, the huge cohort of babies born in the early eighties. As it turned out, TFA was an almost perfect fit with the millennium zeitgeist.

Harvard Business School professor James Heskett describes Gen-Yers as bright, cheery multitaskers who are focused on their own personal development and want an accelerated path to success. He notes that because they are not willing "to pay the price" and have little fear of authority, they are bad bets for long-term employment. In their book *Managing the Generation Mix,* Carolyn A. Martin and Bruce Tulgan report that Millennials demand "the immediate gratification of making immediate impact by doing meaningful work immediately."

William Strauss and Neil Howe, authors of the book *Millennials Rising,* note that trends in youth behavior suggest that Millennials have a much higher regard for family and community than do the boomers or Generation X. Indeed, a survey by the consumer research company Yankelovich released in 2006 indicated that Millennials and their parents had actually "zapped the [generation] gap." Realizing that, TFA added a resource for parents to its website. Like their baby boomer parents, the Millennials were politically interested and socially active. The Higher Education Research Institute at UCLA found that in 2001—the year Rachelle, Phillip, Taylor, and Hrag were college freshmen—a record 82.6 percent of incoming freshmen reported frequent or occasional volunteer work (a requirement for graduation for 28 percent of those polled), and the percentage of students keenly interested in political events made the largest one-year leap (to 31.4 percent) since the 1972 presidential election, the first election many of their parents voted in.

Perhaps the one most defining characteristic of the new generation was its use of technology. Dubbed "digital natives," Generation Y used the Internet as an essential tool for socializing, communicating, and accessing information. Millennials were increasingly wireless, too—and thus constantly connected. Their portables—laptops, iPods, cell phones—allowed them to work, study, play, communicate, and socialize in ways unimaginable to their parents. TFA increasingly turned to its website—not only for marketing, but eventually for online training and teacher development, too.

As it studied the cohort, it adjusted its marketing and recruitment strategies. The trend toward public service played to TFA's strength. But early research suggested that Millennials were not into group gropes; they believed in the power of the individual to make a difference in society. So, like the U.S. Army, which changed its media message to "An Army of One" to speak to a new generation of soldiers, TFA tried to address the idea of the individual as an agent of change. A subtle shift was made in its promotional material. Pictures in which adorable schoolchildren were once dominant gave way to images of individual corps members in classrooms, hard at work with their students.

The new recruiting campaign worked. In 2000, the number of Teach For America applicants was 4,100. Five years later, 17,000 people applied. Many factors accounted for the fourfold jump. But there was little doubt that a more sophisticated and focused recruitment and marketing strategy had successfully changed the way TFA was perceived by a new generation.

TFA remained determined to get better at what it does. The organization began to think about how to identify its best teachers, and what it was that distinguished them from their peers. Obviously, TFA believed that a teacher's value in the classroom was not based on the number of years of service or academic certification; it was determined solely by student outcomes. Kopp's conviction that the teachers getting the best student results were also great leaders became the centerpiece of TFA's approach to selection and teacher training.

TFA moved to both define and measure success. Endless hours of study and debate went into the process. In the end, it was decided that because lower-performing students were so far behind their wealthier counterparts, "significant gains" in academic performance would be required for them to catch up. At the elementary school level, significant gains were defined as a class average jump of at least one and a half grade levels in math and literacy, or two grade levels in math and/or literacy. For secondary content areas, significant gains would mean a class average of at least 80 percent mastery of the subject.

The definition of success in the classroom had a powerful impact across the entire organization. Previously, it was left largely to corps members to decide how best to motivate and move their students. CMs naturally poured energy into those areas that interested them most. Some concentrated on community-service projects, others on mentoring or after-school activities. With the introduction of "significant gains," the collective energy of the entire organization was directed at the same single goal: specific academic gains in student achievement. Within a very short time, worthy but off-the-mark CM activities like painting over graffiti gave way to very purposeful, relentless work aimed solely at lifting academic achievement.

The TFA summer institute was reimagined. Before the creation of the

Teaching as Leadership (TAL) framework, the training text consisted of a 150-page binder containing teaching strategies, articles, and learning theories. Once TAL took hold, it began to inform every facet of training and support. In 2001, a separate TAL text was written for pre-institute prep work; the following year a special course on TAL was added to institute training itself.

The development of the TAL principles was an iterative process that was refined as the data coming in about the distinguishing characteristics of the most successful CMs became more robust. TFA also relied heavily on twice-yearly corps member surveys for insight into satisfaction levels regarding training and support. The two sets of data gave TFA a rich soup of information that helped shape ongoing improvements to the program. By the summer of 2006, analysis of the data resulted in the expansion of the TAL rubric to six principles with twenty-eight related actions.

And that year, in a major leap forward in its drive to improve training, teacher development, and student achievement, TFA began for the first time to track CM on-the-job performance as it specifically related to each of the twenty-eight TAL actions. Now TFA could take the CMs whose students were making significant gains and look at the TAL rubric data to see where on the twenty-eight teacher actions that group was performing. Analysis of the data could yield more insights into the distinguishing characteristics of great teachers, which could potentially lead to the discovery of new selection profiles and further refinements to the training and teacher development programs. "It's like someone turned the light on in terms of shaping our training and support," said Steven Farr, TFA's vice president of knowledge development and public engagement, a 1993 alum and graduate of Yale Law School. "It's a brave new world."

At the same time, rather than teach TAL as a separate course, program designers were working at incorporating that overarching principle into every facet of teacher training. Incoming corps members would be provided with a TAL textbook to establish mind-set before arriving at summer institute. Once there, they would be immersed in the nuts and bolts of teaching.

Afterward, corps members could refer to an interactive website featuring an online TAL textbook, a how-to guide providing new teachers with immediate access to the basics of good teaching. By 2008, TALON, as it was called, was to become a virtual coach to CMs, not only showing with annotated illustrations what works in the classroom, but teaching through online interactions how to adapt those practices and continuously improve. In addition, TFA was planning electronic resource centers for teachers through its online system called TFAnet, which would establish communities for CMs to share ideas and get advice from experts.

Despite the constant push to improve selection, training, and support, identifying its best teachers and accurately measuring significant gains in student achievement remain an imperfect science. Under No Child Left Behind, states are permitted to set their own standards for proficiency, creating wide variances across the country in terms of both the quality and the rigor of curriculum and assessments. A recent Harvard study of student achievement in New York City indicated that TFA's measure of significant gains was reliable, but even by the organization's own reckoning, it was "very messy and unscientific," as TFA's vice president of research, Abigail Smith, conceded in 2006. "We work as hard as we can to norm across regions, but we recognize . . . the apples and oranges challenge." TFA remains underterred. "We can't let 'perfect' be the enemy of 'good,' " insists Farr. "We have got to go with our best hypothesis and move forward."

The reliability of most educational research has always been questionable, with the value of each reform or program seen through the eyes—and innate biases—of the beholder. In 2002, the federal government passed a law establishing the Institute of Education Sciences to foster "scientifically based," federally funded research on which to ground education practice and policy. But the budget for research was small, and the What Works Clearinghouse, set up to review educational research, was quickly dubbed the Nothing Works Clearinghouse, since so few studies reviewed met the rigorous methodological standards set by the government.

Still, the finding that the quality of teaching has the single most profound effect on a child's academic growth is generally accepted as gospel. What is also uncontested is the fact that the amount of research into teacher education and preparation as it relates to student outcomes is "relatively small and inconclusive," according to the American Educational Research Association's 2005 report on research and teacher education, entitled "Studying Teacher Education." Several external studies of TFA's effectiveness in recent years have reached differing conclusions. The largest study, published by the Center for Research on Education

Outcomes at the Hoover Institute, Stanford University, in 2001, looked at student outcomes in Houston public schools and compared TFA results with those of other teachers; it found that the TFAers "perform as well as, and in many cases better than, other teachers hired [by the district]."

A much smaller study by Arizona State University researchers of the Phoenix Public Schools, released the following year, came to the opposite conclusion: it reported that students of TFA teachers "did not perform significantly different from students of other undercertified teachers" and that the students of certified teachers outperformed students of undercertified teachers, regardless of the pathway. TFA objected to the methodology and conclusions of the study, and was frustrated that the media gave it more weight than the organization felt it deserved.

Mathematica Policy Research, Inc., an independent research firm that evaluates socioeconomic issues driving public policy, released its study of Teach For America's effectiveness in 2004. Using a random assignment design, considered the most scientifically desirable—and expensive—method of research, Mathematica compared TFAers with both new and veteran teachers of nearly two thousand students in one hundred first- to fifth-grade classrooms in six of TFA's fifteen regions. The study found that TFA teachers, though lacking traditional teacher training, generated larger math gains than their peers and had the same minimal impact on reading. Mathematica's conclusion: TFA offered an appealing pool of "academically talented teachers" who contributed to the academic achievement of their students. Employing a TFA recruit amounted to a risk-free hire.

Teach For America trumpeted the Mathematica study results on its website and in national press releases. TFA fans and foes alike lauded the study's design, widely regarded as the gold standard in research. But the following spring, Linda Darling-Hammond struck again. In a paper entitled "Does Teacher Preparation Matter?" Darling-Hammond reviewed achievement data among Houston's fourth- and fifth-graders over a six-year span and concluded that uncertified TFA teachers had a significant negative effect on student gains relative to certified teachers. This time, TFA vigorously defended the effectiveness of its program and attacked the rigor of Darling-Hammond's methods, through the media and on its website.

Wendy Kopp, writing in the *The Stanford Daily*, scolded the paper for its coverage of what she believed was a flawed study by Darling-Hammond, who had moved to Stanford University's School of Education in 1998. TFA's Abigail Smith concluded that Darling-Hammond had an "inexplicable, twelve-year vendetta against Teach For America." The Stanford professor stood by her work, calling TFA a "Band-aid on a bleeding sore." The educational establishment was abuzz. But TFA funders were unmoved by the public tit for tat. So, too, were potential candidates: applications soared to an all-time high in 2005.

Internally, the collection and analysis of data continued to fuel the TFA engine. For selection, the idea was to be as accurate as possible on the front end to ensure the very best results at the back end in terms of student outcomes. By 2005, the data from preceding TFA classes on both admissions and CM effectiveness was rich enough for the organization to begin making fairly accurate computer predictions about which candidates were most likely to succeed—rendering unexpected defections like Dave Buehrle's all the more important to study.

TFA's predictive selection model had identified six profiles across the seven competencies that were used to judge potential candidates. A candidate had to be rated at least a 2 (solid) on every competency even to be considered. After that, candidates had to either "spike"—that is, score a 3 (exemplary)—in achievement alone, a very high bar to meet, or spike in two of four other competencies: perserverance, critical thinking, influence/motivating, or organizational ability. (While the two other traits, "respect" and "fit with TFA," were valued, spikes in either or both were not enough on their own to green-light admission.)

Wendy Kopp understood the selectivity piece from the very beginning. In the inaugural corps, only one in five applicants made the cut. TFA's admission policy remained highly selective throughout the first decade, even though the number of applicants averaged only 2,500 a year. In gearing up for growth in the second decade, TFA decided it would expand only if it could maintain, and even exceed, its already high level of selectivity. Though the numbers of applicants were running to five figures by 2002, TFA didn't accept 2,000 corps members until 2005, when 17,000 people applied. The decision to remain highly selective was key to the success that followed.

In 2005, Jim Collins singled out Teach For America for its ability to get the right people, that is, top-flight talent, onto the proverbial bus without relying on money as an incentive. In the Social Sectors mono-

him to rejoin TFA. On his thirtieth birthday, in August 2000, he left his lucrative job with Hogan & Hartson and returned to the TFA fold.

Huffman had no experience in fund-raising, but he saw right away that there were changes in structure and culture that could significantly increase revenues. TFA's regional sites clearly represented a largely untapped source of diversified funding that the organization moved aggressively to exploit. The multiregional setup allowed TFA to figure out the best development practices, quickly share them with other sites, and then execute them. Goals were set, and a rigorous central tracking system built around a high level of skepticism was put in place. Regions were required to do a monthly check-in with the national office to categorize the likelihood that pledges would actually be delivered. The check-ins resulted in brutally honest assessments—both on the reliability of pledges and the proficiency of the fund-raising.

Restructuring the fund-raising effort was easy. The cultural piece was a bit tougher. The focus within the organization had always been on the program—how to build it, improve it, expand it. Fund-raising was seen as a necessary evil, a dirty task that needed to be undertaken in order to do the things that really mattered. Under the five-year plan, fund-raising came to be seen as part and parcel of the mission, an endeavor of elemental importance.

TFA enlisted new funders to be on the ground floor of the expansion at their regional sites. And it began to appreciate the importance of synergy between the private and public sectors. It started to invest more in building personal relationships—especially in Washington, D.C., home to policy makers and federal dollars. It didn't hurt that the new president, like Kopp, was a Texan. During his campaign, George W. Bush had flown Kopp cross-country on his plane to discuss Teach For America. When he took office in 2001, he named Ron Paige, superintendent of the Houston Independent School District, secretary of education. Paige had had a long and happy history with TFA in Houston, and he viewed it as a catalytic force in public education.

"We were still a relatively small nonprofit," recalls Huffman. "We were national in scale but probably not that well known, and all of a sudden we had people in D.C. who thought we were great."

As TFA was figuring out how to engage the power brokers in Washington, it was equally mindful of Wall Street. In 2002 its first national corporate sponsorship fell into its lap when Wachovia Corporation approached TFA to partner up. National corporate partnerships with Lehman Brothers and Amgen followed. In 2002, TFA's annual New York City benefit dinner raised $860,000. Five years later, it raised more than $4 million.

TFA also tapped John Q. Public through Sponsor a Teacher, and continued to seek funding through foundations. The Broad Foundation, the Carnegie Foundation, the Knight Foundation, and New Profit, Inc. were among a dozen or so philanthropies that joined the Pisces Foundation in underwriting the 2000–2005 expansion. By the end of the 2005 fiscal year, operating revenue had grown from $10 million in 2000 to $40 million. Amazon.com named Teach For America one of the country's ten most innovative nonprofits, and the organization received Charity Navigator's highest rating for sound fiscal management.

As the national team worked feverishly to improve the program, the regions worked equally hard executing. Samir and the other program directors were at school sites every day of the week except for Tuesdays. The second day of every workweek was spent in the downtown office, where all the PDs met with managing director of program Felicia Cuesta to assess their work as thought partners to recruits, to share best practices, and to plan ahead for the other programmatic roles they were assigned.

Samir always approached Tuesdays with mixed feelings.

On the one hand, a day at the office was a welcome respite from the stress of a day on the road meeting with harried CMs. He looked forward to seeing his colleagues. Brian Johnson, the Los Angeles region's executive director, Felicia Cuesta, and all six of the PDs in Los Angeles were TFA alums. That in itself was binding—they had all earned their stripes in the trenches, all gained yardage on the battlefield. And like him, they were new to the job—each having been hired after undergoing a typically rigorous TFA selection process. Samir loved them—and trusted them. He considered them his own wise thought partners as he strived to improve his performance as a PD.

But checking in with the regional office could be stressful, too. The PDs shared data on their CMs' performance, which of course was a reflection of their own effectiveness on the job. And there were always new tasks being assigned, new deadlines to meet, new heights to reach.

The meeting on Valentine's Day 2006 started with what the agenda called a "community builder," an icebreaker to get the ten people seated around the conference table warmed up for a full morning of work. Cuesta started off a quick round of personal trivia questions—penciled in for fifteen minutes. To lots of laughter, the group was reminded that when Samir was in elementary school he did not know how to skip, that Felicia toilet-papered houses during slumber parties in junior high, that when Liz was a deejay her stage name was Thunder Bunny, that Ramona craved olives and had a dog named Chile, and that Samir's band was called Stereochemistry.

At nine-fifteen, the team got to work with "personal and professional alignment reflections"—TFA-speak for an update on what everyone was doing. The personal stuff came first: Frank was taking his first day off and leaving at one; Ramona was registering for the San Diego marathon; Liz had gone one day without coffee.

Then came the work updates. Ruth Ann reported on the status of the "excellent school visits" she had been coordinating: CMs, as part of the professional development opportunities offered by TFA, were invited to observe teachers at an "excellent" L.A. school—such as the renowned Harvard-Westlake and the Marlborough School, the all-girls academy that Taylor had visited earlier in the year. The meeting moved quickly over the rest of the calendar and office updates. The team was told of the ongoing push for early placement of the incoming class of CMs, an arduous, months-long process of schmoozing and horse trading. Brian Johnson, a 1999 corps member and Princeton alum, had started the conversation with the area school districts back in October, just after the 2005 school year began.

As TFA's top man in Los Angeles, Johnson had connections. Marlene Canter, president of the LAUSD board, was a TFA fan who had actually donated her annual salary to the cause. (TFA presented her with its Lifetime Leadership Award in July 2006 for her "Commitment to Educational Excellence and Equity.") Five LAUSD school board members had TFA alums working for them; two other TFAers were on the superintendent's staff. Still, negotiating the placement of future CMs required exquisite finesse. Johnson was in constant contact with superintendents, school board members, and human resource officers for the various school districts in the greater Los Angeles area, gingerly balancing supply against demand.

L.A. Unified was by far TFA's largest customer in the Los Angeles area; 200 of the district's 2,347 new teachers in the 2005 school year were TFA recruits, accounting for 8.5 percent of new hires. It cost TFA $12,500 a year to select and train each recruit. The district picked up $3,000 of that. With improvements to the program, the costs kept rising. In 2007 the tab was $14,000 per recruit. By 2010, TFA expected it to cost $20,000 to select and train a corps member.

Johnson had to sell each potential employer on the benefits of hiring a TFA recruit. The problem was, TFA was offering schools the promise of student achievement; what the districts were looking for were "highly qualified" teachers, as mandated by No Child Left Behind. State and federal laws required districts to show proof of progress; the percentage of credentialed teachers was an easy metric to cite. In LAUSD's lowest-performing high schools, where there was an acute shortage of teachers, Johnson had no trouble selling his teachers-to-be. Most principals were happy with warm bodies; a TFAer, though noncredentialed, was almost always preferred to the alternative—a longtime sub. (A 2005 Kane, Parsons & Associates survey found that 84 percent of Los Angeles principals with TFA teachers on staff reported that they would hire another one; 93 percent regarded TFA teachers as more effective than other beginning teachers.) But in elementary schools, where there was no shortage of credentialed teachers, getting a slot for a TFAer often was problematic. When it came down to a choice between a credentialed teacher who could bolster the district's stats and a noncredentialed TFAer, it was no contest—the credentialed teacher tended to get the job.

But TFA refused to entirely cede the elementary school terrain. The need was there: achievement levels among Los Angeles's younger students was alarmingly low, and TFA believed its teachers could perform higher than the average LAUSD hire. TFA insisted that if the mission truly was to close the achievement gap, then it had a moral imperative to be in the lower grades, where it had the potential to have maximum impact. So, TFA and LAUSD worked out a deal. Though LAUSD would still take K–6 teachers from TFA, the numbers would be relatively low, and the teachers could be placed only in schools that already had TFA on staff. What's more, most of the placements would be assigned to sixth grade.

Secondary and middle schools were a different matter. LAUSD was happy to hire TFA teachers for the upper grades for reasons other than the chronic shortage of people willing to work in tough, gritty, urban schools. One of the biggest advantages to hiring TFA recruits was that they tended to pass the test that helped satisfy the NCLB requirement that every child have a "highly qualified teacher," at impressively higher rates than other new candidates. Though the state of California trailed other states in student achievement, it was generally considered to have one of the most rigorous sets of standards. The CSET, the test to demonstrate subject-matter competency, was tough.

"Nobody but the TFA teachers can pass the CSET exams," explains Anthony Thymes, coordinator of new teachers for Locke in 2006. "If TFA weren't here, we would have to hire thirty-five teachers on emergency credentials, and that would make the state come in." There was another advantage to hiring TFAers. They were goal-oriented high achievers, so they tended to work hard and sometimes more purposefully than some of their older colleagues. TFA encouraged CMs to zero in on improving student achievement in their classrooms—a goal that was within their locus of control. Worrying about school dysfunction or other environmental factors that were beyond their power to fix was seen as an unnecessary distraction. So, in the beginning at least, TFAers tended not to complain publicly about overcrowded classrooms or too many preps. And they took on additional work that more experienced teachers, protected by the union, resisted. Often, the more successful they were, the more responsibilities they were given.

Not every school district in Los Angeles laid out the welcome mat. The reforming Long Beach School District, which had declining enrollment, had made so much progress that it no longer needed TFA hires. Compton, though needy, had proven to be a difficult customer. It was one of the original school districts to hire TFAers, but TFA had withdrawn from the troubled district after a dustup over an unwritten agreement to place recruits there went awry. Now TFA wanted back in; Compton was exactly the kind of district that needed TFA the most. Samir, who had taught there so successfully only a few years before, was lobbying school board members hard for a contract. The district was on the fence. Compton, like LAUSD, was desperately seeking math and science teachers. But it didn't need any elementary school teachers. TFA had math and science teachers, but it also needed to find spots for its elementary school assignments. So TFA offered to send ten math and science teachers to Compton if the district signed a contract with TFA to hire ten elementary teachers as well. But TFA was running into a lot of political and union opposition.

The same old objection was being made: *they leave after two years.* Samir considered himself living proof that the argument was specious. After all, he may have left the classroom, but he was still advocating for his students in Compton. He was in a position to bring ten "highly qualified" math and science teachers to Compton. How could anyone argue that TFA bails on its students?

With all the difficulties presented by the big public school districts, TFA was working the charter angle aggressively. It already had CMs working at KIPP L.A. Prep and the Watts Learning Center. Another KIPP charter had recently opened up, and the Green Dot charter schools—many staffed by TFA alums—were popping up all over Los Angeles.

The school-placement update was only one of many items on the agenda. Earlier in the month, the PDs had attended an organization-wide meeting in Las Vegas at which Co-Investigation 2.0 was introduced. The L.A. region PDs had been surveyed on their Co-Investigation needs. It was clear they had no problem analyzing CM data, but they were struggling with the solution and follow-up phases of C-I 2.0.

"The way I scored it," Samir informed the group, "I need a wider range of solutions than I have now." Samir also questioned the need to differentiate the causes—skill, knowledge, or mind-set—of a teacher's problem. "I don't feel it's critical to differentiate between knowledge and skill because the solutions are similar—why debate whether it's one or the other? And I still have to check mind-set . . . and I don't know if I'm comfortable with that. I understand what they mean, but the way it plays out in real time is never that concrete."

Others jumped in, and a spirited discussion followed. The upshot: Cuesta announced that she wanted to tighten up all parts of the Co-Investigation process—from narrowing down and identifying the key teacher problem, a gateway issue, to offering up possible solutions based on causes.

Next up was a matriculation update and a look ahead to the midyear retreat, where the staff would "step back" and look at the big picture—review TFA's core values and strategic plan, gear up for the end of the year, and prepare for the coming one in a smart, disciplined way.

Then it was on to the dreaded stats: at midyear, 19.5 percent of CMs were achieving significant student gains, 24.5 percent away from the L.A. region's year-end target of 44 percent. The key problems and causes were identified, next steps to a solution enumerated, and measures of success put in place.

Cuesta then announced a new program she wanted to pilot in Los Angeles: Co-Investigating the Co-Investigations. She explained that her informal pop-ins to observe PDs at work would continue. But a much more formalized process—straight off the Co-Investigation rubric—would be put in place to assess PD proficiency. Cuesta would oversee the entire Co-Investigation cycle of each PD and a CM of his or her choice. The session would be videotaped, Cuesta would take notes, and then she and the PD would sit down and Co-Investigate the PD's key problem, underlying causes, and possible solutions.

As she explained the new plan, backs around the table stiffened slightly. Program director Amy Cox presumably spoke for the group when she asked for clarification. She explained that she was the type of PD who always invited Cuesta to her most challenging Co-Investigation sessions. "But it's not going to be my cycle of evaluation, is it?"

Cuesta's response hung in the air: "When I say formal, I only mean structured."

She moved on. Next up was a note on the ongoing collection of 2003 alumni data, and TFA's plans to enhance summer institute programming. The institute planning team was harvesting information and feedback from the regions. Early signs indicated that special emphasis would be placed on diagnostics and tracking sessions; institute diversity sessions were historically contentious, and designers were working on improving them, too.

The morning concluded with PDs munching on Valentine's Day cup-cakes, bagels, and grapes as they discussed their nominees for the Sue Lehmann Award for Excellence in Teaching, a five-thousand-dollar prize given each year to an outstanding corps member. At exactly noon, the PDs filed out of the conference room and back onto the battlefield. There wasn't a minute to waste.

CHAPTER TEN

Who Do You Screw?

Who do you screw? It was a question Chad asked himself nearly every day. The other questions that he couldn't get out of his head as he was making the tough calls were: *Is this something I'd want for my kids? Would I be okay with this?* The answer was almost always *no.*

After Dave Buehrle left, Chad had to figure out what to do with five orphaned classes of twelfth-graders. Any way Chad looked at it, someone got screwed; the only thing to be determined was who and to what degree. The obvious and easy solution to the dilemma was to get a full-time sub to take over. But the English department already had two full-time subs. Chad didn't want to take the risk of hiring another.

So he decided to give Buerhle's classes to an underperforming tenth-grade English teacher from one of the other small schools. Chad would disband that teacher's classes and farm out his students. His reasoning was simple: the tenth-graders needed a good teacher more than the twelfth-graders did. After all, the tenth-graders were about to take the California High School Exit Exam (CAHSEE), and if a good percentage of them failed, the entire school's API and AYP scores would be affected.

It was true that the transfer would cause widespread damage to Buehrle's English honors and drama classes. But those kids had already passed the CAHSEE and were on track to graduate. Though it was not a factor in his decision, Chad knew, too, that there was an undeniable side benefit to sticking a crummy teacher in the highest-performing school. Now all the people who had accused him of favoring the School of Social Empowerment over the other learning communities would be silenced; no one in his right mind could interpret that particular chess move as beneficial to SE. So that was that. In the daily battle of who gets screwed at Locke, Buerhle's kids lost. But they knew that the moment he told them he was quitting. Their reaction to the news had been "Why do all the good white teachers leave?"

If they had posed the question to Chad, his unspoken response would have been "Because the school doesn't work." And though he took the position as VP because he thought he could change that, he had been sadly mistaken. He had no power. His job was only a balancing act—between evils. At least when he was a teacher, he had had some fantastic days; in fact, most days were fantastic. Now every time he walked through the door into his office he knew he was entering a no-win zone.

It was maddening to have to make these administrative Hobbesian choices. Kids in suburban schools could live with a couple of duds for teachers, but not the kids at Locke, or any school that looked like Locke, or any school in which a TFA teacher worked. Locke kids arrived with fifth-grade reading levels. A good teacher could move them up one level. A fantastic teacher—a teacher making what TFA called significant gains—could boost them two grades in a year. At Locke, students couldn't afford to have just one or two good teachers. They needed four fantastic ones. And they weren't getting them.

One reason was because schools like Locke were safe havens for lousy teachers. Dr. Wells reckoned that 35 percent of his teachers had no business being in a classroom. But the powerful teachers union, the UTLA, protected tenured teachers regardless of their classroom performance. There was a process in LAUSD to either get rid of bad teachers or make them better—but it required administrators to jump through hoops. Under the rules of the union contract, supervisors were bound to conduct and document repeated rounds of observations and evaluations carried out along a very specific time line, and to offer interventions and remediation through professional development where needed. Even when a convincing case had been built against a teacher, a missed deadline could derail the entire process. The teacher evaluations were divvied up among the administrators at Locke. Dr. Wells took the toughest cases himself. He tried mightily. He had about twenty-two teachers in his sights, but the union contract made tenured teachers just about bullet-proof. Chad didn't get it. *Why are we so concerned about protecting teachers and not kids?*

It was hard to fire a bad teacher, but it did occasionally happen. The terrible irony was that the alternative to a successful dismissal was often worse. Good teachers weren't exactly lining up to teach at Locke, so often the only candidates sending in résumés were district castaways looking for a place to hole up. When Locke couldn't find a permament teacher for a vacant position, it relied on substitute teachers to fill the spot. Noncredentialed substitute teachers in LAUSD needed only to have graduated from college with a 2.7 GPA and to have passed the CBEST, an exam considered easier than the high school exit exam. Some of the subs were okay; many were not. At Locke, if there were only fifteen subs working on any given day, things were looking good. Throughout the 2005–2006 school year, the school had three teacher vacancies and employed seven to ten long-term subs.

Wells estimated that 40 percent of his staff were hardworking, committed educators. And for a long time, Chad had believed that if Locke could get a critical mass of them to stick around, real change could take place. But the dysfunction wore good teachers down and forced them out. With up to thirty teachers leaving every year, some of them TFAers, there was no way to build an enduring culture of achievement. Without that, Locke's numbers might trend up ever so slightly, but for all intents and purposes, the school would continue to flatline.

Locke was on every government education agency's watch list, but the consequences for failing to make the mandated improvements were never clear. The most recent reform, the carving up of the school into small learning communities in 2004, was imposed in an effort to stave off more drastic government action. But the plan was never formally approved and funded by the district, nor was it fully embraced by all of Locke's teachers. In the spring of 2005, the Western Association of Schools and Colleges (WASC), a regional accrediting body for public and private schools, was due to conduct its annual Locke inspection. And a School Assistance and Intervention Team (SAIT), a county auditing group appointed by the state to oversee and support Locke, had recently started to pull together an action plan for school improvement. But the school had been subject to numerous audits and inspections, and countless action plans had been drawn up. It was difficult for Chad to see what anyone could really do to hold the school accountable.

The state could take over the school. But who are they going to send in? The governor? The school could go charter, but who's going to charter a dying public school in the inner city? Green Dot's Steve Barr? He had his chance and took a pass. The school could be reconstituted by firing all the teachers and hiring back only the good ones. But how do you do that? The ones worth their weight might tell you to go to hell, and then Locke would have even more open positions that couldn't be filled. The other big consequence—replacing the administrative staff—has already happened three times since 2001. How is yanking the principal just as he is getting to know the school supposed to improve Locke?

Chad had a daydream. The answer to Locke's problems would come from the students themselves. Locke had 3,100 kids, 5 administrators, and a faculty of 131 or thereabouts; the people being controlled far outnumbered the controllers. The students could rise up and take charge. They could stage a sit-in, call the district, get the media to come, and demand change. If the kids decided they wanted something, they would get what they needed. It could happen.

But the chances were slim.

God knows Chad wanted change. He had tried to be a force for change, a leader. But he couldn't even keep his own job. How was he supposed to support teachers in theirs? After the new vice principal in charge of counseling arrived and took over Chad's office, Wells urged Chad to apply for a newly created position of small-schools coordinator, a job that paid ten thousand dollars more and was perfectly aligned with Chad's ambition. At first Chad was excited about the possibility, but as the weeks passed and nothing happened, he became depressed. Eventually he was advised that he was technically ineligible for the job because he did not have five years of teaching experience. Still, Wells held out the hope that he could find a way around the red tape that was tying up Chad's appointment. In the meantime, Chad became the AP for leftover jobs. He worked out of an empty third-floor room he converted into an office, and from there he found himself shagging all the curveballs that came his way.

Chad didn't feel empowered by Wells, and he in turn didn't feel he was empowering the teachers he supervised. There were no systems in place at Locke. Teachers hoarded supplies, and books that had been ordered and paid for were never distributed. There were no tutors for the two-year-old AVID college-prep program, and the school counselors didn't have functioning computers. There was a budget, estimated to be around twenty million dollars, but nobody ever saw it. Though the school was allocated funds for site improvement, money was wasted—or not spent—at every turn. The adults at Locke were failing the kids. Chad felt increasingly helpless.

And so it was that he began to think that he, too, would join the ranks of Locke's recently departed. He was wracked with guilt. Not the Great White Guilt. He didn't feel guilty because he had come from so much privilege and his kids from so much deprivation. He felt guilty because he had always had a strong faith that Locke would get better if enough of the right people stayed. He felt guilty about abandoning that hope, about walking away from the kids and his commitment to them. But as he evaluated the reasons he remained at Locke, it was more about the guilt he would feel if he left than the hope for the future if he stayed. And that was unhealthy.

Chad contacted Steve Barr, the education reformer who operated the Green Dot charter schools in Los Angeles. Though nothing had come of their meetings a few years before, their long discussions over chips and margaritas had put Chad—and Locke—on Barr's radar.

Barr was an impolitic politico with a knack for the sound bite and a love of the spotlight. He had come to his mission as school reformer rather late in life. The son of an Irish immigrant who abandoned the family when Barr was three, he was raised by his single mother, who waited tables to make ends meet. As a boy, he was a C-minus student in what was then an A-plus school system. But by the time Barr graduated from high school, California had embarked on its inexorable decline from the number one state in student achievement to the forty-eighth. Proposition 13, the taxpayer revolt of 1978, had put a cap on property rates—the death knell for fully funded public education in the state. Twenty years later, California's school system was in shambles, and Barr was in the middle of a midlife crisis.

A writer by trade, Barr had established his reformist credentials in 1990 when he cofounded Rock the Vote, the mostly online movement that encouraged young people to become politically active. Seven years on, he was looking for a new cause. How could he broaden the reach of

Rock the Vote to engage Los Angeles's politically disenfranchised immigrant population? The answer, he thought, was in school reform. Education would connect Los Angeles's youth, many of them new to the country, to the political process—and ensure the financial and social success of the city he loved by making them into an educated workforce.

He resolved to create a prototype of the Great American High School. His effort would be called Green Dot, a reference to the number of wired schools in California at the time. (While researching a story for *George* magazine, Barr had found an online map on which green dots represented the state's wired schools, and discovered that there wasn't a single one in Los Angeles.) His new school would be built on six tenets that the noneducator had identified as key to high-performing schools: they would be small, safe, and autonomous, with high expectations and accountability for students and teachers, an extended school day, parent involvement, and a greater share of government dollars going directly to the sites. The first Green Dot school, Ánimo Leadership Charter High School, opened in 2000. Four more followed. They worked. Graduation rates at the Green Dots averaged 81 percent compared to 47 percent for LAUSD, and API scores on average were up more than one hundred points.

But Barr had never wanted to be an operator of a chain of successful charter schools. His long-term vision was to reform the whole district. The question was: How many green dots would it take to reach the tipping point for all of Los Angeles? By early 2005, he was ready to find out. He began to look for a large, existing high school that he could turn around by using the model that had proven successful in his small schools. He thought of Locke and Chad, and remembered their meetings.

"Chad was a very quiet kid," Barr recalls. "When he walked into a room, you didn't think 'John Kennedy.' But he's one of those guys who rallies people around him by outworking everyone around him. It's amazing how many people follow him, and he does it by example." Given Chad's leadership skills and the school's obvious need, Barr seriously considered making a play for Locke—until another low performer, Jefferson High, erupted in a series of racial clashes. Barr figured that he had to pick the place that would generate the most heat. At that moment, Jefferson was already hot; Locke was not.

So, in a move that enraged the union and the school board, Barr proposed to take the struggling Jefferson High School off LAUSD's hands.

Barr's hostile takeover bid, which he subsequently outlined in a white paper published in March 2006 entitled "School Transformation Plan," called for the deconstruction of Jefferson into a cluster of six autonomous small schools. The four-year process would begin by "incubating" each new school off-site, starting with a ninth-grade class and adding an additional grade each year. Once the schools were at full capacity with four grades, five hundred students, and an established culture of achievement, they would reoccupy the original Jefferson High site and share common facilities. (Because the resulting retention rate would be so high, two entire schools would remain off-site.)

Barr reckoned that his plan could be adopted across the district, transforming forty-six large failing high schools into five hundred discrete high-performing schools within a decade. He argued that nineteen billion dollars in bond money recently raised for new school construction in Los Angeles could be used to finance the incubators and to renovate existing sites to accommodate the new autonomous small schools. When his offer was rebuffed, he was unbowed. He pledged to reform Jefferson anyway. He announced that he would be opening small incubator schools around the Jefferson campus and filling the seats with the kids who would have been Jefferson's incoming ninth-grade class.

Barr got everyone's attention—Chad's included. The union, school board, superintendent, and mayor became locked in a heated battle over Jefferson, at just about the same time that Chad was reaching the boiling point at Locke. When Chad made contact, Barr was eager to see him, and this time the meeting was quite short. After a four-minute interview, Barr offered Chad a job as principal of one of the six new charter schools he intended to open in the fall of 2006. He knew that Chad had been conflicted about leaving Locke the first time he offered him a job. He sensed that joining the shock troops outside the district walls would still be a painful decision for Chad. Barr respected that and felt honored by it.

Chad didn't officially accept the job right away. But he did talk to the six teachers he wanted on his dream team. His first pick was Josh Hartford as vice principal. The rest were other key members of Locke's School of Social Empowerment. Chad got the sense they felt much as he did. They were all ready to jump.

He gave Wells the heads-up a few weeks later. It was late on a Friday when he stopped by the principal's ground-floor corner office before heading home. Chad told Wells that he had been asked to apply for an administrative position with Green Dot, had done so, and had been offered a principalship. When and if he accepted the job, he said, Frank Wells would be the second person to know.

Wells didn't skip a beat. He told Chad it sounded like a great opportunity and he would support him if he decided to accept it. But then he sounded a note of caution.

"I would like you to consider the ethical implications of taking your entourage with you," he said, noting that the new Green Dot schools would no doubt have a wide pool of qualified applicants from which to draw. (In fact, eight hundred teachers—many of them TFA alums— ended up applying for eighty-five positions.) "It doesn't seem right or fair that you would take some of the best teachers in this school with you."

Chad didn't respond. He couldn't trust himself to speak. He objected to Wells's use of the word "entourage," and if Wells wanted to talk ethics, well, he was the one who had an ethical obligation to keep and continue to attract good teachers based on the vision he'd established as principal. *If they leave, it won't be because they blindly follow me; it will because they've made an informed decision based on their experiences here.* Still, it was hard to dismiss Wells's admonition not to poach Locke's best teachers. Chad didn't like the delivery, but he saw his point.

So the internal dialogue he had been conducting for weeks continued:

I would be taking only six people . . . But others might leave, too, once they see the SE exodus.

I care about Locke and I don't want to steal teachers away . . .

But a lot of them would leave anyway, and I could offer them an opportunity that could change the face of public education in Los Angeles.

I'm not hassling them; I only told them I'm interested if they'd like to consider coming on board. If they come, it's their decision . . . But if I hadn't approached them, would they really leave?

Wells is right, there are other qualified candidates in L.A. besides my entourage . . . But I want the most capable people working with me. I'd be remiss not to ask the people I know and have worked so well with.

While key members of the so-called Chad entourage were contemplating the abandonment of the small school they had just built at Locke, Vanessa Morris was planning to create a new one. At that point, Locke had six small schools, only a few of which were actually functional. SE graph to *Good to Great,* he called TFA an "elegant" idea, noting that TFA was able to attract America's elite students to its movement by appealing to their "idealistic passions" and making the process selective. That selectivity led to "credibility with donors, which increased funding, which made it possible to attract and select even more young people into the program," wrote Collins. He said that Kopp understood three fundamental points: (1) the more selective the process, the more attractive the position becomes; (2) purity of mission is a powerful motivator; and (3) *the* number one resource is having enough of the right people committed to the mission.

To ensure the success of the first five-year growth plan, TFA worked on attracting top-quality staffers to grow its organizational capacity and deepen its bench. Staff salaries rose—along with the bar for performance. TFA head-hunted aggressively among its own pool of alumni and their contacts. It was looking for ambitious, goal-seeking staffers, and it rewarded the ones it hired with lots of responsibility. For the underperforming, it was not a comfortable place to work. Many of them self-selected out; others were pointed toward the door or dismissed. Most nonprofits had a greater tolerance for underperformers, a tendency that made frustrated goal-oriented staffers bolt. The staff retention rate at TFA was more differentiated. Staffers, like CMs, were constantly evaluated. The idea was to retain the highest number of top performers and the lowest number of nonperformers. Over 90 percent of the top performers stayed at TFA; the retention rate for the less successful was more like 20 to 30 percent.

Growing its funding base was a key goal in the 2000 five-year plan. TFA wanted to be fully diversified so that it would never again be dependent upon a single revenue stream for its growth—or survival. It approached the development challenge the same way it did every other part of the mission—by setting ambitious targets and doggedly pursuing them.

Kevin Huffman, a 1992 corps member in Houston along with KIPP founders Levin and Feinberg, took on the task of heading development just a few months after speaking on a panel during the tenth anniversary alumni summit in New York. At the time, he had a well-paying job at a prestigious law firm, but being around the old TFA gang again precipitated a full-blown crisis of conscience. Huffman decided he had to get back into the nonprofit world. When Kopp got wind of that, she invited was by far the most successful of the lot, and Morris, the nationally board-certified science chair, thought there was plenty of room at the top. Her idea was to give birth to a technology-heavy small school that would better prepare Locke students for college by offering three years of both math and science, a requirement for admission into the University of California system. She knew the administration would be hard-pressed to refuse her. Kids at Locke tested better in science than in any other subject; 5 percent even scored advanced, an admittedly small number but one that made Morris proud and gave her clout.

She had observed the SE team as they built their school, so she knew the key to success: good teachers. Morris herself was a graduate of UCLA's well-regarded Teacher Education Program, a two-year urban ed master's program. But she was a huge fan of TFA. Over her five years at Locke, she had had only positive experiences with TFAers. They shared her concern for social justice, and they were, without exception, energetic team players. Some of them, like Soleo and Hartford, had become close friends. They had her back and she had theirs. Without them, she wasn't sure how long she would have lasted at Locke. During the week they all worked like crazy; on Fridays they ranted and raved like crazy. Morris considered Friday-night happy hour her form of therapy. In fact, it was better—more fun, and a lot cheaper. So when she went casting about for teachers, it came as no surprise to anyone that she looked to Teach For America first. When she had finally assembled her team and introduced them at a faculty meeting, one teacher quipped: "What is this? A TFA school plus Morris?" Four of the eight were TFAers. Among them were Taylor and Hrag.

Taylor was excited to be joining the team. Morris had invited her and a handful of others to the Olive Garden restaurant for an exploratory meeting, which turned out to be a three-hour working dinner. It had been exhilarating. Ideas were flying around the table, and a vision of what the new school could be took shape. At the end of the night it was decided that the school needed to have a cheer—and a motto. And while they were at it, they joked, maybe they would schedule all the PDs for the new School of Math and Science at the beach. Taylor was hooked. She told Morris she'd do anything she could to help. How could she not? She loved her colleagues, and she really loved teaching. What she didn't like was the disorganization, the chaos, the constant feeling of impending doom waiting outside her classroom door. With a leader like Vanessa Morris, maybe that would all go away. Maybe they could make their little school work.

The ninth-grade academy, the school Taylor was in, sure didn't. It was divided into two "houses," and the classrooms were located in the rows of tacky trailers at the back of the campus along Avalon Boulevard, a big gang thoroughfare. The ninth-graders had been segregated from the rest of the school for the past few years—the gates to the back lot were actually locked shut during the school day and opened only for lunch and the passing time between periods. The thinking had been that the ninth-graders were the biggest at-risk population in the school; they were the hardest to manage and the cohort most likely to drop out. Separating them from the upperclassmen might ease the transition from middle school to high school, foster a better class culture, and keep them at Locke.

The experiment was a nonstarter. There was no coherent leadership, no shared curriculum, and no proven academic benefits. Kids were still dropping out like flies, and the ninth-grade teachers were so disaffected that many didn't even bother showing up for the weekly meetings. As far as Hrag was concerned, they were like every other meeting at Locke: people sat around, argued for a bit, and left. Nothing ever got done. And there was no downside to being a no-show, because there were no consequences. So Hrag ditched the meetings. The only reason Taylor attended was that they were held in her classroom during the lunch hour. She had nowhere else to go.

Morris had conducted her talent search primarily in the ninth-grade houses because she did not want to antagonize other small school leaders by poaching their teachers. But she would have gone trolling in the back lot anyway. That's where many of the TFAers were clustered, because that's traditionally where most of the openings were—veteran teachers preferred not to have to deal with ninth-grade challenges. Morris scooped up Taylor, Hrag, and his roommate, Mackey, along with first-year UCLA grad Jinsue and second-year TFAer Josh Beardall.

Choosing Taylor was easy. She had been teaching only six months and already had a reputation as one of the best English teachers in the school. Taylor was in a state of constant panic—she sweated all day long and had trouble sleeping. But the doubts she harbored about her efficacy in the classroom weren't obvious to her more experienced colleagues. Mrs. Jauregui, who oversaw the two ninth-grade houses, was almost deferential to her, treating Taylor as if she were the head of the ninth-grade English department. Jauregui sent Taylor to special professional training sessions, and when Taylor announced that she wanted to do more literature-based instruction, Jauregui happily ordered the books. Taylor could tell she was getting little perks that the other teachers didn't—like unlimited access to paper—and she suspected she had Jauregui to thank.

Dr. Wells was an unabashed fan, too, though it was unclear to Taylor if he actually knew her name. He called her "lady." When he mandated an intensive after-school CAHSEE prep for seniors, he handpicked the teachers he wanted to lead them. Half were TFAers, among them first-year corps members Phillip and Taylor. Phillip politely declined the offer. Taylor felt like she was ready to take on something new. Only one kid showed up for her first class (she never had more than a handful of students attend), though she sent out a bunch of flyers and phoned the kids on her roster. She thought the CAHSEE prep was a total waste of time, but she got paid two thousand dollars for it, and God only knows how many brownie points she scored. During the presentation of the proposal for Morris's new school, Dr. Wells stopped her and said, "You know, I really like you," to which she replied, "I like you, too."

The literacy coaches from UCLA had spotted Taylor's talents right away. They told her she had the makings of a great teacher, and they took her along to a conference of English teachers out near Disneyland. She had never been to a conference like that before, so she had no basis for comparison. But it made her not want to be an English teacher. The conference was packed with old ladies who taught English, and every time they stood up and read in their English-teacher voices, Taylor winced. *Oh my God! Is that me? That can't be me!*

But she *was* an English teacher, and a pretty good one at that. She had the numbers to prove it. At the end of the first semester in late January, she made her kids retake the Gates-MacGinitie test she had given them in the beginning of the year. Her average student had started ninth grade reading at a fifth-grade level. She was hoping that in the six months they had been in her classroom, they would have advanced two whole grades. The day before the test, she gave her kids a pep talk; they needed to come in the next day with their game faces on. That night she was so nervous she could hardly sleep. The results came back twelve days later. They had done it! Her kids had made what TFA considered "significant gains" by advancing between one and a half and two years in reading.

She was so proud of them—and they basked in the glory. A few weeks later, on Valentine's Day, Taylor got to feel the love. The Locke campus exploded in a profusion of red and pink—some girls hauled giant teddy bears to class; others paraded around campus clutching balloons and flowers and candy. The kids showered Taylor with cards and gifts, and they watched to see if she had any other admirers. They were always curious about her love life; every male teacher who walked into the room was assumed to be a suitor. One girl gave Taylor a valentine written on lined notebook paper, with hearts drawn around the name Miss Rifkin and an arrow pointing down to the name Mr. Brown. Mackey taught in one of the trailers nearby, and it was true that Taylor had been spending a lot of time with both him and his roommate, Hrag. Taylor's college romance had recently ended. Days after the breakup, she and Hrag met for dinner. The following weekend, she invited Mackey and Hrag to join her on a trip home to Santa Barbara. Mackey begged off because of work. Hrag took her up on the offer. Together, they met up with a few of her friends and camped high on the cliffs north of the city, overlooking the ocean. They clicked.

Hrag and Taylor realized they had a lot in common. Both were struggling to find a balance between their professional and private lives. Both believed in the TFA mission, but neither, it turned out, wanted to be martyrs to the cause. And that's how they were feeling—like they were sacrificing their youth on the altar of social justice. They wanted to have fun—to enjoy life. Hrag felt like he had really aged. It struck him one day early in the second semester when he saw his reflection in a store window on his way to work: he was sitting in his little red Ford with a thermos of tea in one hand and a banana in the other. He burst out laughing at his own image: *What a nerd! If my college buddies could see me now, I'd never hear the end of it.*

Taylor's father had advised her early on not to bring work home—he insisted it was important that she maintain a divide between work and leisure. Hrag had figured that bit out on his own. He, too, needed a total disconnect, but it was hard to avoid the carryover. Once, when he accidentally brought home the PAID stamp he used for marking work completed, he totally freaked out. He couldn't bear to look at the thing, so he ended up hiding it until it was time to go to school again. Another time, he didn't realize he had the stamp in his pocket until he was in the school parking lot and ready to take off. Rather than carry it home, he trudged all the way back up three flights of stairs and stashed it in the classroom. When he left at the end of the day, he didn't want to have to think about Locke again until he walked back in the next morning. He and Jinsue no longer spent hours on the phone planning lessons. Now Morris gave them the general outline of how the week should unfold, and they worked it out together at school. That left Hrag's nights free. He took up guitar again and got back to reading. And he went out nearly every night. Even so, school wasn't that easy to shake off. It was always on his mind. And that really bugged him.

The other thing that bugged him was that there was so little appreciation shown for all the work he did. It seemed that nobody ever had anything positive to say. His graduate school coach had recently been in to observe his classroom and all but told him his lesson sucked. The thing was, it hadn't sucked. It was pretty good. Hrag was teaching genetics, and he had the kids doing a celebrity mating game using Punnett squares. He had posted pictures of celebrities—Will Ferrell, J.Lo, Will Smith, Kobe Bryant, Ashlee Simpson—all around the room. The kids had to pick two of them and then cross their genotypes to figure out what percentage of their offspring would end up with certain traits, like hair and eye color, based on their genetic coding. Kobe Bryant got a lot of action, and the kids insisted on mating Hrag with a celebrity, too. It was a really engaging lesson but admittedly noisy; Hrag ended up kicking three kids out of class. Still, all thirty-four of his students seemed to have fun, and he knew that everyone had understood what was going on. Except the LMU guy. He wanted to know why Hrag would plan a crazy lesson like that, and he gave him a lot of crap for throwing the kids out without a note or a referral. Hrag and he got into it, and the guy left the room all red-faced.

Samir didn't exactly do a jig, either, when he watched Hrag teach the next day. With Samir, it was all business, all the time. He sat through the lesson absolutely stone-faced, then left a letter in Hrag's box telling him what a great job he had done. But Hrag was far from reassured.

He had no idea what the administrators at Locke thought of his classroom performance because no one ever came in to observe him. Jauregui had popped in maybe twice, and that was in the beginning of the first semester. In the six months since, not a single administrator had been in his classroom. That worried him, because the longer he went without constructive criticism, the less he welcomed it. At this point, he didn't need anyone else coming into his room giving him flak.

And the kids! Sometimes they made him feel worst of all. He loved them, even the ones who drove him crazy. But every last bone in their bodies was programmed to defy, and it wore Hrag down. They knew he understood Spanish, and often they would purposely go at one another, hurling Spanish insults across the room, just trying to provoke him. Before he became a teacher, if someone got in his face, he'd push right back. Now he had to be cool and calm and rational, even when what he really wanted to do was strangle a kid. He felt so powerless. Being so young didn't help things. After Hrag wrote a note about José to the dean, José accused him of being a snitch. "We don't do that!" he told Hrag.

Hrag couldn't believe his ears. "Who do you think I am?" he asked. "Your homeboy? Get back in your seat before I send you down to the dean again!" He felt like a wuss. He was the authority. But only in name. There were no consequences he could put into play. He could kick a kid out of class, but the kid was always back the next day, ready to spit in his face again.

The students never showed any gratitude, though Hrag knew perfectly well that he had never understood how hard his teachers worked, either. Still, he put on some kick-ass lessons—really good, hands-on stuff that he himself would have loved in high school. As the year went on, he expanded on the curriculum outline that Morris had given him. Hrag took the lessons and made them his own, adding some slick PowerPoint presentations, dropping exercises he felt were too babyish for him to deliver convincingly. Whenever he was about to introduce a new topic with a really cool project, he telegraphed it by saying: "I am about to blow your minds." The kids loved the expression. And they always sat up straighter in their chairs for the "experience."

One of the most "mind-blowing" lessons he did all year was "Who My Baby Daddy?" Morris had given him the idea, and it had been bequeathed to her by another Locke biology teacher who was long gone. Now it was a Locke classic. Hrag took the lesson's basic outline and created a special PowerPoint for it. The idea was that the students had to figure out who, among five class members, was the father of the singer

Ashanti's baby. The kids were given the phenotypes and genotypes for the mother, child, and five suspected dads. Using Punnett squares, they had to cross traits until they found the combination that matched the baby's.

The first photo of Ashanti was entitled "The Mother," and the caption read "Who my baby daddy?" The next picture was of an adorable African American baby, with a caption that read: "WAAAAA!" For the suspects, Hrag took pictures of five boys from each of his classes, altered the eyes and hair with Photoshop, and listed their alibis in captions below. Father #1: "Man, I'm with the sister"; Father #2: "I never seen that girl in my life"; Father #3: "I didn't get her pregnant but my homey here would like to!"; Father #4: "She's just trying to use me for my money"; and Father #5: "She took advantage of me!" The kids had a blast.

Morris had never seen Hrag teach. She didn't need to. She could tell by the way the kids talked about him, and the way he talked about them, that he was a good teacher. He was on a sharp learning curve; it certainly didn't seem like this was his first year on the job. The way he jumped in and contributed to the curriculum impressed her. And she especially liked the way he got frustrated and as a result was constantly trying new things. In the beginning, classroom management was tough for him, and she could see that he took things way too personally. She reminded him that the kids were pretty much the same way every day; it was usually the teacher who was doing the changing, and the kids naturally fed off the instructor's mood shifts. *It's true,* he thought. The students in his fifth period were probably acting out because they could sense his own apprehension about being able to teach them.

Hrag wasn't at the very first meeting of the new School of Math and Science because he wasn't sure he was invited. Morris needed only one biology teacher, and he and Jinsue were a team—they had agreed that neither would join the new school without the other. It took a personal invitation from Morris and an agreement on Jinsue's part to teach chemistry before Hrag would consider it. Even then, he was skeptical. He thought the small schools at Locke had ended up being divisive; the school as a whole had broken up into warring factions of teacher cliques—the veterans, the SE folks, the TFAers, the PE teachers, and so on. After meeting with the School of Math and Science team, he changed his mind overnight. Probably the only way to save the school was to deconstruct it, he concluded. With enough good small schools, Locke as a whole would have to improve—and could eventually even be great. Hrag threw himself into the school planning, agreeing to write the biology proposal; Taylor proofread it. He really liked being a part of developing something new, and it was the first venue he'd found where he could have a say in things beyond his own classroom. The people on the crew were really smart. Even if they didn't all end up staying, maybe they could build something to leave behind.

Until then Hrag had felt uncomfortable around Morris and the SE crowd. They were older and had a long history together. But as he got to know them better over beers and a round of parties, he realized they were people, too—people who sometimes drank too much, used profane language, and did things they regretted the next morning. He felt that he was on their level now, and that was transforming. It made him happier. But he was scared, too, because he could feel himself getting drawn in—to Locke, to teaching, to the camaraderie, to the idea that he was serving the greater good. He knew it would be hard to let go of this, and if he didn't, he might end up being an educator. He wasn't sure why he was so afraid of it; he didn't know what picture he had for himself and his future.

So when he wasn't stressing or destressing about school, he was driving himself nuts thinking about what to do after TFA. One thing he knew for sure: he didn't want to be one of those TFAers who stayed for a third year because they couldn't think of anything else to do. He had to find something he could be passionate about—besides teaching in a low-performing school in the inner city. So he bought himself an LSAT prep book, thinking that law school might be the answer, and when he failed to work up any enthusiasm for becoming an attorney, he considered writing a screenplay. He spent a lot of time on the TFA website, too, looking at the job postings and opportunities open to TFA alums.

And he hung out with Taylor. They were both experiencing these emotional thunderstorms that left them on the edge, constantly freaking out. One day she would need bucking up; the next day it would be his turn. They had similar personalities. They both had a sarcastic sense of humor, and neither was afraid of confrontation. They worked hard (he thought she worked harder than he did), and they played hard. There weren't many TFAers that Hrag could convince to stay out with him till 4 a.m. on a school night, but Taylor was one of them. They saw each other every day at school, and pretty soon they were spending most of their free time together as well. They planned all kinds of weekend adventures—like a spur-of-the-moment jaunt to San Francisco, and a fifty-mile bicycle trip after a night of partying and no sleep at all. Taylor was a tremendous help to Hrag—she got him through the day. And she was happy to do it. They were best friends.

CHAPTER ELEVEN

¡Sí Se Puede!

There were no Friday-night lights at Locke. In fact, there was hardly any football, period. The Locke Saints played only two at-home games all season—and one of those was the homecoming game. It was just too dangerous. Though the campus was relatively safe, the neighborhood wasn't. There were at least four very active gangs within a half-mile radius of Locke, and too often the violence jumped the fence.

It wasn't unusual to find weapons stashed on campus by gangbanging dropouts. In the spring of 2006, well into football's spring training season, somebody found a rusty old nine-millimeter Browning tucked under a backpack on the field where the football players were working out. It looked like a piece of junk; the problem was, it was loaded.

A few weeks earlier, a former student had made his way onto the campus after school let out, gotten into an argument with some kid, and ended up pulling out a gun. There were plenty of students around at the time, and they scattered. A few big guys bolted up the stairs into Rachelle's room, slamming the door shut behind them. She was busy working at her computer and asked them to leave; they begged her to let them stay. "There's a guy with a gun!" they cried. "Call the office!"

They were scared, really shaken up. Once they had calmed down, she got the story. The two kids involved knew each other, argued, and things quickly escalated. One kid slapped the other, and the next thing anyone knew, there was a gun. The kid staring into the muzzle raised his arms in surrender. The would-be shooter lowered the weapon and booked it out of there, sprinting across the crowded quad and scaling the fence onto the street. The students ran, too. Dropping their backpacks, they headed for the main building.

Rachelle gave the kids a snack, and after five minutes or so decided it was probably safe for them to leave. She thought she'd go down to check things out first. Then she came to her senses. *I don't need to see this first-hand. I can't protect them from a bullet.* Thinking about it later, she realized that the kids had known exactly what kind of gun it was; they could identify it even from a distance. It also dawned on her that those three tenth-graders had obviously seen people get shot before. *How crazy is that?*

Soon afterward, there was a gang homicide right on the other side of the fence that enclosed the ninth-grade classroom trailers, just yards away from where the fifteen-year-old student Deliesh Allen had been killed the year before. This time, the shooter was a fifteen-to-eighteen-year-old black male wearing a green sweatshirt and riding a bike. About eight shots went off, and when the cops arrived minutes later, they found a young male dressed in a white T-shirt, facedown between a car and the curb. There was a splotch of blood on the back of his shirt where he had been hit. The officer at the scene could tell that he had died right away because he hadn't bled out—when death comes more slowly, the victims lie in a pool of blood. The shooting occurred right in the middle of the ninth-graders' lunch period, and the gunman had headed north, along the eastern perimeter of the school, to escape. One of the cops radioed the campus police station and asked that the ninth-grade house be put on lockdown. But the lunch hour was crazy that day; Dr. Wells must have been off-site, and the security detail handling the lunch period didn't make it happen. At least the cops were able to get additional police units assigned to dismissal, because when the kids got out of school a few hours later, the body was still there, awaiting the arrival of the coroner.

Violence aside, if you asked Coach Crawford, he would just as soon play all the football games away. Home games were distracting. There was too much going on in the streets and stands for the Locke Saints to really focus on the game. So he preferred to bus his players—and as many fans as they could muster—off campus and out of the neighborhood for the football season.

There was a period when Locke had been a football powerhouse in the city's 3A division. But over the years, the program had declined as more and more of the neighborhood's best athletes opted to be bused out of the neighborhood to better schools. By the time Crawford took over as head coach in 2003, the Locke Saints were considered perennial losers. But that was changing. When Dr. Wells came in, he replaced the old hand-me-down football uniforms from UCLA with brand-new ones. Kids started coming out for the team, and when walking around campus, the players took to tucking their helmets proudly under their arms. In 2005, there were fifty-five varsity players, up from thirty in 2003, and the boys finished third in their conference—the best Locke had done since 1999.

With the exception of a couple of Hispanics, football was the domain of the African Americans at Locke, and far too many of them played it thinking that it would get them out of the ghetto and into the NFL. Crawford discouraged that idea, urging his players instead to get the grades they needed to go to college—a much surer path to success. Not every kid who joined the team had stars in his eyes. Some suited up because they wanted to be a part of something—besides a gang. They may not have been particularly athletic, but Crawford didn't turn anyone away. Kids were getting jumped in at younger and younger ages. After fourteen years of coaching, Crawford had no illusions. The gangs were the real competition his players faced.

While Crawford was trying to breathe new life into the boys' football team, the girls' soccer team was thriving. At Locke, sports mirrored the demographics and the changing culture. Football recalled Locke's storied past, when African Americans were the majority; soccer represented its future, as Hispanics continued to gain ascendancy. The boys' varsity soccer team was okay; the girls' varsity team was great. With Rachelle as head coach, the girls' JV squad ended up dominating, too. She may not have felt totally comfortable teaching special ed, but she was a natural soccer coach. She loved the game and recognized how much it had given her. She believed it could do the same for her girls.

At first, the girls were skeptical. Where did this white girl come off trying to coach them—Latinas who had been playing soccer since before they could even speak? But Rachelle had the skills, and whatever initial qualms the girls may have had, they were quickly replaced by a kind of reverence. The JV girls hung around Rachelle like she was a movie star. They stopped by room 214 before classes, between classes, after classes—often just to chat, sometimes to get help with their schoolwork, too.

Locke atheletes had to maintain at least a 2.0 GPA, and some coaches were grandfathering in a no-fails requirement. Dennis Stein, the boys' soccer coach, offered an academic lunch club during the season, and his kids had to subscribe to his priority list: family first, school second, then soccer. If soccer took precedence over academics, the kid couldn't play. So sports was an effective way to keep students engaged in school.

Playing soccer had worked for Rachelle as a student. Now coaching soccer began to work for her as a teacher, too. She had spent the first half of the year feeling very isolated. That began to change in early February, when the Locke coaches invited her join them on a trip to Las Vegas for a huge coaching clinic at the Flamingo Hotel. Rachelle didn't know what to expect when she said yes. At Locke, there was tension between some of the young, hard-driving teachers who were hell-bent on academic achievement and the athletic coaches, whose players got out of school one period early for practices and games. Folks like Chad Soleo and Josh Hartford argued that the kids at Locke needed more, not less, time in the classroom, and SE had introduced a seven-period day to make that happen. The coaches resented the encroachment on team time, insisting that sports were a proven way to get kids hooked on school. The conflict engendered yet another divide at Locke: the jocks versus the nerds.

Rachelle traveled to and from Las Vegas with Locke's basketball coach, Stephen Minix. Minix, a twenty-eight-year-old six-footer whose family lived in Washington, had been at Locke for four years, making him practically an old-timer. At first Rachelle was hesitant to ride with Minix. Los Angeles to Las Vegas was a six-hour car ride, and she didn't want to be stuck with a total stranger. But they had a mutual friend who helped out with the softball team, and she agreed to accompany them. Rachelle sat in the backseat and listened to the two of them chattering away up front. *He's so nice,* she thought.

Traveling as a member of the athletics department was an eye-opener. Many of her companions on the trip defied all of her preconceived notions. The coaches were smart, dedicated professionals who loved their students as much as she did. Unlike some of the TFAers who were in and out of teaching, these coaches were in it for good; it was what they wanted to do with their lives.

And they knew how to have fun. On the third night, they all got kicked out of the hotel. Somehow, in typical Locke fashion, the reservations had been screwed up and their rooms were booked. The problem was, every hotel in the city was full. So they ended up cruising around the hooker hotels begging for lodging. In the end, they found one room and all piled in for the night. They had a blast. Rachelle found herself bonding with them. They were so *normal.*

They regaled her with Locke stories, and she began to see a side of teaching that seemed to be missing from the Teach For America approach. They didn't talk about significant gains and tracking data; they were more interested in the whole child. Minix, who was the son of a biracial couple, told of how sometimes he would shut the door, forget about "teaching," and just open the floor up to questions. He found that the kids were desperate to find an adult to talk to, someone who actually listened to them and could identify with them. If you happened to be that adult, the kids gave 100 percent back. That approach resonated with Rachelle, and she began to spend more and more time with Stephen and his colleagues.

She was on the field on February 24 for the last game of the girls' varsity soccer season—all the coaches were. Many of the Locke jocks, encouraged by their coaches, came out to cheer the girls on. It was a Friday afternoon, generally a kick-back time at Locke anyway, so Rachelle told the students in her last class that if they got all their work done quickly, they could all make posters and go down to the field to watch the game. It also happened to be Mexican Flag Day, and many kids had come to school wearing sombreros and clutching the green, white, and red Mexican flag. When Rachelle's students arrived at the field, the stands were already filling up; black and brown, boys and girls, even the Hispanic rockers in their tight black jeans and studded jackets were there to watch the show. It was magical. The great divides at Locke disappeared. For this one special game, everyone there was a Locke Saint. Looking back on it, Rachelle considered it the most exciting girls' soccer game she had ever seen.

They were playing Cleveland High School, a good team from the San Fernando Valley. Cleveland was much more ethnically diverse than

Locke; 60 percent of its students were Hispanic, while the rest were a mix of white, Asian, and black. The school ranked relatively high academically, and some on the Locke side detected a whiff of superiority in the air when Cleveland arrived and took the field. "That Valley team came in and thought they'd kick the ball around for a few minutes," recalls Dennis Stein. "They didn't know anything about us. We had been completely overlooked." But as Stein observed: "The one thing our kids know how to do is fight."

And fight they did. The girls played their hearts out. The Saints kept Cleveland scoreless, and when the ref blew the whistle to end the game, Locke was scoreless, too.

The game went into overtime, and the stands were transformed into a churning sea of green, white, and red. Chants burst from the bleachers; drums sounded. The fans were in a frenzy, and still neither side scored.

Now it was double overtime. With a minute of play left, Locke scored, ending the game 1–0. With the ball safely in the net, fans—black and brown—poured out of the bleachers and onto the field. They were laughing, hollering, dancing. One black football player draped himself in the Mexican flag and ran around the field, a scene etched forever in Locke's collective memory. The players wept, and so did many of the coaches and teachers. "It was our little World Cup," recalls Zeus Cubias, who had started the girls' soccer team in 1998. "It was our Brazil, our England." The field was filled with revelers long after the Cleveland buses pulled away. Someone blasted a Latin American *punta* from a boom box, and the kids danced in delirious delight to the ancestral rhythm.

The soccer game was just a curtain-raiser to an extraordinary display of Hispanic pride and passion at Locke a month later. A battle over immigration policy had been heating up for months all across the country as legislators debated the fate of some twelve million illegal immigrants believed to be living in the United States. The issue was particularly pointed in Los Angeles, home to the largest immigrant population in the country. On March 25, more than half a million Angelenos descended on city hall in one of the largest protests in L.A. history. La Gran Marcha was followed the next Monday by a student walkout that left many of Los Angeles's inner-city high schools virtually empty. Unlike the weekend march, the student protest appeared to be hastily organized via MySpace pages and text messages. When word of the walkouts spread, many

LAUSD high school campuses went on lockdown to ensure that students stayed in their seats. Locke was one of them.

Roberto, a senior at Locke, had attended La Gran Marcha downtown that Saturday. It filled him with pride to see so many of his people join in the show of unity: they were good people, hardworking people, whom the government was trying to mess with. The news had said there were 500,000 protesters. That was completely incorrect. Roberto thought there were one million, maybe even two million people at the height of the demonstration. Hispanics were everywhere, as far as the eye could see, and they were all hollering *"¡Sí se puede!"* ("We can do it!"), the motto of the United Farm Workers coined by César Chávez in the seventies. Roberto had never seen anything like it, and it filled his heart with pride.

He and his sisters left City Hall at around two on Saturday afternoon. He had to go to work. It was his duty. He was one of five children born to immigrant parents from Michoacán, Mexico. In his family, the children contributed to the family income. Roberto had begun bagging groceries two years before, in tenth grade. He made $6.75 an hour and worked twenty-two hours a week—usually on the weekends and one day during the week.

When Roberto awoke at six-thirty for school on Monday, he felt unusually calm. To him, the calm had always been a sign of something. He wondered what was up: *Something is about to occur. Something is about to cause chaos in my world.* At that point, his world was full of possibility. With a 3.7 GPA, he was waiting to hear which UC he would be attending in the fall. He was a big man on campus—a track star, actor, poet, and political activist. People knew him. Thin, with an angular face, dark, piercing eyes, and a goatee, he had an intensity that made him stand out from his peers. When he spoke, people listened.

At Locke that Monday, he went straight to his AP statistics class and then on to AP physics with Mr. Hartford. It was in his third-period economics class—his favorite class that semester—that he heard something. It sounded like a rush of air or wind, and it stopped him cold. Then a voice came on over the loudspeaker. The school was on lockdown. All students were to remain in their classrooms; no restroom passes were to be issued. Now Roberto could make out words that seemed to be carried along by the draft of morning air. It was the same chant he had heard on Saturday: *Sí se puede, sí se puede.* We can do it. We can do it. It was faint but getting closer. Roberto was thinking: *Oh, Jesus. Oh, Jesus.* All of a sudden, everyone in the classroom, even his teacher Mr. Crumrine, was looking at him. And then Emilio, a friend, said: "Hey, are we gonna walk?" Roberto didn't respond, but the minute he had heard *Sí se puede* he had pictured how it all would unfold. Maybe it was a flashback to pictures he had seen of 1968, when Chicanos had last made newspaper headlines with a historic march: in his head he had an image of students just walking down the street. It was like a bomb went off in him: *You have to walk. You have to walk for your mom, for your parents, for your pride, for your* patria. *Lead your people.* But they were on lockdown. Frustrated, Roberto said to Mr. Crumrine: "Did we really scare society that bad?"

Crumrine wouldn't engage. He told Roberto and the rest of the class to finish the test they were taking. Roberto returned to his work and, when he was done, sat back and looked at the clock. He could feel the blood rushing through his veins, stopping at his temples and pulsing. Something was telling him: *The time, the time, get up and walk, join your people.* And he looked at all his fellow students and wondered: *Who will walk? How many truly know what we are standing up for? How many have pride?* When five minutes were left till the bell would ring, he held up his five fingers; when a minute passed, he held up four. Just as the period was about to end, when Roberto held only two fingers up in a victory sign, the administration announced that the lockdown was over. Students were free to go to lunch.

Roberto got up, slung his backpack over his shoulder, and headed for the quad. On his way, a friend filled him in on what was happening at other campuses all over Los Angeles. What should Locke do? Without even thinking, Roberto replied: "If you have pride for your culture, you will get on the stage." Then, before he knew it, he was onstage, in the center, looking out and pointing to those Latinos who had not yet joined him. By then, others had taken up the refrain: "If you have pride for your culture, you will get onstage." Someone thrust a big Mexican flag into Roberto's hands, and he stood there, solemnly waving it before the kids standing in the quad looking up at him. Within minutes the stage was filled.

Beside him, Roberto's best friend, Alonzo, said: "Now what do we do?"

Roberto said: "We walk."

And so they did. Hundreds of students formed a column behind Roberto, who, like a twenty-first-century Pied Piper, led them along Saint Street, the internal campus road, to the school gates. To those who wavered or started to head back toward the stage, he said: "If you have pride for your culture, walk with me." The column got longer and thicker. When they finally reached the perimeter, the gates were locked. Roberto announced: "Wait. They will open." In the crowd, approaching him, was Dr. Wells.

For Frank Wells, deciding to open the gates was just part of the plan. In the morning, he and his administrators had discussed their strategy for handling a walkout. They had agreed that they would stop any individual student who tried to ditch or jump the fence. But in the event that a group of kids was organized and decided to leave, they would let them go.

Wells started getting calls from the police and other principals soon after school opened. Students had left other schools and were marching to neighboring LAUSD campuses to rally support. When Wells got word that a group of kids was headed toward Locke, he immediately put the school on lockdown. Soon, students from Fremont stood outside Locke chanting, urging their compatriots to join them in a show of strength. But the Locke kids were penned in and locked down. Stuck.

Wells lifted the lockdown about an hour later, after the Fremont marchers were long gone. Without others inciting them, Wells thought it unlikely that the Locke kids would walk out. Besides, he knew it was going to be tough to keep his kids on lockdown during the lunch periods. They would be hungry and antsy—a bad combination in teenagers. Lunch would proceed; the school would use the student protest as a teaching moment. Students would be encouraged to assemble at the center stage to discuss the politics of immigration.

For a few minutes it looked as if that's how things would go. Until Roberto mounted the stage and started waving the Mexican flag over his head. Wells had assigned his security team to their usual lunchtime positions so that the entire campus would be monitored. Now there weren't enough guards in the quad to stop Roberto once he started walking. When he reached the gate, it was open sesame. It was a matter of safety. If Wells refused to open the gate, he risked setting off a riot. It was not a risk he was prepared to take. As the gates opened, kids rushed to escape.

"We don't have to run today," Roberto said, speaking in both English and Spanish. "Today we walk." As kids poured out onto the street, Wells was right behind him, speaking into his ear: "Control them," he ordered. "Control them."

Roberto wasn't going to promise anything. He would try, but he wasn't sure that anyone could really control what was happening. He stopped, waited for the students at the far gate to be released, and said: "Okay, we start marching."

Zeus Cubias had been at La Gran Marcha on Saturday. He'd supported that protest. But he was against walking out of school. He had already been told that the Latino students planned to meet at the stage during lunch. He had promised to be there to make sure the administration allowed them to hold a peaceful rally. When Roberto began to lead them down Saint Street toward the gate, Cubias tried to dissuade the kids from following him. He walked along with them, urging them to turn around. When he got to the gate, he saw Wells ahead of him.

"Cubias," said Wells, turning to greet him. "Aren't you coming?" Cubias couldn't believe it. He had assumed the principal would have wanted him to get the kids back to their classrooms. Suddenly, his estimation of Frank Wells changed. Wells had done what a movie principal would have. This was like *Stand and Deliver.* Cubias understood the role Wells expected him to play that day. Cubias had to keep the kids safe. Soon other Latino staff joined the parade in a show of solidarity with their students. Mrs. Jauregui was walking, and so was Elissa Salas, one of the TFA resource teachers in special ed. Most important, Dr. Wells was marching, too.

The Locke contingent continued along San Pedro Street. Cubias marched in front with Roberto; Wells stayed in the middle of the pack. Cubias advised Roberto to turn around at Manchester Avenue, a big boulevard about twenty blocks from Locke. Roberto jogged back to consult with Wells. The principal was adamant: Roberto should turn around. The students had made their point, Wells said; now it was time to get back to school. Besides, Wells didn't want Locke students making trouble at Fremont, another big LAUSD high school up ahead. Roberto had led them out of school; now it was his responsibility to lead them back in. Cubias kept the pressure on Roberto. He was afraid things were getting out of control; Roberto had to get a better grip on the kids.

Roberto started to stress. When he got to Manchester he paused and thought: *All right, what should I do? Should I keep going toward Fre-*

mont and break trust with my principal and a really good teacher? Or should I keep going? The answer formed instantly: *You have the whole school behind you. Keep going, keep going.*

He kept going. By now, people were coming out of their homes, some offering the kids food and water, others joining the march. Banners popped up out of nowhere. The Mexican flag floated above their heads. Eventually the TV cameras caught up with them. That's how Roberto's mother came to find out where he was: she saw him on TV. His older sister phoned him. "What are you doing?" she asked.

"I'm leading this march," he replied. Soon groups of students from other schools joined up with the Locke kids. By then, Wells had returned to campus. Zeus decided to peel off, too. He had done his thing on Saturday. This was their thing. He needed to let them do it. He felt like crying. He had forgotten what these wonderful kids are capable of when they are motivated.

When the marchers from the various campuses converged south of downtown, Roberto discovered that two rival OGs (Original Gangsters) were at the front of the march. He knew them from their tattoos. They were probably in their thirties. And here they were, walking together for a common cause. Roberto was astounded. *They fucked up. The senators and the politicians, they fucked up because they are trying to pass a bill that affects all these gangs, and now they are uniting them. They are uniting all of us. We are walking as one people.*

"I'm the leader from Locke," he announced to the old-school gangstas. Then out of his mouth came "We're gonna go to city hall." The OGs were headed that way, too. The march swelled, filling up the streets curb to curb. The paced quickened as they got closer to downtown. Immigrant workers came out of their shops to cheer the marchers on. "You are walking for us!" they cried. Now Roberto was thinking of Exodus: *My people are walking toward significance . . .*

When Roberto actually spoke into the microphone at city hall, the crowd quieted. It seemed impossible. "We have accomplished what our parents and ancestors gave us the will to do," he said into the mike. "To walk for them with all our heart and strength to prove a point. We are the future. We have shown great pride, and that will lead us to even greater strength."

Back at Locke, very few students were in class. And the hallways, usually home to the ditchers not caught in the hourly tardy sweeps, were curiously empty. Most Latino students had walked out; quite a few African Americans had, too. Some marched with the Latinos. "I'm down with my homeys," one black student told Cubias. "I don't want them to send you guys back!" Others saw a golden opportunity to skip school and took it.

Taylor, Hrag, and Mackey missed the walkout. Taylor had thrown herself a birthday bash over the weekend at her Marina del Rey condo. A lot of the Locke contingent had joined in the celebration, which ended only when the cops came to write Taylor up for disturbing the peace with all the noise. Later in the weekend, still in the party mood, she and Hrag had hightailed it up to San Francisco on the spur of the moment. Once there, they decided to take Monday off as a mental-health day. Normally, both would have felt guilty about ditching. But Vanessa Morris was a great believer in mental-health days. She encouraged her teachers to take a day off at least once a month to recharge their emotional batteries. It was something she herself did routinely. It was one of the things that kept her sane and teaching at Locke.

Mackey didn't go to San Francisco, but he took Monday off, too. He felt bad that they had missed being a part of what could have been a turning point in the national discourse about immigration. Hrag had no regrets at all. He didn't think experiencing four kids in his classroom, instead of thirty, would have made him feel a part of anything. He was glad he wasn't there. It was a lost day.

Rachelle didn't teach biology the day of the walkout. Instead she ran off some questions about immigration and public protests and gave them to her students to help stimulate a classroom conversation. But many of them, black and brown, had joined the march.

The walkout came as a total surprise to Phillip. The first he heard of it was when he received a text message from a teacher at a neighboring school. "Is everything okay at your school? Are you on lockdown?" No sooner had Phillip read the message than the announcement of the lockdown came over the PA system. The kids seemed unfazed, and Phillip taught until his third period was over and the lockdown was lifted. But moments after the kids filed out, he heard chanting and loud talking. When he looked down onto Saint Street from his third-floor window, he saw kids running by the side of the building. He strained to see where they were going and what they were saying.

Curious, he joined others in a colleague's room with a better view. He was shocked. Below him in the parking lot were probably a thousand students. The ones on the perimeter were banging on the locked gates. It was hard to imagine how this show was going to end. Suddenly, the walkie-talkie of a security guard standing nearby crackled with instructions: "Go to San Pedro! Open the gate!" It was Dr. Wells. The next thing Phillip knew, the principal and a number of teachers had joined the students as they poured out of the campus and onto the street. Phillip was shocked. *Why? Why would he open the gate?*

He taught to near-empty classrooms for the rest of the day. It was frustrating. In Phillip's mind, nothing should ever get in the way of teaching; he could never support anything that detracted from academic learning time. Was an education something to be valued or squandered? Maybe Phillip was just too straight and narrow, but he thought the whole thing was stupid. It was an entire day wasted for children who couldn't afford to lose a single minute.

What was even more frustrating was that the next day was affected as well. Though teachers weren't alerted, the district mandated that every school open on lockdown. Wells imposed a modified lockdown instead; kids would go to only their first and fifth periods, and those would be extended blocks. He got on the PA system to explain:

"Yesterday, a number of students participated in an organized walk from San Pedro to City Hall. That is done, and we are moving on. I do have to advise you that we have rules and regulations here. Any students engaged in any such action today will be precluded from participating in any senior activities. That's nonnegotiable and you will be subject to suspension and expulsion. . . . I am proud to say that the students who did leave school took part in a meaningful and peaceful march, and you should be applauded for that. But that was yesterday, and today is today. Do not use school as a forum. Don't do it at school. Use your own time."

Wells's handling of the walkout was a matter of debate. Chad Soleo applauded his leadership. Cubias said Wells had performed like a movie-star principal; it was a shining moment. But the TFAers had their doubts. They understood it was a tricky situation, but they wondered about the message that had been sent. How do you, as principal, walk out with the kids one day and the next day declare it an offense punishable by expulsion?

The announcement of the block periods came in the middle of the first period. Taylor was frustrated. Her class was half empty. She had intended to start a new unit, but she knew if she did, she'd be screwing herself, because she would only have to teach it over again the next day when the rest of the class showed up. Apparently, the entire district was on block periods. Taylor couldn't figure out why. But then she couldn't figure out why they had let a walkout happen right under their noses, either: *How could this school think there was any instructional time to lose? I have different priorities. I'm concerned that my kids can't read, and you let them have a walkout.*

She decided to use the extended block time to discuss the march and the issue of illegal immigration. The kids were ready to talk. Her twelfth-graders told her they were scared the day before when they saw so many Hispanic students assembling at the stage area. The stage had traditionally been a flash point for racial disturbances. During the last big one, three years before, kids were throwing chairs, heads were getting busted, trash cans were on fire, and helicopters whirred overhead.

"It seemed like a war," recalled one senior. "The Hispanics were on one side and the blacks were on the other. I remember this little short dude, they threw something at him, and his head was dripping with blood. I was scared. I just kept thinking, 'Oh my God. Oh my God.'" This time, when she saw the students leave the stage and head for Saint Street, she was relieved—and sympathetic to the cause, as were most of the students.

"Without the immigrants, the world would be disorganized," observed one African American girl. "Who would do the things for the whites or the African Americans here?"

A Latina agreed. "I'm not being racist, but no white person gonna be sitting here in the sun and working the fields and doing construction," she observed. "The majority of the people who work for that are Hispanics. Without us, there wouldn't be a lot of work getting done. I'm not saying we are a big part of the U.S., but we are a part."

Another African American girl observed: "For them to say the immigrants are takin' over the jobs, it is not true. They are not takin' over jobs from African Americans. They don't want to do nothin' but sell drugs. They say Latinos are takin' over the jobs, but if a Latino not doin' the jobs, who will? Because the black people don't want to do it."

Then another Latino jumped in: "Hey, there are a lot of Hispanic drug dealers, too. Half of my family, they are drug dealers. Not all Hispanics are the same, and not all blacks are, either. What do you think,

Miss Rifkin?" Taylor confessed that she didn't know the particulars of the proposed changes in immigration law. She urged her students to become knowledgeable about the debate and to think critically about the issues.

"Whether or not you realize it, soon you will be the majority," said Taylor. "It's your time to empower yourselves. Think: Who is in power now? Whites are, and that should piss you off because you are the majority, and it makes no sense. What I'm putting to you is, it is your job to be educated and fill those positions of power, because you are going to become the majority in this city. If you are not seeing people who look like you in power, you should change that. People who say they hate immigrants are ridiculous. This country is a country of immigrants. My family emigrated from Russia—a Jewish family from Russia." The discussion went on for two hours.

Phillip didn't discuss the previous day's events at all. He taught the lesson he had planned and used the extra time in the blocks to meet with each student. It was great. He was able to review their grades with them and get them caught up on missing work. Other colleagues showed movies during the long block. Not Phillip. He had geometry standards to cover.

CHAPTER TWELVE

Rats on a Ship

Dr. Wells always talked about his 911s, those little emergencies that seemed to pop up out of nowhere to demand all his attention. But the school's real problems were actually more like thunderheads—black and menacing—and as the semester progressed they seemed to gather and grow darker.

March was a long and difficult month, a time of reckoning. The CAHSEE, the California High School Exit Exam, was scheduled for March 21 and 22. Until then, there had been no consequences for failing the state-mandated test. But in 2006, it counted; any senior who didn't pass would not be allowed to graduate. So the school had gone all out. In addition to Saturday-morning prep classes, vulnerable seniors had been assigned to mandatory after-school preps. On top of that, for two weeks leading up to the tests, the students scheduled to take the exam were pulled out of their normal classes from 11 a.m. to 3 p.m. each day and enrolled in "CAHSEE boot camp." Taylor, who was teaching one of the after-school preps, thought it was a ridiculous effort at damage control. With three different CAHSEE preps running at the same time, the school was on prep overload, with many teachers reviewing the same material.

Once the kids caught on that the preps were redundant, they ditched. It was way too much, way too late.

In the middle of the frenzied test preparation, the WASC accrediting team (also dreaded) was scheduled to visit. In the weeks leading up to the March 15 date, the district had dispatched two teams to the campus to help administrators prepare. The meetings culminated in a mock WASC visit to various classrooms. The teachers had been forewarned; classrooms were to be tidied up, standards and daily lesson plans were to be clearly posted.

Administrators were on patrol. Taylor got one classroom inspection right before the mock visit. When she heard the knock on the door, she knew immediately that it was the WASC cops. Sure enough, the visiting AP scrutinized every area of the room. The floors were dirty—janitors didn't get back to clean up the bungalows as often as they should—and the classroom was cluttered. But the state standards were posted, and so was the day's agenda. Every teacher at Locke was supposed to have daily lesson plans typed up, but few, if any, ever did. Nevertheless, the visiting AP asked Taylor for her proof of lesson planning and reminded her that it was customary to have it on hand for observations. "If anyone came in and observed this class, they would know that I have a lesson plan," replied Taylor. And, she added, while she understood that classrooms had to be orderly, she was not about to mop her own floors. (As it was, she swept them regularly.) Though the AP had said she was carrying out a routine classroom observation, the note Taylor got later mentioned nothing about her teaching. Instead, it was a scathing indictment of her messy room. The official WASC team ended up visiting Taylor's classroom a few weeks later for thirty seconds. She never heard about WASC again.

Hrag got some company, too. Over a two-week period, four different administrators came to observe his class. One AP visited just as Hrag realized he had screwed up his whole lesson plan. He stood there and carried on, making up DNA strands, faking the entire lesson. If the AP realized it, he didn't let on. Hrag never got any meaningful feedback from any of them; he figured they were just checking to make sure his standards were posted for WASC. He didn't really care anyway. He wasn't trying in the least to impress them. In a way, he was just waiting for someone to say something, because he wanted to unload.

The matter of unissued textbooks at Locke had finally been resolved just weeks before. As one of the terms of the settlement of the lawsuit *Williams* v. *State of California,* which alleged that students in low-performing schools were denied equal educational opportunity, state law required that every student be provided with standards-aligned textbooks or instructional material within two months of the start of the 2005 school year. Until then, it had been common practice among many teachers at Locke and other low-performing schools not to distribute textbooks.

At a December faculty meeting, Wells had described the *Williams* case as "the next best thing since *Brown* v. *Board of Education,*" and ordered all teachers to distribute books to their students under threat of termination. "We're out of compliance," he warned the faculty. "If we fail to adhere, the state can take us over."

He was still preaching the same sermon two months later, at the end of February, a day before the county was scheduled to audit the school for compliance in the *Williams* settlement. "We look pretty good," he advised teachers. "But if even one teacher is out of compliance, that would kill us. It's bigger than me, and it's bigger than you, because we could get taken over. The *Williams* case is not a bad thing. It's because schools like Locke were not providing kids with textbooks for the last two decades that this is happening."

The next day, Rachelle handed out the biology books in room 241. There were only three kids in her fourth-period class, but she decided to do a little role-playing with them, in case a state auditor just happened to come by.

"These are your books," she said. "You can take them home. You now have been assigned a book. I didn't realize you had to have a book—"

"What the fuck?" asked Kenyon.

Rachelle ignored him. "If someone walked in the door with a business suit on and said, 'Please raise your hand if you do not have a book,' would anyone raise his hand?"

When they all responded with a no, she continued: "As a matter of fact, we don't do many things from the book."

"Then why we need a book if we don't use it?" asked Shandrel, a big, husky football player.

It was a good question. The day before, in the faculty meeting, Dr. Wells had observed: "It is not normal to have a class of thirty-five students without books." It was also not normal to have a class of thirty-five students who couldn't read. The biology department got around that handicap by offering inquiry-based, hands-on instruction. Textbooks were not used. Ever. Not for special ed or for general ed. Like Rachelle, Hrag complied with the directive but without much enthusiasm. *Honestly, we don't use them. The kids will take the books home, and we'll be lucky if we get 25 percent of them back. This is such a waste of money and time. Why distribute textbooks that kids can't read?*

Distributed they were, and the school was found to be in compliance. Having dodged that bullet, the administration zeroed back in on the WASC process. Prior to the scheduled visit, the school had to prepare a status report, outlining its problems as well as its progress since the last WASC visit in 2004. The report submitted by one of Locke's assistant principals was a disaster. One district supervisor observed that it looked like a brochure—and not a very good one at that. When Chad saw it, he was appalled. *It could have been written by a third-grader.* Wells agreed.

He put Chad, the self-described vice principal of leftover jobs, in charge of the rewrite. In the end, Chad asked most of his "entourage," plus such stalwarts as Vanessa Morris and English chair Bruce Smith, to help out. They divided the report into sections and took the areas they were most knowledgeable about. But there were some chapters, like school finance, for which no one had expertise. "It was hilarious," remembers Smith. "Some of it was pure fiction. I just wrote what I thought should have happened. All the meetings I referred to? They never occurred. If I told them what really happened, we would have been shut down."

It was a matter of expediency. Locke was a perennial on the state's Program Improvement (PI) roster of schools that do not make Adequate Yearly Progress (AYP) under No Child Left Behind. Loss of accreditation was a real possibility. After all, Crenshaw High had been stripped of its accreditation the summer before, and it had gotten better scores than Locke. It was do-or-die time.

At the same time that the WASC process was unfolding, SAIT was on campus. The SAIT team consisted of a few county education consultants who were brought in to help fix Locke, which had failed to meet agreed-upon growth targets after accepting more than three million dollars in state High Priority Schools Grant Program funding since 2002. SAIT had started out early in 2006 by conducting an academic survey of the staff to identify the school's most pressing needs. The survey was followed by small focus groups. In her group, Taylor let it rip: she suggested that the school institute two-period blocks of literacy instruction. And she insisted that the curriculum needed to be literature-based. The SAIT consultant seemed to like her ideas—particularly since the others spent the time complaining about the administration and crummy teaching conditions.

Based on staff input and team observations, SAIT began to develop an action plan for academic improvement at Locke. This was not the first time the school had been the subject of intervention. SAIT discovered at least five other so-called student-achievement plans gathering dust at Locke. One was actually a draft; no one could find the finished product, if there ever was one. Part of the problem was that there was no institutional memory at Locke. Administrators had come and gone, with not so much as a handoff. The other factor was that the plans and the action steps were all boilerplate, written to meet a requirement. No one at Locke took them seriously, and none of the regulatory bodies appeared to, either.

SAIT published the latest iteration of a corrective-action plan at the end of March. The report painted an alarming picture of a school in crisis. Among the nine key problems listed were a failure to identify and serve students in need of intervention, particularly English learners; the ineffective use of funds for both algebra (600 kids were failing) and English learners (850 kids); a failure of the master schedule to address student needs; and a lack of supplies coupled with inadequate staff training and support. The state required that the team be a presence at the school for at least eighteen months to supervise the implementation of the corrective-action plan they had drawn up.

After so many audits and interventions over the years, it was hard for anyone at Locke to get too worked up about SAIT. Still, if you read—and believed—the fine print, this was the last chance for the troubled school. If Locke failed to implement the SAIT action plan, it would be put into trusteeship by the state. When the SAIT team leader, Marci Perry, addressed the staff just days before the end of school, she didn't sugarcoat things: "You had a ton of money at this school, and this school did not make progress on the API. And so this money [$150 per student, instead of the $400 per student Locke would have received had it made its targets] comes with strings attached, and one of the things attached is me."

Later in another meeting, Perry expanded on the role of SAIT: "When you exit SAIT, you will not have arrived. This is not the thing to get you to the top of the world. This plan is to get you on the right track. These are basic foundational items—Do you have textbooks? Is your master schedule for kids as opposed to adults? Have the teachers had the basic training they need in the adopted curriculum to instruct in that with some kind of fidelity? The collaboration piece—is there time to talk?"

The SAIT team would help teachers and administrators (Dr. Wells would be assigned a principal "coach") install systems that would keep the place running long enough for real improvement to occur. The problem, of course, was that all the research out there suggested that it takes five to seven years to institutionalize positive changes upon which real progress can be built. Would it, could it, ever happen at Locke?

If you had asked some of the teachers, they would have said no, not as long as Dr. Wells was in charge. Over the course of the school year, Wells had become a lightning rod for some of the teacher dissatisfaction. Test scores were on the rise, so were graduation rates, and everyone agreed that he had established a better school environment in terms of safety. After that, the reviews were mixed.

Chad and the SE team thought that Wells lacked academic vision; he was not an instructional leader with established systems in place for academic achievement. They believed Wells did not support—and in fact undermined—real efforts at reform by failing to empower his teachers and his administrators. He ruled autonomously. He didn't even share the budget with the school stakeholders.

Some particularly vocal veterans took a different, more personal view of Wells. They alleged that he favored the young turks on the SE team and a handful of pet teachers. Frank Wells was out to get some of the old-timers, they said. They grieved him again and again to the union—for things big and small. According to Wells, nothing stuck.

A. J. Duffy, president of the powerful teachers' union, came to Locke to address the widespread staff dissatisfaction. Wells had advised the faculty to give Duffy "the good, the bad, and the ugly." But the union rep charged that Wells had intimidated the staff.

Small, with dark glasses and gray, slicked-back hair, Duffy was dressed in a black shirt, white tie, and white suspenders. Speaking in a heavy Brooklyn accent, he got right to the point. "This is a very controversial school," he said. "I've gotten letters and phone calls from a number of people at this school, and they run from 'You have to help us get rid of the principal' to 'Please don't do that.' But if you people really want a change—new principal, new administration, new programs—the only way to get from A to B is for you to sit down together and agree on what you want. The UTLA stands behind you and can make change happen."

Then began a long debate. Wells's supporters applauded him for the positive change in school culture under his leadership. His critics conceded that he was cool—as long as you agreed with him. Some of the newer teachers argued that just because things were *better* didn't mean they were *good*. Back and forth it went, and with each exchange, the discussion became more heated, until finally Duffy shouted: "STOP! STOP! STOP!"

Though meetings at Locke often went that way, no one wanted to miss the upcoming Socratic debate on the merits of the six- versus seven-period schedules. It promised to be a classic showdown between SE and the young reform-minded teachers on the one hand and the old guard on the other. Based on the campus buzz and the intense lobbying that had preceeded it, there were sure to be fireworks.

The battle of the bells had been raging all year. In September, two more schools had adopted SE's longer days–shorter periods model. But the schedule for the seven-period day kept changing—and the length of the extra guidance period kept shrinking—as the schools shaved time off the day to comply with union rules governing teacher work minutes. The result was that the bells at Locke rang seemingly at will. No one could keep track of which periods started when. It was especially hard in classrooms like Rachelle's, where the clock didn't work, or on "banked days," when there was early release for staff development. Wells told a meeting of small-schools coordinators that the multiple schedules were "killing the school." He was determined to get the school on one bell system, and he asked the school leaders to come up with proposals for a revised bell schedule.

They met at the end of March. Seated around a long table in the principal's conference room, the coordinators and department chairs thoughtfully debated the merits of a handful of options. The school's fault lines were exposed for all to see. SE's coordinator, Josh Hartford, refused to budge on the seven-period school day. Others argued that seven periods were too much to ask of students, teachers, and coaches.

"Nobody has gotten urban education right," Hartford said, his voice rising. "If you look around and you're the only one doing it—you might be on to something. If you want lessons on how not to do it, go check out the last twenty years at Locke. I'm getting a little depressed about decisions based on what time teachers get to go home, how athletes feel, and whether there will be missed announcements. This is not about us."

When somebody tried to interject a comment, he barked: "I'm not done yet!" Then he continued: "We're here because it's hard. The easy answer is to leave the hard answers to somebody else. What I want us to do is to think about what it is our kids need and make a school schedule around that!"

More thoughtful discussion followed before Chad stepped in. Noting that there were valid arguments on both sides, he suggested that the entire school staff attend a Socratic seminar in early April at which the merits of both schedules could be presented and debated. An informed faculty vote would follow.

Chad left the meeting on a high. Sitting around the table and hearing all the good ideas and reasoned debate had given him pause. Maybe next year he would be empowered to effect real change. After all, progress had already been made. For one thing, the standardized testing had gone well. The small schools had really had gotten their act together, and fully 95 percent of the students at Locke were in their seats for the exams, a requirement for receiving an API score.

The thing was, testing was the only time that Locke felt like a real school. There were no kids loitering in the halls or skulking about the outer buildings. Administrators were on top of attendance, calling parents, even hopping in their cars to pick up slackers. One VP, Mrs. Walton, actually tracked a missing student to a Bally's gym and had her paged. The student was a senior, and it was her last chance to pass the CAHSEE so she could graduate on time. On any other day, her absence—and that of countless others—would have gone unnoticed. But on testing days, everyone—teachers, administrators, coordinators, even the kids—was on a high-stakes mission, a mission that could be accomplished only through sheer force of will and unity of purpose. What was strange, Chad thought, what was really sad, what was actually *pathetic,* was that the school as a whole chose to accomplish 95 percent attendance only twice a year, during testing. Still, they had done what many thought was impossible. They had proven that if you made attendance a priority, kids would come. And that wasn't nothing.

There were other positive developments, too. There was the inspiring soccer game, the proud and orderly Latino walkout, the upcoming graduation of more seniors (possibly four hundred) than anyone could remember, and the slow but sure uptick in standardized test scores. Then there were all the great teachers Chad had come to know, and, of course, all the wonderful kids he would never forget.

Add to that this very productive coordinators' meeting, which made Chad think that he could help build a schedule of class offerings that actually made sense. Maybe, in line with WASC and SAIT recommendations, the school could offer literacy intervention to the six hundred kids who needed it instead of the eighty who got it now. And maybe he could get teacher buy-in to actually make the intervention courses succeed. It was shocking to look at the courses on offer. Locke had culinary arts and a zillion different music and arts classes, but the school wasn't giving students what they really needed to be successful. The fourteen-year-olds at Locke needed to learn how to read. Once they knew that, they needed to take the required courses to get into college. Here was an opportunity for him to guide the process along.

We could make this happen! There could be a master schedule built completely on student need. Maybe it would be a seven-period decision, or maybe it would be six periods, which would suck. But if the decision was based on stakeholder input, maybe we could all live with it. Maybe, just maybe, it could work!

His reverie didn't last long. He had to remind himself that this was the same old familiar feeling that came over him every spring, when he would get it into his head that maybe *this* would be the year when all the hard work would pay off, when things would kick in and Locke would magically morph from failing to functional.

The truth was, he had already made up his mind to leave. And he had pretty much lined up the team he wanted to go with him. Over the past few weeks he had approached each of his draft picks individually. Each one was a go. Green Dot paid 10 percent more than the LAUSD salary table, and Chad thought that the extra money would be a great selling point. In fact, the teachers he wanted couldn't have cared less. For them, it wasn't about the money. A much more important issue was who else was going to be on the team. When Chad ticked off the names, he could feel a sense of collective guilt settling in. He had recruited six core teachers from the School of Social Empowerment. It was impossible to ignore the fact that without them, there was a good chance SE would collapse. The kids would feel abandoned, betrayed. The teachers got wobbly. They couldn't give Chad a definitive answer.

That came after the April 4 Socratic seminar. There had been quite a buildup to the event. The six-period faction had lobbied heavily, dropping flyers in the mailboxes and handing out candy, too. One teacher showed up at the meeting with a homemade poster adorned with five-dollar and one-dollar bills. The title read BATTLE FOR THE 6's. The chairs in Hobbs Hall had been arranged in a semicircle to facilitate debate. The meeting opened with an impassioned plea by Wells. Sometimes when he spoke—not always, but sometimes—if you closed your eyes and listened to his cadence, you could picture yourself in a church in the Deep South, just waiting to chime in with "Amen!" This was one of those times. He addressed the whole staff, but he might as well have been speaking to Chad and his entourage.

"If you plan to leave, why don't you do something that I think is ethically sound?" he said. "Don't vote. And let me tell you why. Your vote will affect the people you leave behind, and that's not ethically sound. Some of you are already looking, I know, because I get the calls. That's fine. But my call to you is based on ethical behavior. Refrain from voting. Second, we spent a lot of money in training and professional development. We need stability. I am convinced that in two to three years, Locke will no longer be under the state [audit] and we could have a big sign in front of the school that reads 'California Distinguished School.' It could be a reality. I'm only a small part of it. It can't be just me. It has to be me and you. The math department has improved; English is picking up on its rigor. The science department can't be matched. To drop the ball now is going to be really painful."

The seminar began. Chad explained the rules. A certain number of school leaders were seated in the semicircle; empty chairs, which he called "hot seats," were reserved for anyone else who wanted to contribute to the discussion. Each person in the semicircle had thirty seconds to give a summary of his or her position. After that, the floor would be open to thirty-second statements from other members of the staff. There would be no personal attacks, and everyone was to respect everyone else's time. "I have to say, I am really excited," announced Chad. "Because, if it goes well, this is the kind of forum we can use to decide other issues in the future."

The arguments followed a predictable pattern. Those in favor of seven periods argued that more instruction time was the best option for students. An extra guidance period would better prepare them for college; it would also make it easier for them to accumulate the requisite number of credits for graduation. Indeed, the seven-period schedule was one reason the graduation rate at Locke was on the rise. Kids had a way to make up credits they had previously lost through failures.

The six-period folks were having none of it. They argued that students tended to skip school after lunch; adding a period would mean another period ditched. Besides, why would anyone advocate a system in which it was okay to fail ten classes and still graduate on time? Ms. Wickhorst, the UTLA rep, said: "If you guys want to work twenty percent more, and not get paid twenty percent more, then vote for seven periods! I believe the faculty wants six periods. I understand the need to take care of students, but over the last five years we have lost two hundred teachers. How can we retain teachers if we don't respect their wishes for six periods?"

Mr. Twine, the teacher in charge of the tardy room, said: "Where does the responsibility of the student come in? Zero periods, summer school, tutoring—they don't come! How many more classes are you gonna give them that they don't go to? I say the seventh period should be offered after school for more pay!"

One SE teacher who had already been offered a job by Chad spoke about how hard the guidance class had been for her to teach—and how beneficial it had been to her students.

Another teacher, a six-period advocate, practically jumped out of his seat to respond: "I get tired of people saying we have to care for the students. My first year here I spent eight hundred dollars for the students! I don't think you need to bring up how hard you work and how much you care. Most of you aren't gonna be here. Some of the people talking are people I have heard are going to be leaving."

Then the girls' varsity soccer coach weighed in. "The teachers talking within the circle all probably have honors students," he opined. Chad warned him to refrain from personal attacks.

"In PE, we have three hundred forty students out there—per teacher. Do you see us complaining? No, we do our jobs. But by creating a seventh period, you will be creating more hassle within the school itself."

Hartford had his say. Like Wells, he had a way with words. But there were no "Amen"s punctuating his speech. The only interjection was by a dissenting colleague who shouted "Bullshit!" to one of his points. Hartford kept talking.

"I agree with everything those in favor of six periods said, and that's exactly why we need to do seven periods," he said. "You make it [the guidance period] in the middle of the day so they have to do it, and after a year you ask them what they want, and the kids vote one hundred ninety-nine to nine in favor of seven periods. It's hard. But every good thing that has happened at Locke came about because a group of teachers said crap to this. I love Locke students and I hate the way this school works. Let's not pretend that the staff stands for the students, because we all know exactly what's gonna happen. We're fostering a culture of failure. I want to see Locke change!"

The debate ended as it began, with words from Wells. He reminded the staff that regardless of which option they chose, Locke had to be a school that provided kids with academic rigor across the curriculum. "Hey, if you wanted to make a whole lot of money, you're in the wrong place," he lectured. "If you think you can run out of here at 2:52, it ain't gonna happen. Period. Every real teacher worth any salt works before they enter the classroom. It really is hard work being a math or an English teacher. Collecting papers and giving feedback is when you see significant results." Wells insisted that he was neutral on the issue. One teacher accused him of having already made up his mind to vote for seven. But those listening carefully insisted he was a six-periods guy, especially when he said he believed that "less is more."

When Hartford walked out of Hobbs Hall, he knew the battle was lost. *It's not gonna happen. They will never go for seven periods.* He also knew that his time at Locke was over. He was going with Chad—and, he reckoned, after the votes were counted, so would all the others.

The polling took place that Friday. The results were 72–36 in favor of six periods.

Later that day, Chad told Wells that he had decided to leave. He said that he intended to work full-throttle until the end of the year, and if Wells wanted him to, he would work in the summer as well. After a perfunctory thank-you, Wells got right to the point. "Again, I just hope you're not taking the teachers with the most capacity for teaching and leading," he said.

This time Chad was ready with an answer. "There will only be one hundred forty kids in my school. There aren't that many positions. I can hire only six teachers. The teachers who are gonna go are gonna go, and their résumés will go to Green Dot, and I will get them. I'm not going to give you names, but I have a feeling there are probably thirty teachers or more sitting on the fence right now at Locke."

Wells asked for Chad's advice: "How do you think I can get the good ones to stay?"

Chad offered his opinion: "There are some teachers who are going to go, and I don't think you should waste your time trying to get them to change their minds. You are better off giving personal attention to the ones who are still deciding." It was a cordial meeting. Chad was relieved. Wells had not pressed him. But the day of reckoning was fast approaching. Sooner rather than later, Wells would know that he'd been screwed.

The rumors had been flying for weeks. Finally, at the end of April, Hartford and the others could wait no longer. They wanted to give the school enough notice so that their replacements could be found. And they were tired of keeping secrets. At SE's weekly meeting, right before the beginning of open-house night, Hartford told the group that he had had to make a very painful decision. He had been given an opportunity to help start a brand-new school, and he had decided to take it. Then he said all the things they knew and felt themselves—that he was frustrated by a district and administration that wouldn't allow good teachers to make necessary reforms, that he thought the world of his colleagues at SE, that he was sick of fighting. After Hartford spoke, they went around the room and, one by one, the five others announced that they were going, too. There were twelve full-time general ed teachers in the School of Social Empowerment. Six of them were leaving. The news was met with stunned silence.

They told Vanessa Morris next. After all, three of them were science teachers—arguably the best teachers in her department. Hartford and the others filed into her room and just laid it on the line. She was shocked. How and why did they keep it secret from her? Hartford and Chad and the others meant a lot to her—personally and professionally. *We have been side by side in this quest! We were in this war together; we were leading the charge, and now they've decided to retreat. How can I advance without my generals?* Morris couldn't help herself. She started to cry. The next day she stayed home and cried some more. Very few things faze her, but she took the defections personally.

When the kids found out the next morning, there were more tears. Like Morris, they felt orphaned. Hartford and the others cried right along with them.

Wells learned the news from one of the other administrators. He had been off campus when their letters of resignation were left at Mrs. Jauregui's office. He was furious. It was bad enough that he was losing a core group of teachers, but the way in which they were leaving troubled him even more. *It was an abandonment and a violation of ethics.* It had all been done on the hush-hush; and they had shown no remorse, no regrets.

Of course, he had known it was a possibility—Chad was a leader and he had his groupies, a faithful following of excellent, hardworking Locke teachers who were clearly unhappy with the pace of change. That's exactly why Wells had raised the ethical implications with Chad earlier; there was a risk that his leaving would have a domino effect. The thing was, he thought he had gotten through to Chad, whom he knew to be a good and honorable man. Then, to have them all resign at once! On a day when he wasn't there! With no warning! Now, that bothered him.

He confronted Chad immediately. "I'm hearing rumors that these teachers are going with you, and I said, 'No, that can't be true. I see Chad every day, and he would have told me.'"

"Well, actually, it is true," Chad said, just like that.

Wells couldn't believe it. He had gotten a lot of stink from the rest of the staff about SE ever since he set foot on the campus. His take was that the black and brown teachers at Locke thought of SE as a racist school— a pretty much all-white group of teachers who wanted special treatment, a group of elitists who walked around with their noses up in the air. He knew a lot of Locke's teachers, when hearing the news, would think, *Good riddance!*

But there was another group, a smaller group, among which he counted himself, that knew that the defection was a devastating loss. The truth was, SE had more committed teachers than any other small learning community. They were hardworking and their hearts and souls were in the right place. The impact on the school's instructional program was going to be huge. The science department alone had lost three top teachers—

teachers who kept the numbers inching up and the state at bay. *These charter schools like Green Dot are committing highway robbery. Chad gets to take the best teachers, and Frank Wells gets to take what the district provides—which sometimes is a person with nothing more than a heartbeat and a pulse.*

Wells got on the horn to the district right away. LAUSD was sick to death of Steve Barr and Green Dot. Barr not only got the best teachers, he also got to lure the best students from the crappiest schools. Locke had to take whatever kid showed up at the door. The district was looking into taking legal action. Maybe the teachers could be barred from leaving. At the very least, Wells decided, he was going to change the name of SE. Next year it would be known as the College Prep Academy, or something along those lines.

Though he didn't know Chad that well, Hrag Hamalian probably took his leaving the hardest. He was bringing Vanessa Morris a sub sandwich the evening of the school open house when he walked right into the middle of her meeting with Hartford and the others. It was one of those moments. When they saw Hrag, they beat a hasty retreat, leaving Morris alone with Hrag, crying, minutes before parents were due to arrive. Hrag told Morris to go home, that he would tack a note on her door explaining her absence. But Morris said no. She dried her eyes and got through the night. Hrag couldn't believe that the SE team had handled things so badly. It was terrible seeing Morris in so much distress. He didn't feel too cool about it, either: *If they were leaving, the best teachers in the school, what the hell are the rest of us staying for?*

The next day the Green Dot exodus was all anyone could talk about. There was a great deal that had not been explained. Why would they leave a school that they had worked so hard to create? SE wasn't even two years old; how could they just pick up and say they were done? What did this say about where the school at large was headed? If you can't keep your best teachers, what are you doing? The skeletal crew left behind at SE were really confused. Hartford had told them they were the best group of teachers he had ever worked with. If he really believed that, why weren't they all invited to go? And second, why weren't they told this was in the works?

For Phillip and the others, it was hard not to feel like they were just the SE leftovers. The resignations had caused a visible rift in the small school. The Hartford crew was always together; it seemed like their conversations stopped whenever anyone else approached them. The others naturally huddled together, too, trying to figure out how to proceed. Three of the teachers who would be staying were TFAers. Phillip thought that this might be an opportunity to make a distinct TFA school within Locke. SE wasn't going to collapse. He and the other leftovers were not going to let that happen.

When Hrag arrived on Friday, he was still pissed off. But no one else seemed to be angry. He didn't get it. There was such a sense of complacency at Locke. Everyone was supposed to be a martyr and just take stuff. Maybe he was just too volatile. But he felt like the Chad move was going to screw everyone at the school, even more than they were being screwed now. There is a point where you draw the line, especially with your own colleagues. Chad had guided Morris and the new School of Math and Science team through the proposal process, and there had been a clear expectation that he would be there for them when they launched. Hrag told everyone he was going to talk to Chad. Did anyone want to come with him? They looked at him like he was crazy.

Chad was taken aback by Hrag's visit. It hadn't occurred to him that the mass resignations would have an impact on anyone beyond the SE folk. But Hrag's anger was real, and Chad agreed to come Tuesday to the next meeting of the School of Math and Science, to explain his departure and to field their questions.

Mackey started the meeting off by asking Chad to explain to them what had happened. Chad gave them the tick-tock, but the bottom line was, he didn't believe in Locke anymore.

"But you are the light, the visionary," said Taylor. "If you don't believe in Locke, how can I? What's going to happen to us when you leave?"

"The same thing that happened to us when we first came," he replied. "You'll move up into leadership positions, work your butts off, and after three years leave. Like everyone does. Sorry, but that's the reality."

Chad was surprised to find himself justifying his departure to that group, because no one else at the school seemed to care. Nobody had said a thing to him. Not a single person.

After his emotional meeting with Chad the previous Friday, Hrag had nothing left to say. He had already spoken his mind; to say anything more would make him look like a fool. So he zipped it for the meeting. And Chad handled it like a pro. But it didn't change the way Hrag felt. He wasn't comfortable with Chad sucking all the best teachers out of the school. And he still didn't know if they had gone about it the best way. But as he thought about his reaction, he wondered: *Maybe I'm just really tired—emotionally and physically. I don't mean to, but I get in people's faces. You have to at this school or you get totally walked over. I am so sick of things changing.*

CHAPTER THIRTEEN

The Road Show

They said it would happen. The rejuvenation phase would kick in—most likely after the winter break. And sure enough, Rachelle started feeling more comfortable once the second semester was under way in early February. It didn't hurt that a dozen long-stem roses were delivered the first day of the new term. The office called and said there was a delivery for Rachelle. Martel volunteered to pick it up.

"It was a black man, Miss Snyder!" he announced to the whole class as he offered her the flowers. "Ohhh! You got jungle fever!" There was no card attached, so Rachelle called her mother and grandmother—the usual suspects. Neither one claimed credit. *Maybe it was a mistake.*

As the month progressed, the gifts kept coming. On Valentine's Day, she was showered with teddy bears, candy, and a single rose. Her birthday was four days later, and she drove home to San Diego to spend it with her parents and her best friend at a performance of Cirque du Soleil. She enjoyed the rest of the long Presidents' Day Weekend in Los Angeles—playing soccer in a league she had joined and hiking in the Santa Monica Mountains. On Tuesday, when she arrived at school, there were another dozen red roses on her chair. This time, a card was attached. The flowers were from Luis, one of the Latino boys in period four. Luis was a big bear of a kid; at eighteen, he was reading at a third-grade level.

She loved her students. During a lesson on reproduction, Jaime, a Locke soccer player who insisted on being called by his American name, James, said, "You got kids, Miss Snyder? You hidin' something? Ever date anyone?"

"No, never," said Rachelle, smiling, her hair tied back, her gold loop earrings dangling.

"You know that a lie," said James. "Is it true? The ding-dong come to her stomach like that?" he said, pointing to a picture of the reproductive process.

A week later, the boys were on a quest to be "doctors." Like much of what Rachelle did in the classroom, the idea for this had come from Hrag. She had figured out pretty early in the year that her best bet for success was to take the general ed bio curriculum and adapt it to her kids' slower pace and skills. Even then, she spent a great deal of time planning, since she didn't have expertise in special ed, biology, or teaching. It was such an obvious problem: *I'm not the first person to ever teach biology to special ed students. So why is there no established curriculum, no set rules, no lesson plans? It's a joke, a mess.*

The idea behind the doctors unit was that once the kids had mastered the complexities of genetics and understood prenatal testing, they would be awarded doctor certificates. As part of the day's lesson, students were going to act out a couple's trip to the doctor for genetic testing. Luis volunteered to be the doctor. James was the father. And Jesse, one of the toughest kids to control, wanted to be the pregnant mother.

Jesse was a natural. He stuffed a balloon into his shirt and, with one hand on his back, waddled into the room. "I am so damn tired of carryin' this baby!" he exclaimed. "This baby is killin' me!"

"So, how is your pregnancy goin'?" asked Luis, dressed in a doctor's white coat, his brow furrowed in concern.

"It's goin' so good!" Jesse squealed in a loud falsetto. "So, what's it called? This test? Give me that test! I want it for my baby."

Luis was stumped, and he wasn't getting any help from the gallery. Rachelle pronounced the word "amniocentesis," prompting the next question.

"Are there any risks?" Jesse wailed. "My baby ain't gonna die?"

"If I don't touch the baby," said Luis soothingly, with James looking on.

"Thanks for lettin' me know that," said Jesse, now calmed. "Sure, let me do this."

James stood behind the bulging Jesse, hiding a Ziploc bag that contained some water (faux amniotic fluid) and a plastic baby doll. Luis inserted a turkey baster into the plastic bag and put the liquid he had extracted into a test tube—squirting Jesse in the process. The kids hooted in delight. Rachelle reminded them that the amniotic fluid that Luis had just collected contained DNA, which determined the gender and health of the baby. By then, Jesse had burst his balloon and was holding the baby doll in his arms: "My baby is so nice!" he cooed, rocking the light-colored plastic doll back and forth.

"You been messin' with a white lady, Jesse! You got yourself a light-skinned baby!" they teased.

The lesson ended in gales of laughter.

Things got even better as the semester went on. Maybe it was because the course material—genetics, evolution, reproduction—was so interesting. Or maybe it was because she and Stephen Minix were dating. Finally, Rachelle felt supported at Locke. She had someone—a little older and much wiser—to go to when she had a problem. He was especially helpful with her undisciplined boys. Whenever someone was out of line, she reported the kid to Stephen and he handled it later, during PE or at practice, if the kid was on a team. Stephen would work the kid's butt off, and Rachelle's problems would disappear. It didn't feel like a serious relationship because it was so easy and comfortable. But by April they had made plans to fly first-class to Seattle so that Rachelle could meet his family and friends. He was so nice, and she felt so happy, more content than she had in a very long time. After spending the entire first semester trying to figure out what to do with her life after Teach For America, she stopped torturing herself. She liked teaching at Locke. She would stay for at least a third year. After that, maybe she'd look into counseling, or literacy, or something more specialized.

But there were still plenty of down times. Like Valentine's Day, when Rachelle agreed to take on a general ed biology class after another science teacher abruptly quit. Rachelle wasn't qualified under No Child Left Behind—she hadn't taken the CSET exam in biology to prove mastery.

And she had enough to do with four special ed classes, her IEPs, and graduate school. But she felt like she had to say yes, because how could she say no? Hrag and the others were so nice to pass their lesson plans on to her; she felt like she owed them. Besides, Vanessa Morris had promised she'd get paid extra. Rachelle said she wanted to think about it overnight. The next day at the biology department meeting, she told Morris she guessed she could do it.

"Good," replied Morris. "You start tomorrow." Rachelle almost started to cry. Hrag took one look at her and gave her his syllabus. Rachelle crossed out his name, substituted her own, and handed it out the next day. There were forty-eight kids on the roster, more names than chairs in the lab. But a lot were regular no-shows. One girl, seeing Rachelle at the front of the room, said, "Hell, no. I don't want no female teacher," and walked out.

Rachelle had promised herself she would never allow the job to make her cry. But, man, did she come close. Later in February, her advisor from her graduate program at Cal State, Dominguez Hills, came in to observe her fourth-period class and left in shock. The boys were out of control—shadowboxing, singing rap songs, hurling insults. Rachelle barreled her way through a lesson on mitosis, but she did so over a chorus of expletives running from "nigga" and "fuck you" to "homo faggot." The advisor ended up keeping several of the kids after class and lecturing them.

The next day, when the bad behavior continued, Rachelle sat them down for a chat. "I am embarrassed for you," she said. "I'm not gonna get fired over how people behave, but when she makes her report, do you think that behavior reflects well on me—allowing that kind of disrespect? I'm not mad at you. I don't take it home. I'm disappointed. I'm an adult. I don't need to argue with little kids who are disrespectful. I think you guys have a lot more going for you than maybe you even realize. It's okay to be good at something."

No one was paying attention. The more she talked, the more they acted out, with Kenyon and Deangelo slapping each other while the others continued their swearing. Finally Rachelle announced, "I'm done. Pack it up. Your behavior sucks." Then, as the room quieted, she said, "In all seriousness, what do you think we need to do to improve behavior?"

The answer came from Francisco, a Latino boy with a speech impediment: "Behave better."

• • •

Good behavior and good grades became the price of admission for the trip to Catalina Island Rachelle had planned. Though she hadn't been very good about getting her data to Teach For America, she had tracked her kids' progress. She put a chart on the overhead of the first-semester grades for the six kids—out of twenty—who were regulars in period four.

"All six of you got a C or higher," she said. "But my big goal for the entire class was to have eighty percent pass with a C or better, the grades you need to get into college. Did I reach that goal? No. So I need to work harder to make sure all the people understand the material we're covering. What hurts in this class is that the people who don't come bring down the class average. The only ones who failed were the ones who did not come to class.

"Remember," she continued, "Dr. Wells put the payment down for our trip. This semester is really important. I am going to bring the people with good grades and good citizenship. Dr. Wells will not let me bring people with bad grades in other subjects. If I took a bunch of kids and they ended up acting like you guys in period four do, there would be no chance we'd get invited back."

"But we don't act that way on trips," argued Malik, a new addition to the class. "We ain't gonna act like that."

It may have been a moot point. They weren't sure they wanted to go.

"What if somebody gets hurt?" worried James.

"We're goin' to sleep on a boat?" asked Deangelo.

Rachelle explained that the trip was planned for the end of May, a few weeks before school let out. There were going to be special science programs for the class, plus hiking and swimming and snorkeling.

"I don't wanna come back in pieces," said Martel.

Shandrel agreed: "It's not for us."

"Ah, you guys are not adventurous," teased Rachelle.

"You got that right," said Shandrel. "Give us a couple of guns. We go hunting."

"For bears!" said Martel. "They had a movie about some guy who went into the woods at bedtime and he never came back. I'm gonna need a pistol, an AK-47."

"Do you know what snorkeling is?" asked Rachelle, to silence. "It's when you go in the water with goggles and something attached that sticks out of the water that lets you breathe."

"I ain't goin' in the water," said Martel. "You come back with blood all over you. I can't do water. Sharks and that stuff."

"You better kiss your mom before you go away," cautioned one boy. "What if you don't come back?"

Just weeks before they were due to go, Dr. Wells still hadn't signed off on the journey. Rachelle feared he was avoiding her. But there was no way she was going to break her promise to the kids. So she and Jill Greitzer took all the paperwork out to the corner of 111th and San Pedro and tackled Wells during dismissal. He whipped out the school checkbook and paid the fees that day.

Rachelle and Jill had connected at the beginning of the second semester, when Jill had called Rachelle to commiserate about behavioral problems. Jill was a math teacher, and she and Rachelle shared many of the same kids. Rachelle was so happy to get her call. She had wondered all semester long exactly who this Miss G was. The kids often confused Rachelle with her, though they looked nothing alike. The only possible explanation for the mix-up was that they were both white.

On May 31, Rachelle and Jill took twenty special ed students on the three-day trip to Catalina. For many, it was the first high school field trip they had ever been on. The kids all got to school early that Wednesday morning. Rachelle's mother, Lynne, went along as a chaperone, and there was another teacher, Corey Baker, a full-time, uncredentialed special ed sub who had agreed to help out. The kids called him Bake a Cake. He was subbing at Locke while trying to set up a practice as a hypnotherapist specializing in sex therapy. Baker had a way with the kids, especially the males. His theory about classroom management could be summed up in three words: the fear factor. Baker believed kids could smell fear in a teacher and acted on it. He wasn't afraid of them, and they could smell that, too. He had the ability to read their body language and talk them down when they were careening out of control. He prided himself on not sending kids to the dean's office, because for many, that meant jail.

It was a brilliant morning, and the kids were almost subdued as they stood beside their sleeping bags and backpacks awaiting directions outside the front gates of the school. Kenyon stood apart, do-rag on, black hooded sweatshirt pulled low over his head, obviously apprehensive.

They were all teenagers, some as old as eighteen. But they may as well have been in grade school. And they may as well have been going to the moon.

The ride over to Catalina was rough. After an initial burst of energy, the kids were quiet, either sickened by the whitecapped sea voyage or anxious about what lay ahead. But once land came into view, they were mesmerized by the island's rolling green hills, stone cliffs, and high ridges, where palm trees that looked like giant green lollipops stood sentry. The ferry dropped the Locke campers at the base of the science camp. After disembarking, they attended a brief orientation, ate lunch, and assembled at the shore for the first activity of the day: snorkeling.

There were several groups enrolled in the Marine Science Adventures Camp that week. Most of the kids came from suburban schools. And except for the Locke campers, they were all grammar-school-aged. The main facilities—the dining hall, fish hall, conference room, bathrooms, administrative offices—were located at the foot of a long sloping hill, ending at the seashore, which hugged a small, sheltered bay with a dock. A wide and dusty dirt path ran up the center of the incline, dividing the camp into discrete little villages of wooden-floored tents on either side. The Locke kids were assigned the village farthest up the hill on the right, far from the other campsites.

Just hiking up the hill from the beach and mess hall was a challenge for some of the Locke kids, many of whom were overweight from too much junk food and not enough exercise. Locke students scored about the same on the state physical fitness test as they did on the California Standards Test: 3.5 percent of ninth-graders met fitness standards. Before the camp was over, several would have to be helped to their tents, their leg muscles cramped and aching from unusual activity. But a little physical discomfort was a small price to pay for being on Catalina. The air was clean, the hills were green, the water and sky clear blue. The kids practically skipped up the path, free and easy, unencumbered by cares.

Snorkeling was scary. They were being tested—from the minute they were made to don the heavy black wetsuits to the second they had to put their faces in the water. But they did it—even the ones who couldn't swim. That night, the first and only hint of trouble surfaced. The kids were on a "trust walk" in which certain kids were blindfolded and others were designated to be their guides. The walk was interrupted by three camp officials who took Rachelle, Jill, and Corey aside. It seems that some of the boys had been down the hill at another school's bathrooms and had threatened to "get" the little kids later that night. The camp officials were joined by two security guards, who threatened to arrest the offending kids and send the rest of the Locke campers back home. A big lecture from the teachers followed, and the mood went from sweet to sour in seconds.

"It's because we're from South Central," sighed Juliana. The boys reacted to the dressing-down by turning up the volume. Rachelle feared that things were going downhill fast. *I feel like a combination babysitter and parole officer.* Worried about the long, cold night ahead, she ordered everyone to remain in their tents, and she took a few of the girls aside and hammered home the point. She had overheard the boys talking about penis size; they were wondering if they could sleep with the girls. Rachelle did not want to have any Catalina babies!

When the kids awoke the next morning, it was as if none of the unpleasantness from the night before had occurred. After making their own lunches, they went to the plankton lab. When they arrived, one of the camp counselors asked them what group they were in. They started naming gangs and tagging crews, then rapping and break-dancing. The counselors gawked in amazement, and then the rest of the staff filed in to watch the show, too. While it was nice for the kids to get the attention, Rachelle was offended: *I know you all have probably come from someplace like Idaho where you've never seen a black person, much less a dancing black person, but this is not a circus and my kids are not here to entertain you.*

Later, the kids went on a long hike to Catalina's Sandy Beach for a lecture on sea ecology and a swim in the bay. Just minutes into the hour-long hike, when they were climbing a steep ridge, still within eyesight of the camp, the stillness was shattered by what could have been the sound of a gun blast. The kids froze in midstep, their eyes trained in the direction of the noise. Below, they saw a tent, just like the ones they had slept in, crushed by the weight of a huge branch that had broken off from an aging eucalyptus tree. The randomness of the violence, even here, was unsettling. They walked on in silence for a few minutes.

The final adventure was kayaking. The kids all strapped on their orange life jackets and jumped into their very own, very tippy kayaks. It took Shandrel, the man-sized football player, dozens of tries before he got out beyond the shore, and the boat must have capsized dozens more times once he was out there. But he never gave up, not even when confronted by several sharp, protruding rocks that formed a kind of strait leading out to the open water. Navigating through the choppy canal was difficult. Many kids shied away, clearly daunted by the rough water—until Rachelle paddled up, raised her arm in the air, fist clenched, and shouted: "BALLS TO THE WALL!" They all then dutifully fell in line behind her, like ducklings trailing a mother duck, and paddled like mad through the shoals.

They had a campfire each night. The first night, as they gathered on the beach, they lay in the sand and used a laser beam to pick out the constellations—and to find some of their own. Kenyon located a single star for his constellation and called it the "Kenyon Star," because "it looks down on everybody on earth and sees all." Then he saw two stars and called them the "Kenyon Nuts." "Where?" chided Rachelle. "They're so small I can't see!" Everyone cracked up.

Normally, all the different groups attending the camp gathered together on the final night and put on a skit to present what they had learned. Locke was exempted. The Locke campers skipped the campwide awards ceremony, too, holding their own private event in the middle of their tent village. It worked out well, but it was hard to miss the message—intended or otherwise: Locke kids were different.

At the final campfire they had a share circle. The idea was for the campers to confide their biggest fear about the trip. Jovan, an African American boy whose father had died when Jovan was a month old, started off. "I was afraid of the woods," he said. Then came Akira, a tiny child from a renowned gang family. "I was afraid of touching sharks." Deangelo volunteered that he had been afraid of the water. Kendell stood up and said he was afraid to come on the trip without his "homeys." Then he thanked his new homeys, naming every person around the campfire—blacks and Hispanics alike.

When Rachelle spoke, there was absolute silence: "I was afraid of the sharks," she said. "I touched them, but I don't know if I really overcame that fear. But the BIG FEAR, the thing that scared me to death, was being a first-year teacher and having to teach you guys. I was afraid you would eat me alive. I was so scared, and sometimes I got frustrated and pissed off. But I love you all. You have made this the best year of my life. You have taught me so much. I want to thank each and every one of you!"

That night as they made their way back up the dark path to their tents, Pedro, one of the more mature kids on the trip, asked: "How come you so nice, Miss Snyder?"

"They pay me the big bucks, Pedro," she said with a sigh of contentment.

Later, after they had arrived safely on the mainland, the kids were driven back to their homes. One group of four boys begged to stop at the McDonald's, about ten blocks from school, before being dropped off. But not one of them would get out of the car; they insisted on using the drive-through. They explained: they were wearing blue, the color of the Crips, and the McDonald's was located in Blood territory. They did not want to be seen and identified as the enemy. Two of the kids had been jumped before by gangbangers; why risk spoiling one of the happiest times of their lives?

Hrag's kids had a field trip, too. It was an annual affair for the biology department at Locke—at least for as long as Vanessa Morris had been in charge. Every spring she and a cohort of sympathetic teachers took several busloads of kids to Cabrillo Beach to see the amazing grunion runs. The spawning of the grunion, small silver fish, takes place each year from March through August, during high tide, along certain California beaches. It is a you've-got-to-see-it-to believe-it tour de force of nature. The action occurs late at night under a full or new moon, when thousands of grunion swim up the beach, seemingly on cue, wriggle into the sand, drop their eggs, wait for them to be fertilized, and then wriggle back out in time to catch the next wave home. The sight of millions of silvery scales shimmering in the sand under the light of the full moon is simply unforgettable. After a year or two, the field trip had become one of Locke's rites of passage.

This year it had been an on-again, off-again proposition. So much had been going on at Locke that Morris had become distracted. Just as she was feverishly planning for the new School of Math and Science, her best friends at the School of Social Empowerment had announced plans for a wholesale bail. She had a cold, and she didn't feel up to the trip. But the biology teachers had promised their kids and set the date, and it didn't seem fair to cancel for a cold. So it was on. Just. It took a lot of last-minute scrambling to make it happen. Jinsue was out buying the food just hours before they were scheduled to go.

Hrag's sister, Gareen, had flown into Los Angeles the night before. Hrag had planned to take Friday off to spend it with her. But then the field trip was put back on the schedule. Gareen was a sport. She sat through six periods of biology in Hrag's classroom that Friday and happily agreed to tag along to help with the field trip that night.

It was so strange. Hrag had kept the details of his private life secret from his kids all year long. It didn't take him long to figure out that being Armenian was not an issue he had to worry about with the gangs in South Los Angeles, but by then he had already decided his students didn't need to know who he was, or where he was from, or how he came to be teaching them. But it was uncanny the way they picked up on things. They could tell he wasn't *American* American. And they were right. He had been born in Saudi Arabia. When he started kindergarten in the United States—a year too early because his aunt enrolled him and mixed up his birthdate—he spoke no English. So he understood how it felt to be a foreigner, how hard it was not to belong, especially as a kid. It made him particularly empathetic toward the students he now taught, but that was something he had never shared with them. Part of his cover was blown the minute the kids saw Gareen. "Oh, Mr. H, that's your sister!"

Hrag was nervous about having her in the classroom. His lesson for the day was a student-performed play about Darwin. It would be a tough one to pull off, particularly with his rowdy fifth-period class. But the kids poured on the charm for Gareen. They acted like angels the whole day.

The field trip that night was another matter altogether. He was uneasy about it right from the start. The night before he slept badly, tossing and turning until the alarm went off. Things didn't feel right. As the day wore on, he became more and more anxious. In all, some 240 kids lined up after school with signed permission slips. For reasons no one could determine, only three of the four buses they had ordered were available to take them to San Pedro, a beachside town fifteen miles south of Locke. Rather than send some kids home, Morris and the others jammed them all in, eighty to ninety to a bus, for the half-hour ride to the coast.

Hrag was the only adult on his bus, and he stood the whole way. The trip was surprisingly hassle-free. The only incident occurred when some white kids saw the bus and gave his students the finger. The whole bus got quiet, and then one kid turned to Hrag and said: "Mr. H, you should never have brought us!"

"Why?" asked Hrag.

"Because we're ghetto!" he replied. With that, the whole busload of kids burst out laughing.

The buses arrived at around five-fifteen, and the kids piled out and scattered. Within minutes they were everywhere—in the water, in the bathhouses, on the beach, in the tide pools, scrambling up the cliffs of the park. And there was no organized way to keep track of them.

Morris had been picky about which teachers she included. Her team from the new School of Math and Science was invited, but she asked only a few people from the science department, reasoning that it was her field trip and she wanted only those teachers who had made a contribution. The result was some ruffled feathers and, on the trip, too little adult supervision. Though Dr. Wells showed up later that night with two of his children, and some of the SE folk stopped by in a gesture of goodwill, there were never more than ten adults present at the same time over the span of the eight-hour field trip.

For a while, the smell of the barbecue drew all the kids back to the picnic area, where they lined up for hot dogs and sodas at a dollar apiece. The teachers did the cooking and serving. The kids were very appreciative, and when they forgot to say "please" or "thank you," Taylor reminded them. But Hrag remained wary. A strange dynamic was developing between the Hispanics and the blacks. In class, they got along just fine. But here at the beach, things seemed racialized. The kids had completely segregated themselves by race. At one point, Hrag looked over at Taylor and said, "I feel like something's gonna happen, Taylor."

There was plenty of time for things to go awry. They wouldn't be heading back to Locke until nearly midnight, and the schedule was loose. After dinner, the kids would go to the fire rings for a bonfire. Then they would do a tour of the aquarium and watch a short film on the grunions. Finally, it would be back to the beach to watch the fish do their thing until eleven-thirty or so, when the buses would take them back to Locke. Hrag and Taylor were worried. This field trip had it all: water, fire, and darkness—the perfect ingredients for a disaster.

It was at the bonfire that Hrag sensed how quickly things could go wrong. By then, the Locke kids were firmly in their groups, blacks with blacks, Hispanics with Hispanics. And he could see that they were getting bored. There were plenty of marshmallows but no sticks to roast them with. A few kids found wooden planks, plopped marshmallows on top, and stuck them in the fire, but the rest had nothing to do. It was dark, and other schools had shown up, too. Gardena, another inner-city school, was there, and so were a bunch of white kids with beer. A few of his students came up to him, furious, saying some of their things had been stolen. When he noticed some kids wander off, up a big dune and around to the tide pools, out of sight, he followed. But no one else seemed concerned. *Even if I worry my brains out, there's nothing I can do. There are so many places to hide.*

At the aquarium, things started to go south. The Locke kids had been divided into two groups. The students touring the darkened labyrinth of fish tanks were accused of using inappropriate language. Morris ordered them outside and delivered a stern lecture. Meanwhile, the group in the theater watching the film was put on notice, too. The documentary was very dated and had been shot in black and white. The kids talked throughout, their chatter laced with expletives. The manager went ballistic. He berated Hrag for not having better control over the kids.

"Look, I'm doing the best I can," said Hrag; what he was really thinking was: *Screw you and your grunions.* When the movie was over, the kids broke loose and headed for the beach. Hrag was tired from worrying. He stood sentry by the tide pools and then surrendered. Letting down his guard, he sat down in the sand. It was pitch-dark.

The kids who stayed on the beach, waited, and saw the grunions put on their show were enthralled. But the majority of them had grown weary of waiting and wandered off by the time the fish finally did their gyrations in the sand. They had never really come to see the grunions, anyway; they had come to hang with their friends on the beach. When the buses arrived, everyone seemed ready to go.

Hrag stood in front of his bus, checking off names as the kids bounded up the steps. Then, suddenly, all hell broke lose. A chubby, 250-pound black kid named Jarell cut in front of Carlos, a short, stocky Mexican kid who was built like a man.

Hrag knew that Carlos had a short fuse. At the beginning of the semester, he had come into class, sat in the front row, and declared it his new seat. Hrag told Carlos to go back to his assigned seat and to speak to him respectfully. The kid stood up, flipped the desk over, and left. When he returned the next day, Hrag explained that if Carlos had wanted to move his seat, all he had to do was ask. That was it. Carlos smiled, took the front seat, and never gave Hrag an ounce of trouble again. But he kind of scared Hrag, he was so quiet.

When Jarell cut in front of Carlos, he didn't say "Excuse me." Carlos gave him a good shove. In a second, they were tearing each other apart. Hrag had been told never to jump into a fight, but he couldn't not. It looked like they were going to *kill* each other. Hrag tried to put one of them in a hold, and he had the kid pinned with his back against the bus when he slipped. In the scuffle that followed, Hrag got hit a couple of times, hard, in the head. The whole thing was over in thirty to forty seconds; three or four African American boys had jumped in and pulled the boys apart. Gareen had seen it all from the bus, where she was trying to keep the others from jumping off and joining in the mêlée.

Hrag put the two boys on separate buses, and they caravaned back to Locke. It was 1 a.m. before the last student was picked up from school. Weary, Hrag and his sister headed for the faculty parking lot. Even before he reached the car, Hrag could see the shattered glass on the ground. Both his car and Jinsue's had been broken into. The window on the driver's side of Hrag's Ford had been smashed, and more than a thousand dollars' worth of CDs had been stolen. His heart sank. He *loved* that collection; he played his CDs as he drove to and from work, and they made the days easier. *You put so much into this school, and then you get dicked around. This is too much. This school is too much.*

The next day, Mackey took Hrag to a shop in East Los Angeles to get his window replaced. When Hrag returned to school on Monday, shards of glass still littered the parking lot, untouched from the Friday-night break-in. He wrote a letter to Chad Soleo and two deans of the ninth-grade academy, and within two hours both boys were suspended. (He did not report that he had been hit, because he knew that could get the boys expelled.)

Jarell didn't go to school that day but later explained that he had friends who had been jumped by Mexicans, and he was leery of them.

Carlos showed up for class, even though it was May 1 and most Hispanic students had taken May Day off for another pro-immigration protest. He felt bad. He explained to Hrag that he had had no choice but to fight; he could not let someone disrespect him. Carlos gave Hrag his word that it wouldn't happen again, and they shook on it. He was a very solemn street kid, the type of person who would never go back on his word, and Hrag felt satisfied that he had gotten through to him.

Hrag understood exactly how it had all gone down the night of the grunions. Carlos and Jarell were both good kids. It was late, and they were tired. Hrag himself had gotten into his fair share of fights when he was in middle school. But the difference was, with these kids, if they messed with the wrong person, they could get badly beaten. Or shot. Kids told him they got jumped all the time in school—in the hallways, in the bathrooms, in the stairwells. They didn't come back to class bloodied or bruised—on the outside at least.

Once their suspensions were lifted, Hrag welcomed the boys back to class. They sat two desks away from each other for the rest of the year. No one would have known that they had ever crossed swords.

Phillip's only field trip of the year was a lot less dramatic than Hrag's or Rachelle's. It was arranged for all the kids in SE's guidance classes. At SE, guidance was modeled after AVID, a program that teaches the organizational and study skills necessary for college. Chad had headed the AVID program at Locke when it first started. And it was that program, more than anything else, that got him and the other activists connected and thinking about extending their reach, and challenging the status quo. SE actively promoted a college-going culture. To underscore that commitment, its small-school field trip was to nearby University of Southern California and the museum complex adjacent to the campus. The kids got to tour the campus, visit the science museum across the street, and view a movie in the museum's IMAX theater.

SE took some notoriously difficult kids along, and they handled themselves with amazing grace. They kept the profane language in check, asked very intelligent questions, and were perfectly well-behaved in the science museum. It made Phillip think: *We should set higher expectations for these kids. To say that because of their home environment they can't rise to the bar is doing them an injustice. Time and again they have shown me they are capable of great things.*

It was an eye-opener for the kids, too. Many of them hadn't realized that USC was so close—just a seven-mile trip up the freeway. Phillip told them he lived not far from USC, and that surprised them, too. They were blown away by how beautiful the campus was. They remarked on the fact that there was no graffiti on the walls and no trash on the streets. "What would it take to make our campus as beautiful?" asked one student.

Later, when they were all about to sit down to lunch, Phillip left to walk a few students to a nearby McDonald's. When he returned twenty minutes later, the group had finished eating. "What did you guys do? Eat it all?" he teased. One student, Lemarr, handed him a box with half a pizza. "Did you spit on it?" asked Phillip. No, he had not. Lemarr had asked another teacher what Mr. Gedeon would like to eat and drink, ordered it, and saved it for him. Phillip couldn't believe it. "That is the nicest thing a student has ever done for me! Thank you!" he exclaimed.

"You know, I'm not as bad as you think I am," said Lemarr sheepishly.

After that, Phillip and the kids talked about lots of things they could never have discussed during a math lesson, like what it was like to go to college, and how to choose a good one, and whether or not USC would be a good place for them. They wanted to know other stuff, too: why Phillip and most of the teachers were single, how old they were, and where they grew up.

It was a positive experience for everyone involved. It had been so good for his kids to see life outside of Watts. And it had been so good for Phillip to see *them* outside of Watts. He had never been happier. He felt like his kids were learning. If he had a problem at all, it was only how to become a better teacher. He loved to plan lessons, and he thought he was good at it. But he had to get better at instruction, at relaying the information in a way that his students could understand and retain.

After a week of satisfying work, he often treated himself to a drive to Long Beach. He had fallen in love with the waterfront during summer institute and had developed a little ritual there. Instead of taking his clothes to an expensive dry cleaner down the block from his apartment in Baldwin Hills, he would save up his laundry and then drive to a place in Long Beach that charged a dollar an item. He'd drop the clothes off, get a mango smoothie, and pick up a tuna grinder. Then he'd race back up the 405 freeway. He'd become more adventurous since living here. The speed limit was sixty-five miles per hour, but he pushed it to eighty, and he liked to crank up the music. He loved Los Angeles.

It was funny. Two months before, just a few weeks into the second semester, he had endured the worst week of his life. The new term had started out well. The kids knew the routine and there was a rhythm to each period. Finally, his geometry classes were working the way you would expect a geometry class to—in a normal school.

But Locke was not normal. Phillip thought of it as a building pretending to be a school. It had bells and books and all the things a school was supposed to have, except for a true mission that put kids in the forefront and gave them the kind of education they deserved. Every day at Locke, Phillip saw tons of kids not in class, and tons of adults not doing anything about it. There were only small pockets at the school where learning was occurring. One of the pockets happened to be his.

Or so he thought, until the middle of February, when he found himself so angry and confused for three consecutive days that when he left school each afternoon, he told himself he would not return.

The bad luck, or his PMS, or whatever you wanted to call it, had started the week before, when he left Los Angeles for a TFA recruiting trip back to his alma mater, Connecticut College. He hated missing school, and he wasn't looking forward to even a small dose of winter in New England, but he thought it was important to spread the word. He himself had seen the effect Teach For America can have on a school and its students. He wanted to tell potential candidates from Connecticut College about the mission.

It was really just a one-day event, but because of the time difference, it meant two days of traveling. His mother lived only an hour or so from campus, but he didn't know if he would be able to squeeze in a visit. He'd arrive late on Saturday night, rest on Sunday, then work flat out from eight o'clock on Monday morning until seven that night, leaving around noon the next day. TFA had sent him samples of questions that might come up, along with answers he could give. But he didn't feel he had to follow the samples to the letter; if he didn't want to answer a question, he was told he could just say he didn't feel comfortable responding.

He already knew the drill from his previous incarnation as a TFA campus campaign manager. Doing a one-day blitz of the campus as a corps member sounded a lot easier than all the work his first TFA job had entailed. He was on Christmas break when he got the initial e-mails from Teach For America. He had never heard of TFA and, not recognizing the name of the person who sent the message, decided to ignore it. The first deadline for applying for a job as a campus recruiter came and went. Then he got another e-mail, this one more personal. He didn't give that one a second thought, either. During the Easter break the third e-mail arrived. This one almost sounded as if the sender knew him. It was lengthy, and mentioned the names of several other campus leaders. It urged Phillip to apply for a position as Connecticut College's TFA campus manager. Phillip felt compelled to reply, and a phone conversation was arranged. The TFA staffer was persuasive. Within three weeks, Phillip had the job.

He was sent to Washington, D.C., for orientation, and that began the journey that took him to Los Angeles as a 2005 corps member. TFA was never anything he sought. It just kept coming at him, and TFA's persistence finally won out.

Being campus manager was hard work. Phillip was part of a two-member recruiting team, but he ended up being the go-to guy. He did all the brownnosing with the professors and all the research on the students, and it was he who led all the application workshops. TFA had a computerized recruiting dashboard that basically tracked every task he had to do—from getting the academic and extracurricular goods on students to personalizing the invitations to TFA events and meetings. He was required to write a summary of every conversation he had with a prospective candidate and to follow up on each encounter. Once a week, he had to check in with his TFA boss, and was evaluated on whether or not he had reached the goals that had been set. The gig ran from September through June, and when the two application deadlines loomed, Phillip was putting in thirty hours a week. Things slowed down after that, but he was still expected to prepare a list of one hundred names for his successor to pursue the following year. TFA was especially interested in attracting math and science candidates, and minority students, so Phillip's input was important.

He didn't get a good sense that year of what it meant to be a TFA teacher, but he learned a lot about the organization. It was very structured. Impressively so. He loved that the TFA meetings were so efficient. Ambitious goals were set, and data drove the process. It was a good fit for Phillip. He was used to operating in exactly the same way. The year Phillip headed up recruitment, twelve candidates from Connecticut College applied to TFA, a bumper crop.

Recruiting had been a top TFA priority ever since 2000, when the organization embarked on its first major five-year plan. Now TFA had launched the 2010 plan to further ramp up both the number of recruits and the results they achieved. Extensive marketing research was under way to identify changes to the recruitment strategy that could yield a greater number of matriculants. TFA was specifically interested in expanding the number of applications from high-potential prospects (HPPs). In 2006, 10 percent of all prospects it rated HPP had applied; if TFA could attract just 5 percent more of such applicants, it would mean the addition of at least six hundred CMs to the movement.

Galileo, a boutique market research group from the San Francisco Bay Area that specializes in teasing out the considerations that go into complex, high-stakes decisions, conducted qualitative and quantitative research for TFA starting in December 2005. Using some New Age-y research techniques—such as meditation and relaxation with candles and soft music—Galileo conducted focus groups to probe the deeper beliefs and feelings of applicants and nonapplicants, matriculants and decliners. Quantitative online surveys followed, and the results among the four groups were analyzed. Special attention was paid to the nonapplicants, who were further divided into those who had met with a recruitment director and those who had not. The data was cut by ethnicity, gender, degree subject, socioeconomic status, and school type. By June 2006, TFA had identified a number of themes related to how prospects made their decisions about whether or not to apply to TFA. Action plans were developed around each of them.

Galileo had found that applicants were motivated to apply primarily by a desire to "give back" and to have a positive impact on the lives of children—combined with the opportunity for challenge and personal growth. What held them back were concerns that they would sidetrack their careers. They also questioned both their own ability and that of the organization to be effective. Money mattered, too, especially to potential recruits who didn't have a lot of it.

Those key insights reshaped the message TFA was telegraphing. Now four basic understandings would be embedded in all TFA communications, personal cultivation meetings, and website content: though the problem of educational inequality was enormous and grave, it was solvable; the TFA mission was working; each recruit had the potential to make a real difference; and the experience would enable corps members to develop leadership qualities that would lead to a lifetime of impact and meaning.

Teach For America gleaned from the research that in an effort to shed its grassrootsy image from the nineties, it had swung too far in the opposite direction. Now it risked being seen as too corporate, so it moved to reemphasize the importance of the real work it does. Images of kids, which had been downplayed in earlier marketing material, came roaring back. Research showed, too, that the Millennials were savvy to the media—and hated being spinned. TFA learned that it may have over-scripted its recruiters, and that candidates were coming away from meetings not convinced that they were getting the real story. TFA responded by launching a "knowledge building" initiative for recruiters, with field trips to regional classrooms so that they could speak with greater authenticity about the TFA experience. TFA also softened its previous pitch suggesting that it was a springboard to bigger and better things, fearing that recruits would see teaching in an underserved community as a great bullet point to put on a résumé rather than as a truly transformative experience.

In the summer of 2006, TFA redesigned its website and increasingly used it as a major marketing vehicle. Video clips of real people—CMs, alumni, parents—talking frankly about the mission were laced throughout the site, as were testimonials from leaders of America's top grad schools and hottest post-college employers. The list of TFA's blue-chip employer and graduate school partnerships included all the usual suspects: Harvard, Yale, the universities of Chicago, Pennsylvania, and Michigan among the schools; JPMorgan, McKinsey & Co., Wachovia, Google, and GE among the corporate highflyers. TFA offered career services through its Office of Career and Civic Opportunities, and even ran a job bank for potential employers looking to recruit from the ranks of TFA's smart, high-achieving corps members.

TFA built a recruiting framework around the issues the research had probed: brand awareness, knowledge of the issue and TFA's mission, and the considerations that were barriers to joining the program. Campus AKC—awareness, knowledge, and consideration—was further tested in an online Facebook survey of coeds at forty of the four hundred major college campuses at which TFA recruited. The results showed that

62 percent were aware of TFA, 41 percent had a significant knowledge of what TFA does, and 23 percent would consider joining. The takeaway: TFA was missing whole swaths of potential CMs.

Recent alums could play a role in reaching them. Ongoing research indicated that there was a widening gap between campus perceptions of TFA and the realities of the job on the ground. The role of the CM in demystifying the work—without hurting the mission—was crucial to growing the movement. A well-known alumnus like Phillip, who was doing so well as a first-year CM, could help boost the number of Connecticut College Camels applying to help close the gap.

As it turned out, Phillip was a no-show. When he arrived at LAX on Saturday morning, he learned there was a nor'easter due to hit New England that evening. He got as far as O'Hare only to discover that all flights to the East Coast had been canceled. In the storm that became known as the blizzard of 2006, Connecticut received more than two feet of snow, setting state records. After holing up at a hotel near O'Hare that night, Phillip gave up and flew back to Los Angeles on Sunday afternoon.

The trouble started on Tuesday. His eyes welled up with tears just thinking about it. The kids were sassy, even defiant, in periods one and three. Even his best-behaved students were out of whack. Phillip felt like he had lost control and was floundering at sea. And he felt angry. That afternoon he had stayed for the faculty meeting, when what he wanted to do was go straight home to his room. But that wasn't an option; it was his turn to cook for his roommates. He made dinner, but he had taken that bad day home with him, and he couldn't engage in small talk. *I need to be on my own and calm down. I have to get my spirits up so I can go back in tomorrow.*

Wednesday wasn't any better. He was still angry at the kids—and at himself, too, for feeling that way. He decided he had to do something drastic to get their attention. So he made them queue up outside the door, then let them in three at a time.

"This is your warning," he said as each trio entered. "I will call home and kick you out. Go to your chair, sit down, and don't say a word!" Then he started the class. But he had trouble almost immediately with Grant, a special ed student who had recently transferred into period three. Grant had not been assigned a seat, so he chose his own. Phillip insisted he move. Grant refused, saying he didn't like his appointed seat-mate. "Fam, I'm doin' my work!" insisted Grant. "Why are you doin' this? I'm payin' attention."

"Don't call me 'fam,' " snapped Phillip. "It's not my name. What does 'fam' mean anyway?"

"It means you're like family to me," said Grant, his voice rising. "I don't say it to other people."

It was a test of wills and Grant lost. Phillip called Chad and asked him to remove the kid from the class. Then Chrystyna, a usually good student, started in. Phillip had called her grandfather the day before, and she was mad. "Who does he think he is?" she muttered, just loud enough for Phillip to hear. Next up was Paola, the smartest girl in the class, and she wanted to use the bathroom. Phillip refused. Paola, whom Phillip thought of as a hot tamale, just packed up her stuff and left the room. As she was leaving, Phillip was dialing Chrystyna's home number. Seeing that, Chrystyna got up and walked out, too. The next thing he knew, Chad was at the door with Paola, who wanted to be readmitted. She had needed to use the restroom because she was menstruating. Phillip should not have refused her request then, and he certainly could not refuse her request now. He balked. Finally, Chad ordered him to take Paola back. Phillip went home that day even angrier than before. He started calling parents. *I will break these kids, even if I have to call every single parent.*

The parents he phoned that night were supportive; each one urged him to call whenever he had a problem. And most said they had never heard from a teacher at Locke before. The next day, everything was different. The kids all fell in line, and Phillip learned an important lesson: parents have an enormous impact on their children's lives. Kids are afraid of them at some level and want desperately to please them at another.

After that, Phillip had his ups and downs. And so did the kids. But that week was a watershed for him. He never lost control of a class again. In fact, he learned to look past some of the behavior he had once found so disrespectful. Many of his kids had such hard shells covering such fragile interiors; he had to remind himself, as TFA would say, that it wasn't about him. He really did have to understand where they were coming from before he could get them to see things through his lens. So he tried not to take things personally. He knew the kids didn't hate him; it was just the opposite. They liked him because, bottom line, he treated them with respect.

He let loose on the reins. He began to feel more and more like a facilitator and less like a traditional teacher. He got Wells to agree to let him pilot a special geometry class the following year, a class for high-achieving kids that would be entirely student-driven. He was less militant, more familiar with the kids. Some mornings he almost felt high. He'd get up early, grab a Jamba Juice for breakfast, and take the long way to school so he could get a view of downtown from the freeway overpass just as the sun was rising. Then he would play music as the kids entered each period. His favorite song was Destiny's Child's "Stand Up for Love," and he was a big fan of John Legend, the wholesome soul singer. The kids said they hated his music, but he didn't believe them.

CHAPTER FOURTEEN

Significant Gains

Once spring break had come and gone, the campus felt different. The purple blossoms on the jacaranda trees outside the school were dazzling, and the rose garden was in full bloom. The days grew hotter and longer, the kids and teachers more restive.

The garden was somewhat of an anomaly at Locke; a riotous patch of color against an industrial palette of grays and creams. Dr. Wells had planted the garden soon after he arrived in 2004, to mark the spot of that first racial standoff just two days into his tenure. When he suggested it, people thought he was crazy. The garden would never survive, they argued. The kids would destroy it. But Wells insisted, and his boss, Dr. Rousseau, green-lighted the ten-thousand-dollar project. The rose garden thrived and became a special spot, untouched and unspoiled, in an otherwise blemished landscape.

When Taylor stepped off the institute bus and onto the Locke campus for the first time, the garden was one of the first things she noticed. It was a foggy day, and she was dressed in her new professional clothes—her grandmother had taken her to an Express store the day before, and they had practically bought the place out. She was with some of the other new CMs, and somebody exclaimed: "It's not *that* ghetto!"

At first glance, the school didn't look that different from Santa Barbara High. The façade was painted a dark teal and light gray. A marquis outside the main entrance flashed the week's events for LOCKE HIGH SCHOOL, HOME OF THE SUCCESSFUL SAINTS, with a playful halo hovering above. Inside the main three-story building—the last high school to be built by the district in forty years—the gray linoleum floors were polished to a high gloss, and the peachy cream-colored walls looked freshly painted. Bungalows extended from the main building back to the cafeteria and assembly hall, forming an interior, green grass quad with the garden as its centerpiece. The roses were a pleasing distraction—from the chains and the fences, the locks on the doors and the bars on the windows. It wasn't until the corps of 2005 actually started teaching that they began to see those accoutrements of safety as a metaphor for conditions in the community: *locked in and locked out.*

Taylor got her assignment to Locke early, at one of the first TFA job fairs, in May 2005. TFA liked to place the locals right away, before the rush of CMs arrived for institute and things got crazy. The fair started with a crash course in No Child Left Behind, the *Williams* decree, and inclusion—some of the legal issues LAUSD teachers had to be mindful of. Then everyone was given a card with a list of three schools. Taylor's card read: Bell, Locke, and Fairfax. Included on the card was a description of each school, noting size, location, tracks, and the number of TFAers assigned there.

The CMs were corralled in a holding room adjoining the auditorium where interviews were being conducted. When Taylor's name was called, she was taken to the Locke table and introduced to Mrs. Jauregui and another Locke staffer. She was wearing a cute sweater set and a little skirt. She'd been on tons of interviews, and she knew the drill. They asked her about her background, and she glossed over the fact that she had been doing PR for J.Lo. They told her about the new small-schools setup at Locke and asked her a question about classroom management. And that was it. She was hired. She signed the paperwork then and there. She announced the good news to the other waiting CMs, who were as excited as she was. Where would she be working? As soon as she uttered the word "Locke," their faces changed. "Oh," someone said. "I hear that's pretty rough." Taylor couldn't bring herself to look the school up on the Internet. She called her boyfriend and asked him to drive her home to Santa Barbara. She had a raging headache.

A year later, she was well into the second semester and still found herself in the same state of emotional confusion—happy to be teaching but anxious about the circumstances. On the one hand, she knew her classroom was working; she could teach, and her kids were learning. But on the other hand, the novelty of being this young person doing this noble thing had worn off. She could no longer tell her friends and family stories from her great "Adventure in Watts." In fact, she now got offended when they asked. *Yes, the kids did cute things and they were really funny, but at the end of the day, it's not funny when the best seven teachers leave to start a charter school, and your best friend gets punched in the head and has his car broken into.*

Everyone who knew and loved her told her to get the hell out of Locke. She was very close to her family. One brother lived near her in Marina del Rey, and she spoke to her grandparents daily. Her mother, sensing Taylor's unease, sent her a link to a website on anxiety. Her father started trying to find her a teaching job in Santa Barbara. But Taylor had been jumped in. She couldn't go back to the world she once inhabited, and she didn't want to. She was a mass of contradictions. One minute she'd be on cloud nine, and the next, another cloud, a dark cloud, would move in and take over. *Am I happy? Am I sad? I don't know!*

She and Hrag were inseparable. It was great to finally have someone at Locke who "got" it just the way she did. They had a partnership. He calmed her down, and she was there for him. If one of them was having a particularly bad day, the other was just a call or a text message away. *Just hang in there till three.* Then they'd go out that night and decompress until the early-morning hours. Taylor felt responsible for Hrag in a funny way, like a host almost. He was so far from home, and she was a native Californian. So she arranged their road trips.

One Friday night she dragged him down to San Diego, where they slept for four hours before signing up for a wild and crazy fifty-mile bike ride along the coastline of Baja California, Mexico. It was a semi-annual event, much beloved by the college set, which started in Rosarito Beach and ended in a finish-line fiesta down the coast in Ensenada. Taylor was a bike rider from her days at her hippie middle school. Hrag had ridden a total of ten hours in his entire life. It was all spur-of-the-moment. Taylor forgot her fanny pack, so she stuck their money in her sports bra. Hrag's borrowed bike broke, and they had to walk uphill for seven miles. In Ensenada, it was one big party with music and food and plenty of beer.

Taylor had been on the grunion misadventure. She'd left at around nine and missed seeing Hrag get clocked. Good thing. She didn't know what she would have done. It was bad enough seeing the aftermath. Hrag was so disillusioned and disappointed. Like him, she had been uneasy at the picnic. It was like no field trip she had ever been on. When her high school class traveled to Ashland, Oregon, it was *safe*. She didn't know what constituted *safe* for a Locke High trip, but the grunion trip wasn't it. In the scheme of things, nothing truly catastrophic had happened. But the potential for catastrophe had been real and perfectly obvious. After working at Locke for a year and seeing so much go down, both she and Hrag felt like they'd been pushed to the limit.

She had known she was in trouble even before the school year started. She had heard through the grapevine—there never was any official communication between the school and the new teachers—that she was supposed to report to the Locke library for pre-school planning. She canceled the trip she had scheduled and went to work. But only three of the nine teachers in the English department showed up to write the year's teaching units and create assessments—and they were all TFAers.

Taylor had no idea what she was doing. She had left institute just weeks before not really knowing how to plan lessons or write assessments. One of the seven institute binders was called "Instructional Planning and Delivery," and there had been a number of CMA sessions on planning and assessing. But institute was a blur. There had been so much information thrown at them that nothing had been internalized. It didn't matter, she was told by the veterans from other departments. The tests were bullshit. But Taylor and Dan Ehrenfeld and Josh Beardall forged ahead anyway. In retrospect, they should have listened to the others. Nothing they prepared over the summer was ever used during the school year.

When Hrag arrived at the library that summer, he was handed a textbook and told to create an entire year's worth of assessments. But since he was the only biology teacher there, he realized the absurdity of the situation right away. He tried helping Jason Beattie, a second-year TFAer, write the chemistry assessments, but that seemed even crazier—to be planning for a subject he wasn't going to teach. So he spent his time online, buying furniture and looking for a car. Whenever someone came by to ask how he was doing, he said he was doing fine. And he was. He found himself a bed and managed to kit out his whole apartment.

Sometimes Taylor thought about what it would be like to teach at a school that worked, that had systems and set curriculums. At her high school, every department had a curriculum, and the delivery was synchronized, so that every student was learning—and being tested on—the same thing at the same time. The only department at Locke that seemed to have a curriculum was biology—and even that was kind of loosey-goosey, not tightly bound to state standards.

The new English teachers were entirely on their own. Taylor tried to plan with the other ninth-grade teachers, as Chad had urged, but it felt like a bad class project. She got help from second-year TFAer Jessica Miller and the UCLA coaches. When she asked one of the veteran English teachers for plans that had been used in the past, he said he'd look around. But Taylor recognized the evasion right away. *He doesn't have any lesson plans.* So, for the most part, she made up lessons on her own, mapping out what she intended to do six to seven weeks in advance.

She was a quick study. When Samir came to her classroom for the round-three observation, he brought a camera for a videotape observation he was piloting. He hadn't given her any warning that he would be filming her, but she had a great lesson planned that day. Samir was so smart and had been so helpful that she was happy to accommodate him. She had offered to pitch in earlier, in January, when he had mentioned that he was overwhelmed with calls from apprehensive would-be recruits who were still weighing the TFA offer. "Send them my way," she said. "I was in a sorority. I know how to do rush. Just send me the talking points."

Samir demurred. He had just lost two CMs—Dave Buehrle and Dave's roommate, Grant. He didn't want to lose a single one next year. "That's not what I'm looking for," he told Taylor. "I want people to be honest. I want the recruits to know what they're getting into. It's crucial to the success of the mission that they honor their two-year commitment. It has to be about the kids. If you don't want to make a contribution through education, this is not the place for you."

TFA relied on CMs and alums to spread the good word. At public events, like the annual New York City gala or alumni summits, TFA always presented "sparks," the scripted CM testimonials that were part of the welcoming cermony at the Los Angeles institute. TFA also asked corps members to help recruit, raise funds, and talk to the press. The organization wanted CMs to be honest about their experiences, but just as it was counterproductive to be disingenuous about the rigors of the job, it was suicidal to send a struggling or unhappy corps member on the road.

Clearly, corps members had the ability to make or break TFA on college campuses—regardless of whether they were selected to officially recruit. So important was word of mouth to the success of TFA that after the class of 2005's first year, the organization considered adopting a new core value, tentatively named collective responsibility. The draft wording was: "We help and support our colleagues, take the initiative to strengthen our organization, and make choices that are in the interest of our overall goals." The idea was to cultivate the sense that TFA was like family; there may be internecine squabbles and quarrels, but you didn't air the dirty linen. You cleaned it.

Whether or not to add collective responsibility was one of the high-level strategic questions discussed at the thrice-yearly executive directors' meeting in the fall of 2006 in New York. It was thought it might be helpful if CMs understood what an enormous undertaking it was to sustain, grow, and improve TFA across the continuum on the national side. TFA wanted CMs to keep their views in perspective, understanding that most new teachers go through periods of dissatisfaction and become more positive over time. CMs and alumni needed to recognize the power of their words and remember the responsibility they bore for the success of the mission.

Wendy Kopp introduced the question and then led the debate about whether the new core value was needed to further deepen the organization's culture. On the one hand, the hope was that the organization was already fostering a sense of collective responsibility. On the other, as the organization grew, it was important that CMs did not become so focused on meeting their individual goals that they lost sight of the ultimate goal of closing the achievement gap. Kopp conceded that TFA had always had issues around corps member satisfaction but until then had been reticent about telling CMs to think before they vented.

The regional directors jumped in. What would be the downside to adding collective responsibility as a core value? One executive director pointed out that TFA wanted to "get away from a sense of cultishness";

to explicitly add wording on collective responsibility might actually have the opposite effect. Another regional director suggested that to say, in essence, "be careful how you talk" would evoke the feeling of propaganda. But many noted that they heard a lot of complaints from CMs about feeling shut out, not cared about by the organization.

TFA wasn't very touchy-feely. It believed strongly that the focus should be on the goal, not the players. But it was dealing with a new generation of corps members. Market researchers believed that one hallmark of members of Generation Y, the seventy-million-strong cohort of babies born after 1979, was the need to feel appreciated and valued. They had been raised on daily doses of praise from overindulgent baby boomer parents. They were the kids on sports teams on which everyone got a trophy. They expected to be stroked.

The matter was not settled that day; after more thought and discussion in the following months, it was decided not to add collective responsibility to the list of core values. The notion that corps members bore a responsibility to see that TFA reached its ultimate goal was implicit in the culture. Besides, there could be unintended consequences.

The 2005 corps had come into TFA at an important juncture in its history. TFA was in the final year of its ambitious and successful 2000 to 2005 growth plan, in which it saw applications increase fourfold to 17,000, the number of corps members triple to 3,600, communities served nearly double to 22, and operating revenue soar from $10 million to $40 million. In 2010, TFA would be twenty years old. It had to decide what would come next.

As an organization, TFA spent most of 2005 "imagining the possibilities," says Kopp. What it came up with for its twentieth birthday was more of the same—only bigger and better. Its new 2010 plan was to more than double the number and maximize the impact of both its corps members and alumni. By then, TFA wanted to have 7,500 CMs reaching 700,000 students, and a robust pipeline of leaders filled with more than 22,000 alumni. Among the alumni, the goal was to cultivate and empower 600 school leaders and 100 elected officials. Finally, it vowed to become an enduring American institution. To do so, it would once again strengthen its organizational capacity, build its brand, and further diversify its funding base. TFA figured it could reach its ambitious goals by growing its budget to $108 million by 2010—up from its $40.1 million operating budget of 2005.

Every area of the organization geared up for the growth and worked obsessively to improve performance. The organizational structure was readjusted. Now the senior operating team would have six officers reporting to the newly established office of the president. Wendy Kopp would remain the CEO. TFA aggressively head-hunted for talent. One year into the new plan, the national staff had grown to more than six hundred employees, almost doubling in size. The push came with more than a few growing pains, and the L.A. corps felt the burn.

In 2005 the number of incoming L.A. corps—223—had more than doubled, requiring a beefier regional staff. Brian Johnson signed on as the new executive director of the L.A. region, and TFA hired six brand-new PDs to supervise the burgeoning crop of teachers. The rapid increase in corps numbers, coupled with TFA's efforts to widen its impact, contributed to tensions all around. The 2005 institute, which was just a summer shy of a great leap in clarity and sophistication, ended up being rife with dissension, a recognized "hot spot" within TFA. Things didn't improve much in the fall, when the TFA class of 2005 became the first to be subjected to Co-Investigation. The highly structured problem-solving process met with resistance on all sides, and was quietly downplayed the following year. Johnson was brilliant, but he wasn't into hand-holding. He had more pressing matters to attend to, like fund-raising, and finding school placements, and navigating Los Angeles's increasingly charged political shoals.

Stroking new teachers wasn't Samir's forte, either. So not all members of the class of 2005 were happy campers. The end of-the-year survey of Los Angeles CMs showed that 57.9 percent believed TFA's local support network helped make them more effective teachers, compared to the national average of 62.7 percent. And though 78.7 percent of Samir's CMs felt that being part of Teach For America inspired them to strive to achieve significant gains, just 63.8 percent reported that TFA created a welcoming environment, compared to the 75.5 percent national rate. Only 64.6 percent of the L.A. corps reported general satisfaction with Teach For America, compared to 78.5 percent of their predecessors in the class of 2004.

Given the level of dissatisfaction, it was imperative that the L.A. office find the right CMs to be its emissaries. Sometimes the jobs went to the teachers who seemed most eager to do the promo. Often, need dictated the choice. For example, if a funder wanted to see an eleventh-grade math teacher at one specific high school, the job went to the person who best fit the bill. Although Wendy Kopp had always eschewed the notion of charisma as an identifying feature of a leader and designed TFA to be the ultimate data-driven meritocracy, there was an undeniable buzz around certain CMs.

Samir had forwarded Phillip's, Rachelle's, Hrag's, and Taylor's names—among others—to recruitment as potential campus speakers. Rachelle declined and was never asked to do anything again. After Phillip's aborted recruitment trip, he fell off the speakers' circuit, too, though he did apply to be a faculty advisor for the 2006 institute and agreed to write the summer's geometry curriculum. Hrag was never asked to represent TFA at all; Mackey knew somebody in recruitment and got the nod to speak at Boston College instead. In the end, Taylor was the only one of the four who made appearances on TFA's behalf. And she did it again, and again, and again.

Taylor loved that TFA wanted to give an honest account of how hard the work was. After she had charmed her sponsor in December, Samir accepted her offer to chat up the undecided that spring.

In April, she was asked to attend a matriculation event at USC held in a banquet room at the Parkside Commons dorm. She had been invited the previous year, too—as a prospective CM. But at that point she didn't know if she wanted to attend, if she was ready to hear how hard TFA was going to be. So she had walked over, peeked in the window, and walked away. This time she had her doubts, too. She had received numerous e-mails and had sat in on a conference call before the event. She didn't read the twenty-page document with talking points that had been sent to her. She didn't want to spin the experience, and didn't like the idea that the whole event was so scripted, so well orchestrated. She was a professional; she knew how to handle herself. She wasn't going to blow it. But she was going to give it to them straight.

Only a handful of CMs had been invited, and they mingled with the candidates. The point was to determine candidate intentions; if someone had not accepted the offer, it was up to the CMs to find out what was holding that candidate back. Taylor fielded lots of questions—good questions. The undecided wanted to know if there was a written curriculum for new teachers, what the racial makeup of the schools was, what institute was like, what the kids were like. Taylor told them the kids were very raw, very literal, funny but real. If they didn't like what you were wearing, they'd tell you. If you came in with a new hairstyle, they noticed. She was always struck by how canny they were. Once, when she was on the phone, the kids could tell that her laugh was not sincere and scolded her: "You sound like a rich white person, Miss Rifkin!"

Taylor worked the room. If she saw that a person had already signed up, she moved on to someone who was on the fence. And with the ones who were wavering, she was very up-front. She pushed TFA. But she also told them if they had something else they really wanted to do, they should spare TFA the expense and the kids the pain.

After the chitchat, the L.A. recruitment director stood and gave a short speech. Then it was the CMs' turn. Each was supposed to give a thirty-second spiel—something inspiring, short and sweet. TFA liked to move things along. Though Taylor had been advised to jot down some notes, she decided not to. She would speak off the cuff. She had just started the end-of-the-year unit on *Romeo and Juliet* with her ninth-graders, and she spoke about how powerful it was to have the same kids who had come to her in September with fifth-grade reading levels expli-cating quotes from Shakespeare seven months later. She also reminded the candidates that their education at USC was a gift. It was time to give back.

She thought later that she must have looked so pathetic to them. She was practically begging them to do the right thing and sign up. She told them that as difficult and as painful as her experience had been, she felt really lucky to have been given such an opportuntity. And it was true. Sometimes, in the middle of the day, when she had just had one of those unforgettable teaching moments, she'd call Hrag up and say, "What would you rather be?" Hrag would deadpan: "A fireman?" And they would both chuckle because they knew the answer: *There was nothing else they would rather do. It was so empowering to take this on at twenty-two.*

Before her speech was over, Taylor had to stop herself from choking up. When she looked out at the audience, all eyes were trained on her. They were smiling, and she was thinking: *Please, please, God, don't go work for some consulting firm. Do this!*

After she sat down, the group was divided up, and Taylor took the questions specific to teaching high school. When the candidates left, the TFAers sat around a table and shared what they had picked up about the prospects' intentions. They studied all the information that had already been entered into the computer about each potential new teacher, then strategized about which ones needed further assurances and how best to approach them. There was one candidate who was leaning toward law school. Taylor thought that was a done deal; he was not worth pursuing. Same thing with the biz-school candidate—did they really want some schizo who couldn't decide between attending business school and teaching elementary school? What kind of a choice was that? But there was another weighing whether to accept an offer from the Peace Corps. Taylor had argued that she should do TFA first, while she was young and able. The Peace Corps could wait. Taylor thought she had gotten through to her. But someone needed to follow up.

That night, two undeclared candidates signed up to observe Taylor's classroom. One ultimately accepted the TFA offer. Taylor was pretty sure she had scared the other one right off the fence.

Before Taylor left that night, the recruitment director thanked her for her amazing speech and urged her to consider working for TFA after her commitment was up. But as she was about everything else in her life, she was ambivalent about TFA. She wasn't sure she wanted to know what went on behind the curtains. Besides, she still felt that no one could ever match TFA's expectations. It seemed that all the organization cared about was the data that indicated significant gains.

Taylor thought she had nailed them at the end of January, when her kids took the Gates-MacGinitie diagnostic for the second time. On their first try, in early fall, the average reading comprehension score came in at a fifth-grade level. After five months in Taylor's classroom, her students had, on average, jumped almost two grades. One kid's scores had risen by three. When she got the results, Taylor was beside herself with joy. And she couldn't wait to tell Samir. She couldn't sleep all weekend in anticipation.

"Isn't this exciting?" Taylor asked as she showed Samir the numbers. But he was poker-faced. He didn't trust the results. Samir theorized that after the long summer break, the kids were rusty at test taking, and their initial scores must have been reflecting that—not their true literacy levels. He figured the real gains in Taylor's classroom were more like a year's growth. The true test would come in June. Then they'd see if Taylor had achieved gains of the magnitude she was claiming.

Taylor was devastated. Mrs. Jauregui had practically screamed when she saw the scores, and the UCLA mentors were pumped, too. The kids, of course, were psyched. But all of that good stuff was lost to Taylor when she saw Samir's lukewarm reaction. She loved him, but this was too much. She *knew* her kids were learning. Just the other day she was walking to the bathroom thinking: *Okay. My kids have totally learned how to write an essay, a five-paragraph essay with sophisticated transitions—and their reading levels have jumped.* Now her line of thinking changed. *Did they accomplish something, or am I delusional?* She decided that, no, she wasn't delusional. She just had to stop seeking approval from TFA because she was never going to get it. She would just have to forge ahead.

The significant gains measurement was used only internally, but it was imperative that it be as reliable as possible. The data on CM significant gains had an impact on everything from selection, to training and development, to fund-raising. If TFA were to continue to attract support, the program had to be seen as effective; it had to significantly improve kids' achievement levels. TFA's selection model was based on the characteristics of former corps members who had been able to do just that. If the determination of significant gains was wrong—if the CMs with certain key competencies were not actually making significant gains—the selection process would be compromised.

But significant gains was an inherently flawed measurement, because it was based on assessments that were CM-created and self-reported. PDs checked for rigor on the tests on which the submitted scores were based. But sometimes it was a leap of faith. Many CMs questioned the validity of the numbers—and the value in judging corps member effectiveness that way.

Taylor thought it was a completely subjective metric. It was clear to her how important the numbers were to TFA, but when you got beneath them, when you really looked, it was also obvious that the numbers weren't solid. So many things came into play—including something as simple as the way a teacher asked a test question.

TFA had had a lot of trouble getting data from the English teachers. It was a subject in which mastery was hard to accurately assess; it was also a pain for teachers to collect and analyze the results. Even when Samir had the data, it wasn't comparable teacher to teacher or school to school. At Locke, each teacher made up her own curriculum, her own exam, and her own schedule. So Taylor might be testing her kids on persuasive essays when someone else was testing on theme and foreshadowing. Her tests might be hard, theirs easy. Her assessments might be hitting all the state standards, someone else's could be evaluating God knows what. She believed the numbers CMs sent in and TFA crunched were meaningless, unless they were all based on the same assessments scored in the same way. At the end of the second semester, Taylor's kids had averaged 73 percent on her assessments, dumping her into the solid-gains bucket. Good, but not good enough. Not the 80 percent mastery standard required to make significant gains.

Taylor wished they could all Co-Investigate how to measure success. One day she taught a kid how to use a footnote and considered that a major triumph. Maybe she was being too simplistic. But she thought that if TFA strayed off the numbers, it would have more genuine success, more staying power.

Samir was a numbers guy, but he saw the limitations of the metric, too. Some of his very best teachers were not actually reaching significant gains as measured by TFA. Others, whom he thought were on a slower, longer learning curve, were. The only true read he got from the scores CMs sent him was whether or not the teacher had effectively taught whatever it was that was being assessed. He could not say whether one teacher was any better than another.

There was another huge problem with the significant gains measure. It was the source of tremendous stress for hard-charging CMs. Those who didn't make the grade felt like failures and believed that TFA didn't value their efforts.

Phillip belonged in that camp. At the end of the year, his kids had made solid gains, showing 75 percent mastery of the content standards for geometry. On paper, that made Phillip one of the second-tier TFA teachers in terms of student achievement. In reality, he was one of the best in the corps. In his year-end survey, Phillip had noted that TFA did not offer up enough models of exemplary secondary teachers. Samir believed Phillip would make a great model for excellent teaching at the secondary level. He almost willed his students to succeed, and he kept adjusting his style of teaching to meet their needs. Midyear, he slowed the pace, to ensure his kids were mastering the objectives. He focused on the standards, hitting them over and over again, and scores went up. In the weeks leading up to finals, he picked up the pace and the rigor, calling his instruction geometry boot camp. On his final, he deliberately hit each core standard he had covered (fourteen out of twenty) so that the test was exactly representative of the material he had taught. His kids scored an average of 81 percent on that exam. Unlike most teachers at Locke, Phillip based his grading strictly on the results of his weekly assessments—nothing else. Had TFA allowed him to calculate his gains based on the final alone, he would have been in the significant gains bucket.

Phillip was stunned to hear that Samir thought so highly of him. "What?" he said. "I don't think I'd be a model. According to TFA, you have to dazzle."

It was Samir's turn to be stunned. Phillip didn't realize that TFA valued everything he was doing. Samir showed him the TFA rubric. "At what point did I say you needed to be more energetic or put on more fascinating lessons?" he asked. Samir finally understood why Phillip had not appeared to be invested in their meetings, why it didn't seem like they were making much progress: *Phillip always felt he had to defend what he was doing! He didn't realize that our values weren't in conflict with his. He never saw that our goals were very similar.*

At the end of the year, Rachelle felt like she had failed TFA, if that was possible. She was supposed to do the round-three observation before spring break. By mid-May she still hadn't connected with Samir. She figured she was probably the black sheep of the corps. But she didn't care. If she was late getting in her data or sending in her reflective guides—or never got around to it at all—it was because she was busy with more immediate concerns, like teaching kids. She knew she hadn't taken advantage of TFA the way she could have. She found the once-a-month Saturday meetings helpful, and she thought the teacher instruction at institute was a lot better than what she got in the graduate program at Dominguez Hills. But TFA had had no impact on her day-to-day life as a teacher. And she was pretty sure she had had no impact on TFA, either—she was definitely not closing the achievement gap. Her kids couldn't read any better at the end of the year than when they started. If she did anything, maybe it was to get some kids to come to school who otherwise wouldn't have come. Maybe.

Ironically, Rachelle's kids—for all their behavioral and learning problems—demonstrated 80 percent mastery on the tests she gave. Samir was proud of her. She had had the toughest kids to handle, and she had no grounding in biology or special ed. Rachelle had struggled to establish authority in the classroom, and then to teach biology to kids who couldn't read. But she reached out to Miss G for help on classroom management and to Hrag for help on biology. She got around the literacy issue the same way he did—she planned lots of hands-on activities—and in the end her kids internalized some key biological concepts. The highlight of her year had been the trip to Catalina. Rachelle may not have made significant gains in the strictest sense, but Samir had no doubt that she had had significant impact on the lives of her special ed students. That, to Samir, was good enough.

Hrag turned the corner with Samir in February. That was usually the time that new teachers began to feel comfortable, the phase called rejuvenation. It happened after the round-three observation. After resenting Samir's demands on his time all year, Hrag came to see him as someone he could trust and learn from. Together, they pored over Hrag's assessments and then figured out how to give his students multiple ways to demonstrate standards. Once Samir showed Hrag how helpful the data could be, he was hooked. When they broke out the tests and quizzes, Hrag was excited to see that his students were performing even better than he had thought. He really was blowing their minds.

Hrag's final number was 80 percent mastery. He wasn't sure how indicative that was of anything. Locke students weren't good test takers. Often, when he'd give an assessment, they wouldn't be able to understand the questions and would just give up. That's what happened when they took the PSATs in October for practice. His students weren't even halfway through when they realized they didn't know much of what they were being asked. One kid said he felt like jumping off a bridge, but most of them didn't seem to care; at that point they were reduced to doodling on the answer sheets. Hrag knew he was going to lose control of the class if he didn't do something. He didn't give any answers away, but still, he thought that what he did was probably wrong. He went around trying to show them that it wasn't totally hopeless, that if they looked they could find hints to the answers right there in the sentences.

The PSATs made him think about how he was presenting the material, and he began to change the language in his assessments to reflect the questions on the standardized tests. During classroom quizzes, if he saw that the kids were stumped by a question, he found that if he sat there and pointed out the key words and told them to connect the concepts—

if he walked them through how to think critically—they could answer the questions correctly. Was that success?

Like that of many other Locke teachers, Hrag's approach to grades was weighted heavily toward class work: *If the kid does everything you ask of him, how do you fail him?* At Locke, for the most part, students passed if they showed up—and showed interest. How else to explain the fact that it was possible to graduate without really knowing how to read? The problem was, if you didn't do it that way, everyone—with the exception of the three brilliant kids in every class who worked hard and aced the tests—would fail. No one would ever get out of Locke.

Like Taylor, Hrag saw the flaw in the TFA system. A lot of what he had taught wasn't even tied to a standard. It was fun, and it was good to know, but it didn't necessarily correspond to what the state expected the kids to master. He was glad to have achieved significant gains. But he knew that the TFA metric would never pass scientific muster. TFA needed to be able to gauge its effectiveness more accurately. It was doing great things, but it could be doing even better. Hrag began to think hard about how.

He didn't know it, but the national team was doing the same thing. Though outside researchers in New York had looked at TFA's significant-gains data and confirmed that the organization was accurately identifying its most effective teachers, TFA recognized that its internal system had serious limitations. It needed a unified, standardized way to measure corps member impact on student achievement. It took some preliminary steps to improve the system right away. When the class of 2005 returned in September, a much higher standard was placed on teacher-created assessments, and CMs were required to show data for every student's performance on every state standard. The result was a significant drop in the number of CMs achieving significant gains.

A longer-term solution was in the works. TFA determined that it would refine goal setting by linking classroom goals to performance on state tests rather than to 80 percent mastery of standards. It also intended to start measuring student growth, as well as performance. To further enable continuous improvement, TFA decided to pilot a standardized growth assessment developed by the Northwest Evaluation Association the following year. If the pilot proved successful, TFA would be able to make precise comparisons of student learning across grades, subjects, states, and schools—even those in more affluent communities—

in a way that came closer to meeting objective academic standards of rigor.

By turning to an external benchmark to measure gains and ensure more accurate comparability, TFA was headed in Taylor's direction. She made Samir smile. Here was a teacher who had proved him wrong. He'd been skeptical of her results in January because he had never seen that type of increase before. Other good teachers had used the same test, with much different results. So he had reserved judgment on Taylor's apparent significant gains.

Taylor gave her kids a pep talk before they took the Gates-MacGinitie reading diagnostic for the third and last time. By then it was mid-June, and the walls of her classroom had been stripped bare. Gone was the racetrack with her classes' competing scores. The college pennants were down, and so was the poster of the year's big goals. The trash can was filled with the detritus of a year's worth of instruction. Two seniors were cleaning her desk.

"Today's really important," she said. Her kids were drop-a-pin quiet. "Here's why. This is the very last time you will take this test. You have taken it two times already. You have made tremendous growth. You have jumped almost two grades. Remember, that's our goal in this class. From wherever it was. If you were at the fifth-grade level, where do you want to be? Seventh! Are there gonna be people who jump more than that? There are. Will there be people who don't make their goal? Sure. So here's the situation. There are thirty-five questions—all level-one questions. They are right there in the text. Find the answer. This is your last chance to prove to yourself and to me that you can meet our big goals. When I met you, I never believed that we would or could be reading Shakespeare. Did you think we could read *Romeo and Juliet*? One of the most complicated texts? Well, you guys tackled it. You didn't just tackle it, you did it really well. So now is your chance to prove you really can read at two grade levels above. I believe you can do it. You need to believe you can, too."

Taylor was not religious, but as the kids worked, she prayed.

The answer came a week or so later when Taylor learned that her kids had made on average 2.9 years of growth.

When she met with Samir for the last time, she was really nervous. Hrag had just lost his keys, had had to borrow her car to find Mackey at LMU, and was forced to cancel his appointment with Samir. Taylor took it instead. Her kids had scored an average of 73 percent in the class assessments. But they had gained three years in literacy. Which score mattered to TFA? Samir started with a patented generic speech, a "you did it, congratulations, now take time off to reflect and rest" kind of lecture. Taylor thought: *Okay. No problem. I won't work and just relax.*

Then Samir looked at her and said: "Your data. It was really good. I'd be lying if I said it's something I see every day. This is really good, really good."

It took everything in her power not to cry. She had worked so hard, and she had pushed her kids to work so hard, because she knew she could get them to achieve. She had had them take the standardized reading comprehension test on top of her class assessments because she knew it would yield objective, more reliable results. She didn't want there to be any doubt at all about their scores. Once they had taken the test for the third time, she was satisfied. There was no way anyone could say there wasn't real growth there.

Of course, she had considered Samir's theory—the idea that maybe they had scored so high because they had tested in really low—but she didn't believe it. She always thought that her students' gains were for real. The kids explained what had happened. One student, Yemane, who had started at a sixth-grade reading level and ended up at twelfth, said: "I started listening. I had never listened before." A lot of kids just said that no one had ever taught them how to read; once they understood the strategies Taylor showed them, it all made sense. Some admitted that they knew how to read, but Taylor had made them practice, and they got better at it. She didn't know what their experiences had been in middle school—maybe they had had permanent subs for three years. But it was clear to Taylor that if you taught them, they would learn.

Taylor gave a lot of the credit to Samir. Every time he came into her room for an hour, he would immediately see what was wrong and give her a smart suggestion for how to fix it. In the beginning, he told her she didn't have a unit plan, that she needed to know where she was going. The next time, it was big goals. She had to set goals, and get the kids invested by creating a class competition. Then the problem was matching their reading comprehension skills to their performance on tests. These were all things she had been told at institute, but everything was happening so fast then, she'd just missed it.

Before the meeting ended, Samir and Taylor talked about the year to come. She had already come up with her big goal for September. Now she wanted to figure out how to match their performances on the Gates-MacGinitie test with the state standardized tests. Those were the tests that really counted, and that's where her kids were running into trouble. It was unfair. Taylor believed the CSTs were testing white norms. But she wasn't going to make excuses for her kids. Her goal was to help them kick butt.

CHAPTER FIFTEEN

The End

Hrag really liked teaching. One day, toward the end of the year, he had one of those "moments." It happened while he was doing a PowerPoint on sickle-cell trait and paused for a moment. When he looked around, he realized that every single kid in the classroom was looking right back at him. *Wow! They're listening!* The idea was so ridiculous to Hrag that he burst out laughing. And he couldn't stop. He tried, but they were all still watching him, and that made him laugh even harder. It got to the point where he couldn't breathe. The kids didn't know what to make of it. And the more they stared, the more he laughed. Finally, he composed himself. But it took him a while, because the thought that he was teaching and they were listening was such a mind blow: *How are they listening to ME?*

Lots of people listened to him. They had to. He didn't hold back when he had concerns. Whenever the counseling office dumped more students into his room—and they were doing it up until the end of May—he went right downstairs and did something about it. Same thing with the increasing number of lockdowns and block scheduling in the spring. If administrators knew ahead of time that there would be double periods—as they must have known before the well-telegraphed May Day walkout by Hispanics—then they had an obligation to warn the staff so they could be prepared. Then there was the Chad thing with Green Dot. Dr. Wells thought Hrag was a grouch. Hrag considered himself one of the lone voices of reason.

He wasn't shy about calling out Teach For America's shortcomings, either. Hrag argued that new corps members needed to be armed with standards-based lesson plans when they entered the classroom; it was hard enough learning *how* to teach without having to spend time figuring out *what* to teach.

Until then, TFA had subscribed to the Chinese proverb "Give a man a fish, you have fed him for today. Teach a man to fish, and you have fed him for a lifetime." Handing over lesson plans to recruits like so many pieces of fish ran counter to the organization's culture. Planning lessons was something every teacher had to learn in order to succeed. The subject was covered during institute; recruits were expected to execute in the fall. But Samir agreed with Hrag and began to work on developing standards-based curricula and assessments for teachers in the L.A. region. He credited Hrag as inspiration for the initiative.

By the end of the 2005 school year, Samir predicted that Hrag would be taking a leadership role in the new School of Math and Science. In fact, Hrag had already stepped up. He and Taylor had worked on the original proposal for the school and helped write the application for its first grant. Hrag enjoyed running some of the early meetings, and he helped shape both the policies and the vision.

After he got over being angry about Soleo's defection—and the fact that he was taking three dynamite science teachers with him—Hrag decided he wanted some control over how the next year would go. So he asked Morris and Chad if he could accompany them to the Teach For America hiring fair. The science department alone was looking for as many as ten new teachers for the next year. Hrag told them he could offer good insight into the mind of the TFA teacher and help identify the ones best suited for survival at Locke.

The placement fair was held at Bethune Middle School, the same school TFA used to stage its monthly teacher-development workshops. Sometimes the Saturday-morning sessions, which were organized by content area, were helpful. Often they were seen as yet another drain on the new teachers' time. The English teachers at Locke were lucky. Chad Soleo led a professional development session just for them. He was obviously a gifted teacher, and he completely understood the problems they faced.

Chad helped Taylor and the others write their assessments so that they mirrored the format of the state's standardized tests, and then reviewed them for rigor. But the quality of the other sessions varied. Phillip was frustrated because the math sessions were not divided by grade—middle school teachers and high school teachers were lumped in together, and their needs were much different. For him, one of the best things about the mandatory classes was that it gave him a chance to catch up with friends he had made during institute.

The setup for the first of the TFA hiring fairs looked pretty much like the one Hrag remembered. When he arrived, there were about thirty CMs seated outside at picnic tables, waiting to be called into the auditorium for their school interviews. They were the first bunch of candidates, and they were on top of it. They had applied early, had taken the CSETs early, and were gung ho on Teach For America. (They also happened to live locally.) TFA didn't want to complicate the hiring process by giving schools too many choices, so it kept the fair small to ensure a better placement rate. And it offered up only one or two math or science teachers at a time, knowing they'd be scooped up the moment they were on the block. Placement was a finely tuned process. Principals came with their needs, and TFA played Let's Make a Match.

Samir was in charge of putting the first two fairs together at the same time that he was wrapping up the last rounds of Co-Investigation for all fifty of his CMs. The L.A. office was understaffed, and he was strapped. It was important that TFA get as many corps members placed as early as possible. The previous year's placements had not gone smoothly; about a third of the corps had left institute not knowing where they would be teaching. This year the goal was to place 80 percent of the CMs before the end of summer training. Samir and the L.A. staffers assigned to placement had done a few mock run-throughs. As busy as he was, Samir wanted to hit the target.

At the front of the interviewing room was TFA's workstation, with the names and the status of the prospective hirees color-coded on a computer: red for *hired*, orange for *holding*, and yellow for *being interviewed*. CMs were called into the cavernous room and directed to one of the tables where personnel from the interviewing school were seated. If the interview went well, the CM was hired on the spot. The school and TFA then signed an agreement; TFA would not send the teacher on any more interviews, and the school would not fill the position with another candidate. If the CM was not hired (which was unusual), he returned to the holding pen to hope for a better outcome from the next interview.

TFA offered Locke several candidates to interview. Chad, Morris, and Hrag sat at the Locke table, pencils poised over their notepads. Before the interviews began, they had agreed that a bull's-eye drawn at the corner of the page would signal an acceptance. A negative sign would mean a rejection. Hrag came prepared with questions. And they were tough. He wanted to know how the CMs coped with stress, how they would handle themselves in a confrontation, if they had even been in a situation remotely as challenging as teaching in an urban classroom. And even as he was asking the questions, he knew they were kind of unfair; the kids hadn't even been to institute. But he persisted. He really wanted to get a handle on how they would react when their backs were against the wall. Of course, Locke desperately needed teachers, and both Chad and Morris were huge fans of TFA. So they had their bull's-eyes down almost immediately, while Hrag would still be holding out, hammering the prospect with questions. Chad and Morris treated Hrag with the utmost respect. They just sat there, waiting for his bull's-eye. Finally, he would relent, figuring if those two were convinced, who was he to give a thumbs-down. All three candidates were hired. It kind of bothered Hrag. He didn't think any of them was ideal. Then it dawned on him. *Whoever steps up and seems semicompetent will get the job. Why am I here?* He decided his services were no longer needed.

Driving home, he thought about what it was like when he had interviewed. Back then, he had this cocky attitude. He figured if they didn't like him, he probably wouldn't like them, so he wouldn't want to work for them anyway. Hrag was one of the first people called that day, and when he was hired, everyone congratulated him. He was like: *Of course I got it. Why would I not?* Looking back now, if he had been the person interviewing him, he probably would have thought: *Okay. This kid has no idea what he's getting into. I'm glad he's psyched now.* Because that was sort of the way he was thinking about the kids he had just questioned. One of the candidates was this really sweet girl, completely oblivious. When she was hired and everyone was giving her high fives, Hrag was smiling, thinking to himself, *You think you just got this great big "first" by being hired, but not really. They were gonna take you anyway.*

Hrag didn't believe anyone could really predict who was going to be a successful teacher. He thought of the guy across the hall from him at Locke. He was really nice, reserved, almost timid, someone you would think the kids would eat alive. But no. They *loved* him. Then there would be these hard-asses who you would expect would shut the kids down, and the opposite happened. It was weird what they responded to. But he thought he had finally figured it out. He had spent the whole year trying to hide who he was from his students. But if you really wanted to succeed with them, you had to be genuine. You had to be you.

For Chad, the guilt would not go away. But he had a contract with LAUSD that he intended to fulfill, and that meant he still had to work with Wells, who was obviously feeling betrayed. It was tough, and it was only going to get worse as June progressed and the year came to a close. He didn't know how he was going to make it through the senior prom. He didn't even want to think about graduation.

There was plenty to do. Locke had been identified as one of ten schools eligible for a one-million-dollar federal grant to help implement small learning communities. The district needed a sixty-page school-impact report—immediately. With just weeks of school left, Chad was put in charge of it. Ideally, he would not be writing a report of that magnitude on his own. But that's pretty much what it had turned into. The coordinators of most of the small schools showed no interest in helping out, and he didn't want to take teachers out of the classroom. So Vanessa Morris, Josh Hartford, and a few others helped him before and after school. And he worked flat out every day from seven in the morning until eight-thirty at night. In the meantime, he had lots of stuff to do for Green Dot. His new small school was supposed to open on August 25, and they still didn't have a site. But Green Dot would have to wait. Chad couldn't let Locke miss out on a million dollars. Even though there was a good possibility that the money would be squandered, he had to do the work.

Alone in his office, he stewed: *Why am I putting myself through this, driving myself crazy to get this in on time, when it's for them, for their own small schools? Why don't they step up? Because they know I'll sit here till eight-thirty every night writing the damn grant, and if I need help, I'll call on the people I have relationships with. Well, good luck to whoever gets this job next year, because the people who do all the work at Locke are leaving; the people doing the work to hold the school together outside school instruction are going to be gone. Locke is headed for a big crash.*

It would have been nice to have Wells's support. When Chad told him the report was much more work than he had anticipated and would require a substantial amount of time, Wells just told him to go ahead. But Chad didn't hear Wells saying: "Go ahead. I'm the principal, and it's a million-dollar grant, and I'm gonna help you on this." It was nothing like that. Wells had announced the grant at two or three meetings and said that "we" were pursuing it. That was really galling to Chad because: (a) "we" weren't pursuing it, Chad was; and (b) the grant was by no means guaranteed.

Chad was resigned to doing his own thing, and it was apparent that Wells was resigned to moving on without him. As part of the SAIT intervention, Wells had a principal coach who had asked the VPs to fill out a survey on his performance. There was no way Chad was going to fill it out. It wasn't his job to help make Wells a better principal. It was Wells's job to make Chad a better VP, to mentor him. If Wells wanted to have an exit interview with him on his way out the door, fine. Chad had lots to say. But he wasn't going to fill out some anonymous survey.

For a while it looked as if he might be having that exit chat sooner than he thought. Though Chad did the work of a VP in charge of small schools, he had never been given the job. Knowing that Locke was still owed the position, and knowing how important the grant was, Chad asked Wells if he could get someone in that spot for the last weeks of the year. It would tie the person in to the grant and allow Chad to help with the transition.

Wells said no, he didn't think so. Then he laid a bomb in Chad's lap. He suggested that Chad look into getting an early release from the district.

"I know it's only human nature to look forward to the next thing you're going to do, and you're probably starting to check out," said Wells. "Find out if Green Dot will pick up your salary."

Chad was flabbergasted. He didn't know what to make of what he had just heard. If someone else had spoken those words to Chad, he would assume that the person was saying in the nicest possible way: "Get the hell out of my school, and I'll arrange it for you." But with Wells, he wasn't so sure. There was no other AP on campus available to write the grant. Wells would have to be crazy to show Chad the door in the middle of the process.

Chad left the meeting and went straight to Green Dot. "Look," he said. "I can't read him. He could be an empty barrel making noise, or he could be talking to the district and arranging a transfer because he can't fire me under the administrators' contract. I think what he's saying is 'This is the beginning of the end; I'm gonna make your life hell.' " Green Dot was cool. If Chad wanted to quit, they would pick up his salary. If he wanted to see it through to the end, that was okay, too. He had nothing to worry about. Green Dot would support whatever he wanted to do.

That night was the prom. Chad felt terrible, but as an administrator he was required to be there. It was held at the Biltmore in downtown Los Angeles in one of the lower-level ballrooms. The senior prom at Locke was always over-the-top. Chad would never forget his first one: it seemed that all the kids came dressed in purple coats, with canes and hats with feathers. And Ms. Talley, one of the longtime teachers, was there checking out the girls' gowns. When she spotted the ones who had arrived with slits in their dresses up to their hips, she said: "Nope. We're sewing that shut. Come with me." Then she took them upstairs, sat down at a sewing machine, and had them wait while she made them decent.

The 2006 prom was tame by comparison. Kids still pulled up in Hummer limos, and there was the occasional purple fur coat with silver gloves (and one kid in a pink tux and hat to match), but most of the boys wore white tuxedos or tasteful suits. The girls were in gorgeous, one-of-a-kind ball gowns, many designed and sewn by family or local seamstresses. Some couples came color-coordinated, with the boy's shirt matching the girl's dress. They looked beautiful. And maybe it was the clothes, or the occasion, but there seemed to be a measure of gravitas about them, a sense that they had stepped up, that they had a place in the world. Seven or eight hotel security men circulated throughout the ballroom, and two of Locke's own campus policemen were there, too, but they had nothing to do except watch as the strobe lights pulsed and the kids danced in time to the incessant rhythms of reggaeton, rap, and hip-hop.

Even a little dustup over the naming of the royal court didn't spoil the fun. There had been a short campaign on campus before the kids cast their ballots for king, queen, and attendants. The problem was, when the results were counted, the winners were all Hispanic.

"We are a diverse school, and that has to be represented in the court," Wells told the staffers overseeing the counting. One of the senior advisors objected: "They don't see themselves as black and brown. It's the senior class. They voted, and you should honor their vote and let this happen."

Wells stood firm. He decided that there would be two princes, and one of them would be black—the kid who had come in a close second. When the court was announced, the only ones to complain were the two runners-up for Prom Queen. They wanted queen to be a shared title, too.

It had been a very difficult day, and Chad was in a funk all night. When he arrived, it was as if he and Wells had never had that awful conversation earlier in the day. Wells was asking Chad's advice—almost deferring to him: What do you think about this? And how about that? Chad was thinking, *Dude. How about if I just go home, since you told me today to leave.* He stayed as long as he could stand it. At eleven-fifteen he said the hell with it and left.

On his way out, he passed the bar where all the TFAers and other staff were hanging out. They were having a great time. About thirty-five of them had met for dinner downtown before heading over to the Biltmore en masse. They were dressed up, too: the first-years didn't look much older than the students. When the music got too loud and the female teachers tired of being asked to dance, they had moved the party to the bar. It was another one of those moments when Taylor and Hrag and Rachelle and Phillip were all reminded that there were some things that were common across zip codes and cultures. The senior prom was one of them.

The prom happened to coincide with USC's graduation. While Taylor was up at the bar, she bumped into some Greeks she had known from the year before. They looked like they had just walked out of a J. Crew ad—gorgeous, wealthy white kids. When they asked Taylor why she was at the Biltmore, she told them she was a teacher and that she was chaperoning the Locke prom. They were drunk, and they didn't get it; they couldn't understand what Taylor was doing with these black kids dressed up like Lil' Bow Wow. If Taylor needed any reminding of how happy she was to be teaching at Locke, she got it then. *Under no circumstances would I want to be back at USC. These people are so ignorant. My life is so differ-*

ent now—and so much better. This is the richest experience anyone could have right out of college. I am so fortunate.

The days flew by. Once the prom was over, the seniors thought they were finished. But Taylor kept working them. They couldn't read. She couldn't let them out in the world like that; it felt wrong. She didn't let up on her ninth-graders, either. They had started reading *Romeo and Juliet* in April. For Taylor, everything she had been trying to do all year came together then. And there they were, kids who were reading like fifth-graders in September dissecting and interpreting Shakespeare! It was unreal. Her kids from Watts were doing what ninth-graders all over the nation were doing—and doing it well.

She knew from the very first day of *Romeo and Juliet* that the kids were going to get it. She started by having them make a T-chart of all the words in the prologue that had to do with love and hate. "You already know all about foreshadowing and connotations," she told them. "So you know how to analyze a Shakespeare play! Notice, we have positive-connotation words and negative connotations. The point is, we think *Romeo and Juliet* is all about love—but there is hate in there as well." Taylor pointed out that the first word Shakespeare used in the play was "two," and they talked about pairs—how it took two people to love and two people to fight. Who started the fight between the two families? she asked. And could anyone else think of examples where old people start wars their kids have to fight?

Vishon, a really smart African American boy, raised his hand. "The Bloods and the Crips," he said. "The older folks, they put it in their heads to go out there and kill other people that haven't done anything to you. You go shoot them. If it's a park picnic and they see a Blood, they gonna start fighting."

They made the connection. And they were hooked. Over the weeks that followed, Taylor read aloud from the play, stopping after every few sentences to check for understanding with text-related questions. She had the kids act out passages. She played scenes from the Leonardo DiCaprio movie. They wrote essays. She even had them create CDs with songs that best described their favorite character in the tragedy. Everything she did from mid-April until the very last day of school was centered around reading and understanding that play. She knew they had internalized the material when they played a game of *Jeopardy!* in preparation for the final. Her kids could identify lines, characters, scenes, themes, symbols, irony, and foreshadowing. They had a blast—they cheered and jeered, arguing over which teams knew more. *Romeo and Juliet* was their favorite thing they had done all year. They knew it, understood it, loved it.

Before the year was out, Taylor called each student to her desk to review reading comprehension scores over the year. Vishon was the second student up. He had started the year reading at 5.7 and ended at 8.7. "Awesome!" she said. "Your overall growth is three years. What could help you improve even more?"

"Just keep reading," he said. Did he have books at home? He was welcome to take some from the class library. "Congratulations, Vishon. You met our class goals. I am very proud of you."

Not everything she said to every person amounted to a big wet kiss. She told others they could do better: they needed to buckle down, and she would help them.

Throughout June, she deconstructed her classroom bit by bit. By the last day, the walls were bare. And as the classroom grew increasingly more forlorn, she did, too, in a funny way. Part of her couldn't wait for the year to be over; she and and Hrag were going to go camping on Catalina, and then she was meeting a friend in Europe. But the other part of her was worried that she'd miss the drama too much. One day she saw a young woman her age walking a bike up a hill. The sun was shining, and she looked so carefree, and Taylor thought, *That's where I want to be—I want to be on that bike.* But then she'd be having a good time somewhere and one of her kids' faces would pop into her head, and her mind would get the best of her and she'd start worrying: *My God, I wonder what Marisa is doing.* Even the whole notion of teaching was confounding: *I don't know if I'm good enough and I don't know if I want to stay to get better.*

On the last day of class, after the kids had taken their final, she handed each student a glass. Then she passed out Oreos and apple juice. "Listen up, ladies and gentlemen!" she exclaimed. "The reason I gave you glasses is because when somebody does something admirable or congratulatory, you give them a toast. So raise your glasses, please, in a toast to accomplishment!" She reminded them of the two class goals they had set in September: to get 80 percent or higher on tests and quizzes, and to raise reading levels by one and half to two grades. "As a class we met our big goals. So raise your glasses!"

The kids hoisted their cups, and Taylor went around the room until she had clinked every last one.

Hrag gave the final test on the second-to-last day of class so that he and the kids could grade their papers together on the last day, before the party. He was in a great mood. The end was approaching.

The day before, he had been pushed to the limit. He'd been in a fender bender—a result of stress, he figured—and after he picked up the car from the auto-body shop, he had gone for a run. The running was something that he had finally fit into his schedule. He had started the school year overweight and out of shape. His sister had been nagging him about it, so he and Taylor got on a program: no more red meat, yogurt for lunch instead of a sandwich, exercise. It was working. He had lost fifteen pounds. But somewhere on his run his house key had fallen from the drawstring of his shorts. He spent the rest of the day trying to recover. Taylor took his scheduled appointment with Samir, and he ran around in circles trying to right his life.

Now, when the kids were all seated, he asked, "You guys ready? Are you gonna cry? I'm gonna explain how to take the test real fast, but first I want to congratulate you all for finishing your year of biology. I'm extremely proud of you and extremely impressed. This was one of my best classes. My e-mail address is up on the board. If you ever get very sad, when it's around 1:52 in the summer, because you are not getting your minds blown away somewhere else, contact me."

After the kids were done, he gave them ten minutes in which they could ask him any questions they wanted. They had been peppering him with questions about himself all year. Just a few days before, Jordan, a big friendly kid in his crazy fifth period, said: "I think I know your name. It's between Manuel and H-R-A-G."

Another kid, stumbling over the pronunciation, said: "It's Hrag Hamalian, right?" Hrag told him he was close. So it came as no surprise that the first question they wanted answered after the test was "What is your full name?"

"Hrag Manuel Hamalian," he responded.

Next up: How old are you?

"Twenty-three," he said.

"Twenty-three?" they said in surprise.

"Any other questions?"

Jimar, a fifth-period regular, raised his hand. "Can you give me an A?"

"That's it?" said Hrag. "No more questions? If you need to shed a tear for the end of the class, I have plenty of napkins up here!"

And that *was* it. He had spent the whole year hiding his identity, and all they really wanted to know was his name and age.

There were only two half days left, and the kids couldn't stop saying his name. But they had difficulty pronouncing it, until Derrick figured it out. "It's like the Dodge commercial," he said. " 'Like a rock.' "

Before they left for good, a few kids came up to Hrag.

"I thank you, man," said Derrick.

Martin chimed in: "You my favorite teacher, Mr. H. You cool."

"I'm gonna miss you, Mr. H!" said Tiana. "I love you!"

"Well, he love Miss Rifkin," concluded Jimar.

Back in September, a few days before school started, Rachelle had done something that had never been done before at Locke—something other teachers, and even Dr. Wells, mentioned whenever her name was brought up. She had gotten her room assignment, and when she checked it out, room 241 was little bigger than a broom closet—and unbelievably ugly. It was painted the same color as every other room in Locke—a kind of pasty cream, a color that would only ever be seen in an institution.

She couldn't bear the thought of being in that awful little room all day for an entire school year. And she figured that if she felt that way, the kids probably wouldn't enjoy it much, either. So she decided to paint it. She went to the store, picked out a lovely aquamarine paint, and got to work. She didn't have a ladder, so she just stood on a filing cabinet and pushed it from wall to wall until the job was done. Then she decorated the walls.

Everyone who walked into her room was shocked.

"Did you ask anyone?" they asked.

"No," she replied.

"Well, you can't do that!" they insisted.

"Well, nobody told me I couldn't," she shot back. Besides, even if someone didn't like the idea of a teacher painting her own room, Rachelle was pretty certain—even back then—that nobody was going to do anything about it.

After the year was over, she knew for sure. The color of room 241 would be aquamarine till the day they tore the building down.

Even before the trip to Catalina, many of Rachelle's classroom management issues had disappeared. Kids were always in her room during lunch, and though she never allowed them in, they thought of her room as a safe haven, a place to go when they were ditching other classes. Franco and Pedro, quiet boys who were great friends, came to her room every day before school to see if she needed any help, or just to hang. If she had forgotten anything in her car, she would give them the keys, and they would rummage around in the clutter for whatever it was she needed. When she wasn't taking care of her kids, she was helping Stephen with his. Whichever players couldn't fit into Stephen's car would hop into hers, and she'd ferry them to their games and practices.

As much as she had dreaded it, she ended up loving the general ed class that got dumped into her lap on Valentine's Day. It was amazing to see how much easier to handle the kids were, and how much faster the pace. In fact, she had enough extra time to set aside one day a week to discuss social issues with them. One week they took on date rape; another week it would be something else—like drug abuse or safe sex. The kids looked forward to the sessions as much as she did.

One of the very last things she asked the boys in period four to do was write a letter to themselves detailing everything that had happened during the year. It was the same thing a high school teacher had asked her to do when she was their age. Once the letter had been turned in, she never thought about it again—until four years later, when it showed up in her mailbox. Her teacher had mailed it, and it was one of the nicest gifts she had ever received.

So that was going to be her present to these kids. She gave them some prompts: "What did you do this year? What were some major events? What is going on with your family? Did you meet anyone special, do anything new? What is the one thing you want to remember about this year? What advice would you give yourself for next year?"

While they scribbled away, she congratulated them. The year was over. The next class would be the end-of-the-year party. She would bring food, and they were welcome to bring in a movie, as long as it wasn't rated R.

They deserved a party. She had been working them pretty hard, reviewing everything they needed to know for the final. They were having fun, too. The kids had an awesome sense of humor. When they were reviewing Darwinism, she asked the class what happened if you grew the best male.

"You get more girls," came the response.

Then she asked, what happened if you got more girls?

"You get more sex!" they answered.

And if you were able to mate, then what?

"You get more babies." And what did more offspring get you?

"More money!" proclaimed Shandrel, to a roomful of kids who knew all about the welfare system.

Like Taylor, Rachelle decided to play a game as the final prep for the end-of-the-year test. She put her version of *Jeopardy!* on PowerPoint and announced: "Another Rachelle Snyder Production" as the title page flashed on the whiteboard.

"That's your name? Rachelle?" asked one of the boys.

"Yes," she answered.

"But Miss Synder! That's ghetto!"

She gave the kids a choice: they could form teams, or it could be every man for himself. They went solo, and they were amazing. Most seemed to have mastered the material she had taught. Rachelle began to think some of them had actually made significant gains.

She knew she had—in terms of her own maturity. The job had put a lot of things in perspective for her, given her a different lens on society, made her think, *Am I really helping? What do I want to do with my life?*

She didn't know what she wanted to do ultimately, but she did know that in the short run she wanted to get better at teaching. All her life she'd been able to skate. If she was going to stay—and she had decided that she was—then she wanted to do the job right. There were a lot of ways she could improve. She wasn't okay with just being okay.

There were things she could accomplish if she was serious, if she didn't take this as a filler job and committed herself to being a professional. If she stayed in the classroom, she'd have to get more skilled at content. And she would love to learn how to teach reading. She had tried teaching literacy at different points in the year, but not with any consistency. She went back and forth on it. But literacy was the key. Teaching a class that could read proficiently would change everything.

Looking back over the year, Rachelle thought that she probably hadn't helped to close anything—certainly not the achievement gap—but she might have opened some things for her kids when she took them to Catalina. Just to have the experience of seeing something they'd never seen before—at least not in real life—had to be mind-expanding. Mr. Baker had made a videotape of the trip, and she showed it on the last day, for the end-of-the-year party. The kids were transfixed. They wanted to watch it again and again.

Whenever Phillip wanted to get his students' attention, he rearranged the classroom. At the end of May, with just six weeks of school left, he did it again. He had come in over the weekend and moved all the desks into a huge semicircle. When his kids walked in on Monday morning, they knew immediately that something was up.

Phillip announced the beginning of his high-intensity, three-week geometry boot camp, his last concentrated effort to raise achievement. He was using the phrase "boot camp" for a reason. When the brain hears those words, he explained, it understands immediately that "this is something serious; the expectations are very high." Seventeen out of thirty-nine students in period three were failing his course, the highest number of all his classes. Phillip needed the borderline students to prioritize their efforts and energy. If they weren't willing to do that, they should leave. His focus would be entirely on the people who wanted to pass.

"This will be the most intense classroom experience you have ever faced," he explained. "In this last month, I will have no pity on you. It is time to get down to business. That door is always there for you to walk out of. It is time that those students who are here for the right reasons get serviced correctly." He had prepared a PowerPoint, and the "expectations" slide popped up on the whiteboard. Students needed to be on time, be prepared, be respectful, and be their best. Failure to meet those expectations would result in suspension, and a suspension would result in an automatic failure. Phillip handed out photocopied contracts for each student to sign and return.

Boot camp began with a lesson on how to calculate the area of three-dimensional objects. He was a great believer in hands-on activities, and he often used foldables to help his students to visualize geometric concepts. He handed out paper with the outlines of rectangular prisms. The kids took out their scissors, cut along the lines, and folded the papers into their shapes. The room was silent.

Phillip had developed a reputation at Locke. He had heard a lot of it before: he was mean, he was too blunt, he cut students down, he went overboard with his discipline. And he wasn't a team player. At the end of the year, he walked into a meeting of the other geometry teachers. They were planning the final together and hadn't even bothered to include him. And that was okay, because Phillip didn't think their test was very good—it was disorganized and didn't hit enough standards. Other teachers also questioned his grading system. Why would he grade 100 percent by the tests? Didn't he know the majority of students couldn't show what they knew that way? After a year at Locke, all he could say was that his approach was working. He had the test results to prove it.

Phillip might not have been the model teacher that Teach For America—or Locke—expected in terms of classroom management and structure, but he believed he was the teacher that his kids needed and responded to. He had to be assertive. He could not waver. He did what he had to do to make sure he was king of the castle. He wasn't at Locke to be his kids' friend. He was there to make systemic changes and to make them in a short time.

So he didn't think twice about kicking kids out of his class; in fact, he didn't see why the school should be forced to keep them. It wasn't until the end of the year, when there were only a few weeks left, that Locke got rid of the bad apples. The students with straight F's all across the board, who had no chance of passing, were quietly "checked out" of school. School police officers were sent to ticket any kids found wandering the halls without a pass. Phillip thought it was a good thing. By removing the kids who didn't care, it allowed teaching to occur and learning to happen.

Before he had started teaching, he had read all about kids who attend schools like Locke—kids who don't want to learn, who don't want to be in a classroom with high expectations, and who don't respect the teachers who set those expectations. When he signed up for TFA, he wanted to see if those kids could be saved, if urban schools could be saved. And what he had found was, the kids who really deserved to be "checked out" were the exceptions. There wasn't a student in his right mind who didn't want to learn, and Phillip had yet to find a parent who didn't want that for her children. If he had learned anything this year, it was that his power was derived from his students.

Phillip always told his kids he was heartless, but he didn't enjoy being mean. It was hard to put on that poker face every morning and keep it there all day long. He liked to joke around. The truth was, he was an intensely emotional person. And at the end of the year, he was going to let them see that side of him. His human side. On the very last day before finals, he was going to have a party. Once again he would rearrange the desks, and this time he would make the room into a community square. The kids would all bring in food, and then he would say something publicly about each and every student. He felt like there were kids who didn't feel valued or validated at Locke. And he was always on them to be better. Now he wanted them to know how much he appreciated each one of them, and how, on some level, every one of them had improved. It would be a kind of "my bad," to let them know that nothing was done in vain. He wanted to make them cry.

The community square was set up for the last full day of school. "Okay, ladies and gentlemen," he said once everyone was seated. "I want you to stop talking, and I want nothing on your desks. Once everyone's desk is cleared and all of you are listening, we will begin."

He cleared his throat and began to explain the day's proceedings. The kids had forgotten to bring food for the party, so unlike his first period, which had enchiladas, period three would involve no eating. There would also be no bad behavior. He had kicked five people out of the previous two classes; in order to have a farewell, students had to act like adults.

"This is what adults do," he said. "When they leave a job, they have a farewell. People say kids, students, can't handle farewells. But I'm looking at some of you, and I see qualities that resemble adults'. So I am going to believe all of you are adults. This is an opportunity for me to express my appreciation, and I'm not going to be upstaged by anyone!

"Okay, so," he continued, "this is an opportunity for me to convey to you the imprint you will leave with me, and to enjoy the last moment as period three that we will ever have. This moment means a lot to me because it is the only opportunity I have to tell you exactly the level of sincerity and admiration I have for you. So I am going to start off with a quote from someone I love to listen to, and who always has something profound and applicable to say. And the reason I start off with this is that it captures what I think you all have shown. The quote has to do with victory, and it is by Oprah Winfrey: 'Although there may be failures in life, there is always a possibility to triumph—no matter who you are or where you come from, the ability to triumph as a human being is with you always.' "

Phillip took the rest of the period to honor each kid. Damone was someone who challenged him every day to be a better teacher; he would experience great success. Bethany, hands clasped before her face as if in prayer, heard Phillip tell her she was an all-star student. Sergio was a kid who Phillip at first wasn't sure had the drive to succeed; he had proven to have the strongest drive of anyone in the class. David had never demonstrated his true capabilities until this semester; Phillip believed him to be one of the smartest students he had ever come across. Miss Catrina, with her thirst for knowledge, was amazing. Viviana was one of a kind. Cyiarra had a mind of her own; not everyone had the capacity she had to confront a teacher respectfully. Mister Sanchez was a star that shines brightly. Oscar was a silent force in the room. Ramiro was a person who didn't realize how smart he was. Fernando underestimated his own ability to focus; he was humble and always appreciative, an inspiration to all. And on and on it went. He had carefully prepared his remarks. No two people heard the same accolade.

When he finished, Chrystyna spoke for the class: "Quiet, everyone, or I'm not gonna say it. This class, we were forced to come here. You are one of the best teachers, Mr. Gedeon. You explained everything, and let everyone get it. I am happy I was in this class, and I learned so much. I love you all!"

When they filed out of his room, Phillip sighed. It was evident by their reactions that they had never before been told how special they were.

Phillip went to the graduation ceremony at 3 p.m. that Wednesday. He didn't personally know anyone who was graduating, but he wanted to see what graduation at Locke was like. It was a day of suffocating heat. Helicopters circled overhead, their whir an unspoken reminder that Locke was in the heart of the L.A. badlands. It had been a mad scramble to pull the ceremony off. Just minutes before the event was to begin, teachers were still in the community room on the first floor assembling the photocopied programs. Some had been printed without the names of the candidates and had already been distributed to the early arrivals. It was a mess. No one knew with absolute certainty how many, or which seniors, had actually graduated. Wells and other administrators had been dealing for days with hysterical parents insistent that their kids deserved to graduate. It continued up until the day of graduation, when Wells had a lady on the ground, in a faint in his office, upset that her child was not certified to graduate. He found it ironic. The parents you could never get hold of during the school year were the same ones on the floor fainting on graduation morning. He realized something else. It consistently happened with black folks. He couldn't recall ever having a Latino parent on the floor begging him for anything. It underscored how big a thing graduation was to the African American community. The thing was, it was as if graduation was a finalization, not a beginning.

The end of the year was always a stressful time for Frank Wells. But 2006 took the cake. It seemed that he hadn't stopped fighting with the district— or the union—since the second day of his contract, when he kicked all the druggies and gangbangers out of Locke. Admittedly, he had bypassed a slew of things the district required under the auspices of due process. But Wells was working under his own auspices—the auspices of an emergency situation—and in the interest of his kids. He was still dealing with that issue on May 10, when a kid came onto campus and pointed a gun. It was right after school, and there were probably a hundred kids out on the quad. They scattered when they saw what was going down. Some of them ended up in Rachelle's classroom. Eyewitnesses identified the gunman as a Locke student, and Wells immediately expelled him. The next thing he knew, the kid had convinced the district that it was a case of mistaken identity. The mother kicked up a fuss, and Wells was ordered to reinstate the boy.

Wells was sick to death of dealing with higher-ups in the district. During the first week of June he wrote a letter of resignation. He believed that with all the bureaucracy he had to fight and the history of neglect at Locke, the school was doomed to fail. Of course he never sent the letter. He would have been a hypocrite if he joined the rest of the people who were abandoning Locke. He had to stay and fight. *If I don't, who will?*

Locke's graduation was at least something he could be proud of. There were a record number of students graduating this year. And Locke students had been accepted at the big UCs, and even a few Ivies. The stands on the athletic fields, for once, were filled. And a mighty roar rose up when the graduates filed in, mortarboards on, their light blue gowns swishing as they marched single file to their seats on the field beneath a big white canopy. Blue, white, and yellow balloons bobbed in the air. Barely audible strains of Elgar's "Pomp and Circumstance" wafted across the field. The sound system was broken.

Phillip sat with the members of his small school. For the six who were leaving, this was the last Locke graduation they would attend as staff. It was sad. They still felt guilty. It would have been one thing if, after all the effort they had put into the school over the previous five years, Locke was in a better place. But it felt like the school would be in a worse place come September. And it wasn't just them *thinking* it in some kind of self-aggrandizing fantasy; it was everyone else, other teachers at Locke, *saying* it.

The class of 2006 were freshmen when the towering Mr. Osterhaus had first started teaching four years before. Wells had already conducted an exit interview with him. Andy had been frank; he didn't hold back about the formidable problems he saw at the school. The principal was gracious and told him he could always come back.

"Leaving Locke is like going to a planet with a yellow sun," observed another Green Dot defector who sat with Mr. O and watched the ceremony. "Superman was just another guy on his planet. When he got to earth, he was a superhero."

Mr. O explained what his colleague meant. "The idea is, if you think you are a good teacher, and you are brought to a school that functions— that has a yellow sun—you become great." He and the others leaving with him were being given a chance to "rock" as teachers. The painful truth was, having observed other functioning schools, Mr. O thought he was actually a terrible teacher. At Locke, even the so-so teachers were considered great.

Wells kicked off the ceremony with a few words of congratulations. He told the graduates of 2006 that only two years before, fewer than 140 seniors had graduated from Locke. Now more than 300 students had been accepted to universities all across the country. That was news to the teachers in the stands. There were a handful of students going to four-year colleges—Roberto, the leader of the Hispanic walkout, who was headed for UC Riverside, was one of them. But the majority of graduates were only eligible to attend one of California's community colleges, something anyone over the age of eighteen in California had the right to do.

Before the ceremony, each graduate had been asked to write down the name of the college he or she would be attending in the fall.

"Can I write Harvard?" asked one kid.

"You can," said Chad. "I'm not sure anyone would believe you, though."

As they stood to accept their diplomas, each graduate's college destination was announced. There was no way to know that most of the kids would be attending those schools only in their dreams.

But Phillip knew, and he was horrified: *What is this mockery?*

There was no featured guest speaker at the graduation. Scott Braxton, the director of school services who reported to the local District 7 superintendent—who in turn was one of eight who reported to the newly named superintendent of schools, David Brewer—represented the district at the ceremony. He said a few words, then passed the mike to the salutatorian, the valedictorian, and the president of the class. The Saints' choir sang "Stand Up for Love" by Destiny's Child, and the graduates received their diplomas. Then the tassels were moved, the hats were in the air, and the class of 2006 was officially graduated.

Chad Soleo was out on the field seated with Braxton throughout the ceremony. He was mortified. Braxton kept asking him who was in charge of staging the graduation. Why didn't the microphones work? Had there been a rehearsal? Chad just shrugged and said he didn't know. The fact was, the administration had never sat down and had a meeting to discuss the graduation. Instead, at the last minute, every available body was put on an assembly line in the community room, furiously stapling programs together just minutes before the ceremony was about to begin. As for the sound system, the official word was that someone had stolen the extension cord. Chad's reaction was, *Baloney.*

Though there was the little problem of the sound system, Chad didn't think things had actually gone *that* badly. Graduation wasn't a *major* failure. The kids all knew what they were doing, and the procession was fine. The music was well rehearsed, and actually quite good—if only it could have been heard. From his seat in the front row with the other administrators, Chad could see the face of each candidate. He knew most of them. He was so proud of them, and he wanted to savor their success. Instead, he had Braxton sitting beside him carping. What he wanted to say was: *We're up on the stage. There's nothing we can do. Can you just let me enjoy the last couple of times I'm gonna see these kids?* Maybe Braxton could read Chad's mind. After a while, he gave it up.

Chad felt really low. This was not the way he had envisioned leaving Locke. He had wanted to say good-bye to the kids, get into classrooms, and say good-bye to teachers, too. Instead, he had been working until the last minute. Once the grant application was complete, the master schedule for the following year had been thrown at him. Clearly, Wells had not wanted Chad to leave after all. It wasn't until the day before school ended that Chad got around to packing up his office. He was a wreck. Locke had been his life. His identity. His home. His family. It was too much. He couldn't keep it together, and he started crying. Just then, one of his former students walked in and found him.

"You're leaving, too?" she said in disbelief. And then she broke down and cried along with him.

"A Tribute to Locke Staff, an End of the Year Awards Dinner/Delight/Dance Night," was held the evening of the last day of school at a banquet hall in an airport hotel just a twenty-minute ride from Locke. Hrag didn't attend. That day his car had been hit in the school parking lot as he was leaving, by a student, who accused him of being a racist because he insisted on going through insurance to repair the damage instead of following the kid to his uncle's repair shop deep in the heart of Watts. The student hit the exact spot that Hrag had just had repaired. Taylor advised Hrag to get out of town. That afternoon he headed to Vegas.

Close to a hundred staff members showed up at the dinner/delight/dance. Though he was the host, Dr. Wells was delayed—when he arrived home, he had collapsed into a deep sleep. Chad was there. Taylor, Phillip, and most of the other TFAers attended. And so did Rachelle and Stephen. A lot of alcohol was consumed. It was time to forget. And there was a lot to celebrate.

Epilogue

Every year the L.A. region has a culminating event in which the "graduating" second-year teachers are celebrated. The class of 2005 was invited to join the big farewell for their departing colleagues. Executive director Brian Johnson, who presided over the event, exhorted the eighty-two members of the class of 2004 to be proud of what they had done. They had changed lives, he said—their students', one another's, and their own. He issued a rousing call to action, reminding them that they were the fifteenth L.A. corps and that they had begun their commitment on the fiftieth anniversary of *Brown v. Board of Education*.

"Today, in this country, opportunity is determined by the neighborhood in which you grow up," he said. "You are the successors to the civil rights leaders of the past. You, along with the eight hundred L.A. alumni and the ten thousand alumni nationwide, will change the course of history. Because of what you do, a child born in East L.A. will have the same opportunity to succeed as a child born in Beverly Hills. Let's change this town so the quality of our children's education does not depend on zip codes! This is a room of people who can do it, and I am proud to know you!"

Next up was Greg Good, one of the Los Angeles region's first executive directors, a man who liked nothing better than to be "preachin' about teachin,' " a 1992 alum who "begged his way into TFA out of Brown" to teach a class of five-year-olds in Inglewood, California. There were thirty-five of them, he told his audience, and on their first day of school they sat staring in "shock and awe at the big hairy Texan man standing in front of them, who was staring back at them in equal shock and awe." Since his days of ferrying Wendy Kopp around Los Angeles with a TFA cup in hand, Good had gone on to become an actor, a writer, a UCLA law student, and a lifelong advocate for education reform. It all started with Teach For America. And he wanted to share with the folks gathered there the three pillars of his TFA experience.

The first was the "gift"—the gift of teaching, said Good. The inequities that existed in Los Angeles were downright criminal and merited attention every day. But that said, there were glorious treats for TFAers. Like when a kid you taught in kindergarten called to say he had finished his finals at UCLA. Treats like that were "real nuggets of experience that stick in your heart and head and fuel me to this very day," he said.

The second pillar was the "power." Good explained how scared he was when he began teaching and how he lived with a daily feeling of angst—an angst born of the fear that his kids weren't going as fast as they should, and the realization that he was responsible every day to keep them on that journey. That fear and anxiety required him to dive deep into himself. He knew he owed his kids everything he could muster. "I don't mean just working my hardest," he explained. "They needed my A game. And when I faced that, what emerged was the best me in my life. I wasn't the best teacher, probably not even that good, but my kids did achieve, and they deserve credit for that. And as a benefit of being part of their journey, I found the very best Greg Good I ever encountered. I found the Greg Good I wanted to be—as a leader, as a man, as a son, as a brother—challenging the inequities out there and engaging my world. When you tackle the biggest challenge you've faced in your life, you may emerge with a level of personal power that extends past the fear and angst that led to it."

The third pillar was the "responsibility." For Teach For America, student achievement was the bottom line, he said. Students had to achieve, and corps members had to figure out a way to empower them to do that. But the mission didn't end there; it couldn't. The level of inequity was obscene, the level of stratification grotesque and morally reprehensible.

The members of the class of 2004 were part of a corps, an ever-expanding network of warriors. "You are a group of pit bulls—you lock your teeth into whatever you take on and you do not let go until you achieve," said Good. "There is a community to that, and it will feed you. The realities are stark and the stakes are high. In this city, in this state, in this country, we devour low-income kids on a daily basis. This city, this state, this nation is crying for leaders to speak the truth, who will engage aggressively from their experience about the possibility and challenge of low-income kids, who will go full-tilt boogie. I congratulate you all again on this wonderful first step and the colossal task you are only now beginning to address. The movement is contingent upon you humbly and aggressively engaging the issue."

Every TFAer in the class of 2005 got to experience the gift, the power, and the responsibility.

When school started again in September 2006, Hrag was more or less heading up the biology department. For the first months of the school year, he led the professional development workshops for science teachers, too. He became a master to a student teacher from UCLA's teacher education program. Over the course of the year, in consultation with other members of the biology team, he rewrote Locke's biology curriculum to align with the tough California standards and the timing of the state's assessments, and he devised his own simple system for student tracking.

Hrag felt strongly that incoming CMs needed to be provided with workable lesson plans and linked assessments—tied to state standards—if they were to be successful. So he wrote to Brian Johnson, and created a PowerPoint detailing how to effectively collect and share curricula for each subject area across the Los Angeles corps. He also urged TFA to have a heart—CMs' successes needed to be recognized, and so, too, did their travails. Hrag suggested that TFA set up support groups, celebratory gatherings, and stress workshops. He noted that TFA also had to do a better job of tracking alumni—and tapping their talents in support of the mission.

Much of what Hrag suggested regarding curriculum ended up being incorporated into major changes to the Regional Student Achievement Tool Kits (RSATs), the suite of resources each new teacher in Los Angeles received before starting in the classroom in 2007. In addition to a new

and improved national tool kit, the L.A. corps was given electronic curriculum binders that broke California state standards down into teaching
objectives, with unit plans and assessments pegged to the school-year calendar. New CMs were still being taught how to fish; the difference was,
now they were being served some, too.

Working at Locke continued to be a challenge. Things were fine in
Hrag's classroom, but conditions schoolwide seemed to take a turn for
the worse. Hrag now totally understood why Chad and the others left;
every time he tried to do something, he ran into a brick wall. It didn't help
that Green Dot and the school district became locked in battle over the
school's fate. A bid from Green Dot in late fall 2006 to partner with
LAUSD in the running of Locke was rejected. The yearlong tug-of-war
that ensued was a distraction for students and staff alike, and it sapped
the energy and enthusiasm of even the most ardent Locke reformers.

Hrag earned a master's degree in education in the spring of 2006, and
his parents flew out for the ceremony. He graduated with a 4.0 average
and left LMU with a newfound appreciation for its program, which had
been specially tailored to accommodate the time constraints and pres-
sures felt by TFA recruits and was uncommonly forgiving of their short-
ened attention spans.

He spent a lot of time worrying about what to do after Teach For
America. TFA's Los Angeles office sent CMs a regular bulletin filling them
in on area events, providing them with corps documents, posting job
opportunities, and giving shout-outs. The region offered career services
to outgoing CMs, too—ranging from free prep classes for the GREs and
the LSATs, courtesy of Kaplan, to introductions to alumni in various pro-
fessions through casual meetings and conference calls. TFA's Office of
Career and Civic Opportunities also sent out career specific "news-
blasts," complete with job listings and tips on how to navigate the hiring
process. An entire section of the TFA website was dedicated to "After the
Corps."

Hrag read it all. He thought about consulting, and even applied to
TFA to be an assistant to an executive director. But it was at a TFA-
sponsored career fair that he found what he was looking for. Building
Excellent Schools, a national nonprofit that trains aspiring school leaders
to start their own urban charter school, had a table there, and the program instantly appealed to Hrag. He had made up his mind that he
didn't want to work for anyone else—he wanted to be able to blame him-

self for whatever he couldn't do. And he wanted to make a bigger impact. Building Excellent Schools was highly selective and very intense—like Teach For America on steroids. Hrag applied and was accepted, a rare feat for a teacher just out of the corps.

Hrag spent a chunk of the summer traveling in Europe with friends. He began his fellowship in Boston in August 2007; he hoped to open his charter school in Los Angeles in 2009.

Rachelle returned to Locke in 2006 and continued to teach special ed biology in her aquamarine classroom. Things went much more smoothly. She added lots of new projects to the curriculum; her kids even got to dissect a fetal pig. She saved her lesson plans, matching them to the school calendar, so that no other new special ed biology teacher would ever have to start from scratch. She sought out training in the latest techniques for teaching reading and applied the strategies she learned to her classroom, devoting one day a week exclusively to literacy. Rachelle won a mayor's award for excellence in teaching and civic duty for services in the community. She received her certification in mild to moderate special ed K–12 from Cal State, Dominguez Hills, and was awarded her master's in special ed in December 2007.

For the second season in a row, the JV girls soccer squad won the division title. One day, while Rachelle was standing in a grocery line in Santa Monica, wearing a Locke sweatshirt, she met a coach from Beverly Hills High who encouraged her to apply for a job. She wasn't interested in working at Beverly Hills High (she didn't know which was worse: no parents or Beverly Hills parents), but she did jump at the chance to have her girls play on a club team from Beverly Hills. As a result of her advocacy, in 2007, Locke soccer players, boys and girls, became sponsored members of four teams in the West Coast Soccer Academy.

She returned to Catalina with her special ed kids in the spring of 2007. This time, the expenses did not come out of school funds. She raised all the money herself. Her mother went along as a chaperone—and Stephen did, too. Over spring break, Rachelle and Stephen joined her father on a trip to China. During the school year, she helped ferry Stephen's basketball players to games and practices. When their uniforms were dirty, she washed them.

By the end of her two-year commitment to Teach For America, Rachelle knew that she ultimately wanted to extend her reach beyond the classroom. Though she had already decided that she would remain at Locke for another year, she was thinking of pursuing a bigger job in education after that, or perhaps getting into public policy or law school. In her third year, she was looking to coach her soccer girls to a three-peat and hoped to take on more of a leadership role within the school.

In early September 2007, she helped run a professional development session for new teachers. She felt like she was a much better teacher. Sadly, her students seemed worse. Six of her special ed students were reading at a kindergarten–first grade level. Most of the rest were reading at levels no higher than third or fourth grade.

The school felt dangerous. The gangs were back, and students and staff alike felt abandoned by LAUSD. Rachelle was preparing an op-ed piece for the *Los Angeles Times* describing the worsening conditions on campus. She decided that the 2007–2008 school year would be her last at Locke: *Someone is going to die here . . .*

Phillip was back at Locke teaching summer school just weeks after the 2005–2006 school year ended. He loved it. Summer school had block scheduling, giving him time to try new and different things with his students. Though many kids were in his class because they had failed, others were there because they weren't satisfied with the grades they had received; they wanted A's. Phillip had never been around students who actually talked about going to college. It was one of those "moments" for him.

Toward the end of his first year, he had written the geometry curriculum for the TFA summer institute. When he returned to Locke in the fall, he piloted a new math program for advanced students. In 2006, he won LMU's Marva Collins Award for Outstanding African American Educators. He continued his studies at LMU and expected to receive a master of arts in administration by the fall of 2008.

Phillip completed his two-year TFA commitment a fervent believer in the mission. He was extremely grateful to have seen the problems besetting urban education firsthand. But he left TFA feeling underappreciated. The organization was not warm and cuddly. The emphasis was on the kids, not the teachers. In the fall of 2006, he and a few other CMs of color met with Brian Johnson to discuss their concerns about TFA's contentious diversity seminars. Though Phillip had never left a session angry, he did find some of the white CMs' statements offensive. He and the others were also upset that TFA's tough admissions requirements were excluding candidates of color who they believed could have made excellent corps members. Phillip found Johnson sympathetic, open to feedback and improvement. One of TFA's 2010 goals was to increase the number of people of color within the corps to 33 percent, he told them.

In his second year of teaching at Locke, Phillip took on an added role. He became the attendance enforcer—the new Mr. O—for the School of Social Empowerment. But things were different. Without Hartford and the others, the small school was much less proactive—and much more disorganized. By year's end, Phillip could relate to why they had left: *You can be amazing in the classroom but not change anything. And just one group of teachers can't make a huge difference.* He wanted to be a part of radical change, and he could see that radical change was not on the menu at Locke. So he began to look for a school that would give him the experience he needed to reach his long-term goal of taking low-performing schools and turning them around. He decided to apply to West Adams Preparatory High School, a new LAUSD campus scheduled to open in the fall of 2007. He went for an interview one Friday in April and was offered a job the following Monday.

The school opened on September 5, and Phillip was assigned to teach geometry, algebra, and CAHSEE prep. The new principal became his mentor. Phillip was working twelve-hour days and thinking about buying a condo. He had never been happier in his life.

After school was out, Taylor did exactly what Samir had told her to do: she forgot all about TFA and relaxed. She and Hrag headed off to Catalina, where they camped and caught fish for their meals. Then Taylor met up with a friend in Budapest, and they traveled for a month throughout Europe—two girls, a tent, and a car. She came home via New Jersey, where she met Hrag and his family. Then it was back to Santa Barbara and a family vacation in Laguna Beach after that.

Taylor completed her two years with TFA as Locke's lead tenth-grade English teacher. Until just a few days before the 2006–2007 school year was to begin, the English department thought it was going to be using Read 180, a teacher-proof remedial literacy program for its incoming ninth-graders. Then word was received that the program was not district approved. That presented a huge problem: the school had scheduled double blocks for Read 180. Teaching a fifty-minute class without a curriculum was tough enough; teaching for two hours would be virtually impossible for the newly hired. Taylor jumped in and helped to create a plan of instruction. The joke at Locke was that Read 180 was really Read 360. Nothing had changed.

Taylor and Hrag remained inseparable that year. Sometimes she thought they shared a brain. But she knew they had to be careful not to feed off each other's anxieties and frustrations; they didn't want to compound the negativity. Because the truth was, Taylor loved teaching. And though she did not agree with everything it did, at the bottom of her heart she loved TFA, too.

In September 2006, Taylor held a barbecue to welcome the new TFA recruits; her self-appointed job was to make sure they enjoyed themselves and didn't quit. She really liked mentoring the new kids, and she joked that if she stayed a third year she'd end up department chair. She and Hrag also became the point persons for the new School of Math and Science. At Locke, just being a second-year teacher gave you credibility.

Taylor was ambivalent about what to do after Teach For America. She knew she wanted to teach; she just didn't know if she wanted to teach at Locke. Some days she thought: *Oh my God, I could really make a difference here if I stayed.* Then she'd see a kid running down the hall with a bloody face, and it would be: *Coming to Locke is like entering the gates of hell—abandon hope all ye who enter here.* So she sent out a bunch of résumés and was surprised to find how much cachet was attached to the words "Teach For America." She was offered five different teaching jobs. She also applied for a position as a TFA program director. She didn't get it, but TFA did hire her to be a corps member advisor for the 2007 summer institute, a much-improved product over the institute of '05.

In her second year of teaching, Taylor made significant gains once again. And this time she was recognized for them. Taylor was one of three regional finalists for TFA's prestigious Sue Lehmann Award for Excellence in Teaching. She felt humbled by the honor.

In September 2007, she became the ninth-grade English teacher at Ánimo Watts II Charter High School, one of two new Green Dot incubator schools to open near Locke that year. Vanessa Morris was principal. The school was a revelation; it worked. When Taylor visited Locke, just a few blocks away, people told her how lucky she was. One of the school security guards there confided that even he was scared.

· · ·

Samir Bolar left TFA in the summer of 2007 after completing two years as a program director. Every one of his 2007 colleagues left as well; the PD position had never been a pipeline to advancement within TFA. Samir had struggled with the highly structured, step-by-step Co-Investigation model during his first year. In his second year, TFA blew it up; the formal cycle of self-reflective problem solving was too focused on process, and PDs were getting lost executing the steps. In January 2007, TFA zeroed back in on the basics it believes a teacher needs to be successful—a vision, a standards-based plan, and quality assessments—and introduced the concept of backward planning as the way to execute them. The incoming CMs had already been primed for the new approach at institute, where more emphasis had been placed on long-term planning, assessments, and tracking. So the formal rounds of classroom observations and the robotic searches for the single key issue impeding student achievement were quietly shelved, giving way to more organic conversations. PDs were basically instructed to do whatever it took to help CMs get the job done.

The new approach played to Samir's strengths. TFA had already asked each region to contribute models of excellence in the three foundational priorities—a vision, a plan, and assessments—for the National Student Achievement Tool Kits. But Samir wanted to do more. So he took it upon himself to beef up the instructional resources available to the Los Angeles corps, and he got CMs, including Hrag and Phillip, to be leaders in the effort. The result was an online, standards-based road map of long-term planning in each secondary subject.

Samir was accepted into the MBA program at the University of California, Berkeley. He felt he needed to expand his skills set if he wanted to be successful at founding his own educational nonprofit down the road. Only a few months into the program, Samir was already on the Oakland Small Schools Foundation board of directors as a fellow. There was no doubt in his mind. He was in education for the long haul.

Chad Soleo and his team of teachers left Locke in June 2006 and opened the Ánimo Pat Brown Charter High School that August on the site of a failed charter school, across the freeway from the USC campus. Josh Hartford was the vice principal; the five other Locke teachers joined three new hires to make an inaugural team of ten. There were 141 students in the first class of ninth-graders: 94.5 percent were Latino; 8 students were black. That year, the kids at Pat Brown scored 46 percent proficient and advanced in Algebra I, exceeding their goal by 21 percentage points. By contrast, none of Locke's ninth-graders scored advanced in Algebra I and only 2 percent were proficient; 87 percent scored below, or far below, basic. In English, 40 percent of the students at Pat Brown were either proficient or advanced, compared to 11 percent at Locke. In Chad's opinion, accounting for the difference wasn't rocket science. Pat Brown was small, paid attention to the students' needs, and employed quality staff.

The battle for Locke played out throughout Chad's first year as principal. There were moments when he wondered what would have happened had he stayed; about what role he might have had in the inevitable reconstruction of Locke. Green Dot's Barr sought Chad's input, and made the triumphant announcement of Locke's conversion to a charter from Ánimo Pat Brown's cafeteria. But as tempting as it might have been to go back and have a hand in getting Locke right, Chad wasn't going anywhere. He had made a commitment. There was no way he could walk away before his small school was successfully established.

In the fall of 2007, Ánimo Pat Brown added a new class of 142 ninth-graders and moved to a temporary space in Los Angeles's West Adams district to accommodate the school's burgeoning student body of 288. The Pat Brown team was excited and proud of their kids' results on the CSTs. But Chad was coming to the realization that, as essential as it was, quality teaching was not going to solve the problems in urban education on its own. Even at a school like his—a school in a good system, with plenty of support, and with caring teachers who worked relentlessly— it was tough to move students who were so far behind and so burdened by all the beyond-the-classroom issues that come with growing up in poverty. Working at Ánimo Pat Brown made him wonder how he ever survived at Locke.

Dr. Frank Wells did a Saul-on-the-road-to-Damascus-like conversion in 2007 and joined forces with Green Dot to facilitate the reconstitution of Locke High School into a charter school. His change of heart came after a face-to-face meeting with Green Dot's Steve Barr that spring. Before, Wells had been dismissive of Green Dot's success. He had believed that the charter schools got the cream of the crop: they did well because the students who attended them had parents concerned enough with education to go to the trouble to enroll them. Though Green Dot tried to blunt the charge by canvassing inner-city neighborhoods with information about school choice and the charter school option, it was true—it *did* take parent initiative to fill out an application and make sure a child's name was in the lottery for a spot in a Green Dot school. Too many kids at Locke lacked that advantage.

Wells was surprised to find that he and Barr agreed on so much. By the time of their meeting, Wells's relationship with his district bosses had soured. He had spoken out against the district during a visit to Los Angeles by U.S. Secretary of Education Margaret Spellings. And at around the same time, the district notified him that his contract would not be renewed.

He changed sides. Wells allowed—in fact, encouraged—his teachers to collect and sign a petition seeking to convert Locke to a charter school. On May 8, the day that forty-one out of the seventy-three tenured teachers at Locke signed the petition (more than the 51 percent required by law to trigger a conversion), Wells was escorted off the Locke campus and relieved of his duties. The next day, students and teachers alike protested his removal. While he weighed whether or not to take legal action to regain his job and lost wages, he became a consultant to the parent union started by Green Dot. It took nearly three years of fighting the union (and three boxes full of documentation), but in June, just weeks after being removed himself, Wells was notified that one of the twenty-two teachers he had tried so hard to terminate had finally gotten the boot.

In the fall of 2007, Wells was gratified to see that the LAUSD school board had finally approved the conversion of Locke to a Green Dot charter, and he hoped to play an active part in the process. But he was still feeling numb in the wake of his dismissal. The forty-three-year-old administrator was a principal without a school.

When school started in September 2006, safety and security continued to be a priority at Locke. In October, a big wall was erected along the eastern perimeter of the school, the site of at least two homicides in less than two years. Things were relatively calm on campus, but outside a political firestorm was brewing. When the district rejected Steve Barr's offer to partner up at Locke, the school became the object of a nasty yearlong custody battle. After the staff approved the Green Dot plan to take over Locke, the union and the district struck back, successfully lobbying some teachers to rescind their votes and then declaring the petition invalid. As the fate of the school was debated in L.A.'s corridors of power, chaos returned to Locke's hallways. But during the summer, the Bill & Melinda Gates Foundation pledged $7.8 million to fund the transformation of Locke into ten small Green Dot charter schools, and Superintendent David Brewer, who had initially resisted Green Dot's advances, got religion. By September it was a done deal. A newly installed school board voted to approve the new Locke charters.

Amid the squabbling, and against all odds, Locke's scores went up— though not on the scale necessary to meet all state or federal benchmarks. Despite the academic gains, Locke's small schools had become even less functional—just "window dressing," in the words of Frank Wells—and the district considered collapsing them and reverting back to a big-school model. Still, because Locke met the criterion of at least ten points of schoolwide API growth over a two-year period, the school exited SAIT at year's end.

TFA's class of 2005 completed its two-year commitment in June 2007. Every one of the corps members at Locke, with the exception of Dan Ehrenfeld, chose to remain in education. Four of them—Rachelle, Mackey, Heather Fieldsteel, and Erica Rodriguez—decided to teach at Locke for a third year.

When they returned in September 2007, they found a school on the brink of anarchy. Because of reduced enrollment, there was only one lunch period—policed by five fewer security guards. Once a Crips-only school, Locke now enrolled a good number of Bloods. The two rival gangs battled constantly. The entire school was tagged, and packs of kids roamed the halls at will throughout the day. By early October, there had already been a full-on riot, a bomb threat, and an assault on an assistant principal. In announcing the teachers' decision to give Locke to Green Dot, Barr promised to do what had never been done before: turn a large failing urban school around. He had his work cut out for him.

By 2007, the year Wendy Kopp turned forty, she had graced the cover of *Fortune,* been named one of America's top twenty-five leaders by *U.S. News & World Report,* and, in what she jokes was the scariest moment of her life, appeared on *The Colbert Report.* (The media attention frightens her; she is mindful of the laws of gravity.) *BusinessWeek* ranked Teach For America tenth among undergrads' top twenty-five most-wanted employers. The Princeton Review recognized it as one of the country's top launching pads for college graduates seeking entry-level jobs. And on some of the country's top campuses, such as UCLA, Smith College, and Vanderbilt University, TFA was the number one post-grad employer.

TFA's largest-ever corps—more than 5,000 members—was teaching in twenty-six regions across the country. The newly admitted corps members numbered 2,900, a 19.5 percent increase over the size of the 2006 corps. They were serving more than 440,000 students.

But by TFA's own reckoning, there were thirteen million children in the United States living in poverty, the majority of whom were being educated in underperforming schools. Even with its remarkable growth spurt, TFA could never reach them all. If the organization was ever to close the achievement gap—and even some of its most ardent admirers had their doubts—it had to depend on the realization of the second part of Kopp's theory of change: its alumni, the leaders TFA had incubated and then embedded in society's professional classes, had to rise up.

In 2007, there was evidence that that was beginning to happen. The *Washington Post* called it the "TFA insurgency." As early members of the movement were coming of age, they were assuming positions of power within the burgeoning education reform movement—and within the ranks of the rich philanthropies that increasingly funded it. They all knew one another, and some were even married to each other. Kopp's husband, Richard Barth, one of her first TFA hires, was CEO of the successful KIPP schools, which had been founded by two TFA alums. The Education Trust, an education advocacy group based in Washington, D.C., was packed with TFA alums. And the New Teacher Project, a TFA spin-off from the late 1990s, was headed by Michelle Rhee, a thirty-seven-year-old TFA alum who had taught in Baltimore as a member of the 1992 corps.

Over the years, TFA had groomed more than two hundred school principals, and had infiltrated numerous local school boards, but for the most part it had been on the outside trying to push for reform within. In June 2007, the appointment of Rhee as chancellor of the troubled Washington, D.C, school district had the potential to change all that. Her nomination was a breakthrough for TFA, a marker indicating that the young teaching mavericks had arrived. Rhee filled some key positions in her cabinet with fellow TFA alums, among them Jason Kamras, the 2005 National Teacher of the Year. TFA was determined that Rhee's ascension would be just the beginning of the fulfillment of the second half of the mission. By the end of the decade, it planned to have eight hundred school leaders and one hundred elected officials among its more than twenty thousand alumni.

In the midst of implementing its 2010 plan at home, TFA announced that it was going global: a new organization called Teach For All, in concert with Teach First, its British adaptation, would support similar TFA initiatives in India, South Africa, Estonia, Israel, and Germany. The Dell Foundation, which had contributed to the second TFA expansion plan, pledged $2.5 million toward Teach For All's effort in India.

TFA continued to have its critics, who charged that the millions of dollars raised to get high-flying do-gooders to teach poor, underperforming kids could have been better spent reforming the recruitment and training of career teachers. Although TFA kept detailed records on its corps members, its tracking of alumni was less rigorous. Of the 57 percent who responded to the 2007 alumni survey, 67 percent said they worked in education. (The definition was a broad one, as it included those who were studying full-time in the field of education.) Funders appeared to be less concerned about TFA corps members' abbreviated classroom careers than was the educational establishment. In 2006, TFA's operating campaign raised $57 million—a 40 percent increase over the previous year's effort. Wachovia alone committed $6 million over three years.

As she looks ahead to the year 2010, when TFA will be twenty years old, Kopp plans to grow the TFA corps in size, effectiveness, and leadership, making TFA an enduring American institution. Knowing that the dream of closing the achievement gap is so far from being realized, she is driven by a sense of urgency. "There is so much more to be done," she says. "We are not yet the success we have the potential to be." She remains in relentless pursuit.

Acknowledgments

I am indebted to so many people.

First, heartfelt thanks to Phillip Gedeon, Hrag Hamalian, Taylor Rifkin, and Rachelle Snyder for allowing me to accompany them on their first-year journey with Teach For America. Without their candor, courage, and commitment, this book would not have been possible. Not only did they teach their children well; they taught me so many things, in so many ways. I must also thank Chad Soleo, who was tremendously helpful and always forthright. And I am grateful to Dr. Frank Wells, who opened wide the doors to Locke High School for me and gave me free rein to record "the good, the bad, and the ugly." His perspective was invaluable. I want to express my gratitude to the dozens of Locke staffers who shared their individual stories and experiences with me—and to the entire staff for their patience and generosity of spirit. And last, but certainly not least, I want to thank Locke's students for putting up with Miss Donna. Though their names have all been changed, their stories stay with me.

Of course, I am enormously grateful to Wendy Kopp and her team at Teach For America, especially Steven Farr, Melissa Golden, Brian Johnson, and Matt Kramer. Special thanks goes to Samir Bolar for giving so freely of his time and keen insights. It took a great leap of faith and a supreme act of confidence for Teach For America to grant me the unprecedented access I received. Thank you.

I am grateful to Emily Foote for introducing me to Teach For America, Liza Levine for introducing me to Locke High School, and Betsy Streisand for getting me started and keeping me going. I am indebted to Emily Yoffe for her wise counsel, Mark Miller for his wide shoulders, Patricia King for her empathetic ear, and Patty Gibson for her way with words. Big thanks to Martha Groves, Jill Cherneff, and Olga Mohan for their unwavering support; to Carol Dietz for our music; and to Lori Altshuler for our walks. I am grateful to Becky Kordones and Laurell Schweneker for their nourishment, and to my brothers, sisters, and father for their encouragement. Thanks to Ruth Tenenbaum for her research, Rebecca Dameron for her review, and Lily Evans for her editorial assistance.

I am indebted to the Mac Geniuses at the Manhattan Beach Apple store, who helped me organize my reporting and saw me through my technological meltdowns. My gratitude, too, to the staff at The Kettle, who graciously allowed me to monopolize a table during their busiest shifts, and to the crew at Noah's for my daily dose of bagels and caffeine.

I am especially grateful to Annalyn Swan for believing in this project and for introducing me to my agent, Peter Bernstein. A huge thank-you to Peter for shepherding me through this process, and to my editor, George Andreou, for bringing this book to life.

Finally, the biggest thanks goes to my husband, Jim Shalvoy, and my son, James, who endured too many take-out dinners and long absences during the making of this book—and did so with uncommon grace, love, and good humor.

A NOTE ABOUT THE AUTHOR

Donna Foote is a freelance journalist and former *Newsweek* correspondent. She lives in Manhattan Beach, California, with her husband and fourteen-year-old son.

A NOTE ABOUT THE TYPE

The text of this book was set in Sabon, a typeface designed by Jan Tschichold (1902–1974), the well-known German typographer. Based loosely on the original designs by Claude Garamond (c. 1480–1561), Sabon is unique in that it was explicitly designed for hotmetal composition on both the Monotype and Linotype machines as well as for filmsetting. Designed in 1966 in Frankfurt, Sabon was named for the famous Lyons punch cutter Jacques Sabon, who is thought to have brought some of Garamond's matrices to Frankfurt.

Composed by Creative Graphics, Inc.,
Allentown, Pennsylvania

Printed and bound by Berryville Graphics,
Berryville, Virginia

Designed by Soonyoung Kwon